D1620659

Dispersed Democratic Leadership

Dispersed Democratic Leadership

Origins, Dynamics, and Implications

Edited by
John Kane, Haig Patapan, and Paul 't Hart

OXFORD
UNIVERSITY PRESS

OXFORD
UNIVERSITY PRESS

Great Clarendon Street, Oxford OX2 6DP

Oxford University Press is a department of the University of Oxford.
It furthers the University's objective of excellence in research, scholarship,
and education by publishing worldwide in

Oxford New York

Auckland Cape Town Dar es Salaam Hong Kong Karachi
Kuala Lumpur Madrid Melbourne Mexico City Nairobi
New Delhi Shanghai Taipei Toronto

With offices in

Argentina Austria Brazil Chile Czech Republic France Greece
Guatemala Hungary Italy Japan Poland Portugal Singapore
South Korea Switzerland Thailand Turkey Ukraine Vietnam

Oxford is a registered trade mark of Oxford University Press
in the UK and in certain other countries

Published in the United States
by Oxford University Press Inc., New York

First published 2009

British Library Cataloguing in Publication Data

Data available

Library of Congress Cataloging-in-Publication Data

Dispersed democratic leadership : origins, dynamics, and implications / edited by
Paul 't Hart, John Kane, and Haig Patapan.
p. cm.
Includes index.
ISBN 978-0-19-956299-2 (hardback)
1. Democracy. 2. Political leadership. 3. Comparative government.
I. 't Hart, Paul. II. Kane, John, 1945 Apr. 18– III. Patapan, Haig, 1959–
JC423.D6625 2010
321.8—dc22 2009026428

Typeset by SPI Publisher Services, Pondicherry, India
Printed in Great Britain
on acid-free paper by
the MPG Books Group, Bodmin and King's Lynn

ISBN 978-0-19-956299-2

Contents

List of contributors

Professor **Stephen Bell**, School of Political Science and International Studies, University of Queensland, Australia

Professor **Jos de Beus**, Department of Political Science, University of Amsterdam, the Netherlands

Professor **Glyn Davis**, Vice Chancellor, University of Melbourne, Australia

Professor **Douwe Jan Elzinga**, Department of Constitutional Law and International Law, University of Groningen, the Netherlands

Professor **Erwin C. Hargrove**, Department of Political Science, Vanderbilt University, USA

Professor **John Kane**, Department of Politics and Public Policy, Griffith University, Australia

Professor **John Keane**, Centre for the Study of Democracy, University of Westminster, UK

Professor **Haig Patapan**, Department of Politics and Public Policy, Griffith University, Australia

Professor **Hillel Schmid**, Centre for the Study of Philanthropy, Hebrew University, Israel

Professor **Michael Schudson**, Department of Communication, University of California, San Diego, USA

Dr **Geoff Sharrock**, L. H. Martin Institute, University of Melbourne, Australia

Associate Professor **Patricia Lee Sykes**, School of Public Affairs, American University, USA

Professor **Paul 't Hart**, Research School of Social Sciences, Australian National University, and Utrecht School of Governance, Utrecht University, the Netherlands

Karen Tindall, Research School of Social Sciences, Australian National University

List of contributors

Professor **Mark Tushnet**, Harvard Law School, Harvard University, USA

Professor **John Uhr**, Crawford School of Economics and Government, Australian National University

Professor **Bertjan Verbeek**, Institute for Management Research, Radboud University Nijmegen, the Netherlands, the Paul Nitze School of Advanced International Studies, Bologna, Italy, and Crismart, Swedish National Defence College, Stockholm, Sweden

List of Tables

List of Abbreviations

BCA	Business Council of Australia
CFC	Chloro-Fluoro-Carbons
DATA	Debt AIDS Trade Africa
ECJ	European Court of Justice
EPA	Environmental Protection Agency
EMU	Economic and Monetary Union
EP	European Parliament
EU	European Union
FATF	Financial Action Task Force
FSF	Financial Stability Forum
IAEA	International Atomic Energy Agency
ICTY	International Criminal Tribunal for the Former Yugoslavia
IGO	Intergovernmental Organization
IMO	International Maritime Organization
LPF	List Pim Fortuyn
MAD	Multiple Accountabilities Disorder
MCR	Merger Control Regulation
MMP	Mixed Member Proportional Representation
NAFTA	North American Free Trade Agreement
NPO	Non-Profit Organization
PLP	Parliamentary Labour Party
PR	Public Relations
WTO	World Trade Organization

Chapter 1

Dispersed Democratic Leadership

John Kane, Haig Patapan, and Paul 't Hart

Dispersed leadership in democracy

We tend to take it for granted that liberal democracies foster political pluralism, where political decision-making is not solely the business of constituted government but the concern of a variety of organizations and individuals interested in exerting influence upon it (Dahl 1961; Connolly 1995). Liberty of speech and association and the legitimacy of dissent in democracies make such pluralism inevitable. What is less often noted is that the broad distribution of influence and authority implies a distribution of the public leadership function throughout society. Leadership is not concentrated in a ruling elite nor in a single monarch or tyrant but broadly dispersed. This makes political leadership in a democratic polity very difficult. Elected leaders with large responsibilities must try to govern effectively amidst a multitude of critics and opponents with contradictory ideas and intentions who cannot simply be commanded.

Political science, when it studies leadership, tends to focus primarily upon the elected government, and particularly upon the figure of the chief executive. This is a very important topic, and this volume will certainly not ignore it. The central argument of this volume, however, is that, since many public leaders help shape debate and policy in a democracy, it is important to balance the usual person-centred approach with one that is more contextual, institutional, and relational. How does the dispersal of leadership in a democracy affect good governance? Business leaders in market economies are assumed to wield significant political power, but do they, and how? Media moguls similarly pretend to influence, and are assumed moreover to have a democratic responsibility for scrutinizing governments, but how effective are they and how do they understand their leadership role? Non-governmental organizations proliferate for various specific purposes and are sites of leadership for people who wish either to call governments to account or to supplement their services, but what is the nature and consequence of their political interaction? Anyone in a democracy with a cause or a grievance, from a right-wing populist to a celebrity singer to a retired American president, may take up a leadership role and effectively mobilize people either to support or challenge elected governments, but how much do we understand of their prospects and power? Constitutional monarchies curiously preserve an ancient and non-democratic form of leadership which is assumed to be harmlessly ceremonial, but is the monarch's role more significant than this?

All these and other topics will be addressed by individual contributors to the present volume. It will become clear to the reader who delves into these chapters that the sheer number and variety of contemporary leadership avenues in liberal democracies has produced a political system that is both complex and opaque. It is one that contains both ancient and newly emergent loci of leadership, institutionalized and ad hoc ones, political and self-consciously apolitical ones. We are likely to assume, as democrats, that this is a good and proper thing, but is this really the case? The dispersal of sites of leadership may be an inevitable thing in a democracy, but is it always and necessarily a good thing? This is a question we will address and try to answer after having reviewed the fascinating set of chapters collected here. Let us first set the scene by examining the problem of democratic leadership and the dual causes of democratic dispersal.

Leadership: a blind spot in democratic theory

Democracy is founded upon the core principle of popular sovereignty, implying that the people should rule themselves. In practice, this idea results in a twofold challenge for leadership.

The first challenge is the problem of democratic leadership itself. Democracy needs good leaders but, because of its egalitarian commitments, possesses no clear theory of leadership to counteract its inherent suspicions of strong leaders. The consequence is that the practice of democratic leadership is perpetually fraught with alternating hope in leaders and challenges to their legitimacy. Because it is difficult or impossible, except in the case of very small communities, for the people to rule directly, democracies empower elected representatives to rule on their behalf. Such leaders possess the extraordinary authority that comes from a grant of the popular will, and they rule by consent and ostensibly on behalf of the people. Yet, because democracies fear that their leaders will turn themselves into de facto sovereigns, they constantly challenge their authority and attempt to rein it in. The shadow of democratic illegitimacy haunts every leadership act and decision.

The second challenge arises partly as a consequence of the first. If in a democracy no one has natural or God-given right to lead, then everyone may equally be a leader. With political authority granted but permanently questioned, democratic citizens are at liberty to find other opportunities for effective public leadership. The idea of popular sovereignty, in other words, works to actively disperse offices and sites in which leadership can be exercised, and contemporary democracies are thus characterized by many avenues for gaining the attention and approval of the sovereign people. This tendency is significantly enhanced in liberal democracies by the liberal–constitutional division of powers that distributes authority among political branches. Liberalism, by definition, fears the danger to individual liberty of concentrated power, including the concentrated power of 'the people', and uses the division of offices to curb the potentially powerful democratic impulse to rule without sufficient attention to the rights and concerns of individuals. Pluralists, meanwhile, appreciate the many opportunities that liberal democratic dispersal provides for 'venue shopping'.

The fact that the permanent tension between leaders and the sovereign people noted above is, in principle, irresolvable gives democratic leadership its special character, explaining both its remarkable strengths and acknowledged weaknesses. Democratic leadership is, indeed, uniquely challenging because it must be most carefully exercised under conditions of peculiar constraint and constant distrust. This is an important subject inadequately addressed in the scholarship, which indeed constitutes a permanent blind spot for most modern students of democracy (Kane and Patapan 2008).

Democratic solutions to the problem of leadership

We may discern two fundamentally opposed tendencies in attempting to cope with democracy's fundamental ambivalence about leadership. So-called elitist theorists resolve the tension in favour of leadership at the expense of popular sovereignty, the most famous formulation of their position being that oligarchic rule is an 'iron law' of politics. More democratically inclined scholars react to this elitist challenge by trying to resolve the tension in favour of popular sovereignty. They do not so much solve the problem of democratic leadership as pass over it in embarrassed silence, typically pursuing more ideally 'democratic' political forms that envisage wider or even universal citizen participation in political processes and decisions. The thrust of these strategies sometimes seems to be to eschew the need for leadership altogether but, since this is impractical, they might be alternatively conceived as attempts to disperse an indispensable leadership function as widely as possible. If the dispersal of leadership is taken as characteristic of democracy, then it must follow that the more widely dispersed it is the more democratic the polity.

Thus deliberative democrats note the many sites of deliberation that exist in democracies and seek to disperse authority more widely by creating more of them (Dryzek 1990; Fishkin 1993; Gutmann and Thompson 2004; Gastill and Levine 2005). Students of executive governance note that modern democracies are not characterized so much by fixed hierarchies as by networks in which individuals exercise forms of linked yet distributed leadership (Kickert, Klijn, and Koppenjan 1997; Rhodes 1997). Other scholars argue that leadership in democracies is best understood in terms of a 'lattice of leadership' that describes the dispersal and mutual influence of various forms of leadership (Uhr 2005, 2008). Yet these are merely modern articulations of a fundamental insight regarding democratic politics that has an ancient provenance.

British historian, statesman, and diplomat, James Bryce (Bryce 1921: I, 3–14), surveyed six modern democracies – France, Switzerland, Canada, the United States, Australia, and New Zealand – to see how well they confirmed Tocqueville's observations on the nature of democratic government, and captured succinctly the consequences of modern democracy for leadership.[1] Bryce argued that, 'where legal supremacy belongs to the multitude actual power is exerted not only by the persons to whom it delegates its legal authority, but by those also who can influence the multitude itself, inducing it to take one course or another, and to commit executive functions to particular persons'. Consequently, those who form public opinion, for example journalists and authors, also exercise leadership in democracies (1921: II, 605).[2] If the sovereign feels justified in listening to a range of opinion other than that of authorized political leaders, then popular sovereignty by its nature must tend to disperse leadership to a variety of people who may not hold office but who are capable of influencing public opinion.[3]

This tendency for democracy to disperse leadership was strengthened by liberal thought. In Montesquieu's *Spirit of the Laws* we find one of the most famous and influential accounts of how the separation of powers – in effect the dispersing of authority and therefore leadership – provides a guarantee of individual freedom. Through his influence on the American founding and thereby modern liberal democratic constitutionalism, Montesquieu's theoretical justification for dispersal as an essential means of securing liberty by defraying and fragmenting power became a powerful support for the democratic impulse towards dispersion. Thus modern liberal democracies can be said to have both liberal and democratic impulses or drives towards dispersing leadership. But, as all students of American government and modern constitutionalism recognize, such dispersion comes at a cost of considerable inefficiency, policy incoherence, and occasionally logjam. Dispersion is consequently opposed by countervailing impulses founded upon arguments of expertise, efficiency, expediency, and tradition. The result is a distinctively democratic dynamic of countervailing forces that require delicate balancing, and which presents a permanent challenge to all leaders in a democracy.

Moreover, because leadership is both desired and distrusted in a democracy, dispersed leaders confront the same challenges as do elected leaders to their basic legitimacy. They will be questioned on their democratic credentials if they seem not to defer sufficiently to the popular will, either procedurally or in substance, or if their actions display undue arrogance or seem to deny democratic authority. They must be prepared at any time to justify their leadership before the bench of democracy while contending with other leaders similarly free to speak and challenge. The liberal–democratic dispersal of authority thus results in a twofold politics that any leader must engage: a politics of the democratic dynamic and a politics of democratic legitimacy.

Democratic leadership: new perspectives

Leadership is pivotal in all political systems. Leaders have extraordinary influence, for better or worse, in invigorating and transforming established institutions, policies, and routines. The scope and depth of this influence and authority can be gauged from the range of functions that leadership may undertake, such as fundamentally defining the character of communities; interpreting opportunities and dangers; articulating and preserving public values by selecting and defending norms and standards; and coping with non-routine challenges and public emergencies by finding pathways to absorb, transform, and learn from them.

Despite being pivotal, public leadership has been described by James McGregor Burns (1978) as 'one of the least understood phenomena on earth'. Prescriptive, exhortative treatises in the Machiavellian tradition advising executive leaders how to behave are not hard to come by (Meltsner 1988; Lord 2003; Keohane 2005), but empirically the field is unevenly developed. Though our understanding of political leadership has increased significantly in the three decades since Burns issued his rallying cry (e.g. Elcock [2001]), the developing subfield of leadership studies still suffers from an important bias in both its locus and its focus.

In terms of the *locus* of study, public leadership entails four major domains: political, administrative, judicial, and civic leadership ('t Hart and Uhr 2008). Each entails a distinct set of roles, which can be embedded in a variety of public offices and performed by a broad range of individuals and groups, not just elected representatives or public office-holders (see Table 1.1). For too long, too many political scientists have equated the study of leadership with the analysis of political leadership, particularly the study of executive elites. Heads of government top the bill. We have countless studies – individual and collective biographies, institutional histories, national and cross-national comparative analyses – of presidents and prime ministers (Rose and Suleiman 1980; Elgie 1995; Sykes 2000; Helms 2005). There are also considerable literatures on cabinet ministers and legislative leaders. Within the field of public administration, there is ample attention for administrative leaders and leadership (Kaufman

Table 1.1 Public leadership types and roles

Political leadership
1. Identity entrepreneur: mediating collective identity
2. Selector: (re)directing government agendas
3. Decision-maker: choosing rules and policies
4. Crisis manager: regulating collective stress

Administrative leadership
1. Servant: advising and facilitating government
2. Guardian: safeguarding administrative processes
3. Manager: crafting, sustaining, and adapting public organizations
4. Implementer: delivering public value

Civic leadership
1. Advocate: challenging and exhorting government
2. Watchdog: monitoring and evaluating government
3. Service provider: circumventing and complementing government

Judicial leadership
1. Arbitrator: resolving public disputes not effectively dealt by or directly involving government
2. Steward: preserving democratic regime values by interpreting constitutions and laws

1981; Terry 1995; Theakston 1999; Weller 2001; Page and Wright 2007), often highlighting the delicate relationships that exist within the executive branch between political and administrative office-holders (Savoie 2003; Hood and Lodge 2006; Lewis 2008). By comparison, we have relatively little comparative insight into the dynamics of other forms of leadership and their interplay. Nor do we know much about the dilemmas involved in asserting these various forms of public leadership within the context of (representative) democracy.

This volume tries to remedy this imbalance. It covers a wide range of forms and loci of public leadership, and examines their interrelationships. We sample the extraordinary range of offices permitted – indeed encouraged and supported – by democracy. By thus broadening the *locus* of leadership studies in politics we make an important addition to our understanding of democratic leadership, highlighting loci and forms of democratic leadership that remain relatively unexplored. For example, the focus on executive political leadership has not been matched by equally detailed examination of other categories of political leader, for instance those exercising the craft of opposition or indeed the enduring role of monarchs. Likewise, the judicial branch has been widely acknowledged as a crucial 'check' on executive power, but surprisingly few studies offer insight into the 'life world' of senior judges whose beliefs, decisions, and arguments actually shape this 'check'. To be sure, much is written about the political role of the courts, but we know much less about how this role is understood and elaborated by actual judicial leaders. And although Putnam's work has stimulated much debate about the pivotal role of 'civil society' for democratic viability, the roles that various types of civic leaders – activist, religious, charitable – can and do play in 'making democracy work' demand detailed exploration.

The chapters in this volume cover both executive and non-executive democratic leadership. They juxtapose office-based and informal types of public leadership. They study how these various forms of leadership gain and maintain authority within the context of democratic polities. They examine the inherent tensions as well as the potential complementarities between them.

In terms of the analytical *focus*, many students of leadership concentrate on grasping the impact of the character and capacities of leaders – their traits, styles, judgement, choices, and relationships with followers – on their agility in exploiting the possibilities of, mostly, the executive offices they hold. Much of this work borrows concepts and theories from psychology to study individual office-holders (Hermann and Wilburn 1977; Paige 1977; Simonton 1987; Brett 1997; Greenstein 2000; Post 2003). The other cluster of leadership studies in political science focuses instead on the institutional structures leaders inhabit, and which enable and constrain them in exercising leadership. Thus we get comparative studies of cabinet government (Blondel and Muller-Rommel 1993; Weller 2007), the office of prime minister (Henessy 2001; Rose 2001), the presidency (Neustadt 1992; Waterman 2003; Rockman and Waterman 2008), or socio-anthropological accounts of leadership as a product of 'culture' (Wildavsky 1984, 1989; Ellis and Wildavsky 1989).

Yet, as Hermann (1986) and Hargrove and Owens (2002) rightly observe, public leadership in fact arises from the interplay of 'skill' (people with their capacities and styles) and 'context' (institutions, cultures, situations). It is this crucial interplay that has received comparatively little sustained attention (but see, e.g., Skowronek [2008]). Where the interplay between the two is seriously addressed at all – for example in studies of democratic government by political theorists – it is usually in terms of the limitation of executive leadership by the separation of powers (after Montesquieu), or by the 'caging' effect of modern rational–legal structures (after Weber).

We argue that the Montesquieian and Weberian approaches, though revealing important aspects of the dynamics of office, limit our overall understanding of public leadership in democracies. This collection of essays instead aims to examine how democracy not just needs but actively produces and disperses public leadership possibilities. We seek to enhance our appreciation of the variety of possibilities of active leadership (and therefore citizenship) that modern democracies foster, and indeed require, if they are to be intelligent and resilient in addressing complex public problems and socio-political conflicts. Each chapter explores a particular leadership 'office' or role. Some of these forms of leadership, like the executive and the judiciary, are legally and constitutionally entrenched. Others exist by convention. Some wield ambiguous authority to challenge or oppose orthodox structures. Each chapter studies how the various offices and role sets create expectations and possibilities for, but also place limitations on, the people inhabiting them.

We have asked international experts from a range of disciplines to reflect on the interplay between key public leadership roles, the interpretation of those roles by the people performing them, and the broader normative and institutional setting of democratic governance in which both these roles and actors are embedded. Taken together, these essays help us reflect in new ways on the old concern of democratic theorists (what leadership might do to democracy), but more importantly enable us to examine the often-ignored reverse question: what democracy does to leadership.

Volume overview and acknowledgements

The volume does not begin with a set theory of democratic leadership, nor does it aim to develop one. It instead seeks to highlight the dynamics and ramifications of dispersed democratic leadership. It studies multiple forms of public leadership which have emerged as products of democratic design or democratic commitment to pluralism and toleration. Each chapter examines a particular form, and explains how its practitioners tend to perceive, interpret, and negotiate the possibilities and constraints of their roles. We begin in the heart of conventional political leadership studies – heads of government – and follow the thrust of democratic leadership dispersal to trace ever more non-executive and/or informal forms of public leadership. The last of the essays takes us full circle, by focusing on the increasingly activist and visible role of the ultimate non-office holders: retired heads of government.

The final chapter reviews the major arguments that emerge from the work as a whole. It shows how the two main doctrinal thrusts of democratic leadership dispersal – popular sovereignty and liberal constitutionalism – have operated and continue to do so. It also shows how the very prevalence of leadership dispersal has generated challenges for each of the various leadership forms thus created: how to relate to other offices or loci of leadership, and how to cope with the inherent trend to further fragmentation of power and authority. If democracy encourages and tolerates ever further proliferation of leadership venues and roles, how in the end does the system hold together?

This volume has been a joy to make, in no small measure due to the wisdom and professionalism of our chapter authors, recruited from far and wide to perform what to many of them may have seemed a rather unstructured and ambiguous task. We thank them for their commitment and creativity. We gratefully acknowledge the financial and logistical support offered by the Utrecht School of Governance of Utrecht University, in particular its research director Mark Bovens, in hosting a highly productive authors' meeting in March 2008. Jaap van der Spek and Wouter Jan Verheul provided a useful summary of the workshop discussions. Haig Patapan and John Kane enjoyed financial support from the Australian Research Council. Invaluable editorial support was provided by Karen Tindall, without whom the production of this volume would have been much more arduous.

Notes

1. Bryce discusses 'Leadership in Democracy' in one chapter (II, LXXVI, 605–17) of his two-volume book. Tocqueville's famous *Democracy in America,* one of the first and most profound studies of modern democracy, is arguably a subtle and extended meditation on the unique opportunities and challenges faced by democratic leaders. Tocqueville seldom addresses leadership in explicit terms. For him, America was the nation where the democratic revolution – an irresistible and universal advance of equality – had been most fully and peacefully realized, where the sovereignty of the people had been put into practice in a direct, unlimited, and absolute way. He examined America because, as he admitted, 'he saw in America more than America; it was the shape of democracy itself'. The problem of leadership comes implicitly into play in his accounts of the sovereignty of the people (I, I, 4), tyranny of majority (I, II, 7 and 8), and the influence of equality and freedom (II, II, 1). There are, in addition, specific references to, for example, the nature of government (I, I, 8; I, II, 5), parties (I, II, 2), and public speaking (II, I, 18 and 21).
2. The remainder of the chapter considers the question of what are the 'qualities which fix the attention and win the favour of the people?' (1921: II, 606).
3. Bryce was no doubt alluding to the famous Platonic image of the 'ship of state' which outlined the character of democratic regimes. Socrates in Plato's *Republic* depicts a ship owned by a shipowner who surpasses everyone on board in height and strength, but is somewhat deaf and short-sighted, with limited knowledge of seamanship. The sailors, according to this account, are crowding around the ship-owner, persuading, begging, and fighting each other to take over the piloting of the ship (*Republic* 488a–489a). In such a struggle, according to Socrates, the true pilot – the person skilled in navigating the ship – is neglected in favour of the man 'who is clever at figuring out how they will get the rule, either by persuading or forcing the ship-owner'. This Platonic image of democratic politics confirms an important insight about democracy as rule of the people: democracies make possible a contest for leadership.

Bibliography

Blondel, J. and Müller-Rommel, F. (eds.), *Governing Together: The Extent and Limits of Joint Decision-making in Western European Cabinets* (Basingstoke: MacMillan, 1993).

Brett, J. (ed.), *Political Lives* (Sydney: Allen & Unwin, 1997).

Bryce, J., *Modern Democracies* (London: Macmillan and Co., 1921).

Burns, J. M., *Leadership* (New York: Harper Colophon, 1978).

Carter, A. and Stokes, G. (eds.), *Democratic Theory Today* (Cambridge: Polity Press, 2002).

Connolly, W. E., *The Ethos of Pluralization* (Minneapolis, Minn.: University of Minnesota Press, 1995).

Dahl, R., *Who Governs?* (New Haven, Conn.: Yale University Press, 1961).

Dryzek, J. S., *Discursive Democracy: Politics, Policy and Political Science* (New York: Cambridge University Press, 1990).

Elcock, H., *Political Leadership* (Cheltenham: Edward Elgar, 2001).

Elgie, R., *Political Leadership in Liberal Democracies* (Basingstoke: MacMillan, 1995).

Ellis, R. and Wildavsky, A., *Dilemmas of Presidential Leadership* (New Brunswick, New Jersey: Transaction Publishers, 1989).

Fishkin, J. S., *Democracy and Deliberation: New Directions in Democratic Reform* (New Haven, Conn.: Yale University Press, 1993).

Gastill J. and Levine, P. (eds.), *The Deliberative Democracy Handbook: Strategies for Effective Civic Engagement in the Twenty-First Century* (San Francisco, CA: Jossey-Bass, 2005).

Greenstein, F., *The Presidential Difference: Leadership Style from FDR to Clinton* (New York: Free Press, 2000).

Gutmann, A. and Thompson, D., *Why Deliberative Democracy?* (Princeton, New Jersey: Princeton University Press, 2004).

Hargrove, E. C. and Owens, J. (eds.), *Leadership in Context* (London: Rowman and Littlefield, 2002).

't Hart, P. and Uhr, J., 'Understanding Public Leadership: An Introduction', in P. 't Hart and J. Uhr, *Public Leadership: Perspectives and Practices* (Canberra: ANU E Press, 2008), 1–24.

Held, D. (ed.), *Prospects for Democracy* (Cambridge: Polity Press, 1993).

——*Models of Democracy* (Cambridge: Polity Press, 1996).

Helms, L., *Presidents, Prime Ministers and Chancellors: Executive Leadership in Western Democracies* (Basingstoke: Palgrave Macmillan, 2005).

Henessy, P., *The Prime Minister: The Office and Its Holders Since 1945* (London: Penguin, 2001).

Hermann, M., *Political Psychology* (San Francisco, CA: Jossey-Bass, 1986).

——and Wilburn, T. W. (eds.), *A Psychological Examination of Political Leader* (New York: The Free Press, 1977).

Hood, C. and Lodge, M., *The Politics of Public Service Bargains: Reward, Competency, Loyalty – and Blame* (Oxford: Oxford University Press, 2006).

Kane, J. and Patapan, H., 'The Neglected Problem of Democratic Leadership', in P. 't Hart and J. Uhr, *Public Leadership: Perspectives and Practices* (Canberra: ANU E Press, 2008), 25–36.

Kaufman, H., *The Administrative Behavior of Federal Bureau Chiefs* (Washington, DC: Brookings Institution, 1981).

Keohane, N., 'On Leadership', *Perspectives on Politics*, 3 (2005), 705–22.

Kickert, W. J. M., Klijn, E. H., and Koppenjan, J. F. M. (eds.), *Managing Complex Networks* (London: Sage Publications, 1997).

Lewis, D. E., *The Politics of Presidential Appointments: Political Control and Bureaucratic Performance* (Princeton, New Jersey: Princeton University Press, 2008).

Lord, C., *The Modern Prince: What Leaders Need to Know Now* (New Haven, Conn.: Yale University Press, 2003).

Meltsner, A., *Rules for Rulers: The Politics of Advice* (Philadelphia, Penn.: Temple University Press, 1988).

Miroff, B., *Icons of Democracy: American Leaders as Heroes, Aristocrats, Dissenters, and Democrats* (Kansas: University Press of Kansas, 2000).
Montesquieu, *The Spirit of the Laws,* A. M. Cohler, B. C. Miller, and H. S. Stone (trans. and eds.) (Cambridge: Cambridge University Press, [1752] 1989).
Neustadt, R. E., *Presidential Power and the Modern Presidents* (New York: The Free Press, 1992).
Page, E. and Wright, V. (eds.), *From the Active to the Enabling State: The Changing Roles of Top Officials in European Nations* (Houndmills: Palgrave, 2007).
Paige, G. D., *The Scientific Study of Political Leadership* (New York: Free Press, 1977).
Pennock, J., *Democratic Political Theory* (Princeton, New Jersey: Princeton University Press, 1979).
Plato, *Republic,* trans. A. Bloom (New York: BasicBooks, [360BC] 1968).
Post, J. M. (ed.), *The Psychological Assessment of Individual Leaders: With Profiles of Saddam Hussein and Bill Clinton* (Ann Arbor: University of Michigan Press, 2003).
Putnam, R. D., *Making Democracy Work: Civic Traditions in Modern Italy* (Princeton, New Jersey: Princeton University Press, 1993).
Rhodes, R. A. W., *Understanding Governance: Policy Networks, Governance, Reflexivity and Accountability* (London: Open University Press, 1997).
Rockman, B. and Waterman, R., *Presidential Leadership: The Vortex of Power* (New York: Oxford University Press, 2008).
Rose, R., *The Prime Minister in a Shrinking World* (Oxford and Boston: Polity Press, 2001).
——and Suleiman, E. (eds.), *Presidents and Prime Ministers* (Washington DC: American Enterprise Institute, 1980).
Ruscio, K. P., *The Leadership Dilemma in Modern Democracy* (Cheltenham: Edward Elgar, 2004).
Savoie, D. J., *Breaking the Bargain* (Toronto: University of Toronto Press, 2003).
Shapiro, I. and Hacker-Cordón, C. (eds.), *Democracy's Edges* and *Democracy's Value* (Cambridge, Cambridge University Press, 1999).
Simonton, D. K., *Why Presidents Succeed: A Political Psychology of Leadership* (New Haven, Conn.: Yale University Press, 1987).
Skowronek, S., *The Politics Presidents Make: Leadership from John Adams to Bill Clinton* (Cambridge, Mass.: Belknap, 1997).
——*Presidential Leadership in Political Time: Reprise and Reappraisal* (Lawrence, Kansas: University Press of Kansas, 2008).
Sykes, P., *Presidents and Prime Ministers: Conviction Politics in the Anglo-American Tradition* (Lawrence, Kansas: University Press of Kansas, 2000).
Terchek, R. J., 'Teaching Democracy: A Survey of Courses in Democratic Theory', *Perspectives on Politics,* 1/1 (2003), 147–55.
Terry, L. D., *Leadership of Public Bureaucracies: The Administrator as Conservator* (Thousand Oaks, CA: Sage, 1995).
Theakston, K., *Leadership in Whitehall* (London: Macmillan, 1999).
Uhr, J., *Terms of Trust: Arguments over Ethics in Australian Government* (Sydney: University of New South Wales Press, 2005).
——'Distributed Authority in a Democracy: The Lattice of Leadership Revisited', in P. 't Hart and J. Uhr, *Public Leadership: Perspectives and Practices* (Canberra: ANU E Press, 2008), 37–44.

Waterman, R. W., *The Changing American Presidency: New Perspectives on Presidential Power* (Cincinnati, Ohio: Atomic Dog Publishers/Thomson Learning, 2003).

Weller, P., *Australia's Mandarins: The Frank and the Fearless?* (Sydney: Allen and Unwin Australia, 2001).

——*Cabinet Government in Australia 1901–2006* (Sydney: University of New South Wales Press, 2007).

Wildavsky, A., *The Nursing Father: Moses as a Political Leader* (Alabama: University of Alabama Press, 1984).

——'A Cultural Theory of Leadership', in B. D. Jones, *Leadership and Politics: New Perspectives in Political Science* (Kansas: University Press of Kansas, 1989), 87–113.

Chapter 2

Evolving Executive Authority in Anglo-American Democracy: Coping with Leadership Dispersal

Erwin C. Hargrove

Conceptions of executive authority

In some ways, all democratic presidents and prime ministers swim against the tide of the democratic dynamic noted in the introductory chapter of this volume: over time, democracy proliferates offices and other loci of public leadership that vie for prominence and legitimacy with the traditional executive authority accorded to heads of government. How do they manage? How have the leadership efforts of successive heads of government altered the nature of executive leadership in their countries? This chapter explores these questions. It compares traditional conceptions of executive authority in America and the United Kingdom and contrasts them with new theories and practices which may have superseded or threaten to replace the dominant conceptions. It takes a bird's eye view of political leadership in these two countries, looking at the predicaments, instincts, and accomplishments of post World War II government leaders in both countries. It does so through the lens of two ideal–typical models of executive leadership – the collegial and the dominant executive – each of which captures the core features and inner logic of each set of arrangements (Aberbach and Peterson 2005: 530).

In the US version of the *collegial model*, the president works within a formal constitutional system of, in Richard Neustadt's terms, 'separated institutions sharing powers' (Neustadt 1992: 29). Presidents have the political responsibility for formulating national programmes and proposing them to Congress, but the legislature, not only disposes, but is the source of much independent legislation. The president leads by building political coalitions in the country, Congress, and in wide circles of affected interests. The institutions of the national government – executive, legislative, and bureaucratic – are loosely coupled and the president has no guarantee that his or her programme will be either enacted or implemented (Dahl 2006).

Collegial policymaking in the United Kingdom works through party government that unites the prime minister and cabinet with the majority party in the House of Commons. The prime minister leads the cabinet as the 'first among equals' by leading, guiding, and coordinating the government for legislation. Ministers of State are his chief advisers. The prime minister must have an eye to important constituencies within his or her party and within the larger polity. The prime minister has more legislative authority than the president but he or she is the leader of a team of colleagues with diverse goals, interests and sometimes factional ties who must be consulted regularly.

These two conceptions of government have had strong support within political science, not only as description, but also as ideas of how government should work. The logic of the American model is for dispersed leadership within loosely coupled institutions. The logic of the British model is for collective government within political constraints. Notwithstanding this, some theorists but most of all practitioners of senior executive government have felt a growing discomfort with the perceived dilution of executive authority at the core of government. Many a president or prime minister has baulked at the self-reinforcing dispersal of power and leadership that democratic regimes facilitate (emancipation, decentralization, participation and international collaboration all conducing to 'hollowing out' of the heart of state power), and which contemporary technological revolutions ('the network society') have exacerbated. This has led to the rise of a second model, that of the *dominant executive*.

In the United States this model is characterized by claims by the president and his executive entourage to primacy over Congress and administration. The president organizes the executive so that subordinates in the Executive Office of the President control and oversee key actions of bureaucracy to make them consistent with presidential policy. Presidents value the 'responsive competence' of their White House assistants more than they do the 'neutral competence' of the professional bureaucracy.

Richard Nathan has called this the 'administrative presidency' (Nathan 1986). A number of devices to control policymaking and implementation are used: oversight of regulatory rules, presidential appointments, insistence of loyalty to the president, and agreement with presidential ideology. The president may turn to Congress for needed legislation but, in case of frustration, policy is made through executive orders and rule making whenever feasible. Congressional followers are expected to follow, not lead. This general strategy is favoured by presidents who seek to scale back domestic government and yet at the same time, enhance the power of the national security state. A more recent version is called the 'unitary executive' which asserts the primacy of the president, without restraint of Congress or the courts, in spheres that he reserves for himself, especially in national security policy.

The dominant executive conception in the United Kingdom depicts the prime minister as the undisputed (often mistakenly referred to as 'presidentialized', revealing a fundamental misunderstanding of the traditionally soft, negotiated and contingent power of the US president) leader of the cabinet and executive institutions (Foley 1993). The addition of expert staff in Downing Street, some from outside government and some from the civil service, strengthens the prime minister's hand with ministers and the higher civil service in policy development. The use of such assistants violates the traditional injunction that prime ministers must receive their advice from Ministers of State. As in the United States, 'responsive competence' crowds out 'neutral competence'.

These models are clearly ideal types but they help one ask a series of questions that will guide this chapter. There seems to have been a shift in both countries' executive leadership practices away from the former and towards the latter model. Is this really the case, and if so why has it happened? How temporary or permanent are changes of this kind? And what are the pros and cons of each model in practice? In exploring these questions, I shall draw upon my own four decades of researching the presidency and to a lesser extent the British prime minister (Hargrove 1966, 1974, 1988, 1998, 2008; Hargrove and Nelson 1984; Hargrove and Owen 2001), as well as on classic and recent studies by others. I adopt a bird's eye view throughout, dealing briefly with virtually all holders of these offices since 1945. So I trade off within-case detail against the allure of a largish-n trend analysis. I start with the US case.

The institutional presidency

The idea of the presidency as an institution emerged slowly in the first half of the twentieth century. The Budget and Accounting Act of 1921 gave the president direct authority over departmental budgets for the first time. The Executive Reorganization Act of 1939 gave President Franklin Roosevelt six White House assistants and moved the Bureau of the Budget from the Treasury department to a new Executive Office of the President. At the same time Congress rejected a presidential request for reorganization of the executive departments along functional lines because it would endanger lines of control from existing congressional committees. The Bureau of the Budget assisted the president in developing a legislative programme and overseeing the administration of programmes. The six assistants were staff to the president without specific assignments.

Harry Truman and Dwight Eisenhower (1945–52; 1953–60)

The institutional presidency gradually developed in the Truman and Eisenhower years in ad hoc ways in response to new government responsibilities and foreign policy crises. The National Security Act of 1947 sought to override wartime fighting among the services by creating a Department of Defense. The Central Intelligence Agency fell within the Act, primarily as an agency to provide intelligence, with only implied powers to engage in the secret use of force. The National Security Council was created to unify policy under the president and key cabinet officers, with a small staff. A Council of Economic Advisers was also created by the Employment Act. Truman had a small White House staff, much like Roosevelt's, with the Bureau of the Budget providing most of the legislative and administrative expertise.

Truman used his authority decisively but in a collegial manner. He had hoped to lead Congress toward reform legislation, but seeing the weakness of the Democratic coalition, he compromised the Fair Deal programme in order to win support for his Cold War policies. The signs of an 'imperial presidency' were visible but latent in his failure to get congressional approval for fighting in Korea. Eisenhower's White House staff was small and he relied on the Bureau of the Budget for programme development. He created a larger National Security Council staff to coordinate policy development with the departments and a parallel staff to oversee policy implementation. But The Secretary of State held sway, and the president was his own Secretary of Defense. Domestic policy for the last six years, when the Democrats controlled Congress was worked out with Speaker of the House Sam Rayburn and Senate majority leader Lyndon Johnson. The president asked for a limited amount of legislation, received most of what he wanted, and guarded tight budgets, his chief concern. He certainly operated within the limits of the collegial model on the surface. However he was willing to secretly use the Central Intelligence Agency to reverse the overthrow of the Shah of Iran and to drive a radical regime in Guatemala from office.

The development of new institutions within the Executive Office is not to be confused with claims that came later of the authority of the president to act within his own sphere without legislative or judicial oversight.

John Kennedy (1961–3)

Democratic presidents stand in the footsteps of Franklin Roosevelt as reformers. Domestic reform requires legislation and the mastery of Congress. Kennedy had a reform programme, much of which had germinated among Democrats in Congress in the 1950s. He also used a number of 'task forces' in policy areas to develop fresh ideas. They were composed of academics and government officials, mostly from the budget bureau. Kennedy lacked the votes to pass his

New Frontier programmes. The 'conservative coalition' of Republicans and southern Democrats still ran the Congress. He hoped to win a large re-election majority in 1964 to enact his programme. His White House staff was not large but he used them aggressively as a ginger group against the departments, to get information and spark innovation.

Lyndon Johnson (1963–9)

Johnson wanted to be the greatest president ever, and to him this meant passing laws in Congress. He would outdo Roosevelt and in fact he did. The torrent of domestic reform legislation that was passed in five years was incredible. Policy ideas were developed by outside task forces and then refined within the government. The White House lost control of the implementation of many new programmes in the vast federal bureaucracy and federal system but legislative passage was the Democratic goal. Republicans later reversed those priorities.

Johnson brought the same furious energy and ambition to the conflict in Vietnam. On his first day as president he told associates that he would not be the first president to lose a war. He knew from the beginning however that the war was a trap for him. He could withdraw from Vietnam and face the politics of the 'loss' of China, as Truman had, or he could escalate American involvement. The Gulf of Tonkin resolution in 1964 authorized the president to act, as he chose, against 'aggression' in South East Asia. Johnson promised Senate leaders that he would ask for approval for the use of troops but he never returned. His problem was that he gambled on a short war and lost.

As the war continued, historians and political scientists began to write about the 'imperial presidency' (Schlesinger 2004). The image of the presidency had been a progressive one, part of the progressive theory of American history. The president was chief reformer and guardian of the national interest. The war reversed this image among presidential scholars. There was a great deal of writing about the importance of 'presidential character' (Barber 1985). Johnson's personal insecurities were seen as at the root of his rigidity in pursuing the war. Character was fitted into the larger framework of the American crusade against communist aggression that had characterized policy since Truman. The 'imperial presidency' seemed a reality.

Richard Nixon (1969–74)

We see a watershed with Nixon. The administrative presidency came into its own during his tenure in full-blown form, to be repeated by Ronald Reagan, and later by both Bush Presidencies. Republican presidents are more sceptical of domestic government and accordingly want less from Congress than Democratic presidents. When Congress has frustrated their requests they have turned to executive means to secure their goals.

Nixon saw an opportunity to build a Republican majority by creating a broad middle class alliance, including southern whites, in an appeal to 'forgotten Americans'. The federal government's role in society was to be cut, and a number of programmes were to be reorganized and administered by states and local governments with minimal federal oversight. Congress rejected these ideas. He also impounded funds appropriated by Congress until the courts stopped him. Nixon asked Congress to permit him to reorganize the federal bureaucracy into large departments of human resources, natural resources, economic development, and community development but Congress ignored him. Congress was not about to permit its regular ties with agencies, through its committees, to be severed (Nathan 1986).

At the beginning of his second term Nixon returned to executive reorganization by creating a two tier cabinet in which the Secretaries of the Treasury, Health, Education and Welfare, Agriculture, and Housing and Urban Development were to be special assistants to the president with authority over other cabinet officers. Nixon also reduced the size of the White House staff and sent many of them to sub-cabinet positions in departments and agencies where they would be more responsive to the White House than career bureaucrats (Nathan 1986).

As the Watergate affair began to balloon the Administrative Presidency was abandoned and, as the president was increasingly distracted by his personal problems with Watergate, the Office of Management and Budget, which was the Bureau of the Budget with a new emphasis on oversight of department administration, kept the government steady and gave cues to the departments. The Administrative Presidency, as Nixon conceived it, could not have lasted because cabinet officers would not have taken direction from other cabinet officers, and Congress would not have permitted it.

The number of crimes under the label of Watergate – burglaries, electronic eavesdropping, secret payments of cash to indicted burglars – were a response to Nixon's inability to achieve peace in Vietnam and his hostility to critics, many of whom he regarded as 'enemies'. At the end of the day he failed because he held to the illusion of total control (Genovese 1999).

Gerald Ford and Jimmy Carter (1974–7; 1977–81)

The presidencies of Gerald Ford and Jimmy Carter reflected popular unhappiness with the 'imperial presidency' of Vietnam and Watergate. Both presidents promised honesty and transparency in government and did their best to follow through on their promises. Both were doomed to underdeliver, as their presidencies, Carter's in particular, imploded in a way that is characteristic of presidents committed to a political regime that has lost ideological and popular appeal (Skowronek 1993).

Ford was a child of Congress who had been an open and accessible minority leader in the House. He was liked and trusted by Democrats and recommended by House Democratic leaders for the vice presidency when Nixon queried them. His domestic presidency was characterized by a very high number of successful vetoes against congressional spending bills and uneven attempts to fight simultaneous inflation and recession. But ultimately his authority was undermined early on, when he pardoned Nixon and tainted himself with the smell of the very administrative presidency he was expected, and to some expected committed, to reverse.

Jimmy Carter was serious about rolling back executive dominance. Having run on a 'I am not a Washington insider' ticket, he carried his own bags, stopped the playing of Hail to the Chief, and sought to be a citizen president. He sent an ambitious legislative programme to a Democratic controlled Congress, and, after considerable struggle, was able to achieve energy conservation programmes and treaties relinquishing the Canal to Panama. Yet he was also plagued by stagflation, and too committed to the Keynesian paradigm to successfully combat it. A time of troubles in his last year – hostages in Iran, the Russian invasion of Afghanistan, and oil price increases – sealed his defeat, and heralded the end of the post-Vietnam, post-Watergate attempts to return to a more collegial presidency.

Ronald Reagan (1981–9)

Ronald Reagan envisioned a Republican realignment around conservative policies of reducing dependence on government and tax cuts to stimulate a lagging economy. He got his tax cuts, and the deficits that followed, but very little else was achieved. His administration sought to reduce the federal bureaucracy and promoted administrative deregulation. There was no Republican electoral realignment because most voters, despite their liking for Reagan, had not turned into ideological conservatives.

His major foreign policy achievement was the negotiation of an arms-control agreement about nuclear weapons in Europe with Mikhail Gorbachev of the Soviet Union. His principal lieutenant was Secretary of State George Shultz. Reagan operated best with a close adviser who could clear the path for him.

His style failed him when it came to covert action. His CIA Director William Casey launched covert operations all over the world and made an art of dissembling about them to congressional intelligence committees, and lying if necessary. The president's decision to sell weapons to Iran, which was at war with Iraq, was illegal because Iran was officially named a 'terrorist' nation. He had legal discretion on this but never informed Congress as he should have. The secret diversion of funds from the sale to the Contras fighting against the Sandinista government in Nicaragua was a scandal that reduced confidence in Reagan. Reagan was a solo operator who often failed when not presented with good advice and in this case his advisers misled him.

George H. W. Bush (1989–93)

Bush served Reagan's third term. His chief campaign promise was 'no new taxes', which was a campaign ploy rather than serious policy. He presented modest proposals to Congress and skilfully signed on to congressionally initiated ideas for revision of the Clean Air Act, renewal of the Civil Rights Act, and the new American Disabilities Act. But he then took administrative action to dilute the implementation of new laws. Vice President Daniel Quayle chaired the Competitiveness Council that guided Office of Management and Budget (OMB) oversight of new departmental regulations. The White House counsel, C. Boyden Gray, gave Bush a large number of signing statements that questioned the constitutionality of new laws for the environment, safety, and health.

Bush won the approval of Congress to drive Iraqi forces from Kuwait after considerable debate but said clearly that he would have gone ahead if they had refused, and was willing to risk impeachment. There might have been a constitutional crisis except that the war was short and it succeeded. He was effective in creating the coalition of nations that fought in that action and was very effective in working out a START arms-control agreement with the Soviet Union. Again, this was bargaining behind the scenes. He was comfortable with the administrative presidency (cf. Mullins and Wildavsky 1991). He came close in his public statements to confirming the theory of the 'unitary executive', which claimed that the president had sole authority over the executive branch against the interference of Congress (Tiefer 1994).

Bill Clinton (1993–2001)

Clinton yet again sought to reverse the administrative presidency because he was a Democrat whose idea of leadership was to pass reform legislation. For example, his great achievement was to win congressional support over a period of five years to balance the federal budget and create surpluses. His greatest failure was to launch a too ambitious national health care plan. The complexity of the plan, strong opposition from the health care industry and Republican determination to deny him a political victory were more than he could overcome. One result was the election of a Republican Congress in 1994. Yet he did not give up legislative leadership but learned how to achieve some successes through playing the two parties in Congress off against each other to his own credit. For example, he achieved welfare reform, but not as Republicans wanted it, but also in a moderate way that many Democrats opposed. As a believer in persuasion and bargaining rather than executive prerogative, Clinton was trapped – as Bush had been before him – by the polarization of congressional parties.

George W. Bush (2001–9)

George W. Bush entered the White House with the determination to fulfil the Reagan 'revolution' by reversing the direction of big government. He lost the popular vote in 2000 but won the electoral vote. Bush immediately rejected the idea of appealing to a bipartisan or moderate centre in favour of his conservative agenda. He wanted to move policy to the right and congressional Republicans simply played dead as he rolled over them. He used OMB oversight of administrative regulations to loosen controls over environmental law, and conservation. He also increased the number of signing statements saying that he would reserve his own judgment of legislative intent in terms of his authority as commander in chief (Campbell and Rockman 2004).

He became a warrior president after the 9/11 attacks by signalling the defeat of terrorism as his central mission. Action to drive the Taliban and Al Qaeda from Afghanistan won high approval and strengthened congressional Republicans in the 2002 elections. His foreign policy had been for the United States to go it alone in international relations and to avoid 'nation building,' but the invasion of Iraq forced him into nation building by necessity. The invasion, which was justified as action against the 'weapons of mass destruction' which Iraq presumably had, was redefined as an action of nation building for democracy for Iraq and in the region, after no weapons were found (Woodward 2002, 2004).

What appeared to be a quick victory has been drawn out in a long guerrilla war which has become increasingly unpopular with the public and driven Bush's public approval down. The Democrats won control of Congress in the 2006 election but the result has been an impasse between the majority in Congress and the president who has been able to veto all efforts to restrain him in war or force a compromise.

For Bush the Republican, the administrative presidency beckoned. It appeared most visibly in actions taken by Bush on behalf of national security. Bush was armed with congressional approval that he use 'all necessary powers' against terrorists who planned the 9/11 destruction or agents of subsequent terrorists. A 'war' against terrorism was launched by the president without any stipulation about when it might end. He and his lawyers justified any action they might take as justified by the powers of the commander in chief in wartime. His lawyers argued that his actions as commander in chief were not subject to congressional oversight or judicial review. The National Security Agency wiretapped the telephones of American citizens without the court approved warrants that the law required. 'Enemy combatants' captured in Afghanistan and other places were imprisoned, and sat in a legal limbo.

Bush would not compromise with his conception of his constitutional role. But the war was so unpopular by 2007 and his standing was so low that he seemed, much like Johnson, to have undermined his own authority as president with an unpopular war. As with both Nixon and Johnson, war and issues of national security were associated with presidential claims to power which may challenge the constitution itself, but create backlash against the president. When the subprime mortgage crisis escalated to a collapse of the banking system in September 2008, Bush's weakened position – lame duck, deemed ineffective, unpopular – became painfully clear.

Conclusions: the ebbs and flows of presidential authority and style

The gradual strengthening of the institution of the presidency since Roosevelt's executive reorganization should not be confused with the Administrative Presidency which began with Nixon and was pursued by most Republican presidents. The question is whether future presidents will continue this presidency because they find it in their political interests. Political scientists have argued that this is the case. Terry Moe (1985) contended that presidential institutions must be congruent with presidential incentives. Presidents face popular expectations that are not easily fulfilled in a politics of dispersed authority and the fragmentation of pluralist representation. The traditional constitutional checks and balances are an impediment to presidential effectiveness. Therefore presidents maximize their policy effectiveness as much as possible by centralizing 'responsive competence' in the White House, OMB, and the upper reaches of the departments and agencies as much as possible.

Theodore Lowi takes the argument to another level. The nation has developed plebiscitary politics and a 'personal' presidency in which the president stands alone in elections and the executive is divorced from parties and other institutions (Lowi 1985). Not only do presidents centralize authority in their own hands, they substitute image for reality in their propaganda strategies to meet the expectations of publics that they will be effective. This leads to oversell, particularly in foreign policy, which is the one area in which presidents can make their mark, but image may cancel out reality. Lowi despairs of returning to constitutional checks and balances and advocates a third party which would check presidents and require bargaining in government policy-making as a substitute.

My own analysis presented earlier suggests a less linear pattern. There are underlying institutional trends, but much depends on the political identity (Democrat or Republican) and personal style (persuader or doer) of incumbents, as well as their placement in political time (Skowronek 1993). But before passing final judgment, let us turn to our British comparisons.

The British political executive

Three models of British government are in good currency at the present time among UK political observers and researchers (cf. Bevir and Rhodes 2006). The first two are squarely in the collegial and dominant executive moulds. The third most closely approximates the notion of dispersed leadership that is central to this volume. We keep all of them in mind as we examine the prime-ministerial case studies that follow.

Cabinet government

The simple model of the prime minister as chair of a committee who pulls agreement out of discussion is not realistic, and perhaps never has been so except in quiet times. Prime ministers must contend with ministers who are rivals with each other and with the first minister. The prime minister is not an executive in this model but does the political work of leading the party, setting an agenda, reconciling conflicts, and presenting a united front for the government (James 1999). To do this work they need the steady support of cabinets, which, once lost, is hard to regain. Lloyd George and Winston Churchill, Margaret Thatcher, and Tony Blair, achieved temporary dominance but were eventually brought down either by the electorate or by senior colleagues. George Jones uses the image of the 'elastic band' which, if pulled too hard by a prime minister, will snap back toward more collegial government (Jones 1991).

The British presidency

The gap between public expectations of government and the cumbersome character of cabinet government in achieving policy action has prompted prime ministers to fill the gap by taking command of the party and the cabinet by creating a personal political persona through which they win elections and keep the attention of the public as more than first among equals. Such leadership is most likely to occur when prime ministers are determined to make fundamental changes in the society and polity. The mass media love the personification of government. The British 'presidency' cannot become an American presidency. Institutions will not permit it. But mass politics is moving in the same direction in both countries (Foley 1993; Heffernan 2003; see also Poguntke and Webb [2005]).

In this model, the prime minister is much more than the head of a cabinet but becomes a national figure in his own right against which his or her government is judged by the public. The PM must tread a delicate balance between being the leader of a team and standing outside the team. One may refer back to the insights about these factors in American politics put forth by Terry Moe and Ted Lowi discussed earlier. Centralization of administrative control within government and the search for personal approval and popularity go together. Prime ministers violate the constitutional principle that they should receive their advice from ministers and civil servants and rely on personal staffs housed at Number 10 (Foley 1993, 2000).

Peter Hennessy acknowledges these changes but asks a hard question. The job of prime minister is so stressful that its occupants will be tempted to pull all authority to themselves because they believe in themselves and 'self-belief is the greatest spur, and in that lies the potential temptation and deformation of excessive prime ministerialism' (Hennessy 2000).

The core executive

A complex, differentiated executive, in which government officials must invent strategies to win and bargain with each other as coalitions for action are formed is a new conception but not a new reality, for either American or British governance. One is easily beguiled by the hierarchical structure of British government in which prime minister, cabinet, and civil service all collaborate on the surface. But, just as ministers are rivals, politics is everywhere. The prime minister has advantages here but must bargain to win. The logic of institutional incentives and interests dominates the model in which individuals play roles, not so much as individuals, but as office holders. Cabinet government or prime ministerial dominance does not describe reality; bureaucratic politics inside and around the core executive as well as wider policy networks may be equally powerful loci of decision, action, and interpretation (Bevir and Rhodes 2003). Success in negotiating the complex structures of what is in effect a 'differentiated polity' depends on 'the tactics, choices, and strategies they (the players) adapt in using their resources'. In such a polity, the prime minister does not necessarily dominate – although power may well be asymmetrically distributed from time to time. Even from the vantage point of the Cabinet Office, pivotal parts of government have been delegated away from the centre (Flinders 2008) And amidst all of this complexity, cabinet has become a 'dignified' part of the constitution with a limited functional role (Smith 1999; Marsh et al. 2001).

Clement Attlee (1945–51)

Attlee was deputy prime minister in Winston Churchill's wartime government and brought that experience to office. He was a collegial but firm PM who kept a tight hand over a cabinet of strong personalities. He once said: 'Democracy means government by discussion but it is only effective if you can stop people talking' (Hennessey 2000: 148). He let his cabinet ministers talk and argue and doodled while they talked, but he was the only person who could work with all of them. His government introduced the comprehensive welfare state to Britain but it was done through strong ministers overseen by the prime minister. Attlee had no interest in the media as an instrument of politics and was a conservative about precedent and procedures. His ideal prime minister was Stanley Baldwin who presided over governments of the 1920s and 1930s by subtly steering a path forward by balancing ministers. Like Baldwin he was 'a deeply reassuring figure' (Hennessey 2000: 174). He once wrote that 'a fairly egocentric cabinet minister can get along, but an egocentric prime minister can't' (Hennessey 2000: 175).

Winston Churchill (1951–5)

Churchill returned to office in 1951 at age 77. He told John Colville, his assistant, that he would serve one year and then give way to Anthony Eden, the Foreign Secretary (Gilbert 1991: 900). Churchill wanted to restore the wartime alliance with Russia and reduce the Cold War but he found President Dwight Eisenhower, who was elected in 1952, lukewarm on the idea, even after Stalin's death in 1953. As the goal receded he stayed in office, hoping still for success; he also had doubts about Eden, and, as old politicians do, feared that he might die if he gave up office (Hennessy 2000: 206).

He had a small arterial spasm in February 1952, which was kept secret, and he increasingly found it difficult to read materials for cabinet meetings. But he was still able to prepare for debate in the House of Commons and spoke well (Gilbert 1991: 904). From time to time small groups of Ministers approached him to suggest that he give way to Eden but they were rebuffed, and when Eden nearly died from botched surgeries in 1953 Churchill took on the Foreign Office, having relinquished the Ministry of Defence. Eden sought a commitment on resignation after his return but with no success.

A prime minister may be ousted by his cabinet, especially if a successor is agreed upon, but Churchill, a national hero, was special. He was also a traditionalist about cabinet government who left domestic policy to his ministers and admitted that he knew little about economics. He continued to importune Eisenhower about a summit meeting and, in 1953, as the president hesitated, Churchill planned to visit Moscow to talk with Stalin's successors. Eden was against the trip and opposed it in the cabinet. He prevailed and Churchill did not go (Gilbert 1991: 930). In June 1953 Churchill suffered a stroke and was temporarily paralyzed on his left side but presided over the cabinet the next day. The illness was again kept secret (Gilbert 1991: 928). An increasing number of ministers wanted Churchill to resign. Yet he went to the south of France to work on book revisions. Eden was desperate for a decision but the prime minister was brilliant in the House debate on his return, so he stayed in office to continue to seek a summit meeting.

In the autumn of 1954, Churchill, now 80, promised to go in 1955 in time for Eden to campaign in the general election of that year. Colville wrote in the spring of 1955 that Churchill was aging month by month. He read only the newspapers. When Eden asked for a resignation date he was rebuffed again, but after a group of ministers came to see Churchill he realized that they wanted him out and he resigned in April, reluctantly (Gilbert 1991: 933–4).

Anthony Eden (1955–7)

In 1993 Lord Thorneycroft, a colleague, wrote of Eden and Suez: 'It's very difficult to challenge a Prime Minister, but to challenge a Prime Minister on foreign policy, if that is his real strength, is very difficult indeed' (Hennessy 2000: 207). Eden had been the bridesmaid in waiting for so long that many people were deceived by 'the politics of appearances' (Hennessy 2000: 212–13). He looked like a prime minister and the public so regarded him as he increased the Conservative majority in 1955. Colleagues were not so sure. Ministers and civil servants called him a great 'fusser' because he poked inappropriately into the work of his ministers, had temper tantrums over small office difficulties, and did not always receive bad news from civil servants graciously; indeed they often withheld it for fear of the response. He was ill much of the time. The fevers that followed his operations returned and he suffered from bile duct infection and side effects of medicines meant to help (Hennessy 2000: 212–15). He stood alone without personal or political friends; he avoided the smoking rooms in Parliament and refused to join the clubs that politicians frequented. Harold Macmillan wrote in his diary in July 1956 that the government was not working because Eden provided no leadership; of course Macmillan was a rival (Hennessy 2000: 217).

Cabinet government was collegial because the prime minister focused on his own foreign policy interests and had little knowledge of either domestic or economic matters. The Europeans began to create what became the Common Market but he held to the traditional idea about Britain at the centre of Europe, the Commonwealth, and the United States with an autonomy of its own. When Colonel Gamal Nasser, the Egyptian dictator, seized control of the Suez Canal in 1956 Eden reacted in a highly emotional way. He wanted to drive Nasser from power, retake the canal, and foster a new Middle East in which Britain would be the influential power, and keep the Soviets out of the area. Here he did seek, and manage, to dominate cabinet (Verbeek 2003) and involved Britain in a secret invasion plan with France and Israel, with disastrous results.

President Eisenhower had consistently told Eden not to use force and, after force was used, the American Secretary of the Treasury, told Harold Macmillan, the Chancellor of the Exchequer, that the United States would no longer guarantee British credit with the International Monetary Fund, which would have put sterling in jeopardy. Macmillan essentially took over and the prime minister was forced to withdraw British forces from Egypt. An ill man, he went to Jamaica for vacation. After his return in December Eden lied to the House of Commons that he had no prior knowledge of the intentions of Israel, and under pressure from his colleagues, he resigned in January, and Macmillan became prime minister (Epstein 1964: 31–7).

It was clear, in retrospect, that Eden and a few key ministers acted as a chief executive throughout (Verbeek 2003). Eden had plenty of warning that he might fail. Norman Brook, the cabinet secretary, told him that cabinet procedures for discussion were not followed. The Conservative Central Office warned about public uncertainty, Eisenhower made his opposition clear from the beginning, the military professionals complained about lack of guidance from the Government about what to do after the invasion (Hennessey 2000: 243). The Suez story is quite similar to Neville Chamberlain's appeasement debacle in 1938 and 1939. Chamberlain failed to act against Hitler and Eden overreacted. But in both cases the prime minister had such tight control of his government that dissent was muffled. When disaster struck, in both cases, opposition overflowed (Parker 1993).

Harold Macmillan and Alec Douglas-Home (1957–63; 1963–4)

Macmillan dramatized himself as prime minister and ran his government very much in terms of electoral appeals. He did not try to be a 'president' but his dominance of his cabinet was maintained until his fall. Macmillan supported the Suez adventure in 1956 but as Chancellor he learned quickly of the economic price and led the way out, becoming prime minister in the process. He easily established his authority. His colleagues were impressed by his intelligence but he had no friends in the cabinet and relied heavily on Norman Brook, the secretary of the cabinet, and a handful of personal assistants brought into Number 10. He loved being prime minister and, as Anthony Sampson put it, he was 'an isolated man, like an actor' (Sampson 1967: 169). But he did not try to be a British 'president' because he was a traditionalist about institutions.

He pushed the Treasury hard to stimulate the economy before the 1959 election and forced one obdurate chancellor to resign in favour of a compliant one (Lamb 1995: 50). He fought the 1959 election on the theme 'you never had it so good,' and won a great victory. He also established a grip on the public as 'Super Mac', the apostle of affluence. The long run result was a boom that overheated the economy with inflation. But Macmillan had become the personification of government. He was his own foreign secretary in valiant, but unsuccessful attempts to ease the East–West divide in the cold war and win entry for Britain into the Common Market. This was solo work, with cabinet support.

An expansionary budget in 1961 created a crisis in sterling requiring a raise in interest rates and efforts at a 'pay pause', which were ineffective. Matters drifted until the summer of 1962 when Macmillan became frightened and suspected a plot against him from within the government. His response was to sack his chancellor and six other ministers in the 'night of the long knives'. Jeremy Thorpe, a Liberal leader, proclaimed 'Greater love hath no man than that he lay down his friends for his life' (Lamb 1995: 446). A generation of younger Tory leaders was brought into the cabinet and Macmillan set about to revive Tory fortunes. Unfortunately De Gaulle said no to Britain in Europe, the Americans withdrew their offer of the Skybolt missile without informing the British government in advance, and the scandal of the Secretary for War who lied to the House about his sexual escapades rocked the government. At this point Macmillan was hospitalized with prostate cancer. Thinking that he was dying, which was not the case, he resigned, and in the hurried rush to find a successor through party consultations Lord Alec Douglas-Home was chosen who resigned his peerage to do so and held office for a year, returning to a quiescent kind of cabinet government.

Harold Wilson (1964–70; 1974–6)

Wilson was influenced by John Kennedy's use of White House staff for policy innovation. He thought that cabinet government needed loosening to permit fresh ideas and brought outside advisers into Downing Street to be a ginger group. He headed a cabinet that was split between right and left and was also required to balance potential rivals like James Callaghan, George Brown, and Roy Jenkins. He believed that he was the key to winning elections (Pryce 1997: 59, 65). Wilson's hopes for economic planning were never fulfilled because of continual difficulties with the pound and the balance of payments. The government was continually caught in short terms crises, such as the devaluation of the pound in 1967.

Labour lost the 1970 election but returned in 1974. Wilson had said privately that he would serve only two years. His cabinet was more experienced than before and, again, he had to guard carefully against rivals. He dropped the idea of being 'presidential' and encouraged full discussion in the cabinet. Affairs were managed at the top among the PM, James Callaghan, Roy Jenkins, and Dennis Healy at the Treasury. Wilson brought Bernard Donoughue from the London School of Economics (LSE) into Number 10 to head a small policy unit which worked with the cabinet office and unofficial advisers throughout Whitehall. Donoughue reports that relations in Number 10 were nonhierarchical and informal; and that the prime minister was accessible (Donoughue 1987: 31). The account sounds much like the relations among a president and his close advisers.

Edward Heath (1970–4)

We backtrack to Heath. He was a managerial person who believed in rational discussion and had little interest in politics or public opinion. His credo was to get on with the job. The cabinet met regularly for discussion but Heath was stiff with others and lonely at the top (Hennessy 2000: 341). He created the Central Policy Review Staff, a small group of experts to serve the Cabinet Office with expertise. It was resented by civil servants but tamed by the cabinet office (Hennessy 2000: 338–41).

He dominated the cabinet most of the time (Hennessy 2000: 333). But he seldom linked policy to politics and was aloof with the press (Pryce 1997: 101). He lacked the intuitive skills of a good politician and never found a language of popular persuasion (Taylor 2004: 189). He entered office with the intention of loosening regulations on industry, and encouraging economic investment, which he saw as essential for entering Europe. But western economies were entering a period of stagflation, and declining productivity. When Rolls Royce engines were about to go under and Upper Clyde ship builders were on the rocks the government saved their bacon with economic help (Cairncross 1996: 140). This was the famous U-Turn which Prime Minister Thatcher was later to denounce in 1981 by saying 'the lady is not for turning'. The OPEC oil shock of 1973 shattered Heath's hopes for a stable incomes policy and the miner's strike of 1974 made his situation impossible. He offered a pay plan which the miner's unions rejected and thereupon called a general election on the question of 'who governs'. He lost the election contrary to his expectations. The Tory belief in a place for government in bolstering industry was bankrupt. His successor as Tory leader Mrs Thatcher was to bring something new, as well as a new style of prime-ministerial leadership.

James Callaghan (1976–9)

Callaghan was a collegial leader who took issues to the cabinet. His major problem was that the cabinet, the parliamentary party, and the party in the country were deeply divided between those who hungered for socialism and those who sought a middle way. Trade Union leaders had cooperated with the government on wage restraint but they were beginning to lose control of their unions through revolts of militant shop stewards. Callaghan steered the cabinet through hard negotiations for financial help from the International Monetary Fund in return for promises of wage and price stability. But he was unable to win agreement from the Trades Union Congress leaders (Donoughue 1987: 176–80). His downfall was the 'Winter of Discontent' of 1978–9 with an eruption of strikes in transportation, manufacturing, hospitals, food services, railway, and water workers. Ministers lacked the nerve to oppose strikers if they were in nationalized industries. Donouhgue called the events 'a curiously feverish madness affecting industrial relations' (Donoughue 1987: 171).

Labour lost a vote of confidence in the House by one vote in March 1979 and lost the subsequent election. Both parties were now discredited. The 'One Nation' Tories had failed and Labour was in shambles. The advent of Margaret Thatcher and Tony Blair was the response to this intellectual exhaustion. Fresh policy ideas required strong leadership to break conventional moulds in government and society. The modest innovations of cabinet government in previous years were insignificant (Kavanagh 1990: 246–80; 2004: 321–34).

Margaret Thatcher (1979–90)

Thatcher intended to lead and for others to follow. She once said that she would rather be president than prime minister. She was a minority in her first government because she had to appoint many senior shadow ministers. However, within a year most of them were gone, replaced by younger, more amenable colleagues. The key economic posts were held by her apostles from the beginning. Geoffrey Howe at the Treasury cut back spending by 5 per cent, increased interest rates, and announced that 'full' employment was no longer an objective. Interest rates were increased and taxes were raised against inflation. The immediate result was a recession with high unemployment. Inefficient industries like ship building and mining were hit hard but not rescued. The 'wets' in her cabinet protested but were soon dispensed with. She kept her ministers on the defensive about spending in their departments often making flying visits to level hard questions at civil servants. Her approval rating sank to 23 per cent in 1981. But yet, as with Reagan's recession, many voters understood that all other alternatives to economic growth had failed.

The Falklands war of 1982 ensured her re-election in 1983. She worked with a small war cabinet and the military chiefs, and gained considerably in self-confidence (Hennessy 2000: 412–18, 421–2). She eventually learned that she could dominate her cabinet. Ministers were happy to run their departments with side agreements with her (Hennessy 2000: 431). Her style in cabinet was argumentative. She would make an assertion and challenge disagreement, holding to her position and seldom giving way. Discussion was a waste of time to her. Tory men were not used to such women and were almost speechless.

She governed through rows with her own ministers, sometimes in cabinet and sometimes publicly (Young 1989: 430–1, 550; Hennessy 2000: 401). She did nothing to cultivate mutual trust and support so, at the end of the day, there was no loyalty to her (Hennessy 2000: 398). Her closest advisers were Anthony Powell, on temporary duty from the Foreign Office, and Bernard Ingham, her press adviser (Pryce 1997: 181–2). She took advice from them and a few loyal ministers. The cabinet became increasingly a hole in the government.

In her second term she began the privatization of nationalized industries, sold council houses to their tenants, set demands and controls on universities for productivity, abolished the London County Councils and other county councils, which were Labour strongholds, broke the back of the National Miners Union, and continued the reform of labour law to weaken union leaders. She continued with monetary policy and reduced inflation (Young 1989: 212–15, 227; Hennessy 2000: 425). She was not wildly popular at the time of the 1987 election but the Conservatives won 43 per cent of the vote, doing particularly well among skilled workers.

She experienced defections in her third term. Howe had been moved to the Foreign Office and Nigel Lawson appointed to the Treasury. But in 1989 Lawson demanded that Alan Walters, a British economist at Johns Hopkins University, who had set up shop in a bedroom in Downing Street as her economic adviser, be sacked. Lawson argued that it was constitutionally required that she take her advice from the Treasury. Walters stayed and Lawson resigned. She got into a row with Michael Heseltine, her Defence minister, about whether to award a defence contract to a European or American firm. He stood up in the cabinet meeting and walked out declaring that she had not permitted full discussion on the question. Geoffrey Howe was moved from the Foreign Office to leader of the House because he was thought to be too European.

She stubbornly insisted on replacing property taxes with a poll tax shared by all citizens. This was very unpopular because all households paid the same tax. The Tories began to lose by-elections. The final straw came in 1990 when she denounced European Union plans for a single currency. It was 'cloud cuckoo land' she said and accused the European Union of being against 'democracy'. This was too much for Howe. He resigned and accused her of cutting Britain off from Europe. He also criticized her for her neglect of cabinet government, and invited others to voice their opposition. Heseltine immediately stood against her, and lost, but her support was too low and John Major became prime minister.

The question for this paper is whether Margaret Thatcher needed to be so authoritarian as prime minister. Her intransigence at the end finally destroyed her credibility. She may have paid a necessary price, but was it necessary?

John Major (1990–7)

The new prime minister was a collegial leader who tried to turn the clock back to cabinet government. He was good at listening, consulting, and compromise. His competitors for the job were given special responsibilities. He kept in touch with the parliamentary party (Foley 1993: 199). His great difficulties were surmounting the conflicts within his cabinet and party, particularly over Britain's role in Europe, and his inability to project a favourable image of his qualities of leadership in the new politics of personal leadership. He followed

Margaret Thatcher, fought hard and tried, with only limited success, to isolate his leadership from the pattern of expectations set by her dominant style of leadership, and indeed from her ever-watchful and increasingly critical eye. Winning the 1992 election unexpectedly, he was eventually eclipsed by Tony Blair (Foley 2000: 81–8, 146–84), and so was the attempt to revive cabinet government.

Tony Blair (1997–2007)

Tony Blair became the protagonist of 'New Labour', that is, a centrist party that would combine a renovated, more efficient welfare state with the vitality of the market. As prime minister he replaced conventional cabinet government with a system of concentric circles with himself at the centre. To some extent it fit the 'core executive' model except that Blair provided strong direction and animation on issues he cared about. The inner circle consisted of himself and a few close, unelected advisers who worked on policy and press relations. The next circle added Gordon Brown, Chancellor of the Exchequer, and one or two other Minister advisers, and so on. Gordon Brown oversaw economic policy by agreement with Blair. The two men made economic policy by themselves, and informed the cabinet what it was to be. Jack Straw, the Home Secretary at the time, told Peter Hennessy's students: 'The prime minister is operating as chief executive of... various subsidiary companies and you are called to account for yourself' (Hennessy 2000: 523). The energy in the system came from Blair. He told a BBC interviewer that, contrary to report, he did discuss policy with ministers but criticized previous Labour governments where the cabinet would sometimes meet for two days to resolve an issue: 'I've got a feeling with this thing that is you have a strong idea of what you want to do and believe in pushing it through, then you're...a dictator. And if not then you're "weak"... You pays your Money and you takes your choice' (Hennessy 2000: 519–20).

As the central figure in government Blair articulated national policy, not in parliament, but through the media, primarily by speeches. His leadership had plebiscitarian traits; he confirmed Wilson's insight that the prime minister's connection with the public was the key to effective influence. Ministers managed their departments and policy as usual was negotiated in networks beyond Whitehall but he was out in front on the big issues: Northern Ireland, the Balkans, Europe, and the war in Iraq. Policies to improve education and health services were delegated to ministers.

Blair's role in the war in Iraq is far too complex to be dealt with in this chapter (Kampfner 2003; Seldon 2007). He thought that Britain was the only country that might advise the Americans well, even constrain them. He was also a 'conviction politician', who saw right and wrong in the world and wished to stand with the right (Seldon 2004: 489). He believed that the only way that Britain could work on the world stage was in concert with the United States. George W. Bush was grateful for his support but set policy by his own stars. Public opinion in Britain about going to war was always shaky. Nor was the media particularly supportive. One hundred and thirty nine Labour backbenchers voted no. The cabinet was divided and uncertain but Blair used the threat of weapons of mass destruction to carry them. The Foreign Office was less than enthusiastic. Blair carried the day by force of personality (Seldon 2004: 504, 573, 580, 595–6).

The increasing unpopularity of the war coincided with Gordon Brown's restlessness about Blair's promise to resign before the next election and eventually led Blair to resign in 2007. He had hoped to stay on but yielded to the facts of politics.

Conclusions: executive centralization and its limits

The temptations to centralize the political executive in both systems are strong because in part they are driven by popular politics: leaders must succeed or appear to succeed. Centralization has been at work in the development of the institutional presidency but for most of those years, the White House and departments have worked together, in varying degrees, to develop policy. The attempts to control all policy from the White House began with Nixon and has been taken to great lengths by George W. Bush, but the pattern in the period in between has been uneven. There is certainly no monotonous trend: some presidents accept the realities of dispersed democratic leadership and try to navigate them as best they can. Only a few, Republicans mostly, try to supersede them by flexing their executive muscles – with varying degrees of success.

Bush has gone beyond the administrative presidency to insistence on the unitary executive, which in a variety of forms claims presidential dominance. The traditional constitutional idea is that the president executes the laws, along with congressional oversight and judicial review. Some advocates of the new executive claim that the president may judge the constitutionality of laws as well as the Supreme Court (Yoo 2005). Others claim that the president's authority as commander in chief is not subject to either legislative or judicial check (Savage 2007). An extreme claim is that the president has authority to do what he likes in administration without any scrutiny. This has all to be sorted out but the extreme claims are not likely to live.

Undue centralization may fail. Such close control of affairs permits too many policy mistakes because there is too little debate and discussion at the centre. The handful of policy makers at the top are blindsided by events. Future American presidents, especially Democrats, will require large coalitions in Congress and the country to win support for their policies. The George

W. Bush presidency has perhaps taught future Republican presidents that it is hazardous to try to govern with 50 per cent plus 1.

The British presidency thesis gained support on the back of first the early Wilson, then the Thatcher and most recently the Blair leadership styles, as well as an institutional analysis of the growth of the Cabinet office, and special advisers around the prime minister. To the extent there is presidentialization in the British system it is largely of an informal kind. The prime minister does not have the constitutional authority of a president but skilful public leadership, innovative policy ideas that challenge conventional wisdom, joined to election victories and parliamentary majorities, permitted two leaders to dominate their cabinets and place policymaking in a few hands responsive to them. But it is important to note that both Thatcher and Blair as leaders were eventually repudiated by their own followers. We should also remember that the prime minister wedged between them, John Major, managed to govern for seven years in a more classic collegial style.

The British case is less clear than the American one. There is, for example, no party-political pattern there, whereas in the States executive dominance attempts have consistently been the work of Republican presidents. Future patterns appear to depend more upon the leadership styles of future prime ministers than on path-dependent institutional imperatives. But there are institutional features of British government that offer opportunities for prime ministerial dominance. Both the House of Commons and the Cabinet find it difficult to restrain a popular prime minister; there are more checks and balances further removed from the centre, for instance, in the negotiated orders of the many policy networks that are the engine rooms of low-politics governance. It is, however, not clear how a classic model of 'cabinet government' could be recovered given the growing pressures on governments to act quickly and decisively in high-politics crises. And yet, the elastic band may still hold, even though the centre of gravity is closer to the top.

Bibliography

Aberbach, J. and Peterson, M. A., 'Control and Accountability: Dilemmas of the Executive Branch', in J. Aberbach and M. A. Peterson (eds.), *The Executive Branch* (Oxford: Oxford University Press, 2005), 525–54.

Ball, S. and Seldon, A. (eds.), *The Heath Government, 1970–1974: A Reappraisal* (London: Longman, 1996).

Barber, J. D., *The Presidential Character: Predicting Performance in the White House* (Englewood Cliffs, New Jersey: Prentice-Hall, 1985).

Bevir, M. and Rhodes, R. A. W., *Interpreting British Governance* (London: Routledge, 2003).

——— *Governance Stories* (London: Routledge, 2006).

Cairncross, A.,'The Health Government and the British Economy', in S. Ball and A. Seldon (eds.), *The Heath Government 1970–1974* (Harlow and London: Addison Wesley Longman, 1996), 107–38.

Campbell, C. and Rockman, B. (eds.), *The Bush Presidency: First Appraisals* (Chatham, New Jersey: Chatham House Publishers, 1991).

———(eds.), *The George W. Bush Presidency: Appraisals and Prospects* (Washington, D. C.: Congressional Quarterly Press, 2004).

Dahl, R. A., *Preface to Democratic Theory* (Chicago: University of Chicago Press, 2006).

Donoughue, B., *Prime Minister: The Conduct of Policy under Harold Wilson and James Callaghan* (London: Jonathan Cape, 1987).

Epstein, L., *British Politics in the Suez Crisis* (Urbana: University of Illinois Press, 1964).

Flinders, M., *Delegated Governance and the British State: Walking without Order* (Oxford: Oxford University Press, 2008).

Foley, M., *The Rise of the British Presidency* (Manchester: Manchester University Press, 1993).

——*The British Presidency: Tony Blair and the Politics of Public Leadership* (Manchester: Manchester University Press, 2000).

Genovese, M., *The Watergate Crisis* (Westport, Conn.: The Greenwood Press, 1999).

Gilbert, M., *Churchill, A Life* (New York: Henry Holt and Company, 1991).

Hamby, A., *Beyond the New Deal: Harry S. Truman and American Liberalism* (New York: Columbia University Press, 1973).

Hargrove, E. C., *Presidential Leadership: Personality and Political Style* (Toronto: The MacMillan Company, 1966).

——*The Power of the Modern Presidency* (Philadelphia, Penn.: Temple University Press, 1974).

——*Jimmy Carter as President: Leadership and the Politics of the Public Good* (Baton Rouge, Louisiana: Louisiana State University Press, 1988).

——*The President as Leader* (Lawrence, Kans.: University of Kansas Press, 1999).

——*The Effective Presidency: Lessons on Leadership from John F. Kennedy to George W. Bush* (Boulder, Col.: Paradigm Publishers, 2008).

——and Nelson, M., *Presidents, Politics, and Policy* (New York: Knopf, 1984).

——and Owens, J. (eds.), *Leadership in Context* (London: Rowman and Littlefield, 2002).

Heffernan, R., 'Prime Ministerial Predominance? Core Executive Politics in the UK', *British Journal of Politics and International Relations*, 5/3 (2003), 347–72.

Hennessy, P., *The Prime Minister: The Office and Its Holders Since 1945* (London: Allen Lane, The Penguin Press, 2000).

James, S., *British Cabinet Government* (London: Routledge, 1999).

Jones, G. W., 'Presidentialization in a Parliamentary System', in C. Campbell and M. Wyszomirski (eds.), *Executive Leadership in Anglo-American Systems* (Pittsburgh: Pittsburgh University Press, 1991), 111–37.

Kampfner, J., *Blair's Wars* (New York: Simon and Schuster, 2003).

Kavanagh, D., *Thatcherism and British Politic: The End of Consensus?* (Oxford: Oxford University Press, 1990).

——'Conclusion: Reading and Misreading Old Labour', in A. Seldon and K. Hickson (eds.), *New Labour, Old Labour: The Wilson and Callaghan Governments, 1974–1979* (London: Routledge, 2004), 321–34.

King, A. (ed.), *The British Prime Minister*, 2nd edn. (Basingstoke: Macmillan, 1985).

Lamb, R., *The Macmillan Years: The Emerging Truth* (London: John Murray, 1995).

Lowi, T., *The Personal President: Power Invested, Promises Unfulfilled* (Ithaca, New York: Cornell University Press, 1985).

Marsh, D., Richards, D., and Smith, M. J., *Changing Patterns of Governance: Reinventing Whitehall?* (Basingstoke: Palgrave, 2001).

Moe, T., 'The Politicized Presidency', in J. E. Chubb and P. E. Peterson (eds.), *The New Directions in American Politics* (Washington D.C.: The Brookings Institution, 1985), 235–71.

Mullins, K. and Wildavsky, A., 'The Procedural Presidency of George Bush', *Society,* 28/2 (1991), 49–59.

Nathan, R., *The Administrative Presidency* (New York: Macmillan, 1986).

Neustadt, R. E., *Presidential Power and the Modern Presidents* (New York: The Free Press, 1992).

Parker, R. A. C., *Chamberlain and Appeasement: British Policy and the Coming of the Second World War* (New York: St. Martin's Press, 1993).

Pimlott, B., *Harold Wilson* (London: Harper Collins, 1992).

Poguntke, T. and Webb, P., *The Presidentialization of Politics: A Comparative Study of Modern Democracies* (Oxford: Oxford University Press, 2005).

Pryce, S., *Presidentializing the Premiership* (New York: St. Martins Press, 1997).

Sampson, A., *Harold Macmillan: A Study in Ambiguity* (London: Allen Lane/The Penguin Press, 1967).

Savage, C., *Takeover: The Return of the Imperial Presidency and the Subversion of American Democracy* (Boston: Little Brown and Company, 2007).

Schlesinger, Jr., A. M., *War and the American Presidency* (New York: W. W. Norton, 2005).

Seldon, A., *Blair* (London: The Free Press, 2004).

——and Hickson, K. (eds.), *New Labour, Old Labour: The Wilson and Callaghan Governments, 1974–1979* (London: Routledge, 2004).

——(ed.), *Blair's Britain: 1997–2007* (Cambridge: Cambridge University Press, 2007).

Skowronek, S., *The Politics Presidents Make: Leadership from John Adams to George Bush* (Cambridge, Mass.: The Belknap Press of Harvard University, 1993).

Smith, M. J., *The Core Executive in Britain* (New York: St. Martins Press, 1999).

Taylor, R., 'The Rise and Fall of the Social Contract', in A. Seldon and K. Hickson (eds.), *New Labour, Old Labour: The Wilson and Callaghan Governments, 1974–1979* (London: Routledge, 2004), 70–104.

Tiefer, C., *The Semi-Sovereign Presidency: The Bush Administration's Strategy of Governing Without Congress* (Boulder, Col.: Westview Press, 1994).

Verbeek, B., *Decision-Making in Great Britain during the Suez Crisis. Small groups and a Persistent Leader* (Aldershot: Ashgate, 2003).

Weiner, T., *Legacy of Ashes: The History of the CIA* (New York: Doubleday, 2007).

Woodward, B., *Bush at War* (New York: Simon and Schuster, 2002).

——*Plan of Attack* (New York: Simon and Schuster, 2004).

Yoo, J., *The Powers of War and Peace: The Constitution and Foreign Affairs After 9/11* (Chicago: The University of Chicago Press, 2005).

Young, H., *The Iron Lady: A Biography of Margaret Thatcher* (New York: Farrar Straus, and Giroux/The Noonday Press, 1989).

Chapter 3

Incomplete Empowerment: Female Cabinet Ministers in Anglo-American Systems

Patricia Lee Sykes

Dispersed leadership can provide significant opportunities for marginalized groups to seek emancipation and secure representation, but leadership dispersal can also pose unique challenges for political minorities. In the historical development of Anglo-American nations, the success of women's movements propelled women into cabinet posts, especially during the late twentieth century. In fact, a 'Britonnic network' of reformers generally linked women's movements across the Pacific and the Atlantic throughout Anglo-American history (Belich 2001: 167). The achievements of women's movements demonstrate the broader 'democratic dynamic' that contributes to leadership dispersal, which the introductory chapter of this volume identifies. At the same time, however, aspects of political development have restricted the ability of female ministers to actually lead the way in promoting policies that advance the interests and enhance the status of women as a group. In general, women have moved into cabinet at a juncture in political development when both ideological and institutional trends constrained their authority. Female cabinet ministers have achieved greater descriptive and symbolic representation, but they have made much less progress in bringing significant changes to the substance and process of public policy. As a result, their experiences constitute cases of leadership dispersal with incomplete empowerment.

Anglo nations share common legal and philosophical roots, which have given rise to similar institutions, and the experiences of their female cabinet ministers largely converge into a single story of the unfulfilled promise of leadership dispersal.[1] Even though Anglo systems often present themselves as models of democracy, women remain under-represented in government, especially in positions of executive leadership. To a great extent, women encounter obstacles that stem from the high degree of 'masculinism' that traditionally characterizes adversarial, Anglo systems (DiStefano 1983; Duerst-Lahti and Kelly 1995). Deeply embedded in the rules, expectations, and norms of executive leadership, masculinism systematically serves to privilege masculine attributes in leaders and places women executives at a distinct disadvantage.

A concept commonly used in gender studies, masculinism provides a contrast to feminalism. Whereas masculinism privileges attributes associated with men, feminalism (its conceptual counterpart) prefers traits associated with women. Feminalism also assumes female agency and includes women's own preferences in its construction. It differs from feminine, a concept constructed by men, which treats women as weak and inferior to men and masculinity. Finally, feminism comprises an ideological element of feminalism that, among other aims, seeks to enhance women's power and to achieve equality between women and men. (Duerst-Lahti 2002). To succeed in Anglo systems, female cabinet ministers have generally needed to put aside feminalist priorities and preferences and embrace the masculinism that Anglo institutions require.

The leadership of female cabinet ministers reveals the gender-specific nature of both ideological trends and institutional developments. Simply by virtue of being male, men bring a degree of authority to almost any ideological or institutional context, but women usually struggle to satisfy the masculinist norms and expectations of political leadership. In general, leadership dispersal should favour feminalist leadership styles, which are more participatory, open, and engaging than traditional, masculinist leadership. When leadership is dispersed within Anglo, adversarial governments, however, women encounter substantial difficulties as they lack the personal clout to compensate for limited institutional authority. To succeed in cabinet, women who wish to pursue change require a favourable ideological climate and substantial institutional integrity. Most female cabinet ministers have failed to enjoy either of those conditions. In particular, two highly masculinist macro-trends have affected the content and process of executive government in their countries in recent decades.

First, women in cabinet have had to contend with the global wave of neo-liberalism that produced a profound impact in Anglo countries where individualism had already established deep roots. The prevalence of this policy paradigm in the cabinet rooms of these countries created obstacles for women seeking to advance classic feminist causes or adopt feminalist approaches to leadership. Of course, it created opportunities for women politicians who shared its ideological commitments, most notably Margaret Thatcher (though she achieved her goals as prime minister rather than as a mere member of cabinet). Female cabinet ministers who endorsed neo-liberalism generally proved able to exercise more effective policy leadership than others. Yet neo-liberal women failed to contribute to leadership dispersal as a democratic dynamic by forging a broader set of values and principles that serve the interests or enhance the status of women as a politically marginalized group.

Second, the 'presidentialization' of the executive – the tendency towards increasing and concentrating prime-ministerial authority in and over cabinet – provides another macro-trend that has affected female ministers. Indeed, that phenomenon has been bad news for leadership dispersal in general, arguably altering the constitutional balance of Westminster style cabinet systems and effectively limiting the influence of all cabinet ministers.[2] More directly relevant to this chapter, just as women reached cabinet level in greater numbers, the leadership opportunities associated with that office were eroding.

At first glance, it might appear that women who become prime ministers would benefit from presidentialization and gain greater latitude to push feminalist agendas and styles, but that view overlooks the fundamental masculinism of the top spot in Anglo systems. The legal foundation and political structure of most Anglo systems pose distinct challenges for women because their adversarial institutional arrangements are highly masculinist. To facilitate programmatic change, adversarial systems concentrate power in the executive, and to ensure accountability, they rely on combat between two major political parties. Women leaders in such systems usually need to show they are capable of being strong, determined, and decisive.

Prime Minister Thatcher, the best known and most influential woman leader in the Anglo world, proved she was capable by practising masculinist leadership – in substance and style. Thatcher insisted that she alone had a remedy for the problems that plagued the United Kingdom, and she promoted her public philosophy in highly masculinist terms by extolling the virtues of rugged individualism and fierce anti-communism. Moreover, she developed a distinctly masculinist style, which she described in the confrontational, combative language of 'conviction politics' (Sykes 2000). It was her aggressive style as much as the substance of her leadership that conjured up the image of Boadicea – the ancient warrior Queen – and earned her the appellation Iron Lady. The first and only woman British prime minister satisfied masculinist norms and expectations by displaying a decisive and divisive demeanour and avoiding any association with classic feminist causes. As this chapter shows, the neo-liberal substance of recent political regimes and the presidentialization of parliamentary systems have only intensified the masculinist character of executive leadership in Anglo systems. Consequently, these trends have limited the leadership momentum of the women's movement and obstructed the empowerment of female ministers with classic feminist agendas and feminalist leadership styles.

Women leaders in neo-liberal times

Primarily in the 1980s, Anglo nations experienced a resurgence of conservative movements and political ideas. More universally labelled 'neo-liberals', the reformers rolled back the state and revived nineteenth century free-market principles. (In some but not all Anglo nations, neo-liberal reformers have also advocated social conservatism by encouraging a return to family values and traditional roles.) As an ideology, neo-liberalism limits women because its market-oriented ideology shifts public policy away from the goal of equality to equity (fairness and impartiality), reinforcing the bias of classical liberal theory that fails to recognize differences between men and women.[3] Just as important, in a neo-liberal period of fiscal conservatism, budgetary constraints have made it difficult for women leaders to promote new social and economic programmes or protect existing ones from cuts (Bashevkin 1998). As a result, neo-liberal times have imposed limits on the ambition and creativity of women as increasing numbers of them move into cabinet posts.

Most female ministers in Anglo systems have occupied posts that deal with domestic policies and programmes. As women have traditionally dealt with the 'domestic' in the home, heads of government have put them in charge of similar duties in cabinet. In particular, politicians, the press, and the public often consider subjects such as education, health, and welfare as 'women's issues', and polling data consistently show that women do care about these issues more than men do. In cabinet, many of these positions threaten to become regendered as the 'women's posts'. Both the public and politicians increasingly view these posts as 'feminine' – or more accurately 'feminalist', the opposite of masculinist. They appear to favour attributes associated with women – collectivism, caring, and compassion. As a Minister for Education in Ireland declared, 'I can go to a European Council meeting now, and all the Education Ministers are women. It's kind of a branding almost' (Interview, Mary Hanafin, 24 June 2005). In the case of female cabinet ministers in the last several decades, they have also been the areas that endured the most severe budget cuts or diminished rates of funding. As a consequence, the political costs of implementing the neo-liberal agenda have outweighed many benefits women might have derived from fitting into feminalist slots.

The United Kingdom

In the United Kingdom, budget cuts in education started in the 1970s and continued until the twenty-first century. Ironically, Thatcher was the first woman Secretary of State for Education who was forced to endure the unpopularity of budget cuts. When the Conservative government decided that older elementary school children should no longer receive free milk, the popular press vilified 'Thatcher the Milk Snatcher'. Despite her media image as mean and miserly, Thatcher generally sought to defend her department and its programmes in the face of budget cuts. Her performance as Education Secretary provided few hints of the radical neo-liberal assault she would later level against the welfare state. To the public and the press at the time, what mattered more was the fact that a woman deprived the children of their milk. Several subsequent women ministers in charge of feminalist domestic policies such as education, health, and welfare would suffer similar fates.

Thatcherism lingered long after her premiership, and when Labour returned to government after eighteen years in opposition, its female ministers continued to endure the political costs of budget cuts. Dubbed 'Blair's Babes' by the *Times* (of London), 101 women Labour MPs won seats in the 1997 election. The Labour party had taken several affirmative steps to increase the representation of women, adopting women-only shortlists for parliamentary candidates and reserving at least three spots in the shadow cabinet. The party required Prime Minister Tony Blair to bring members of the shadow cabinet into government, and predictably he placed all but one of the women in domestic posts. The first time a British government included many female ministers, the prime minister put them in positions where they would encounter stringent fiscal constraints and substantial political controversy – as the case of Harriet Harman illustrates.

First in the shadow cabinet and later in government, Harman repeatedly ignited public controversy, but even earlier she incurred the wrath of many members of the parliamentary Labour party (PLP) as a proponent of the positive discrimination (affirmative action) reforms. While the women-only shortlists encountered resistance from the constituency parties, reserving spaces for women in the shadow cabinet sparked opposition from men in the PLP. As Harman recalled 'the hysteria' generated by the rule that three of the twenty seats must go to women, she explained: 'Anybody would think it was like the death of a first born. It was so controversial and the hatred for the people who were advancing this argument was absolutely profound' (Interview, Harriet Harman, 12 July 2004). She and several other women entered the cabinet when and where male colleagues already resented their presence.

As Secretary of State for Social Security (1997–8), Harman was responsible for cutting benefits for single-parent households, a policy New Labour called the New Deal for Lone Parents, essentially a neo-liberal programme that substituted workfare for welfare. Gender clearly coloured much of the criticism directed at Harman. As she described the 'flack' she got, she conveyed the tone of the attack when she recalled her critics' comments that:

> 'You're forcing mothers to work. You don't value motherhood'... It was a woman cutting women's benefits. I mean if I had been a gray anonymous man, then I could have got away with it. But I was incredibly high profile.

The prime minister might have thought that a woman could more easily institute these cuts and soften their impact, but instead the media magnified the maternal role and Harman's failure to fulfil it.

Admittedly, as part of the New Labour movement, Harman had supported the party's commitment to maintain fiscal restraint. In its manifesto, Labour promised to adhere to the Conservative spending limits at least for the first two years in government. That electoral pledge helped to modernize party policy and proved successful at the polls, but it also placed the Minister for Social Security in a politically untenable position, conceivably the worst spot in the New Labour government. Harman explained:

> I inherited a budget that was going down. So I had to stand in the dispatch box, newly elected as the new government and say, 'Hello. We're Labour. We're here to cut your benefits'. Well you can imagine that was not very popular... [I]t caused absolute turmoil and uproar.

Harman believes the policy ultimately proved successful once she had 'been sacked and [the government] started putting benefits up', but to achieve that success, she served as the sacrificial lamb on the altar of electoral expediency and in the name of economic efficiency.

Other women ministers in the New Labour government also struggled to succeed under the pressures of continued neo-liberal restructuring, and once again a female Education Minister suffered. A former teacher herself, Secretary of State for the Department of Education and Skills (2001–2) Estelle Morris tried to defend the interests of her department and clientele groups such as the teachers unions. According to her cabinet colleagues, she was popular with educators and their advocates but engaged in a tug of war with the prime minister and his staff. In addition, she was beset with business-like obstacles in managing a department with limited resources. The department failed to achieve standardized literacy and numeracy targets, became embroiled in controversy concerning the marking of A-level papers, and got stuck with delays vetting teachers for the new school year. Ultimately, the public will prove more likely to remember Morris's resignation than her beleaguered tenure in office. During her resignation press conference, she broke down in tears and declared that she did not feel 'up to the job', as she read from a script that the Number 10 Downing Street press office prepared. The popular press used her experience to confirm the worst stereotypes about women overwhelmed by serious work and unable to shoulder weighty responsibility.

Ireland

In Ireland during the period of economic reform in the 1980s, one woman minister Gemma Hussey successively occupied all three of the highly sensitive, feminalist posts: Minister for Education (1982–6), Minister for Social Welfare (1986–7), and Minister for Health (1987). For Ireland, the 1980s provided a period of social liberalism, but the economic crisis – and fear of the International Monetary Fund's intervention – forced the government to adopt stringent spending limits and budget cuts. From 1982 to 1987, the Taoiseach (prime minister) Garret FitzGerald led a coalition composed of

Fine Gael (the more liberal of the two major parties) and Labour (a minor party). Originally an Independent member of the Seanad (senate) in a university seat, Hussey had joined Fine Gael and served as Government Leader of the Seanad, before she moved into the Dail (lower house) and into cabinet. Her quick elevation to the cabinet sparked resentment among male ministers. 'There was a lot of jealousy', she recalled. 'A lot of talk about she's only there because she's a woman' (Interview, Gemma Hussey, 7 June 2005). Despite her meteoric rise, the Taoiseach had hardly elevated her to an enviable position.

Instead, the economic crisis meant that the first woman education minister would be responsible for implementing policies construed as harmful to children. Hussey described getting her appointment as being 'given a poisoned chalice', a term women leaders frequently use to depict the sorry state of their selection. She continued:

> Education was going to be – it was one of the big spending ministries – therefore, there were going to be problems. Because there were going to have to be cutbacks as there were going to have to be in health and social welfare. They were the big spending ministries and so the whole time we were in government, I was embroiled in endless public controversy... Because of the fiscal constraints, from day one I was thrown into the deep end... You go into the Dail everyday and you're faced with the howling mobs – and the teachers unions, the parents associations. I was the villain, the number one villain for most of the time.

When Hussey needed to cut one of the teachers training colleges, she recalled, 'You'd think that I had declared WW III. The reaction was so (pause), I was never off the front page, it seemed to me'. Inevitably (and to her dismay), the mass media compared Hussey with her nemesis Thatcher.

From the beginning, Hussey would have preferred an appointment in foreign affairs, an area where she had ample experience and relevant skills. When FitzGerald reshuffled his cabinet in 1986, he promised her the proposed post of Minister for European Affairs, the result of dividing the Department of Foreign Affairs to deal with Northern Ireland separately. He broke his promise, however, when the Minister for Foreign Affairs (from Labour) refused to leave his position. In her diaries, she recorded her disappointment and wrote, 'Garret has made the most appalling mess of the re-shuffle and I am the victim to expediency' (Hussey 1990: 197). In an interview almost two decades later, she explained that when she moved from education to social welfare, her situation went from bad to worse. As she put it:

> [I] found myself suddenly transported to social welfare – about which I knew nothing and in a situation where the Minister for Finance was looking for a list of cuts. It was a nightmare. The social welfare brief was a nightmare.

Her diaries record her constant struggle to combat proposed cuts. While she managed to achieve some limited success, after a brief period at health, her tenure in cabinet – and that of the Fine Gael–Labour coalition – came to an end.

Mary O'Rourke followed Hussey as Minister for Education and expressed similar sentiments. When she took over, she recalled, 'It was a time of huge cutbacks in education and in health. We had come in in 1987 when the world was crumbling around us, and it looked as if we were going bankrupt' (Interview, Mary O'Rourke, 15 June 2005). In successive Fianna Fail dominated coalition governments (the largest party and more socially conservative), O'Rourke occupied several ministerial positions in addition to education: Minister for Health (1991–2) and then some economic posts. In particular as Minister for State for Public Enterprise (1997–2002), she managed to convince the government to spend money to improve the safety of the railways – following a tragic accident that drew national media attention. While the media magnified the need to fund her measure, she also benefited from an improved Irish economy.

By the twenty-first century, another woman Minister for Education Mary Hanafin, inherited a different fiscal environment. With the 'instant acceptance of a woman being in a social policy area', Hanafin could also reap the rewards that went with Ireland's economic prosperity. Enthusiastically, she announced, 'Obviously, when you've got money, it's a good time to tackle things you've never tackled before, like special needs. [And] it's a good time to focus on the disadvantaged as well – and pump more resources into it'. Less subject to the ideological limits of neo-liberalism and more pragmatic, the Irish government in the twenty-first century has proven willing to spend more on social programmes. In this instance, the early struggles of women ministers helped set the stage for success at a later date in development when the ideological climate started to change and economic opportunities expanded.

Australia

In Australia, Margaret Guilfoyle served successively as Minister for Education (1975), Minister for Social Security (1975–80), and Minister for Finance (1980–3) – and she expressed some of the same views as Harman and Hussey when she discussed her first two posts. Trained as an accountant and working in a Liberal government (the conservative major party), she was nonetheless a reluctant participant in the early cutbacks that presaged the neo-liberal revolution. According to Guilfoyle:

> [T]he challenging part in my case [at Education and Social Security] was probably to maintain the system that was there and not have it reduced.... When we went in in '75, there was a move that you had to, as the Prime Minister termed it always, 'reign in expenditure'. And as my department was the largest spender, of course it was very vulnerable to cabinet decisions to change and to reduce (Interview, Margaret Guilfoyle, 13 March 2003).

Comparing social security to finance, Guilfoyle recalled, 'It is a very different role. At the Social Security Department, you'd feel, you'd wake up every morning thinking, "Who hates us today?"' As she described her promotions, she observed the irony that 'after being the biggest spending minister', she 'became the finance minister to stop all of the other spending'.

Guilfoyle found the transition from the feminalist posts to the masculinist one of finance relatively easy for some special reasons. Among other things, when Senator Guilfoyle moved to finance, she shared responsibilities with John Howard who was then the head of the Treasury and a member of the lower house. Being paired with Howard probably helped to dissipate doubts about the ability of a woman to handle the job. In addition, Australia avoided the most extreme cuts and declined to dismantle massive parts of the state that provide social services.[4]

Social conservatism

Neo-liberal policies entailed more than just spending cuts, and other aspects of the agenda presented additional obstacles in some Anglo countries more than others. Social conservatism constituted a significant part of the neo-liberal programme in Australia, Canada, and the United States. As the Australian Minister for Family and Community Services and as Minister for Women (2001–3), Senator Amanda Vanstone frequently found herself in the awkward position of releasing reports that would document the disproportionately harmful impact that ostensibly 'family friendly' tax policies had on women (Summers 2003). When interviewed in 2003, Vanstone said less about her accomplishments in that post than what she had achieved earlier as Minister for Justice (1997–2001), a post outside cabinet (Interview, Amanda Vanstone, 27 March 2003). As the Canadian Minister for Justice and Attorney General (1990–3), Kim Campbell had to contend with competing social forces surrounding moral issues such as abortion and rape (Campbell 1996). In the United States, Secretary for Health and Human Services (1993–8) Donna Shalala drew fire from religious groups for advocating access to the abortion pill RU486. The large rural (and morally conservative) communities in these three countries might make them especially receptive to the religious right.

The United States experience

The United States provides a somewhat distinctive case in yet another respect. The opposite of Australia which maintained a relatively large public sector, the United States has always had a substantially smaller state to roll back. Perhaps for this reason, women who occupied positions dealing with education, health, and welfare suffered much less than many of their Anglo counterparts.

On the other hand, one controversial position did become regendered and feminalized in the neo-liberal era. Deregulation made women administrators of the Environmental Protection Agency (EPA) extremely unpopular – with either the public or the president. An eager participant in the Reagan revolution, from 1981 to 1983 Ann Burford gained notoriety in the press and the public by cutting the EPA's budget by 200 million and slashing the staff by 23 per cent (before she slid into the Superfund scandal that forced her resignation). Twenty years later, former governor of New Jersey Christine Todd Whitman, as administrator of the EPA (2001–3), clashed repeatedly with the administration of President George W. Bush. When she resigned she gave personal reasons, but later she alleged that she refused to ease pollution controls as the administration wanted (Whitman 2005). Of course, as these two very different women indicate, whether neo-liberal reforms provide opportunities or constraints depends to some extent on the particular woman and her political views.

'Neo-liberal feminists': New Zealand

Women ministers in tune with neo-liberal times proved able to accomplish many of their goals, and a few of them consider themselves feminists. These women believe that a free market economy stimulates competition, increases opportunities, and rewards merit – in ways that allow women to secure greater equality. Whether neo-liberal policies produce such results is debatable, but neo-liberalism garnered enthusiastic support from some self-described feminists.

In New Zealand, two women from National (the conservative major party) zealously pursued neo-liberal reforms while continuing to declare themselves 'strong feminists': Jenny Shipley (Minister for Social Services and Minister for Women 1990–3, and Prime Minister 1997–9) and Ruth Richardson (Minister for Finance 1990–3). Neo-liberal restructuring had actually started in the 1980s during the fourth Labour government and under the leadership of Roger Douglas as Finance Minister. By the time National formed its government in 1990, Shipley and Richardson entered a reform environment where 'Rogernomics' (the New Zealand equivalent of Reaganomics) prevailed. In contrast to many of their pragmatic predecessors in Labour, Shipley and Richardson ardently advocated neo-liberal principles, and they hoped to increase the rate of rolling back the state.

Both women emphasized how neo-liberal ideals informed their politics and guided their goals. 'I'm not a wish list politician', Shipley declared. 'I actually believe people do best when they have a lot of money in their own pocket, not someone else's hand in it' (Interview, Jenny Shipley, 29 April 2003). She continued to explain:

> When I was Women's Minister, you know I had every bleeding heart telling me what we should be doing for women, usually patronizing them and making them dependent. Or reinforcing their dependence on either their family or the state or whatever... I made it very clear that both my philosophical belief, the party I belong to, but also my commitment to those women was that if we were spending any money, it was to provide them with ladders – so they could both develop skills and then grow their own success.

Like many women sent to social ministries, Shipley initially considered her appointment a Machiavellian manoeuvre on the part of her prime minister, James Bolger. After only three years in politics, Shipley moved 'to one of the largest ministries, in fact the largest ministry. Highly controversial', as she described it. And she added, 'People thought "He's trying to bury Jen by giving her impossible tasks all the time" '. As it turned out, Shipley buried Bolger in an intra-party leadership coup, but forced to lead a coalition and then a minority government, her premiership proved precarious and short-lived.

Richardson's period in government was even shorter, but as Finance Minister she made the most of it. As she summed up her philosophy, she announced, 'My creed from day one has been around the celebration of liberty in all of its forms, and I have sought in my private and political life to pursue policies that would basically enhance and promote liberty' (Interview, Ruth Richardson, 25 April 2003; see also Richardson [1995]). When she took office, she recalled there was a growing view of the state that 'it's broke [and] it's got to be fixed'. According to Richardson:

> We had high unemployment, we had a big structural problem with the labour market, we had low levels of productivity. So we said, 'You're going to be free to work, we're going to dramatically free up the labour market'. Then our campaign message was 'our current arrangements are a jobless structured machine, you've got to choose a market alternative'... We did it very quickly. Speed never kills a reform. Uncertainty kills reform. So you know the people of New Zealand were prepared to take the medicine.

As Finance Minister, Richardson did enact dramatic change, and New Zealand continued to move from one of the most extensive state-controlled economies to a wide open market. Yet the dose of medicine eventually proved too much for the public who sought to remedy the situation by adopting mixed member proportional representation (MMP). MMP put an end to radical restructuring – and to Richardson's political career. As Bolger described his decision to take the finance portfolio from her, he explained that after the MMP referendum:

> I didn't believe her skills – her interpersonal skills – were the ones that were going to be necessary to manage that portfolio in a coalition government. It was as simple as that. She had a very strong – some would say bombastic style. She clearly wasn't a person who would be comfortable working in a coalition government (Interview, James Bolger, January 2002; see also Bolger [1998]).

Not surprisingly, the media portrayed Richardson as distinctly Thatcherite – tough, determined, and decisive – but by 1993, Anglo governments no longer wished to convey that image. In New Zealand with the major restructuring complete and a sense of 'reform fatigue' in the public, Richardson had outlived her usefulness. When the prime minister refused to give her the finance portfolio, she resigned her seat in parliament. Richardson might have been Thatcherite, but she lacked Thatcher's institutional authority and, like so many of her Anglo cabinet counterparts, she served at the pleasure of the prime minister.

Women ministers in masculinist cabinets and departments

In all six countries, few women have occupied the highly masculinist cabinet posts pertaining to finance, justice, and foreign affairs. Masculinist norms and expectations have always pervaded these positions, but neo-liberalism seemed to intensify and exaggerate the need for masculine virtues of strength, toughness, and hard-heartedness. Finance ministers in the neo-liberal era needed to make cold, calculating cuts in public expenditures, leaving little room for 'bleeding hearts'. Justice Ministers had to convey their ability to maintain 'law and order' more than ever, and even when a woman managed to meet masculinist standards, the media might well mock her for her masculinity. (American readers will remember Attorney General Janet Reno's character on Saturday Night Live.) In foreign affairs, the global status of the nation affects the degree of masculinity demanded of a minister, but neo-liberalism in international politics has generally required a leader willing to fight fearlessly for freedom. The two female Secretaries of State in the United States – Madeleine Albright and Condoleezza Rice – have had to walk a fine line between maintaining their femininity and meeting masculinist expectations. In 2008, US President-Elect Barack Obama announced his intention to nominate a third woman, Senator Hillary Clinton. Predictably, presidents placed these women at the Department of State, not Defense. While Secretary of State has not necessarily been regendered, the US view of diplomacy makes it somewhat feminalist in the field of international affairs.

Regardless of their position, most women describe the atmosphere within the cabinet room as distinctly masculinist. Women ministers use words such as 'boysey' and 'blokey' to characterize cabinet conversations. While admitting they must scramble to stay in the 'scrum', women ministers also tend to dismiss or joke about the implications. Many believe that discussions in cabinet meetings matter very little – when compared to the significance of decision-making among presidents or prime ministers and their personal staffs.

Women ministers do express a high degree of satisfaction and sense of gratification when they discuss leading their own departments. Across political systems and across policy areas, all the women cabinet members interviewed conveyed their enormous respect for the talent and dedication of civil servants. This is somewhat surprising, because (male) politicians tend to blame bureaucrats for their failure to execute policies. Women ministers appear to appreciate the professionalism of civil servants and often contrast it to the behaviour of men in cabinet. Unfortunately, women ministers also express concern that presidents or prime ministers frequently disparage civil servants' skills and bypass their departments' expertise. Whether women discuss the dynamics of cabinet or the nature of their departments, they point to the increasing presidentialization of their political systems.

Cabinet membership in the context of presidentialization

For several decades, social scientists, political journalists, and politicians have been documenting and debating the creeping centralization and concentration of authority in the executive. Initially considered 'prime ministerial' government (Crossman 1972), more recently the phenomenon has become known as the presidentialization of parliamentary systems (Foley 1993, 2000; Poguntke and Webb 2005). In the United States, observers first detected the development of the 'administrative presidency' (Nathan 1983) and then its politicization (Moe 1985; Dickinson 2005). Whether parliamentary or presidential, this institutional trend traces the increasing tendency of chief executives to go their own way by relying on their personal staff and circumventing the institutions of the legislature, parties, and cabinet. Furthermore, within this development the individual prime minister or president has moved to centre stage, adding an element of personalization (Campbell 1998). Several factors fuel presidentialization, including the erosion of social cleavages, the decline of political parties, the internationalization of politics, growth of the state, and changes in mass communications (Poguntke and Webb 2005).

Admittedly, the presidentialization thesis is sometimes stated in terms that seem too sweeping and oversimplified (Rhodes 2006, 2007). Some factors can halt or even temporarily reverse the trend, including political circumstances and the personal preferences of the prime minister. Moreover, the extent of presidentialization varies among Anglo nations. Nevertheless, most scholars agree that when presidentialization occurs, it diminishes the authority of cabinet ministers. Unfortunately for female ministers, the trend has happened when and where women were starting to increase their representation in cabinet.

Women ministers during the Blair 'presidency'

British Labour Governments under Blair's leadership demonstrate how presidentialization can erode the authority of cabinet as an institution and restrict the influence of individual ministers. Secretary of State for Northern Ireland (1997–9) Mo Mowlam reflected on the success she achieved outside cabinet while expressing the frustration she felt within it. In particular, she emphasized her belief that a feminalist approach to management enhanced her ability to negotiate among the conflicting parties in Northern Ireland.[5] According to Mowlam, 'I think [being a woman] made a difference because I was used to listening. Men don't listen well. And I was used to accommodating... It's natural [for women]' (Interview, Mo Mowlam, 14 July 2004; see also Mowlam [2002]). By contrast to the atmosphere she nurtured in the negotiations, cabinet provided a distinctly different environment in which a single man dominated.

While Mowlam joined the other women who believed 'the cabinet was not functioning as cabinet government should', she also expressed her regret that the prime minister's presidential style prevented women from making their unique contribution. She explained:

> I mean I can give you the line that Tony is sympathetic to women. You know what the line is, but he doesn't listen to anybody [in cabinet] but Gordon Brown. And Gordon Brown is even worse. I don't think any of them actually fundamentally thinks they need women there. And they do. I think women are better politicians. They're better conciliators. So I think there are a lot of advantages women bring to politics, but [the men] don't necessarily benefit from them... My views are quite jaundiced because I think they use us for window dressing, and they haven't actually accepted us as bone fide women MPs.

Mowlam's experience led her to acquire that jaundiced view. After she successfully concluded the agreement that produced the Good Friday Peace Accord in 1998, Blair sacked her and put his personal friend Peter Mandelson in the post. In her memoirs, she recalled the distinctly gendered 'whispering campaign' conducted against her at the time. Like many other ministers, she described how the Number 10 press machine enables prime ministers to quell opposition and discredit opponents – within the government. As a consolation, Blair offered her the health portfolio (though she requested defence), but Mowlam opted instead for a post she described as 'easy' – as head of the Cabinet Office.

Among the women in Blair's governments, Secretary of State for International Development (1997–2003) Clare Short proved to be the staunchest, most outspoken critic of his leadership. As she described it, 'Tony doesn't run a cabinet of equals... [He's] a very, very great centralizer and dominator'. Moreover, Short extended her critique beyond the prime minister's personal style. She understood fully the implications of presidentialization for women in cabinet when she recalled:

> It wasn't just the women who were being excluded, but as women took their place in parliament, took their place in cabinet, power moved. I don't think it's cause and effect, but it does have consequences for women. You have your own departments,

> but now I think you've got this overruling of departments on some questions by Number 10 and all these clever young people he employs (8 July 2004).

Instead of cabinet ministers, 'little groups in Number 10 decide on policy initiatives that [the prime minister] thinks will triangulate well', and Short added, 'It is notable that the inner group have no women in them'. By the time women arrived at the cabinet room, power had moved to 10 Downing Street, a club that remained reserved for men.

The shift in power has had wider, more profound consequences for the constitution, according to Short. When Blair decided to go to war in Iraq, she resigned and in her resignation speech, she warned parliament that the United Kingdom had achieved the worst of two worlds: presidential leadership with large parliamentary majorities, producing an excessive concentration of power in the hands of the prime minister (Hansard, 12 May 2003). Among the negative consequences of Blair's presidential style, Short also emphasized that the prime minister's ability to go his own way led him to overlook the expertise and advice of departments as well as cabinet ministers. While acknowledging that this development had started before 1997, Short added:

> But it's leapt under Blair. Obviously I wasn't in the Thatcher cabinet, but I listen to civil servants. Even then, there was more attention to the proprieties, you know, of cabinet government. The meetings were longer. (Pause) We have this prestigious committee for big foreign policy questions, chaired by the prime minister, and all the big ministers plus heads of the intelligence agencies plus the chief of the defence staff, and it never met. I mean it's shocking. And everything was so informal. It leads to bad decisions.

According to Short's assessment, a combination of factors has produced a perilous period in politics, and the British prime minister's decision to go to war in Iraq provides 'the most spectacular example' of the dangers.

The US president and politicization

On the other side of the Atlantic, critics of the US president's decision to attack Iraq have rendered a similar critique, although in this case they call the culprit politicization rather than presidentialization. In the politicized presidency, chief executives trust their own staff in the White House more than the professional, permanent bureaucracy. Several accounts document how President Bush and a few close associates (including only one cabinet member, Defense Secretary Donald Rumsfeld) planned the war while circumventing conventional channels, bypassing bureaucratic expertise, and excluding a cabinet member as significant as Secretary of State Colin Powell (Woodward 2004). As National Security Advisor, Condoleezza Rice should have played a central role; yet she increasingly moved to the margins of the inner circle – from 9/11 to the decision to invade Iraq.

At the start, Rice appeared to have a close relationship with Bush, and unlike Blair, the US president had some prominent women among his personal staff (though only Rice ever played a serious policy role). The only woman among the foreign policy players inside the White House also seems to have been the only one who expressed doubts about the decision to go to war. By most accounts, Rice's voice as an honest broker gradually weakened until she fell silent (Burke 2005). While anyone in that lonely position might have done the same, it must have been especially challenging for the only woman to take a softer stance and still struggle to be heard by the president's men. After the decision to go to war, the president moved her out of the White House and over to the State Department. The mass media celebrated the symbolic significance of her appointment as the first black woman to become Secretary of State, but Rice's step outside the White House and into cabinet constitutes a step down from her previous proximity to the president.

The other Anglo systems

The chief executive has become increasingly dominant and personalized in Canada as well as in the United Kingdom and in the United States, although some distinctive features of each system affect the consequences. The US system of separate institutions often creates divided government. In theory, that should check executive authority, though in practice, divided government rarely matters (Mayhew 2005). More significantly, federalism in the United States, Canada, and Australia can impede presidentialization. Effective opposition occasionally comes from the provinces, states, and territories where the concentration of power in the executive occurs again at the sub-national level. Yet even studies that consider the importance of federalism tend to conclude that presidentialization facilitates the concentration of power in the prime minister's control of the national party, parliament, and cabinet (Poguntke and Webb 2005: 199–220, especially 199, 217).

By contrast to most Anglo systems, a greater degree of institutional integrity remains in the Australian (Weller 2007) and particularly in the Irish cabinet. In the latter, women ministers (though few) have benefited as a result. Ireland has had coalition governments since 1989, and the distribution of portfolios constitutes a significant part of coalition negotiations. As a result, a great deal of debate and conflict continues to occur in cabinet, and it rarely renders a rubber stamp for the Taoiseach (Connolly and O'Halpin 2005). Cabinet meets weekly and the Taoiseach presides over the meetings as a chairman of the board. At least one woman cabinet member expressed shock at the experience of women in Blair's cabinet. According to Hanafin, 'The Taoiseach would never do that', and she added, 'I mean he's very conscious of trying to promote women'. In her view, inter-party rivalry overrides the gender dynamic that characterizes much of the boysy behaviour elsewhere. As Hanafin speculated,

'I think insofar as there's a dynamic in a coalition, it's between parties. I just wonder if you had a cabinet meeting all of the one party, would gender play a greater difference?' Perhaps, gender difference dissipates when inter-party competition prevails. Certainly, coalition government makes cabinet more important and constrains the ability of a prime minister to go his – or her – own way. Nevertheless, even as cabinet remains viable, Taoiseach Bertie Ahern became a much more prominent public figure than his predecessors, and Ireland remains subject to some of the same external factors that foster presidentialization in other systems.

Presidentialization under women prime ministers: New Zealand

New Zealand also differs from other Anglo systems, and its development has taken some unusual twists and turns. Until the adoption of MMP, it had a pure Westminster system that allowed the cabinet to dominate parliament (McLeay 2006). In fact, the purity of New Zealand's Westminster system – with its party duopoly, strong party discipline, and a small single chamber – might have made the nation less susceptible to presidentialization back in the 1980s. As the discussion in the early part of this chapter indicates, Finance Ministers could wield extraordinary influence, and they sometimes played an even greater role than the prime minister in initiating and enacting the neo-liberal agenda. In response to enormous ministerial power, proponents of proportional representation intended to check the executive by replacing the Westminster system with coalition governments that would enhance the role of legislators. Initially, the post-MMP governments of Bolger and Shipley seemed to satisfy the reformers' aspirations, at least by weakening the executive – both cabinet and the prime minister.

Under the premiership of Helen Clark, cabinet continued to meet weekly and the meetings consumed much of her time, but Clark clearly dominated both cabinet and parliament. After the 1999 election, she managed to parlay poll results in 2002 and 2005 into presidential leadership. If those elections had produced governments whose survival depended entirely on the support of more than one party, then cabinet might have mattered as much in New Zealand as it has in Ireland. Clark's old inter-party adversary Shipley described the decline of cabinet as follows:

> In fact one of the characteristics of the government of the 1990s was that if you went out on the street and asked who was in government, they'd be able to quote senior ministers just like that [snap of fingers]. If you go down on the street now and ask how many people they know in the current government – if you choose ten people – you won't find any who can quote a senior minister.

Clark herself admitted, 'What's happened I think is that the parliamentary systems are transforming themselves into presidential systems'. Then she added, 'Well, we're the head of government as prime minister just as the American president is the head of government. So there are certain functions that go with being the head of government – and sitting around parliament for hours isn't one of them' (Interview, Helen Clark, 14 April 2003). If cabinet has declined in significance as both Shipley and Clark suggest, then the relatively high representation of women in Clark's cabinet (approximately 30%) mattered much less than generally assumed. The adoption of MMP might have stalled presidentialization, but it has not prevented it.

As Clark's experience indicates, many factors can foster or impede presidentialization, including the political environment. A contrast to the masculinist, domineering approach of Blair, his predecessor John Major reversed the model of prime ministerial dominance and ran classic cabinet government. Unlike Blair or Thatcher, Major presided over a weak government whose survival depended on Unionist support. Without large parliamentary majorities, prime ministers might prove more likely to resume the role of first among equals and restore cabinet collective decision-making.

The prime minister's personal style and preferences also matter. As Taoiseach, Bertie Ahern adopted a much more feminalist approach to leadership. In addition to encouraging women in politics and government, he engaged the participation of his ministers and appeared to welcome their input. As Canadian prime minister, after Brian Mulroney's masculinist dominance, Kim Campbell tried to restore the cabinet's integrity by practising 'the politics of inclusion' (Campbell 1996). She led for only a few months before she faced and failed to win a general election. Such a short premiership is too brief to test the success of her approach, but her limited experience suggests that a woman executive who adopts a feminalist approach runs the risk of appearing weak. Paradoxically, the cliché 'Nixon goes to China' might apply here: it could prove easier for a male prime minister or president to be feminalist than for a woman. Without the personal authority that men automatically bring to office, most women must struggle to meet the masculinist expectations of executive leadership that so often prevail in Anglo systems.

Conclusions: from symbolic representation to executive leadership

In sum, in Anglo-American systems, while women have been increasing their numerical representation in cabinet, they have also encountered numerous obstacles, especially when they attempt to engender change. More women in cabinet clearly enhance representation in descriptive and symbolic ways, and those types of representation have some value. A government that looks like the nation it serves is one that ordinary citizens can more easily relate to and identify with. Moreover, symbolic representation can signify fundamental national principles and reflect changing values. In the case of gender, the symbol of a female cabinet minister might signal progress towards making gender equality a higher national priority. Nevertheless, if women are going to make a fundamental difference in politics and policy, they need to secure greater substantive representation.

Instead, at least since 1980, the dominant public philosophy of neo-liberalism has placed severe limits on the ability of female ministers to initiate and advance their interests in substantive ways. In the 1960s when governments were spending money, women had few career prospects in politics. After the women's movement gained momentum and the number of women in cabinet increased, meagre resources remained in the public sector. Presidents and prime ministers who appointed women to cabinet sent most of them to feminalist posts that deal with domestic welfare in a period of severe budget cuts and extreme fiscal restraint. As a result, women found themselves in the most politically untenable and publicly unpopular positions. Female ministers who wished to establish or expand programmes specifically designed to assist women as a group were swimming against the ideological tide of neo-liberal individualism.

The twenty-first century shows some signs that the tide might be starting to turn, as issues such as health and education have once again become national priorities in Anglo systems. If so, then female ministers in the near future will find greater room to practise innovative and effective feminalist leadership. In some Anglo countries, change in the ideological climate has already opened new opportunities for female ministers. Following the 2007 Australian election, the Labor Government led by Prime Minister Kevin Rudd included many women cabinet ministers in charge of significant portfolios – education, industrial relations, indigenous affairs, the environment, health, and housing. The number of female ministers has enhanced the representative character of Australian government, and, at the time of writing, it appears that women will play a significant role in shaping progressive public policies in the twenty-first century. Even earlier, across the Tasman Sea, New Zealand Prime Minister Clark started to shift the agenda away from neo-liberalism and towards greater social spending, especially on programmes designed to benefit women. Signs of change in Australia as well as New Zealand might provide the first ripples in a new wave of reform that will wash across the Anglo world (Sykes 2008*b*).

In the past several decades female ministers have also gotten hit by a wave of institutional change that has eroded some of the ground women gained when they entered cabinet. Presidents and prime ministers (male and female) have increasingly concentrated and increased their authority at the expense of cabinet. While the prime minister's personal preferences and political circumstances affect the pace and progress of presidentialization, when it occurs, it reduces the integrity of cabinet and restricts the influence of ministers. Subject to the ebb and flow of ideological and institutional developments, the movement of women into positions of political leadership is not a story of steady, ever increasing influence. It is more a story of stepping forward and then being pushed back by features of the ideological and institutional context in which they must operate. As a consequence, the empowerment women might have achieved when they moved into cabinet remains incomplete.

Finally, the experience of female cabinet ministers serves as a reminder that the gendered nature of institutions and ideas make different forms of leadership gender specific as well. Dispersed leadership – like any other type of leadership – is not gender neutral. Leadership dispersal has helped drive the democratic dynamic of the women's movement in significant ways. Practised in the context of a social movement, dispersed leadership has opened opportunities for women to adopt feminalist styles of leadership that invite and increase the participation of women as a group, while it has also provided the means to advance feminist agendas. Within the structures of government, however, it has proven considerably more difficult for women to promote feminalist policies or processes in positions of dispersed leadership. Lacking the personal clout that most of their male counterparts carry, female leaders need access to the formal authority that institutions can provide. Even more than men, women depend on institutional integrity and viability to establish the credibility and legitimacy of their leadership. Yet even when women gain that formal authority, they must struggle to advance feminalist priorities in the highly masculinist environment of Anglo-American political systems.

Notes

1. This research is part of a book (in progress) on women leaders in six Anglo-American systems: the United Kingdom, the Republic of Ireland, Australia, New Zealand, Canada, and the United States. I would like to acknowledge the Australian National University for providing two opportunities to conduct research for my book, as a Visiting Fellow at the Research School of Social Sciences in 2003 and as the Fulbright-ANU Distinguished Chair in Political Science in 2008. I also presented some of the research here in a public lecture sponsored by the Australian Senate (Sykes 2008*a*).
2. In theory, the US cabinet is distinctive because its members serve primarily 'at the pleasure of the president' and lack independent political stature, whereas the prime minister is supposed to be only 'first among equals'. In practice, however, the erosion of cabinet's decision-making authority and the tendency of prime ministers to go their own way in parliamentary systems now make it more reasonable and fruitful to compare the US cabinet with its Anglo counterparts (see Hargrove, this volume).
3. Liberalism constitutes the dominant ideology in Anglo countries, and it is a distinctly masculinist ideology in both its classical form and its neo-reincarnation. In classical theory, liberalism embraces the concept of a disembodied, genderless individual, making it more difficult for women to seek redress under the law for the concrete ways that their experiences differ from those of men. In Anglo nations, women leaders are likely to be liberal (or neo-liberal) feminists, if they are feminists

at all, and so the liberal ideological framework limits the degree of change they seek even in the best of times.

4. Nevertheless, later neo-liberal restructuring did rearrange or dismantle much of the Australian femocrats' policy machinery (see Sawer [2007]).
5. Several women attributed their achievements to their feminalist management style, which they described as open, engaging, and accommodating. For example, Clare Short recalled, 'I think that in my old department the whole management style of the organization changed in this broad, inclusive, energizing way. Now that I think is a woman thing. That's what I expect more women in politics to create – those kinds of changes right through the system. And you do see some of that in different places when women break through – a more human style of management and so on, more inclusive' (Interview, Clare Short, 8 July 2004).

Bibliography

Bashevkin, S., *Women on the Defensive: Living through Conservative Times* (Chicago: University of Chicago Press, 1998).

Belich, J., *Paradise Reforged: A History of the New Zealanders* (Honolulu, Hawaii: University of Hawaii Press, 2001).

Bolger, J., *Bolger: A View from the Top* (Auckland, NZ: Viking, 1998).

——Interview with author, January 2002.

Burke, J., 'The Contemporary Presidency: Condoleezza Rice as NSC Advisor: A Case Study of the Honest Broker Role', *Presidential Studies Quarterly*, 35/3 (2005), 554–75.

Campbell, C., *The US Presidency in Crisis: A Comparative Perspective* (Oxford: Oxford University Press, 1998).

Campbell, K., *Time and Chance: The Political Memoirs of Canada's First Woman Prime Minister* (Toronto: Doubleday, 1996).

Clark, H., Interview with author, 14 April 2003.

Connolly, E. and O'Halpin, E., 'The Government and the Governmental System', in J. Coakley and M. Gallagher (eds.), *Politics in the Republic of Ireland*, 4th edn. (London: Routledge, 2005), 249–70.

Crossman, R., *The Myths of Cabinet Government* (Cambridge: Harvard University Press, 1972).

Dickinson, M., 'The Executive Office of the President: The Paradox of Politicization', in J. Aberbach and M. Peterson (eds.), *The Executive Branch* (Oxford: Oxford University Press, 2005), 135–73.

DiStefano, C., 'Masculinity as Ideology in Political Theory: Hobbesian Man Considered', *Women's Studies International Forum*, 6/6 (1983), 633–44.

Duerst-Lahti, G., 'Governing Institutions, Ideologies, and Gender: Toward the Possibility of Equal Political Representation', *Sex Roles*, 47 (2002), 371–88.

——and Kelly, R. M., 'On Governance, Leadership, and Gender', in G. Duerst-Lahti and R. M. Kelly (eds.), *Gender Power, Leadership, and Governance* (Ann Arbor: University of Michigan Press, 1995), 10–37.

Foley, M., *The Rise of the British Presidency* (Manchester: University of Manchester Press, 1993).

Foley, M., *The British Presidency: Tony Blair and the Politics of Public Leadership* (Manchester: Manchester University Press, 2000).
Guilfoyle, M., Interview with author, 13 March 2003.
Harman, H., Interview with author, 12 July 2004.
Hanafin, M., Interview with author, 24 June 2005.
Hussey, G., *At the Cutting Edge: Cabinet Diaries 1982–1987* (Dublin: Gill and Macmillan, 1990).
——Interview with author, 7 June 2005.
Mayhew, D., *Divided We Govern: Party Control, Lawmaking, and Investigations, 1946–2002* (New Haven: Yale University Press, 2005).
McLeay, E., 'Cabinet', in R. Miller (ed.), *New Zealand Government and Politics*, 4th edn. (South Melbourne, Australia: Oxford University Press, 2006), 8–105.
Moe, T., 'The Politicized Presidency', in J. E. Chubb and P. E. Peterson (eds.), *The New Direction in American Politics* (Washington, D. C.: Brookings Institution, 1985), 235–72.
Mowlam, M., *Momentum: The Struggle for Peace, Politics and the People* (London: Hodder and Stoughton, 2002).
——Interview with author, 14 July 2004.
Nathan, R., *The Administrative Presidency* (Upper Saddle River, New Jersey: Prentice Hall, 1983).
O'Rourke, M., Interview with author, 15 June 2005.
Poguntke, T. and Webb, P., *The Presidentialization of Politics: A Comparative Study of Modern Democracies* (Oxford: Oxford University Press, 2005).
Rhodes, R. A. W., 'Executives in Parliamentary Government', in R. A. W. Rhodes, S. A. Binder, and B. A. Rockman (eds.), *The Oxford Handbook of Political Institutions* (Oxford: Oxford University Press, 2005), 323–44.
——'Blair and Governance', in R. Koch and J. Dixon (eds.), *Public Governance and Leadership* (Wiesbaden: Deutscher Universitäts-Verlag, 2007), 95–116.
Richardson, R., *Making a Difference* (Christchurch, NZ: Shoal Bay Press, 1995).
——Interview with author, 25 April 2003.
Sawer, M., 'Australia: The Fall of the Femocrat', in J. Kantola and J. Outshoorn (eds.), *Changing State Feminism* (New York: Palgrave Macmillan, 2007), 20–40.
Shipley, J., Interview with author, 29 April 2003.
Short, C., Interview with author, 8 July 2004.
Summers, A., 'The End of Equality? Australian Women and the Howard Government', The Pamela Denoon Lecture delivered at Australian National University, Canberra, 6 March 2003.
Sykes, P. L., *Presidents and Prime Ministers: Conviction Politics in the Anglo-American Tradition* (Lawrence, Kansas: University Press of Kansas, 2000).
——'Women Leaders and Executive Politics: Engendering Change in Anglo-American Nations', *Papers on Parliament*, 49 (2008*a*), 11–23.
——'Gender in the 2008 Presidential Election: Two Types of Time Collide', *PS: Political Science & Politics*, 41/1 (2008*b*), 761–64.
Vanstone, A., Interview with author, 27 March 2003.
Weller, P., *Cabinet Government in Australia, 1901–2006: Practice, Principles, Performance* (Sydney: New South Wales Press, 2007).
Whitman, C. T., *It's My Party Too: The Battle for the Heart of the GOP and the Future of America* (New York: Penguin, 2005).
Woodward, B., *Plan of Attack* (New York: Simon and Schuster, 2004).

Chapter 4

Parliamentary Oppositional Leadership

John Uhr

Dispersing leadership by organizing opposition

One of the fascinating paradoxes of democracy is that while theories of democracy emphasize the dispersal of power among sovereign citizens, existing democratic regimes display increasing concentrations of power in political executives (Blondel 1997; Crick 2005). The promise of democracy rests on de-concentrations of power away from traditional political authorities; actual democratic regimes, however, tend to re-concentrate power in newly authorized political centres, with heads of government demonstrating their leadership leverage through their assignment of shared leadership responsibilities across their executive team. Analysts of democracy entertain at least two prospects for dispersed leadership. The first prospect is related to the underlying democratic norm of 'people power' with close alignment between norms and forms of government, both promoting one version of dispersed leadership through widely shared public participation in government. The second prospect is related to emerging practices of 'the team at the top' with heads of government performing as collaborative leaders, dispensing powers among chosen executive favourites on terms and conditions that reflect the very concentrated quality of leadership available for conditional dispersal.

These two leadership prospects can coexist, either unresolved as two worlds of 'theory' and 'practice' or as an operational amalgam of core concept and administrative convenience. My theme relates to a third prospect for leadership dispersal found in parliamentary democracies: dispersed leadership through organized political opposition. This third prospect is characteristic of parliamentary forms of democratic government and uncharacteristic, or at least less characteristic, of non-parliamentary (e.g. presidential) forms of democratic government where there is certainly *dispersed* opposition but less *leadership* of opposition. What is common to all three prospects is some type of power-sharing. What is distinctive about this third prospect is the dispersal or sharing of quite significant public powers between leaders of governing parties and leaders of non-governing parties. By contrast, models of dispersal in 'people power' relate to the constitutional powers of a sovereign people; and models of dispersal in 'the executive team' relate to the powers of executive government. Opposition models relate to legislative powers which in parliamentary settings are dispersed across all parliamentary representatives, with significant opportunities for public leadership open to non-government leaders. My argument is that democratic analysts have generally ignored the role of opposition leadership as a bridge between the normative principle of popular sovereignty, where the people are expected to choose who rules, and the operational principle of the executive team, where the head of government shapes the network of shared executive powers (Mair 2007). I argue that the task of those exercising the share of public leadership open to parliamentary oppositions is to reshape relationships between voters and governing parties to the political and policy benefit of the opposition. I will show that in some parliamentary structures, such as classic Westminster adversary systems, opposition leaders reshape this relationship in the interests of 'the alternative government' with the aim of winning public confidence to replace the party in government (Hargrove and Owens 2002; Burns 2003). In other parliamentary settings, such as consensual systems, I will show that opposition leadership takes different forms, enlisting public confidence to broker preferred policy outcomes while not necessarily competing for government office.

This chapter investigates different leadership roles emerging in research on parliamentary opposition. The reference to 'research' is deliberate, as this chapter is limited by the lack of comprehensive coverage of opposition options in current parliamentary research. Although political opposition is a lively and important practice in all contemporary democracies, opposition is a relatively neglected topic in the study of democracy and dispersed leadership, with very limited comparative study of opposition practices. Three possible explanations account for this relative neglect. First, political studies have moved on from traditional interests in constitutional forms and practices favoured by earlier generations of comparative politics, as one can see by comparing the prominence of constitutionalism, including forms of parliamentary opposition, in such earlier scholars as James Bryce with the preference for electoral and party politics in such outstanding contemporary comparativists as Arend Lijphart. The further researchers stand back, the more it is that forms of opposition appear as secondary, although valuable, components of the party system.

Second, the rise of interest in the multiplicity of governance networks has displaced much of the traditional interest in binary relationships between government and opposition, even in such flagship political science journals as *Government and Opposition*. The focus on democratic governance moves attention away from legal formalities to surrounding relationships of power that have grown up beneath and around the formal architecture of state.

Third, the main research interest in democracy and political opposition has moved outside the confines of conventional institutional politics to the sphere of civil society and particularly the extra-parliamentary world of social movements. Opposition struggles by non-state actors are often regarded as having more democratic integrity than the conventional bargaining over power and place by ambitious but allegedly compromised party elites operating inside the narrow pathways of the mainstream legislative process.

Despite these limitations, there is much that can and should be said about the contribution of formal opposition to dispersed leadership in democratic systems of government. This chapter is a step in that direction offered partly as a report on the state of play and also as a stimulus to further research by other scholars. This chapter is not intended as a comprehensive literature review of the field of parliamentary studies of opposition, which would be an immense task. Practices of opposition vary within as well as across the many types of parliamentary regime and each practice seems to have attracted its analysts who emphasize the many exceptions to every rule in the political study of opposition.

My main aim here is to keep the focus on the theme of leadership which moves in and out of the larger field of opposition studies. I try to simplify this diverse world of parliamentary oppositions by examining two main worlds of leadership evident in political studies of parliamentary opposition: the surprisingly diverse Westminster set of parliamentary democracies, which I present in terms of four quite separate models; and the equally diverse set of non-Westminster European parliamentary democracies, which promote quite different forms of opposition leadership. Sticking to my story about 'parliamentary oppositional leadership', I provide less attention to the so-called mixed or semi-presidential systems, and even less to the US and cognate presidentialism systems, despite the interesting emergence of research on 'the opposition president' operating in a system of divided government where the legislature is frequently controlled by the party opposed to the chief political executive (Crockett 2000; Helms 2004: 40–5).

Varieties of oppositional leadership: medium and media

Like many other forms of political activity, political opposition lends itself to the study of 'leaders' and of 'leadership', with the implication that not all opposition leaders measure up to the often-unstated benchmarks of 'leadership'. One practical application of this distinction is that we can identify many opposition leaders who perform opposition functions but at levels or in measures that fall short of 'leadership'. Similarly, there can be legislative and policy leadership from non-government legislators who have no formal status as 'Opposition Leaders'. The use of the term 'Opposition Leader' refers to only one of a number of types of opposition leadership. Each type has a distinctive test of its leadership performance, each with a different media profile.

We can start by noting three mediums where oppositions perform their tasks and the different ways that each form relates to the mass media. The success of oppositions depends in general on their capacity for 'position-taking': in some types, this capacity requires careful alliance with the news media, yet in other types it requires different skill in media management including minimizing public exposure of sensitive cross-party negotiations. We can think of these three mediums as exemplary situations of oppositional leadership. One exemplary type is opposition leaders in Westminster systems, where the primary practical test of leadership performance is replacing the leader of the government, either at the next available general election or, more rarely, through victory in a parliamentary vote of confidence that results in a change of party in government. This type of opposition activity is highly dependent on supportive media exposure.

But for opposition leaders in many non-Westminster or modified-Westminster systems, the practical test of leadership performance can be quite different. Consider then two additional types of opposition leadership, both arising in multiparty parliamentary systems that differ in fundamental ways from the classic two-party Westminster norm. One type is the leader of a political party operating as a junior partner in either a formal or an informal coalition with other governing parties. Many European parliaments establish executive governments through so-called 'oversized coalitions' which share executive offices among more political parties than are strictly necessary for the sustained parliamentary support of the government. This coalition arrangement is often explicitly designed to minimize unwelcome forms of opposition leadership by inviting potential adversaries 'inside the tent' where their opposition can be kept within bounds. Examples include many smaller, often temporary and often quite narrowly ideological parties of the right or left, depending on whether the governing coalition at the time is from the right or the left. These parties are often splinter groups which break away from larger parties but remain as a supporting chorus group to parties intent on forming governing. Classic 'independents' often fall into this category of splinter groups whose leadership is tested by the ability to use the institutional powers of 'opposition', often exercised well behind the scenes, to extract concessions for favoured constituencies.

A third exemplary type is the opposition leader of a more intractable minor party with a more highly defined party ideology which refuses to 'enter the tent' and instead prefers to use its parliamentary power to extract policy and legislative concessions from the governing party or parties in exchange for institutional support when considered appropriate. Examples include post-materialist political parties like many of the Greens parties which see themselves as the political wing of a more fundamental and indeed oppositional social movement. This third type of opposition leadership can include carefully staged strategic episodes of highly publicized opposition to serving governments, designed less to shame the governing parties and more to consolidate and grow the base of party supporters. Many of these party supporters are suspicious of the mainstream parliamentary model of 'leadership as leverage' and subscribe to an alternative social-movement model of 'leadership as legacy': honouring and protecting vulnerable ideological commitments, as well as current and future collective resources, like the environment, that should not be traded away. This third type of opposition leadership depends on positive media publicity almost as extensively as the classic Westminster type, but clearly for quite different purposes.

This gallery of three types of opposition leadership is one way of correcting the standard Westminster bias towards 'The Leader of the Opposition' which tends to dominate the literature on parliamentary opposition. The Westminster bias reflects a very traditional institutional framework featuring an increasingly rare electoral system relying on a contest between two dominating political parties using 'first past the post' mechanisms to translate popular votes into parliamentary seats. The supposedly 'majoritarian' qualities of this electoral system refer to its effect in transforming winning electoral pluralities into commanding parliamentary majorities. By terming alternative parliamentary systems 'consensual', analysts not only set themselves up for overlooking the more subtle nature of interparty rivalry and government–opposition relationships in those systems, they also define the Westminster model by its alleged non-consensual or adversary nature. This adversarial core is legitimated and also mitigated by a quaint but noteworthy form of power-sharing where the governing party confers prestige and valuable speaking rights on the chief adversary: the Leader of the Opposition and associated 'shadow ministry'. This 'alternative chief minister' leadership position is filled by vote of the parliamentary members of the 'losing' party and has evolved into a highly paid public office whose incumbent is most regularly seen at work when holding the government to account during parliamentary Question Time.

The test of leadership of this type of opposition role – I shall come back later to the role of opposition in consensual systems – is fundamentally one of *publicity*: using routines such as Question Time to undermine public confidence in the government of the day and to build up public trust in the opposition party as the 'alternative government' ready to take on the responsibilities of office as the next government. The management of publicity includes trying to take advantage of media interest in the failings of government, with the unsettling knowledge that the government too will be trying to take advantage of the media's equally pressing interest in the failings of the opposition.

The prominent reliance on the powers of publicity in this classic form of opposition means that Westminster opposition leaders are deeply dependent on their skills in media management and are more likely than other types of opposition leaders to risk being managed instead by the media, which is perhaps the most powerful form of non-parliamentary opposition in contemporary democracies, equally at home in oversighting the opposition as well as the serving government. Scholars acknowledge the mass media as 'potential veto players' with the capacity to act as the 'veritable functional equivalent of a powerful opposition party' (Christiansen and Damgaard 2008: 70–1; Helms 2008*b*: 27).

The paradox of opposition leadership

We can begin to drill deeper into opposition leadership by examining a leadership paradox that is largely ignored by the research community (but note Helms [2004]; Tuffin [2007]). This paradox is that the studies which deal most prominently with questions of opposition leadership tend to isolate 'the opposition leader' from the legislative institution, mainly because of the lack of hard evidence of opposition leaders' influence over legislatures. Examples of this approach include many of the studies of Westminster-derived parliamentary oppositions. These studies typically concede that Westminster-style opposition leaders have little real power to shape process or outcome of their home political institution: parliament (Ghany 2001). The other side of this paradox is that those (typically non-Westminster) studies which deal more directly with the capacity of oppositions to influence process and outcome in legislative institutions tend to ignore the role of opposition leaders, noting but rarely explaining the presence of diversified leadership practices exercised by a large number of participating legislators. Examples of this second approach include many of the studies of consensus or multiparty parliamentary oppositions.

The paradox is that the models of parliamentary opposition that elevate 'the leader' often have little hard evidence of parliamentary leadership, while models that do demonstrate evidence of opposition power over institutional process and outcomes rarely include 'the leader' in their accounts of opposition politics. This paradox maps on to a core division in parliamentary studies between models of 'adversary' politics (two-party systems) and of 'consensus' politics (multiparty systems). This spills over into a division between models of a 'binary opposition' involving the party in government and 'the alternative government', and models of shared parliamentary decision-making involving coalitions of political parties often, but not always, operating in unstable working relationships (Crick 1971; Sartori 1971).

Of course, neither Westminster nor its alternative are unified or cohesive sets of parliamentary behaviour. Below I will unpack the Westminster type into a number of leadership models reflecting the wide range of operational realities found in different Westminster-derived systems. So too the consensual systems vary markedly and lend themselves to a variety of emerging leadership models as I will try to show. But one can still appreciate the logic of the separation of parliamentary regimes into 'Westminster' and 'other': the

Westminster-derived set have leadership models that derive from an historic governance model of two-party government, where the two main political parties function as the primary adversaries in a two-party electoral contest. The Westminster opposition leadership story is about a relationship between the opposition party and the electorate, with the opposition leader using the available institutional power to win public confidence that the alternative government is fundamentally 'an office-seeking opposition' or indeed an 'office-expecting' opposition and is a responsible party ready to govern (Punnett 1973: 4, 10, 13). The so-called consensus or non-adversary parliamentary systems generate different leadership models based on different institutional relationships. These non-Westminster systems are more immediately concerned with managing cross-party relationships in the parliamentary arena than managing extra-parliamentary relationships with voters as part of a long-term campaign to win office in their own right.

Given this rough and ready divide between adversary and consensus systems, we can see that the paradox takes a deeper turn when we note that the influential model of 'responsible opposition' is one associated with the isolated opposition leader with little hard evidence of capacity to use the office of opposition leader to shape parliamentary process or outcomes. The standout example here is the venerable doctrine of 'responsible opposition' associated with 'the Westminster model' of parliament: a doctrine classically formulated by mid-twentieth century authorities like Jennings (1957) and Wheare (1968). In this model, a responsible opposition is one that manages its anti-government activity in ways that demonstrate that it is ready for government, the proof of which is that it is prepared to be judged by the acceptability and feasibility of its declared programme of intended policy, and that it is not tempted to engage in 'opposition for opposition's sake'. In this model, 'destructive' opposition is conduct which destroys the reputation or hold of a government on office, when that conduct is performed in the manner of 'spoilsport' intent on undermining one's political enemies but not intent on taking over the responsibilities of government, or on implementing its declared policy programme that has been put to the electorate for public judgement.

The leadership theme is evident in this open contract with the electorate. Thus a 'responsible opposition' refers directly to the opposition party's programme of selling itself as ready to take over the responsibilities of executive government (Punnett 1973: 29–32). A responsible opposition engages in 'constructive' rather than destructive political strategies, committed to act on its own publicly stated policies if it wins government. As 'the alternative government', a responsible opposition will certainly oppose the ruling government's policies, programmes, and personnel but it will do so in ways that demonstrate its readiness to replace rather than simply displace the governing party. The model of leadership in this approach is the model of the alternative government, with the opposition leader promoted as the alternative head of government, and the opposition party promoted as a team of 'shadow ministers' at arm's length from the governing party but ready and able to take control of government.

The corresponding models of leadership found in the non-Westminster schools of opposition studies are of constructive engagement by non-government parties intent on amending law and public policy to reflect their own party interests. Typically, the focus is on the period between elections, in contrast to the 'responsible opposition' schools which study the opposition's preparation for the next electoral test. The leadership model here varies across the many types of non-Westminster parliaments but a common theme is the negotiation of alternative policies and programmes, in contrast to the promotion of an alternative government-in-waiting. The test of opposition leadership is not so much the electoral test of gaining an increased share of popular votes, but instead the capacity to 'work the system' and structure parliamentary relationships with other political parties in and out of government in order to build winning policy and legislative coalitions. These coalitions might match the state of the parties in a governing coalition; or then again, they might be irregular interruptions of any governing coalition. In this school, the leader of 'the opposition' recedes because the binary division of government and opposition recedes, replaced by potentially shifting coalitions of political parties. Each managing their distinctive relationship with core stakeholders (parliamentary parties and extra-parliamentary supporters) over the classic parliamentary struggle over bargains and tradeoffs to be made when supporting governing parties in exchange for concessions.

Models of opposition leadership

Traditional political science often approached the distinguishing qualities of parliamentary systems, including opposition arrangements, through such crudely bipolar divisions as 'Westminster and Washington', as though British and US political systems were the standout candidates for and against parliamentary systems. More recent literature on parliamentary government is an improvement in that it now tends to separate the parliamentary field into two worlds of Westminster and non-Westminster parliaments. But even better is the latest school of comparative analysis which treats Westminster and non-Westminster as loose clusters of parliamentarism, each with many variations (Helms 2004; Helms and Norton 2008). In keeping with this latest approach, I will unpack the first of these two clusters and begin to unpack the second. Why the priority for unpacking the traditional Westminster cluster? The answer is that if we can demonstrate that this putatively cohesive category of parliamentarism is increasingly diverse in its gallery of types of opposition leadership, then it should come as less of a surprise that the non-Westminster cluster also contains a spread of emerging types of opposition leadership. All of this should serve to enrich our collection of opposition leadership forms, our understanding of the roles of opposition in contemporary democracy, and our understanding of the leadership functions performed by democratic oppositions.

Classic Westminster: UK models

Norton claims that the UK model is 'a paragon of the opposition mode': a claim that he makes in an edited collection that includes a rival conclusion that: 'There is no such thing as a Westminster pattern of parliamentary opposition' (Kaiser 2008: 36; Norton 2008: 241). Read carefully, Norton really means that the UK model of opposition leadership is a standout case of negative rather than constructive oppositional politics, practised by the most ambitious non-government party that remains unreconciled to its minority status in parliament.

The Westminster medium encourages high media publicity. Opposition leadership is tested as much by media management as by parliamentary management. The parliamentary careers of Margaret Thatcher and Tony Blair illustrate many of the leadership characteristics that define successful Westminster opposition leaders (Foley 2002: 198–202). Blair's time as leader of both opposition and government has parallels with that of Margaret Thatcher, who also obtained a reputation for remaining too long in executive office. But although Thatcher spent around the same time as Blair as Leader of the Opposition (four years to Blair's three), Thatcher's time between entering parliament and becoming prime minister was around double that of Blair (twenty years to Blair's eleven). Thatcher illustrates the traditional pathway to the top; Blair, who learned so much from Thatcher's style of party leadership, illustrates a more contemporary pathway. Blair's Labour party lost office to Thatcher's Conservative party at the 1983 elections. During the Conservative period of rule between 1983 and 1997, the Labour party looked to four party leaders (Foot, Kinnock who became the longest serving UK opposition leader that century, Smith, and Blair) and lost four elections in a row before regaining office. This matches the experience of many parties in opposition in contemporary Westminster systems, including the Conservative party opposing Blair and his successor, Gordon Brown. Blair eventually secured what Thatcher had earlier earned from her time in opposition: 'a mass-based mandate' which in Blair's case benefited from a modernized party with his personal command of 'a publicity machine of matchless quality' (Foley 2002: 110, 193).

Both Thatcher and Blair rose as public figures rather than simply party mouthpieces; but both left office once their parties had calculated that a governing party cannot afford to carry diminishing opinion-leaders for fear that a fresh opposition leader will emerge to bring the opposing party to office.

Political parties make hard calculations about which internal leadership candidate has extra-party public appeal, and even harder calculations about when to discard once-successful party leaders once their opinion-leadership fades. We now think of Blair as a prime minister who, whatever his claims to greatness as a head of government, almost stayed too long in prime-ministerial office, a leader who nearly lost his reputation for leadership by holding on to office for too long, threatening to erode public confidence in his own party even though he had won three electoral victories. But we also tend to forget that Blair at the time of his first great electoral win in 1997 had already clocked up over a decade as a backbencher, slightly longer than his tenure as prime minister. Three of those pre-prime-ministerial years were as Opposition Leader, a time used by Blair to stamp his modernizing mark on his party and his acceptability on the public mind. As Blair warned his party colleagues: '...don't elect a leader and not allow him to lead. You can't do that in modern politics' (Foley 2002: 116).

Westminster features so prominently in part because it has developed over so long a period of history. The literature on the institutional development of British parliamentary opposition is rich in its historical description of the rise of 'Her Majesty's Loyal Opposition' (now listed on the House of Commons web site 'HM's *Official* Opposition') in the early eighteenth century, where the theme is the reactive nature of parliamentary opposition (Foord 1964: 121–6, 153–9; Turner 1969: 2–18; Parry 1997: 459). The initiative is, as always, with the political executive: Walpole as the first real prime minister established the preconditions for the eventual rise of the opposition, loyal to the monarchy and the regime of constitutional monarchy established with the 1688 Revolution, but opposed to the government of the day (the 'ministerialists') and prepared to solicit and accept an invitation by the monarch to replace the serving ministry (Schumpeter 1976: 176).

Note the team theme: the opposition puts itself forward as an anti-ministerialist team, as an alternative government or a government-in-waiting (in contrast to a government-in-exile which would be disloyal opposition). This was termed 'formed' or 'organized' opposition, as distinct from mere rebelliousness. This concept of opposition is a constitutional doctrine on the importance of party in parliamentary government (Ionescu and de Madariaga 1968: 50–6). An important claim of the first-wave opposition was that Walpole's title of 'prime minister' was itself unconstitutional and that the opposition was truer to the appropriate constitutional norms of parliamentarism. Originally, proponents of a doctrine of opposition made few if any claims about the role of an opposition leader; and the early practices of opposition politics were mainly about the claims of the team of 'outs' compared with the team of 'ins' (Johnson 1997).

British parliamentary opposition is historically grounded in a critique of executive supremacy, reinforced by Walpole's tendency (followed by almost all subsequent chief political executives) to establish a new system of 'court' politics against which the opposition reacts with a defence of the deeper constitutionality of 'country' politics, closer to the people whose interests deserve to be represented in parliament. The larger point is that the original impulse of opposition is to justify itself as 'constitutional' opposition, which means defending the constitution against the unconstitutional expansions of executive power by the serving government. The chief eighteenth-century architect of this political theory of constitutional opposition is 'the wayward genius' Bolingbroke, whose concept of 'the patriot prince' refashions executive power in the guise of a constitutional monarchy ruling through a cabinet of parliamentary ministers who only face an opposition when needed: that is, only when the cabinet succumbs to the corruptions of a chief minister like Walpole (Foord 1964: 113; an alternative account traces the oppositional checks and balances back to Montesquieu: see, e.g., de Jouvenel [1966]). What is the big lesson that Bolingbroke leaves for later students of opposition? The answer is the importance of power politics, in the sense that the performance test of an opposition is its ability to get hold of the power of government by replacing a corrupt party holding government. As originally understood, a 'constitutional' opposition is not an exercise in constitutional engineering to establish a permanent set of intra-parliamentary checks and balances but part of an argument that the country urgently needs those 'constitutionalists' in opposition to replace the 'unconstitutional' party in government (Foord 1964: 145–51).

Opposition predates 'Her Majesty's Opposition', a term which does not come to light until 1826, and even then as something of a term of jest at the arrogance of the very idea. But the opposition emerged as a modern version of the Roman tribune, acting as 'the constitutional critic of all public affairs', sobered by the partisan ambition to use the criticism to build public confidence about the merits of the claims of the alternative government (Todd 1892: 82–3; Foord 1964: 1; Maddox 1982, 2000). Criticism is all well and good but the overarching theme is that the pursuit of office is the primary purpose of 'the opposition' (Foord 1964: 317). The question of partisan strategy is how to use parliamentary power to get the greater power of executive office. The answer rests with the language of leadership exercised by the opposition, as political realists have long understood, noting that 'politicians fire off words instead of bullets' as the core strategy to win public confidence in their constitutional cause of restoring uncorrupt government (Schumpeter 1976: 279, cf. 269–73).

In power politics, the power of words matters. Among the most hard-nosed analysts of democratic leadership are Weber and Schumpeter, both of whom relate the Westminster story of opposition leadership back to the contest between mid-nineteenth-century British statesmen, Disraeli and Gladstone (Schumpeter 1976: 275–6; Weber 1994: 342–3, 351). Although Weber and Schumpeter are classic realist proponents of power politics, both identify the distinctive oppositional power as the power of public (and not narrowly parliamentary) speech. Disraeli initiated the practice with his use of publicly directed parliamentary speeches (Punnett 1973: 27–8). Gladstone's defeat of Disraeli's government in the so-called Midlothian campaign of 1879 marks the real arrival of an opposition leader as an electoral campaigner, taking the case against the government 'out of doors' into the public arena where voters rather than elected members could determine who should govern. The fascinating aspect of this development in public oppositional power is that Gladstone simply assumed a leadership role among the non-government forces: at that stage there really was no designated leader of the opposition. Disraeli is credited with first recognizing the need for leadership of an organized opposition party but Gladstone gets the prize for ushering in the modern era of electoral politics by opposition parties (Hanham 1971).

Weber gets to the heart of the matter when describing Gladstone as the exemplary modern demagogue whose commitment to plebiscitary democracy reflects the needs of oppositions to circumvent governing parties by winning public confidence as the basis for office, which would in turn be sustained by the new-found parliamentary confidence. Thus the confidence-vote that really matters for oppositions is the vote of public confidence. Subsequent commentary on British practices of parliamentary opposition spells out the detailed implications of this original nineteenth century model of opposition leadership, anchored in an electoral system reinforcing a two-party contest and a parliamentary system reinforcing this adversary arrangement between two competing parties. Surprisingly, the literature includes little in the way of detailed analysis of the internal parliamentary strategy of the 'front bench opposition', although there is slightly more attention paid to the extra-parliamentary or party-political strategy of the opposition party (Punnett 1973). For all the public attention claimed by 'the shadow cabinet' (a term apparently first used by Churchill), researchers have paid little attention to the various leadership roles performed by those leading opposition representatives who support the designated leader of the opposition, whose role and performance does attract considerable research attention. The prevailing research theme is that the leadership capacity of an opposition is explained by the persuasive capacity of the opposition leader when using parliamentary opportunities like Question Time (not to be discounted, according to Kaiser [2008: 28]) to erode public confidence in the serving government, and when using public opportunities like media presentations to broadcast a leadership image of public trust.

Two problems plague the Westminster model of opposition leadership. One persistent challenge to Westminster ways of managing the opposition function is the role of third parties in the parliamentary and party-political process (Punnett 1973: 20–7). Justifications of so-called 'responsible opposition' emerge against the backdrop of the allegedly irresponsible opposition of Irish 'home rule' radicals in Westminster in the late nineteenth century. Parnell's parliamentary leadership deserves note, as a primary example of effective obstructive opposition (Hanham 1971). Irish radical representatives discovered, then mastered, the power of procedure to stall and defeat government business. Among the 'weapons of the weak' in many parliamentary systems are the inherited procedures allowing minorities opportunities to be over-represented in many core parliamentary processes (e.g. Question Time where the opposition are by convention allocated half of the questions: Johnson [1997: 491–8]; Durkin and Gay [2006*a*]) and so can delay and obstruct government initiatives. The Westminster experience was that the good will and patience of successive governments were worn down by the guerrilla tactics of the Irish radicals who inverted the classic minority ploy of support in exchange for concessions, so that it became opposition (which would only cease) in exchange for concessions. The fallout of this era of competitive party politics was the consolidation of an institutional bias in favour of a two-party adversary system with rewards for the Official Opposition and few if any incentives for the other minor non-government parties (Johnson 1997: 506–7). The resistance to any form of a proportional electoral system, demanded by minorities since the late nineteenth century, robs third parties of much of their representative strength. This system persists today, making the leadership potential of the Liberal Democrats (a party which won 10% of the House of Commons seats with 22.1% of the vote at the 2005 election: Durkin and Gay 2006*b*) very difficult to deliver. Critics continue to label these minor non-government parties as part of 'a constitutional but non-responsible opposition' (Norton 2008: 243).

Another persistent challenge to Westminster ways of managing the opposition function is the potential of the House of Lords to invade and even 'crowd out' the field of legislative and policy opposition. Everywhere bicameralism complicates by duplicating parliamentary opposition, in Asia as much as Europe (Miyoshi 1998: 86–8; Uhr 2006). From a Westminster perspective, reforms over the last decade to the House of Lords have had the effect of strengthening the second chamber's institutional capacity to review government initiatives. This upper-chamber opposition has little to do with the classic opposition appeals to the country to 'throw the rascals out' at the next election. But the non-government forces in the Lords (including independently minded government party members) have been very effective in managing one important opposition function, which is reviewing the detail of proposed policy and legislative initiatives and pursuing their preferred amendments. A kind of division of labour emerges, where even the Official Opposition manages the primary opposition function of holding the government accountable through such publicly relevant lower house practices as Question Time, while opposition members in the upper house focus more on the sight-unseen matters of policy and legislative detail, performing the unsung but valuable oppositional role of 'fault-finding' (de Jouvenel 1966: 173).

Modified Westminster: Canadian models

Canada is a rich field for studies of parliamentary opposition. The use of the term 'House of Commons' for the national lower house suggests the desired continuity while the use of 'Senate' for the national upper house conveys the discontinuity caused by federalism. Federalism complicates opposition by diversifying the sources of anti-government power; further, as Friedrich notes, federalism increases the frequency of electoral contests which are the preferred mediums of oppositional campaigns for public confidence against governments (Friedrich 1966: 295). Canadian federalism provides the first big modification of Westminster models of leadership, with a structure of institutionalized opposition between federal and provincial levels of government, with ample potential for Ottawa-based non-government parties to use their provincial power-bases to leverage support for the anti-government cause. When federalism is mapped on to pre-existing linguistic/cultural divides, as in Canada, then the potential for federal/provincial opposition is vastly increased. When federalism reaches into the parliament and establishes a bicameral legislature, additional complications arise from the separations of power between the two houses, each of which might be dominated by separate political parties. Canada adds value to the federalism story by anticipating inter-cameral conflict and denying substantial public legitimacy to the legally powerful but conventionally tame appointed Senate (Friedrich 1966: 296; D. Smith 2007).

But Canada's value does not stop there: Canada is an archive of variations on Westminster modes of opposition, one of which has been the use of the formal offices of Official Opposition by the separatist Quebec party, the Bloc Quebecois. This novel period only came to an end when the Opposition Leader returned to provincial politics to take up the real work of Quebec self-government. There are many other examples of Canadian innovation in Westminster arrangements: such as the frequent occurrence of minority governments in Ottawa (e.g. 1957, 1962, 1963, 1965, 1972, and generally since 2004: Strahl [2004]); the famous Opposition two-week parliamentary boycott known as the Bells Crisis in the late 1980s; the episodes at provincial level, such as in New Brunswick in 1987, where elections have returned no opposition seats, which is one interpretation of the Westminster bias towards strong party government; or where governments have responded to total seat control by appointing a government party representative as opposition leader pro tem; or where the non-government parties have been deadlocked, resulting in a fascinating tradition of Speakers' rulings allocating the rewards of opposition office to different parties on different criteria under different circumstances; or where there is an attempt to avoid any designated opposition in the consensual parliaments in the new Northwest Territories and Nunavut (Hyson 1988, 1998; Michaud 2000: 73).

As often happens, colonies can institutionalize parliamentary conventions well before the metropolitan power commits them to the black letter of formality. Consistent with this, doctrines of 'responsible parliamentary government' were first formulated in Canada before being exported back into Britain when the occasion later arose to identify the spirit of constitutional modernization associated with the emergence of strong party government (and strong party opposition) at home. Admittedly, it was a member of the House of Lords, Lord Durham, who used his time in the 1830s as colonial administrator in Canada to formulate the constitutional doctrine of responsible government, drawing particularly on his radical Whig sympathies for parliamentary self-government free of regal or vice-regal intervention. In keeping with this Canadian innovation, it is notable that the first recognized leader of the official opposition occurred in the Canadian province of Nova Scotia as early as 1848 and the first paid office of Leader of the Opposition was established in Ottawa in 1905, well before its formal recognition as a paid public office at Westminster in 1937 (Michaud 2000: 71; Kaiser 2008: 24).

Westminster observers now look to Canada mainly to learn about the procedure for managing minority governments (they could also look to India: see Kashyap [2004]), and the Ottawa parliament has many lessons for students of the role of oppositions under minority governments. Canadian researcher Smith (2007) has used this experience to chart the 'rival theories of democracy' (parliamentary, constitutional, and electoral) at work in the Canadian parliamentary system, creating institutional instability from three competing sets of community expectations. In this environment of high flexibility, occasionally the opposition seizes the moment, such as when the Martin government lost a confidence vote that sent the government to the polls in late 2005. Under the former Martin government, the official opposition was the New Democratic Party which managed relationships with the government according to a charter of mutual expectations. But under the successor Harper government, the various opposition parties have taken their turn in supporting or attacking the government, making parliamentary confidence quite unpredictable (Kaiser 2008: 30). Yet despite such a rich recent history, Smith notes that 'one of the larger gaps in scholarly research in Canada is study of the opposition' (D. Smith 2007: 92, 126). Would that Canadians wrote more about the Canadian experience of opposition, especially with the remarkable innovation of the 2008 general election initiated by the serving Harper government when, in effect, it 'lost confidence' in the opposition parties based on their refusal to move confidence motions against the minority Harper government. It is one thing for opposition leaders to determine when to move confidence motions against governing parties. But it is quite a novel development for a governing party to dissolve the parliament when it loses confidence in the willingness of opposition leaders to play by the traditional rules of the parliamentary game.

Westminster reshaped: Australian models

Australia shares with Canada the formal architecture of federalism and of bicameralism. But the similarities end there. Australian governments expect little from the official opposition in the lower house and fear much from the unofficial opposition in the upper house. As one of the very few parliamentary systems not possessing a charter or bill of rights, Australia might derive great benefit from a constructive opposition. But the major political parties have learnt to live without such help. As a consequence, the official opposition party spreads its bets by investing heavily in the main game of election preparations and the minor game of using its party-political power in the Senate to work with other non-government parties to modify government initiatives. There is little scholarly research on the leadership repertoires deployed in the first area but a growing body of research on the shared leadership across non-government parties found in the Senate (Uhr 1998; Bach 2003; Tuffin 2007).

Internationally, Australia is noted for having 'two different patterns of parliamentary opposition' (Tuffin 2007; Kaiser 2008: 23). Most students are more interested in the evidence of a Westminster-like bipolar form of opposition in the lower house or House of Representatives, but the real evidence of opposition power derives from the existence of the multipolar form in the upper house or Senate. In Kaiser's recent ranking of four national opposition schemes, Australia emerges as much less powerful than either the minority-government systems of Canada or New Zealand and quite behind the majority-government system at Westminster. A symbol of the problem confronting Australian official oppositions is the remarkable weakness of the speaker in the lower house who exercises few of the independent powers of the Westminster Speaker, and so contributes little to the promotion of balanced cross-party parliamentarism celebrated as core Westminster (Kaiser 2008: 26–7). Why? 'Small house, large parties' is the standard answer. Contrast the multipolar arrangement in the Australian Senate, perhaps the most powerful elected upper house covered in this chapter: 'small house, many parties'. Elected through a form of proportional representation (PR) which almost always robs major parties (government or opposition) of effective control, the Senate operates as a multiparty chamber which shares the opposition functions among all non-government senators. The existence of an independent presiding officer, lacking in either Australian parliamentary house, seems unnecessary to this development (Uhr 1998; Bach 2003).

Westminster overhauled: New Zealand models

At the time after the Second World War that Australia was reforming its upper house through the adoption of a new electoral system based on PR, New Zealand abandoned bicameralism. Many years later, after the experience of highly energized government with apparently little opposition capacity to moderate government initiatives to modernize the state and economy, New Zealand engaged in substantial electoral reform to restructure the parliament around a German-derived system of PR. A decade later, New Zealand is increasingly described as entrenching 'persistent Scandinavian-style minority government constellations' (Kaiser 2008: 23). All governments since 1999 have been minority (but unlike Canada) *coalition* governments, with increasing emphasis on formalized structures of cross-party negotiation over various forms of power-sharing.

This institutional development has many implications for opposition leadership. Many of the traditional leadership platforms, such as Question Time, continue to privilege the official leader of the opposition as head of 'the alternative government'. But many other platforms of parliamentary power confer leadership on smaller non-government parties. The official opposition as an actor in its own right 'has to accept a status of powerlessness', because it alone lacks the power to veto anything (Kaiser 2008: 33). Some of the newer platforms are formal power-sharing contracts between the political executive and, for example, the Greens to establish conditions of government survivability in the circumstances of a minority government. Other platforms confer power and hence leadership potential on whichever non-government parties can negotiate their place at the relevant parliamentary committee responsible for case-managing legislative or policy initiatives, still (as in classic Westminster) predominately the responsibility of the government of the day (Kaiser 2008: 32–3).

Non-Westminster models

One particular regime type is singled out for special attention in this final section: the so-called 'post-consociational' parliamentary democracies of the Netherlands, Belgium, and Austria. Changes over recent years in the ways that oppositions have used their parliamentary power suggests that the non-Westminster model of 'consensual' parliamentarism is no longer as stable as once described. My suggestion is that if this world of exemplary 'consensualism' has moved away from its traditional consociationalism, then we can expect that less formalized versions of consensual parliamentarism will also have become more flexible and less predictable in the ways that opposition parties contribute to parliamentary government (Helms 2008*a*). Overarching this is one important structural difference between Westminster and non-Westminster parliaments which helps explain different approaches to opposition leadership. Adapting Arter (2007), we can suggest that the operational priorities for Westminster revolve around 'holding government accountable', whereas many non-Westminster parliaments often have a different operational priority revolving around 'representativeness'. The former approach encourages institutional checks and balances conducive to an adversary mode of opposition leadership. The latter approach encourages a form of give and take in the name of institutional inclusiveness, facilitating a quite different mode of opposition leadership. Few non-Westminster parliaments have established 'leader of the opposition' positions, although more than a few have followed Sweden's example and begun to arrange their party coalitions around a more explicitly adversarial axis of government and non-government blocs (Arter 2007).

Take the Netherlands as the most discussed example of consociationalism, with contemporary research on parliamentary opposition in the Netherlands providing important contrasts with these Westminster-derived developments (Andeweg, de Winter, and Muller 2008). The Netherlands features prominently in contemporary studies of opposition, originally as an example of consociational and now in some quarters as an example of post-consociational forms of parliamentary opposition (Lijphart 1968, 1999). According to past models of consensus forms of parliamentary government, consensus processes rise when adversary relationships fall. As a consequence of this commitment to consensus, the strict separation of government and opposition fades when many political groups participate in the slow, steady, and hard work of determining outcomes acceptable to all recognized parties (Ionescu and de Madariaga 1968: 92–102).

But the emerging argument is that the earlier wave of consociationalism is passing in response to the 'de-pillarization' of, in particular among this set of three countries, Dutch society. Pillarized (or socially segmented) societies promote a form of parliamentarism where representative elites work out power-sharing arrangements that respect and reflect the veto claims exercised by each social pillar or recognized cultural group. The earlier era of so-called 'grand' (or 'oversized') coalitions produced a model of multiparty government with parliamentary power shared among recognized peak groups. The grand concept implied that it made better political sense to have more players on board (or 'in the tent') than strictly necessary for government formation. One consequence was a low profile for anything like a Westminster official opposition or leader of 'the alternative government'. Opposition parties might well exist, but they tended to be quite removed from 'the loyal opposition', with a preference in many cases for constitutional disloyalty consistent with 'anti-system parties' like many European communist parties in the 1950s and 1960s (Dahl 1973: 1–18; G. Smith 1987: 59–63; Daalder 1996; Norton 2008: 239).

With social change comes institutional innovation (von Beyme 1987; Helms 2008*a*). The modernization (usually defined in terms of the spread of secularism and individualism) and de-pillarization of Dutch society has allowed non-pillar interests to use the proportional electoral system to enter parliament, in the guise of new minor parties typically away from the centre on the right or left of the centrist governing coalitions. One institutional consequence is the tendency to devise new parliamentary mechanisms of more immediate use to opposition parties than to governing parties. An important example is the annual 'Accountability Day' debate over government performance, which nicely fits in between Westminster platforms designed to maximize an opposition's electoral competitiveness and traditional consociational devices of shared executive power. Here is a parliamentary platform allowing opposition parties to retain their distance from executive government, decline to present as 'the alternative government', yet appear as responsible parliamentary players by making constructive criticisms of those exercising executive power. In keeping with this institutional innovation, the Dutch parliament has experienced a dramatically increased trend in successful opposition legislative amendments in the post-pillarization period, and large increases in questions to government and inquiries into government by parliamentary committees. Scholars conclude that this increased opposition impact reflects more a new parliamentary professionalism of cross-party negotiation rather than the adoption of an anti-government oppositionalism as such (Holzhacker 2005: 440–4; Andeweg et al. 2008).

The Scandinavian countries are acknowledged as having the highest impact of opposition parties on government decision-making, a situation deriving from the sustained shared experience of 'minority governance' (Christiansen and Damgaard 2008). Not all opposition parties try to exercise the same modes of parliamentary leadership: some see themselves as support parties for the governing group, others act more strategically to support some but not all of the government's initiatives, still others drift in and out of explicit oppositionalism. The recent trend has been for an informal version of a majority coalition government to overtake past reliance on minority governments, through more stable blocs of support (often hammered out publicly in the lead-up to an election) from those opposition parties sharing mutual policy interests with the governing minority party. Given that the opposition parties usually reserve their rights to dissent from the policy of the governing party, opposition leadership practices are rather unpredictable, reflecting in large part the changing prominence of different policy issues. The result is that differently situated opposition parties exercise very different types of parliamentary leadership, covering the range from the sort of leadership expected of a junior coalition partner to the self-proclaimed (and self-justifying) independence of fringe parties.

Conclusions: rethinking oppositional leadership

Standing back from the many details of parliamentary opposition, we can discern a number of general research themes that arise from the specifics investigated in this chapter. One research theme is that the study of parliamentary opposition provides a very practical focus on dispersed leadership. Democracy is a grand but often nebulous theme, yet here we have a very concrete set of practices that tell us much about the effective operation of parliamentary democracy: when it works, how it works, and why it works. So too notions of 'dispersal' can swirl around, loosely referring to any form of networked relationships, however distant and indirect. But a focus on policy activities managed by prominent elected representatives preserves the value of 'articulation' that is implicit in concepts of dispersed leadership. That is, what is of real research interest in the type of dispersed leadership exercised by parliamentary oppositions is the role and value of the political and policy relationships articulated by opposition leaders. By 'articulation', I here mean both the Westminster style of public rhetoric used by opposition leaders intent on becoming heads of government; and also the consensual-style of policy collaboration favoured by party leaders working in parliamentary coalitions that impact on government even when the party leaders do not particularly want to be part of 'the government'. Researchers still have much to do in plotting and charting the world of dispersed leadership, but I think that this future research task is more promising precisely because of the practical illustrations of concepts of dispersal and leadership found in the study of parliamentary opposition.

Another general research theme is the importance of the distinction between leaders and leadership. Studies of dispersed leadership emphasize the importance of differently located sources of public leadership. Theses studies rightly note that many leaders occupying offices away from the centre of government provide valuable public leadership missing from those mastering the central machine of government. But I think this chapter's study of opposition leaders opens another research dimension in this distinction between leaders and leadership. The study of parliamentary opposition can generate a gallery of types of prominent public figures. This gallery ranges from leaders of 'the alternative government' who, without strong displays of political leadership, inherit government office in the wake of the fall of inept governing parties, through to those figures who possess relevant leadership qualities which are never properly appreciated either by party colleagues or by voters at large (Hargrove and Owens 2002). To be leader of a party in opposition is an opportunity to display public leadership, and the research community might begin to display some of its own leadership if it placed priority on investigating and explaining how some leaders bring leadership to positions of power while others simply bring power to the leader's position. Opposition leaders have many ways of joining power and leadership, from the heights of 'the leader of the opposition' to the back rooms of parliamentary party negotiations in non-Westminster systems. Researchers can help by exploring the democratic potential of each type of opposition leadership.

A final general research theme is the one with which I began this chapter: leadership as power-sharing (Crick 2005). By itself, 'dispersal' can convey simply a sense of distance, as in some meanings of a leadership dispersal when that phrase is used to suggest scattered resources and a lack of appropriate concentration. But I think this chapter has shown that opposition leadership is a good example of the value of dispersed leadership to democracy, precisely because opposition leadership is a study in power-sharing rather than power dispersal. At one level, opposition leaders help rulers and the ruled appreciate that their relationship is one of shared power, with the governing parties holding offices of trust for the benefit of those they represent. At another level, opposition leaders actively participate in the power game by insisting on their own rights and responsibilities as holders of parliamentary office with constitutional claims to share in the management of legislative power. Opposition leaders can thus be tested by their commitment to defend not just their share of public and parliamentary power but their rights to participate as co-custodians of the legislative power of the democratic state. Researchers can take this notion of leadership as power-sharing much further than I have in this chapter by teasing out the constitutional implications of the public standing conceded to political oppositions in parliamentary democracies. As I have tried to show in this chapter, the quality of opposition leadership is defined by its ability to extract such concessions from political executives reluctant to share power with what they see as their adversaries, their antagonists, and their opponents. It is no small feat for a parliamentary democracy to encourage governing parties to treat political competitors honourably as 'the opposition', with its own role to play in public leadership.

Bibliography

Andeweg, R., De Winter, L., and Muller, W., 'Parliamentary Opposition in Post-Consociational Democracies', *Journal of Legislative Studies*, 14 (2008), 77–112.

Arter, D., 'From "Parliamentary Control" to "Accountable Government"?', *Parliamentary Affairs*, 61 (2007), 122–43.

Bach, S., *Platypus and Parliament: The Australian Senate in Theory and Practice* (Canberra: Department of the Senate, 2003).

Barker, R. (ed.), *Studies in Opposition* (London: Macmillan, 1971).

Blondel, J., 'Political Opposition in the Contemporary World', *Government and Opposition*, 32 (1997), 462–86.

Burns, J. M., *Transforming Leadership* (New York: Atlantic Monthly Press, 2003).

Christiansen, F. J. and Damgaard, E., 'Parliamentary Opposition under Minority Parliamentarism: Scandinavia', *Journal of Legislative Studies*, 14 (2008), 56–76.

Corrales, J. and Penfold, M., 'Venezuela: Crowding out the Opposition', *Journal of Democracy*, 18 (2007), 99–113.

Crick, B., *The Reform of Parliament* (London: Weidenfeld and Nicolson, 1964).

——'On Conflict and Opposition', in R. Barker (ed.), *Studies in Opposition* (London: Macmillan, 1971), 38–44.

——*In Defence of Politics*, 5th edn. (London: Continuum, 2005).

Crockett, D., 'The President as Opposition Leader', *Presidential Studies Quarterly*, 30 (2000), 245–74.

Daalder, H., 'The Netherlands: Political Opposition in a Segmented Society', in R. A. Dahl (ed.), *Political Oppositions in Western Democracies* (New Haven: Yale University Press, 1966), 118–236.

Dahl, R. A. (ed.), *Political Oppositions in Western Democracies* (New Haven: Yale University Press, 1966).

——(ed.), *Regimes and Oppositions* (New Haven: Yale University Press, 1973).

De Jouvenel, B., 'The Means of Contestation', *Government and Opposition*, 1/2 (1966), 155–74.

Durkin, M. and Gay, O., *Her Majesty's Opposition* (London: House of Commons Library, 2006*a*).

————*The Other Opposition Parties at Westminster* (London: House of Commons Library, 2006*b*).

Foley, M., *John Major, Tony Blair and a Conflict of Leadership Collision Course* (Manchester: Manchester University Press, 2002).

Foord, A. S., *His Majesty's Opposition, 1714–1830* (Oxford: Oxford University Press, 1964).

Friedrich, C. J., 'Federalism and Opposition', *Government and Opposition*, 1/3 (1966), 286–96.

Ghany, H., 'The Office of Leader of the Opposition', *Journal of Legislative Studies*, 7/2 (2001), 105–22.

Hanham, H. J., 'Opposition Techniques in British Politics: 1867–1914', in R. Barker (ed.), *Studies in Opposition* (London: Macmillan, 1971), 130–45.

Hargrove, E. C. and Owens, J. (eds.), *Leadership in Context* (London: Rowman and Littlefield, 2002).

Helms, L., 'Five Ways of Institutionalizing Political Opposition', *Government and Opposition*, 39 (2004), 22–54.

——'Studying Parliamentary Opposition in Old and New Democracies: Issues and Perspectives', *Journal of Legislative Studies*, 14 (2008*a*), 6–19.

——'Governing in the Media Age: The Impact of the Mass Media on Executive Leadership in Contemporary Democracies', *Government and Opposition*, 43 (2008*b*), 26–54.

——and Norton, P. (eds.), 'Parliamentary Opposition in Old and New Democracies', *Journal of Legislative Studies*, 14 (2008), 1–250.

Holzhacker, R., 'The Power of Opposition Parliamentary Party Groups in European Scrutiny', *Journal of Legislative Studies*, 11/3 (2005), 428–44.

Hyson, S., 'Where's "Her Majesty's Loyal Opposition" in the Loyalist Province?', *Canadian Parliamentary Review*, 11/2 Summer (1988), 22–5.

——'Nova Scotia and the "Problem" of Minority Government', *Canadian Parliamentary Review*, 21/4 (1998), 11–15.

Ionescu, G. and de Madariaga, S., *Opposition: Past and Present of a Political Institution.* (London: Watts, 1968).

Jennings, I., *Parliament*, 2nd edn. (Cambridge: Cambridge University Press, 1957).

Johnson, N., 'Opposition in the British Political System', *Government and Opposition*, 32 (1997), 487–511.

Kaiser, A., 'Parliamentary Opposition in Westminster Democracies', *Journal of Legislative Studies*, 14 (2008), 20–45.

Kashyap, S. C., 'Executive-Legislative Interface in the Indian Polity', *Journal of Legislative Studies*, 10/2 (2004), 278–94.

Lijphart, A., *The Politics of Accommodation: Pluralist Democracy in the Netherlands* (Berkeley: University California Press, 1968).

——*Patterns of Democracy* (New Haven: Yale University Press, 1999).

Maddox, G., 'Responsible and Irresponsible Opposition', *Government and Opposition*, 17 (1982), 211–20.

——'Opposition', in G. Maddox (ed.), *Australian Democracy in Theory and Practice* (Sydney: Longman, 2000), 269–94.

Mair, P., 'Political Opposition and the European Union', *Government and Opposition*, 42 (2007), 1–17.

Michaud, N., 'Designating the Official Opposition in a Westminster Parliamentary System', *Journal of Legislative Studies*, 6/4 (2000), 69–90.

Miyoshi, A., 'The Diet in Japan', *Journal of Legislative Studies*, 4/4 (1998), 83–102.

Mujica, A. and Sanchez-Cuena, I., 'Consensus and Parliamentary Opposition: The Case of Spain', *Government and Opposition,* 41 (2006), 86–103.

Norton, P., 'Making Sense of Opposition', *Journal of Legislative Studies*, 14 (2008), 236–50.

Parry, G., 'Opposition Questions', *Government and Opposition*, 32 (1997), 457–61.

Punnett, R. M., *Front-Bench Opposition* (London: Heinemann, 1973).

Sartori, G., 'Opposition and Control, in R. Barker (ed.), *Studies in Opposition* (London: Macmillan, 1971), 31–7.

——*Parties and Party Systems* (Cambridge: Cambridge University Press, 1976).

Schumpeter, J. A., *Capitalism, Socialism and Democracy* (London: Allen and Unwin, 1976).

Smith, D., *The People's House of Commons* (Toronto: University of Toronto Press, 2007).

Smith, G., 'Party and Protest: The Two Faces of Opposition in Western Europe', in E. Kolinsky (ed.), *Opposition in Western Europe* (London: Croom Helm, 1987).

Stepan, A., 'Democratic Opposition and Democratization Theory', *Government and Opposition*, 32 (1997), 657–78.

Strahl, C., 'Politics and Procedure in a Minority Parliament', *Canadian Parliamentary Review*, 27/4 (2004), 7–9.

Todd, A., *Parliamentary Government in England* (London: Sampson Low, Marston & Company, 1892).

Tuffin, K., 'Opposition', in B. Galligan and W. Roberts (eds.), *The Oxford Companion to Australian Politics* (Melbourne: Oxford University Press, 2007), 377–80.

Turner, D., *The Shadow Cabinet in British Politics* (London: Routledge, 1969).

Uhr, J., *Deliberative Democracy in Australia* (Melbourne: Cambridge University Press, 1998).

——'Bicameralism', in R. Rhodes, R. Binder, and B. Rockman (eds.), *Oxford Handbook of Political Institutions* (Oxford: Oxford University Press, 2006), 474–94.

Von Beyme, C., 'Parliamentary Oppositions in Europe', in E. Kolinsky (ed.), *Opposition in Western Europe* (London: Croom Helm, 1987).

Weber, M., *Political Writings*, P. Lassman and R. Spwirs (eds.), (Cambridge: Cambridge University Press, 1994).

Wheare, K. C., *Legislatures*, 2nd edn. (Oxford: Oxford University Press, 1968).

Chapter 5

Populist Leadership

Jos de Beus

The populist revival

Populism is a technical term for mobilization of resistance against a ruling class alias establishment, pursuit of absolute majority rule (with contempt of deliberation and compromise), display of popular and militant nationalism, electoral opportunism (following polls and the given policy preferences of relevant voters), and manipulation of the public – either stirring up dangerous emotions of the crowd or pleasing an irrational crowd (Canovan 1981, 1999, 2005; Riker 1982; Taggart 2000, 2002; Mackie 2003; Mudde 2004; Stoker 2006: 132–45).

Populism seldom advances as a unified force. Its features contradict each other. An anti-establishment agenda may polarize the electorate rather than accumulate support of the middle class. Popular nationalism may hinder foreign policy success. Rejection of comprehensive ideologies, carried by mainstream parties, turns populists into chameleons. Some of them are left-wing, others right-wing; yet others defy such categorizations as they seek to redefine the political space (Kazin 1995; Phillips 2003). Populist conservatism became legitimate in the United States due to the innovation of President Reagan, the realignment of the Republican Party, and the combativeness of President George W. Bush (Wilentz 2008). To date, it is resented by mainstream parties in Western Europe, mainly out of an aversion steeped in Europe's dark mid-twentieth-century history (Rifkin 2004; Lukacs 2005; Albertazzi and McDonnell 2008).

Political scientists draw a distinction between populism by outsiders with a claim to representation of oppressed and excluded members of the polity (grassroots populism) and populism by insiders with a claim to use of the state apparatus in accordance with the will of ordinary citizens (government house populism). Some argue that stable liberal democracies are marked by alternation of populism and pragmatism (Hirschman 1982; Unger 1987; Notermans 2000). Pragmatism is non-populism in the sense of continuation of rational public policy, liberal pluralism (respect for minorities and dissidents), elitist administration of the nation state, politics as professional business insulated from the cycle and buzz of elections, and control of the public by means of mitigating rhetoric and moderation.

Populism will be articulated by new politicians seeking office via offensive campaigning and radical change, and by old politicians whose office holding is losing the support of major constituencies and who stick to power by defensive campaigning and preservation of the status quo. Pragmatism will be articulated by cooperative and flexible leaders of opposition parties as well as by incumbent politicians whose office is both vested and popular. For example, during the crisis of stagflation and overload of the Keynesian welfare state in the 1970s populist leaders preferred growth of public expenditure and social entitlements to austere fiscal policy and balanced budgets, while pragmatic leaders made the opposite choice (Buchanan and Wagner 1977; Frey 1978; Goldthorpe 1984).

Political theorists draw a distinction between authoritarian and democratic populism (Spengler 1928; Habermas 1992; Rawls 1993, 1999: 97; Chambers 2004, 2005; Dworkin 2006). Demagogues and dictators are false friends of the people who apply the dirty means of plebiscitary politics to shape hegemonic power and make plans that can only be realized in a regime without the rule of law and civil rights. Liberators and statesmen are true friends of the people who apply the noble repertoire of deliberative politics to create public authority and make plans that are conducive to closure of the gap between the democratic ideal and the real world. Populism indicates either liberal democracy's corruption and decline or its promise and resilience (Dahrendorf 2002; Panizza 2005). In a perspective of decline, populism is modelled as a backlash against cartel behaviour or excessive convergence among vested parties (Katz and Mair 1995; Aucante and Dézé 2008).

This chapter introduces a perspective of resilience. It discusses the contemporary revival of the populist aspect of leadership in Western democracies by focusing on the office seeking and office holding of prominent politicians in two-party systems (the American President Clinton, the American presidential candidate Perot, and the British Prime Minister Blair) as well as in multiparty systems (the Italian Prime Minister Berlusconi, the German Chancellor Schröder, and the Dutch candidate for parliament Fortuyn). All these men entered politics in order to become leaders of national government and tread in the footsteps of great leaders in the universal history of democracy, say Roosevelt, Churchill, de Gaulle, Attlee, or Adenauer. They renewed political communication by turning the political party and the executive branch of government into machines for continuous and sophisticated campaigning in a public sphere with highly competitive parties and media outlets. They drew on spray-on charisma, that is, dramaturgical competence and aura on the television screen (Rieff 2007: 3–13). All of them were, and still are, controversial politician-celebrities (see further 't Hart and Tindall, this volume). Some of them were accused of weak leadership, marked by private money, deceit, gesture politics, narcissism, and impotence as to running the public sector and improving its performance.[1] They seem to fit in De Bonald's old sketch of the theatre king, 'who lays down scepter and diadem after the show and who, having returned to his original estate, blends the habits of a servant with the grandiloquent language of his role' (De Bonald [1796] 1845: 126–7).

There are good reasons to track populist leadership in unexpected places, that is, respectable capital cities of Western countries today. First, the standard claim of political science that populism is a viable option for radical new politicians and besieged old ones (yet an inferior option for leaders of regular opposition and successful incumbent leaders) warrants fresh evidence on a par with such evidence about emergent nationalist persuasion by rival elites in processes of transition from autocracy to democracy (Snyder 2000; Mansfield and Snyder 2005). Does it still hold for mature democracies that populist opponents are unable to govern wisely, while pragmatic incumbents are unwilling to enchant the public mind?

Second, the dispersal of agents and sites of credible popular representation in mature democracies – networks of public advocacy, journalists as spokespersons, independent authorities and non-governmental associations both domestic and across the border, corporations, and lobbyists going public – may go in tandem with diffusion of populism among all eligible and elected politicians. Populism is no longer limited to third party challengers in the United States, *personalismo* in Latin America, and recurrent movements of discontent in post-totalitarian Europe. It may well become durable in the 'audience democracy' and 'populist-bureaucratic regime' that characterize established democracies today. In fact many observers of contemporary presidents and prime ministers note that they rely on a plebiscitary mode of public policy-making (Manin 1997: 218–35; Skowronek 1997: 53; Keller 2007: 3).

Third, the realist view of leadership needs testability and falsification. In realism, national leaders are populists by definition. They invent popular interests, mobilize large masses, and organize their unified power. They leave the administration of party and government to trusted and like-minded agents. They compete with other (potential) leaders in state and community building. Realists neglect the significance of pragmatism for administration of complex institutions and the making of cohesive coalitions backstage, out of the eye of journalists, voters, and opponents (Burnham 1943; Mansfield 1996; McCormick 2001, 2006; Samuels 2003).

Fourth and finally, the idealist objection against contemporary right-wing populism needs qualification. Some scholars argue that individualization and mediatization of society promote a cynical and fanatical populism that fears and hates libertarians, secular believers, immigrants, profiteering welfare state clients, owners and managers of global corporations, cosmopolitans, supporters of European integration, and greens (Elchardus 2002; Mény and Surel 2002;

Mazzoleni 2003; Davies 2008; Hall Jamieson and Cappella 1997, 2008). I disagree. Neoconservatism does not coincide with populism. Some neoconservatives try to temper populism, while some new progressives try to imitate it. Antiglobalism, including dissatisfaction with multicultural policies, is not an exclusive privilege of telegenic radicals of the right.

Populist office seeking

The process of office seeking comprises the path to professional politics, candidacy, and first gain in national campaigning. All my cases involve leaders who tried to end the reign of an establishment. Clinton in 1992 wanted to break the rule of Republicans since 1980 and the unravelling of New Deal Democrats and liberalism since Johnson's retreat in 1968. Perot, a dissatisfied Republican and rival of Clinton, wanted to dismantle the Washington consensus on globalization. Berlusconi in 1994 wanted to abolish the post-war *partitocrazia* of Christian Democrats, Socialists, and Communists and its capture of the public sector and protection of vested industries.

Blair in 1997 wanted to break the rule of Conservatives since 1979 and the implosion of Labour in the clash between cadre radicalization and the crisis management by Prime Ministers Wilson and Callaghan (1974–9). Schröder in 1998 wanted to break the rule of Kohl's Christian Democrats since 1982 and transcend a protracted division and confusion within the German Social Democratic Party with respect to German unification and welfare state reform. Fortuyn in 2002 wanted to dissolve a 'cartel' of mainstream parties in the Netherlands, manifest during two lib–lab cabinets since 1994, and get rid of the Dutch consensus on multiculturalism and Europeanism.

But there are major differences between the hard populism of Perot, Berlusconi, and Fortuyn – three angry businessmen with a simple message – and the soft populism growing out of a search for popularity by third way modernizers such as Clinton, Blair, and Schröder, three members of a new generation of party politicians (Clinton and Schröder as state governors and Blair as Member of Parliament). For example, Perot and Fortuyn loathed polling and campaign consultancy, while the others tried each new development in public opinion research. Let me first turn to the hard populism of Perot, Berlusconi, and Fortuyn.

Ross Perot

Ross Perot was an independent candidate during the American presidential elections of 1992 with 19 per cent of the popular vote (Kazin 1995: 269–86; Posner 1996; Wilentz 2008: 315–17, 320–2). He was a former manager of IBM who made his fortune by selling computers to the federal government and gradually committed himself – in an effort to counter the movement against the Vietnam war – to the cause of prisoners of war, war veterans, young drop-outs, and chronic drugs users. Perot left the Republican Party because of his rejection of the war in the Persian Gulf. He cultivated a public reputation of national heroism and non-partisan statesmanship. He tried to perform as a plain-speaking common man rather than charmer or crisis manager. Focusing on American workers and middle class households as alleged victims of global free trade North American Free Trade Association (NAFTA) and military interventionism, he presented himself as a rich capitalist who felt guilty and ashamed about economic failure, social corruption, and political opportunism of many of his own class and who would reform the rule of federal agencies and big corporations without class warfare.

Perot organized *United We Stand*, a national movement of volunteers, with an agenda for balancing the federal budget (through expenditure cuts rather than increased taxes), winning the war on drugs, protectionism, and direct democracy by means of 'electronic town halls'. On moral issues, Perot was not the sturdy, reactionary Texas rancher. He did not see abortion as a criminal act and supported gay rights and gun control. His policy ideas in the best-selling *United We Stand: How We Can Take Back Our Country* (1992) seemed strongly influenced by a classical liberal morality. Perot did not warm to Christian fundamentalism.

Perot faced fierce opposition from Reaganite media such as Limbaugh's talk radio and *The Wall Street Journal*. His liabilities in the press, his own campaign team, and his fluid constituency were paranoia, obstinacy, patronization of black Americans, and bullying. Perot's methods to overcome such obstacles and to achieve the best third-party result since Theodore Roosevelt in 1912 were anti-Washington rhetoric, spokesmanship for a moderate, non-ideological majority of citizens, patriotism, simple and funny messages ('We own the country', 'I am Ross and you are the boss', 'It's just that simple'), and considerable debating skills. Perot's campaign was a parade of cable television appearances in both serious and frivolous programmes, facilitated by free television time and unlimited personal funds.

Silvio Berlusconi

At the time of writing, Silvio Berlusconi is Prime Minister of Italy in his third term. Between 2001 and 2006 this mogul from Milano presided over Italy's longest administration since the Second World War. He needed two campaigns, in 1994 and 2001, plus an instructive failure of his first and short-lived cabinet in 1994–5, to reach the political top. Berlusconi was the richest man in his country and a famous owner of a conglomerate of television channels, print media, telecommunication, soccer, and real estate. His political commitment was rooted in visceral anti-communism, a belief in the American model of free enterprise and consumer sovereignty, and the intuition that Christian Democracy was exhausted and could no longer preserve Catholic values and institutions. Berlusconi presented himself as a smart businessman with many talents and good luck, caring father of the Italian clan writ large, ruthless saviour of the national economy and national prestige, and naughty Italian male (Ginsborg 2004; Stille 2006).

Berlusconi created his own formation *Forza Italia* and forged an alliance with Northern separatists and Southern neofascists without a specific agenda. His first campaign boiled down to the claim that only he could clean up the mess of leftist state failure, treason, and immorality, and then restore the post-war spirit of economic miracle, European unity, and American cordiality. His second campaign was the opposite and promised a detailed mandate on the rise of old-age pensions, halving the unemployment rate, public works, cutting taxes, and lowering the crime rate.[2]

Berlusconi had to deal with certain risks and liabilities: energetic judges in antitrust and criminal law cases, Mafia infiltration in his projects, his membership of a secret Masonic lodge, lack of experience and agreement in his movement and party coalition, and conflict between his private interests and public policy purposes. Berlusconi's methods to turn necessity into virtue and lead the largest bloc of governmental parties in 1994 and 2001 were: a cultivated self-image of the lonely, honest, disinterested, responsive, and eternally young outsider; a quasi-majoritarian arrangement of continuous presence on prime time television, exploitation of news monopoly, and shrewd coalition building backstage; nationalism without remorse about the fascist past or shame in the picking of friends (such as Putin's Russia) and of enemies (courts, the European Commission, immigrants, Muslim societies, and gypsies); advanced public opinion research as integral part of corporate marketing; and omnipresence in the public sphere via campaigning techniques, such as the soccer metaphor.

Pim Fortuyn

Pim Fortuyn was a Dutch academic and pundit who financed an extravagant lifestyle by means of polemic books, columns, and public lectures on the state of Dutch society and politics (Pels 2003; Wansink 2004). He presented himself as a prophet and entrepreneur. In 2002, he became leader of *Leefbaar Nederland*, a union of local protest parties. After a quarrel concerning Fortuyn's main message about the danger of Islamization of the West and an electoral victory in Rotterdam as leader of the local party branch, Fortuyn and his sponsors in real estate began the *List Pim Fortuyn* (LPF). On 15 May 2002, this party gained 26 out of 150 seats in the Dutch lower house; by that time Fortuyn had been dead for nine days, assassinated by a member of the extreme animal liberation movement. Yet his political vehicle, LPF, joined a centre-right cabinet with four ministers. Although the cabinet lasted for only eighty-seven days and the LPF faded away in two successive general elections, Fortuyn's wake-up call and his liquidation stand for a critical juncture in the Netherlands, comparable to September 11 in the United States.

After serial flirts with all mainstream parties, Fortuyn began to express a basic critique of consensus democracy during the 1990s. He referred to the core of Dutch government and business as a conspiracy of 'our sort of people' that constituted the real enemy of ordinary citizens. Such citizens were victims of multiculturalism, corporatism, Europeanism, cosmopolitanism and, most menacing, Islamism. They comprised the self-employed, employers of small firms, the middle class in social and public services (policemen, nurses, and teachers), and, last but not least, self-reliant immigrants outside the mosque.

Fortuyn's agenda was articulated in a book, *The Ruins of Eight Years Lib-Lab*. This was a mixture of electoral manifesto, autobiography, vilification of opponents, and cultural studies. It contained broad visions and detailed proposals on health care, schools, security, welfare reform, agriculture (with infrastructure and public utilities), administrative reform, immigration policy, and foreign policy (with defence and European integration). Fortuyn advocated strict border control, strong government, and renationalization of European policies. He welcomed commercialization of public services and internationalization of corporations, while rejecting the cult of managerialism and scale enlargement within organizations.

Fortuyn was demonized by nearly all his rivals and observers in the press as a pupil of Mussert (the leader of Dutch Nazi's during the German occupation) and a kindred spirit of the European radical right today (Dewinter, Haider, and Le Pen). His liabilities were open homosexuality, lack of experience in parliament and public administration, and a lukewarm approach of the popular royal House of Orange. Fortuyn's ultimately effective methods to cope with all of this included: intimate knowledge of the flaws of the elite consensus and the problems of the mass of voters; an explicit and reflexive idea about the Dutch nation; mercurial performances, eloquent rhetoric ('At your service!', 'the left church'), superb debating skills, and a secret pact with the Christian Democrat Jan-Peter Balkenende, the Dutch prime minister since 2002.

Bill Clinton

Turning now to the three 'soft populists' discussed in this chapter, I begin with Bill Clinton, a tenaciously ambitious governor of a small southern state, prominent modernizer of the Democratic Party, and champion of flexible synthesis between liberalism and conservatism. Clinton became the forty-second American President – with 43 per cent of the popular vote – after a protracted struggle in bumpy primaries and cut-throat contests with two contenders,

President George H. W. Bush and Perot (Hamilton 2003, 2007; Wilentz 2008: 317–27). Clinton, a policy wonk par excellence in many social issues, endorsed a novel view of the centre-left based on the acceptance of free trade, balanced budgets, expansive monetary policy, workfare (forced labour participation of the poor, called 'empowerment'), public regulation of the markets for social services, particularly education and healthcare, and repressive policies of criminal justice. Announcing his candidacy in October 1991, Clinton argued that 'People out here don't care about the idle rhetoric of "left" and "right" and "liberal" and "conservative" and all the other words that have made our politics as a substitute for action'. His manifesto *Putting People First* made a minor pragmatic case for public deficit reduction and a major populist case for a tax cut for the middle class, a surge of spending on public works, and $60 billion of outlays in healthcare, education, and childcare.

Clinton was adept at exploiting his assets: his intelligence, natural persona and superb communication skills, good looks, stamina and lust for campaigning, team of first-rate consultants (including his wife Hillary), and network of rich sponsors. His constraints were equally diverse. The Democrats after Reagan and the end of the Cold War were still in need of a policy programme and linkage with their old constituency that suffered from low wages, unemployment, and healthcare costs yet disliked the dominant Democratic approach to race, rights, and taxes. The issue of character was raised, both with respect to decadence of the '1968' generation of baby boomers which Clinton epitomized (Fortuyn, Blair, and Schröder had to account for similar sins of youth) and through the course of his life (slick, adulterous, draft-dodging, smoking but not inhaling pot). There were doubts of fellow Democrats and leading journalists about the vagueness of Clinton's words and proposals. Hence, Clinton was widely portrayed as a populist of the wrong kind, a pandering politician without moral compass.

Clinton had to inject some populism of the right kind. His approach included simplification ('It's the economy, stupid'), a competent running mate (Al Gore), informal campaigning (bus tours, talk show appearances, and town hall meetings), avoidance of libertarianism (sticking to the death penalty, accusing hip-hop artist Sister Souljah of inciting racist violence), and lots of empathy face-to-face and into-your-face (television) based on chats, stories, simple emotional arguments, simple statistical data, and biographical stuff (playing with black kids and attending black religious services).

Tony Blair

Tony Blair, an Oxford graduate in law from Scotland, social liberal, Christian moralist, and maverick in the British socialist tradition, won his first national campaign as Labour Party leader in the spring of 1997, and remained prime minister until the summer of 2007, based on two more electoral victories

(Seldon 2001, 2007; Seldon and Kavanagh 2005). Blair wanted to end the post-empire period of national decline since the 1950s and complete Thatcher's reform of class society and the welfare state. He sought to prepare his compatriots – the widest constituency in a procedural sense – for globalization by restoring British capitalism in the current informational revolution, improving the focus of the public sector on the preferences and opportunity sets of citizens, and redefining a moral mission of community building in domestic politics and foreign policy.

Blair's leadership of the opposition since 1994 had been revisionist. Clause IV of the party's constitution on nationalization of basic industries was rewritten and New Labour invented. Blair abolished the block vote and introduced the rule of one member, one vote. New Labour buried the history, ideology, and organization of the labour movement. It created a centralized campaign party, adapted to the new market economy, media, and post-Thatcher generations.

Could Blair beat the Tory Prime Minister Major, a cautious and colourless rival, and mobilize, on the one hand, repugnance against exhausted conservatism, and, on the other, enthusiasm for New Labour? Many Members of Parliament chose Blair for selfish reasons. They expected a man with energy, charm, and good looks to restore their power and promote their careers. Could he stop the end of organized socialism and turn the party into a winner in the middle of the electoral space? Could he break the hegemony of conservatism and replace it with moderate and practical policies by the left?

Blair had a number of assets. First, his faith and family life made him acceptable to core constituencies of both his own party and conservatives. Blair articulated certain widespread complaints about excessive individualization of the nation. Restoring the British urban community was neither left nor right, but common sense. Second, Blair's resolute will to abolish left traditionalism and modernize Labour was widely acclaimed by mainstream media and favourably impressed the electorate. Blair's middle way between the old left and new right entailed salient yet undisputed values: equal worth, opportunity for all, personal responsibility, and community. Third, Blair's youthfulness, flair, rhetoric, and seemingly natural knowledge of urgent popular concerns were conducive to the credibility of his goals, standpoints, and proposals. As some of his early supporters put it: 'The image of the young man in denim jeans and casual shirt sitting with his family at the kitchen table at home in the fashionable London district of Islington was just what they wanted' (Stephens 2004: 45). Finally, Blair abandoned the view of capitalists as arch-enemies of the working class. He stressed the values and functions of a strong market economy, albeit within the bounds of decency, tolerance, and fairness. He met with captains of industry. He created a widening circle of rich supporters, friends, and party sponsors.

Blair's first and crucial campaign achieved the largest party victory since the 1930s with a New Labour majority of 178 seats. With hindsight, we may observe a joint product of Blair's dual anti-establishment view (against Tories and trade unions), will to shape New Labour's entry in British state institutions, communitarianism, opportunism ('tough on crime, tough on the causes of crime'), and selling of policy ideas. The campaign was based on imitation of Clinton's techniques of soft populism of, by, and for an intended vital centre. New Labour started a permanent and militant campaign in the media based on targeted mailing, voter focus groups, candidate media training, adequate intelligence, and instant response to the policies and statements of rival candidates.

According to Blair's closest advisors, party victory involved a change of language and tone. Labour needed to connect with the voters by using a non-political tone and stressing patriotism. As a symbol, the party chose a bulldog because they saw it as an animal with a strong sense of history and tradition. New Labour wanted to articulate the shared understandings of the British nation. Blair's speeches included sentences like 'I love my country' and 'I am a patriot'. The campaigners positioned New Labour as the coming people's party in a cohesive and creative society. The identity of the centre-left, its leader, and the country boiled down to youth and its virtues of entrepreneurship, optimism, and upward mobility.

One of the crucial consequences of the 1997 election campaign was that the Labour Party was tamed ideologically, becoming chiefly a vehicle for the leader's politics of communication during party conferences, meetings with the press, televised meetings with the people, public policy announcements, local visits, international trips, and, of course, Lower House debates. Blair's famous performances, such as his reactions to the murder of the young boy Bulger in February 1993, and, later, the death of Princess Diana in August 1997, and the London subway bombings in July 2005 – came across as brilliant idiosyncratic improvisations. In point of fact, they were well-prepared, well-organized, and thoroughly professionalized acts of leadership to reach the hearts and minds of well-examined audiences. The Labour Party started to make extensive use of opinion polls and focus groups, both during and between elections. Great events and crises in daily politics were occasions for Blair to give meaning and direction to his government, display populism of the centre, make short-term issues in the media central to the agenda setting of all ministries (his 'eye-catching initiatives'), and legitimize a quasi-presidential mode of decision-making. Communication was the means by which Blair gained absolute power in party, parliament, cabinet, civil service, and local government majorities.

Gerhard Schröder

Gerhard Schröder, a libertarian lawyer with a lower labour class background, was the first Social Democrat in the chancellery of Berlin between 1998 and

2005 (Meng 2002; Egle, Ostheim, and Zohlnhöfer 2003; Hogreve 2004; Egle and Zohlnhöfer 2007). His first and successful campaign was the outcome of a long march through the bastions of the Social Democratic Party (SPD) – the oldest mass-membership party in the world and an integral part of the establishment of post-war Western Germany. First, local party activist, then chairman of the radical Young Socialists, then backbencher in the *Bundestag* (the Lower House in Bonn), then chairman of the Hanover party district, and, finally, Minister-President of Lower Saxony, and member of the party presidium and shadow minister. Candidate Schröder insisted on the world's recognition of Germany as a 'normal nation state' and self-confident member of the European Union, NATO, and the United Nations. To reduce unemployment, control costs of German unification, and break through the aversion to reforms during the last terms of Kohl's administration (*Reformstau*), Schröder reformulated the Bad Godesberg orthodoxy of the SPD. He joined Blair's Third Way in a *Neue Mitte* and promoting overhaul of the welfare state and – to a lesser extent – the corporate economy in Rhenish capitalism.

Schröder engendered considerable hostility. In Lower Saxony, he had invented a specific style. On one hand, Schröder became the pragmatist and public sector Chief Executive Officer who depoliticized tradeoffs between economic growth, employment, social justice, and the environment (no speed limits for cleaner cars). On the other hand, he became the populist who sold regional protectionism as the new mode of post-socialism (what is good for business exports is good for progressive citizens). Schröder's performances were sometimes sensitive, sentimental, and provincial. But they could also be tough, calculating, provocative, and anti-bourgeois. The results were equally ambivalent. Schröder turned into a national politician-celebrity and exemplified a new generation of modernizers in German – indeed, Western – social democracy. Nevertheless, Schröder's open pursuit of hegemony, opportunism, and realism also engendered major resistance and scepticism among fellow leaders and the rank and file of the SPD as well as in mainstream liberal media. How did Schröder overcome the massive rejection of his chameleonic behaviour, that is, changing masks in front of distrustful voters and impertinent journalists?

First, Schröder allied himself to Lafontaine, the influential and popular chairman of the party who rejected the Third Way and advocated control of supercapitalism and reinforcement of the role of central government in Germany and the European Economic and Monetary Union (EMU).[3] Second, he tried to convey the message that he was a winner and the first contender who could beat the great Kohl – after three SPD defeats in a row. Schröder sported tailor-made Italian suits, red and white ties, and expensive cigars. He presented himself as a *Genosse der Bosse* (comrade of the bosses). There was a distinct transformation in outward appearance, facial expression, phonation, gestures, and locomotion. Here stood a potential national leader (Dieball 2005: 84–94, 115). In April 1998, more than 93 per cent of the party members chose Schröder as their chancellor candidate. Their confidence in his electoral prowess was greater than their suspicion of his programmatic credentials.

Finally, Schröder's campaign was well-orchestrated. He promised a new Berlin Republic, substantive reduction of the 4 million unemployed, economic recovery, fairness of welfare state reforms, continuity of foreign policy, and administrative competence. He avoided the issue of European integration (such as the abolition of the German Mark) and resisted the temptation to disqualify his petrified opponent. The campaign itself was personalized (*Deutschland braucht einen neuen Kanzler*) and based on the campaigns of the left American and British modernizers, such as the introduction of rapid rebuttal units at party headquarters. The SPD attained 40.9 per cent of the vote and 44.5 per cent of the seats in the Lower House. Schröder won in both the East and West. He drew support from many economic groups, except for the self-employed and farmers, who remained loyal to the losing Christian Democrats.

Populist office holding

Office holding by leaders of national government comprises recruitment of strong and loyal ministers and officials, implementation of distinctive and problem-solving policies, obtaining support and compliance of influential elites and major organized groups of citizens, and maintenance of international standing and prospects of re-election. In mature democracies, the demands of office holding include the capability to govern (effectiveness) in an unruly and multiform public sphere as well as responsiveness (taking the electoral mandate seriously), accountability (explaining hard choices afterwards), and credibility (eliciting popularity and positive public opinion between elections).

All three cases discussed under this rubric (Perot and Fortuyn never reached executive office) involve protracted government, namely, Clinton's two terms, Blair's three terms, Berlusconi's five years – a feat of arms in Italy, and Schröder's two terms. Such stability suggests a daily diet of pragmatism and inevitable containment and dilution of populist passions and dreams within the real world of international relations, bureaucracy, business, and conventional morality. What is left, then, of the constructive impulse and promise of 'change' that populist leadership entails? To answer this question, I analyse below how these three leader-centred regimes cope with moments of leadership crisis, when either new legitimacy is warranted or existing legitimacy is weakened.

Bill Clinton

Clinton survived two crises: the triumphant control of Congress by the Republican firebrand Gingrich in 1994–5 after Clinton's squandering of the public's backing of a grand health care plan; and the impeachment procedure during the Lewinsky scandal of 1998–9 (Jacobs and Shapiro 2000: 75–152; Wilentz 2008: 323–407). The mid-term election of 1994 was a disaster. Clinton and his party were shocked and demoralized. Not since 1952 had Democrats lost control of Congress. Major television networks granted presidential airtime to Gingrich, not to the guy in the White House. Nevertheless, 1995 and 1996 became a moment of grace in Clinton's leadership, resulting in his re-election, the first Democratic President since Roosevelt. The terrorist bombing of a federal building in Oklahoma, which killed 168 people, was a turning point. Clinton gave a moving speech at the memorial service and defined the case against extreme anti-federalism (militias). He joined a budget battle with the Republican establishment of Gingrich and Dole and called their bluff during a shutdown of federal government buildings in Washington in the Christmas period of 1995.

More generally, Clinton turned necessity into virtue by what he and his consultants called 'triangulation'. He crafted policies and messages with respect to salient issues at a distance from ideological and overstretching politicians in both parties, such as the bill on workfare, a follow-up of Reagan's Family Support Bill of 1988. Clinton became the national leader of opposition against the usurpation of Gingrich, the quasi-presidential leader of the House of Representatives. This tactic of role reversal worked. In 1996 Republican Dole received 41 per cent of the popular vote, independent Perot 9 per cent, and Clinton won more than 49 per cent, with 379 electoral votes to Dole's 159. A more focused Clinton emerged in 1997, campaigning for further reduction of the federal budget deficit, earned income credits, environmental rules, and pacification in the Balkans, the Middle East, and Northern Ireland. Clinton tried to sell bipartisan plans, or, to put it bluntly, he adopted Republican ideas and framed them as a coherent public philosophy of New Democrats.

The second crisis began, of course, in January 1998 with the revelation of his affair with Lewinsky, a White House intern, by the writer of the online *Drudge Report*. This became the greatest trial to date of the politics of authenticity that politician-celebrities make. Most Republicans and media outlets promoted a climate of opinion in which Clinton would be forced to resign, either voluntarily or via impeachment. Clinton tried to control the bad news by clever statements, crowded substantive agendas, and reinforcement of his ties with constituencies in race and gender issues. Public opinion remained strikingly unperturbed and sophisticated in its distinction between private evil (the harm to his wife, daughter, and young mistress) and public good (Clinton's low-key control of the economic cycle). After the crisis, Clinton tried to restore his prestige by confessions of guilt and shame as well as by shaping a legacy (such as the failed meetings in Camp David with Ehud Barak and Yasser Arafat).

It is hard to rate the strategy of a spent leader in his final quarters and compare it with his strategy of comeback in 1995 and 1996. It boiled down to disciplined management of a booming, globalizing US economy (creating a public budget surplus and reducing income and wealth inequalities) and due reluctance to use of military force in foreign affairs (e.g. in Rwanda and, for a long time, in former Yugoslavia, yet in the end bombing and sanctioning Serbia and Iraq). Both after Gingrich and after Lewinsky, Clinton relied on soft populism in an era of optimism about peace and the democratic future of failing poor states and intelligent authoritarian states, with the modal American voter longing for prudent guardianship and accommodation rather than aggressive ideology and polarization.

Tony Blair

Blair survived one crisis during 2002 and 2003. It concerned his early, full, principled, and unflinching support of the unpopular American war against the dictator Saddam Hussein and the start of a bloody occupation of Iraq with a prominent role of British soldiers. On many other contested issues, such as British entry of the EMU, Blair used to anticipate the mood of the public, exploit occasional agreement with the weakened Conservative Party, and win by delay, adaptation, personal earnestness, magnetism, and office power. The Iraq crisis was different. Blair was accused of lying, misleading parliament and the British people, politicization of intelligence and diplomatic services, propaganda and manipulation of free news media, subjection of the British nation to an American empire, and provocation of domestic terror by radicalized Muslim immigrants. Leading Labour politicians disputed Blair's leadership. New Labour's victory in 2001 had been less impressive than its first one. Hence, Blair's militarism began to jeopardize the electoral base and unity of Social Democrats, irrespective of the prolonged ongoing economic miracle in Britain.

Blair responded by stretching the constraints of government house populism. He used each opportunity in parliament and on television to spell out his new strategic doctrine of national interest (connecting antiterrorism with the Palestine question and the global fight against nuclear armament, genocide, poverty, and organized crime) and demonstrate his moral integrity and love of truth ('doing the right thing'). He accounted for his foreign policy in front of reluctant party representatives and several special commissions of scrutiny. He laboured all the harder to promote Labour's domestic agenda in education and improvement of public services. His last campaign in 2005 was called the 'masochism strategy' – putting himself into situations where the public could vent their anger (Mulgan 2006: 203). He won mainly because the Conservatives still looked unelectable, but the thrill was gone.

In his short and difficult last term (2005–7), Blair tried to mitigate the unexpected negativism with respect to his political personality. Forced by an increasingly vocal and impatient faction of 'Brownites' within his party, he announced and clarified his moment of departure. He publicly supported his successor notwithstanding relentless publicity about their years of alleged rivalry. He explained the irreversibility and long-term, steady-state net benefits of British globalization (also compared to the post-war experience of loss, retreat, and instability). And he continued to push a new agenda (African development, Middle East and British Islam pacification, global warming, and nuclear energy). On certain occasions, such as the eventful July 2005 week that saw the Live 8 concert, the London Olympic bid succeeding, and the bomb attacks by young home-grown terrorists, Blair showed his Churchillean gift of defining the situation. But overall, Blair could not stop the rot in his self-made constituency. His farewell tour of speeches and visits in the spring of 2007 was met with lukewarm responses. He had clearly overstayed his welcome.

Silvio Berlusconi

Berlusconi's case is special since he did *not* face a leadership crisis when in office, with simmering corruption allegations never quite fully catching up with him.

He tinkered with media ownership systems, popular elections, and criminal law in accordance with his personal interests. The most important laws of his second administration concerned labour market liberalization, school innovations, tax reform, abolition of compulsory military service, large infrastructural projects, bans of public smoking and embryonic stem cell research, and strict assignment of driving licences to promote traffic safety. One of Berlusconi's peaks was the new (2004) Constitutional Treaty of the European Union signed in Rome. Yet only one promise to his people was honoured: raising minimum old-age pensions. Many observers pointed at the poor design of welfare state reforms and the stagnation of the Italian economy during Berlusconi's reign (an average of 0.7% economic growth). So why and how did Berlusconi avoid a leadership crisis, while he arguably did not deliver the goods? (In April 2006, he suffered defeat against Prodi's rambling left bloc by the narrowest margin. In April 2008, he made a comeback.)

First, there were no leaders waiting in the wings in Berlusconi's party and cabinet, no Lafontaine to taunt him or Brown to haunt him. Second, Berlusconi showed that grassroots populism could turn into government house populism. Many voters saw his policy record as satisfactory – whether in domestic policy (migration control) or in foreign policy (antiterrorism), without illusions about Berlusconi's megalomania as well as his vulgar jokes, blunders, and tricks.[4] Third, many citizens accept corruption as a fact of life in a nation of intelligent and inventive individuals. Fourth, the opposition of left-wing parties and social movements was weak in terms of both policy substance and access to news media. Finally, Berlusconi had strong allies in the United States and the EU who remembered the failure of the Haider boycott of Austria (2000) and were willing to neglect his abuse of power.

Gerhard Schröder

Schröder experienced two crises of leadership, one in the early stages of his campaign for re-election and one in the process of reform of the labour market. In the summer of 2002, the *Medienkanzler* was lagging in the polls due to his failure to reduce unemployment and speed up economic recovery and the prestige of the Christian Democrat candidate Stoiber as governor of the booming Bavarian economy. Yet he managed to exploit the Elbe flood and the public's mood of pacifism and anti-Americanism during Bush's preparation of regime change in Iraq to turn the trend around (Katz and Mair 1995; Albertazzi and McDonnell 2008; Aucante and Dézé 2008; Bytzek 2008). He blew up the alliance with fellow modernizer Blair and shaped one with the Gaullist Chirac, and was therefore accused of opportunism in international relations. But Schröder enforced continuity of his government coalition, albeit with a narrow margin. The SPD lost 2.4 per cent of the popular vote, while the Christian Democrats and liberals won. Yet, the gain of his ally Joska Fischer's Greens turned out to be sufficient to deliver Schröder's red–green coalition a narrow majority in parliament: 50.7 per cent of the seats versus 48.9 per cent for the black–yellow coalition of Christian Democrats and Liberals.

Schröder's second crisis involved his masterpiece as a policy-maker in 2003, namely, *Agenda 2010*, a set of measures to reduce benefits for the unemployed and poor, liberalize dismissal of employees, centralize wage bargaining, improve vocational training, modernize crafts, rationalize healthcare systems, and efficiently tax households, corporations, and municipalities. Public outlays for social policies did not decrease in the short run, while macroeconomic advantages of reform surfaced in the long run (indeed, in the period of Chancellor Merkel who presided over a booming economy in 2006 and 2007). However, Schröder had to face alienation among his party members, rejection among his potential voters, increasing unity and obstruction of right-wing opposition parties (strengthened by the gradual decline of regional red–green cabinets and the federal constitution of Germany), the establishment of a new party combination on the left (with the help of Schröder's estranged former ally Lafontaine), growing distrust of media as to his macho style of celebrity politics, and irritation of some governments in Germany's many neighbouring countries.

Schröder's final act of leadership was a Clintonian role reversal and a characteristic and effective one, taking his dire circumstances into account. During the election campaign of 2005, he behaved as if he were leader of the opposition party and Merkel (his main contender) responsible for all public policy disasters. He acted as if he were the outsider in Germany's media system and Merkel the real insider. His final campaign was manic rather than panicky. He attacked Merkel's proposed Minister of Finance in a negative campaign, arguing that the Christian Democrats concealed their real intention of introducing ruthless American capitalism in a unified Germany. Schröder managed to reduce the loss of his party to 3.5 per cent of the national vote and twenty-nine seats in the *Bundestag*. On election night, he even claimed victory over the opinion polls and primacy in the coming process of cabinet formation vis-à-vis astonished leaders of other parties and moderating journalists. In the end, he faced the fact of his own political expendability and facilitated a relatively swift transition towards a great coalition between Christian Democrats and Social Democrats.[5]

Conclusions: causes and credentials of the new populism

In this chapter I attempted to demonstrate that populism is not only a leadership style of radicals and fools at the margins of the democratic space, but also a leadership style of both dissident and mainstream politicians in the heart of the legitimate and constitution-based process of office seeking and office holding in Western mature democracies. I did not, however, intend to claim empirically and historically that populism dominates pragmatism today, nor that populism is rising with some speed and pattern of diffusion without break or backlash.

Nevertheless, it is striking to find current varieties of populism (grassroots and government house, hard and soft, left and right) in two of the oldest democracies of the world (the hegemon United States and the small state of the Netherlands) and in two of the world's core states with a totalitarian past (Germany and Italy). Such variety requires some concluding considerations about the causes and credentials of the new populism.

I note a cluster of causes. Globalization of commerce, labour, news, entertainment, disease, terror, and crime goes in tandem with the politics of national identity and the politics of group fear, two breeding grounds of grassroots populism. International and supranational governance of globalization, such as European integration, is a process of scale enlargement that strengthens the representative role of heads of government, hence government house populism. Governance has also become an important method of domestic politics. It is marked by delegation of competences to independent authorities, networks, and regulated markets. The impersonal and technocratic nature of governance engenders a reaction of grassroots populism.

Furthermore, mass membership parties (the American Democratic Party, the German SPD, British Labour) are turning into campaign parties, while new formations start *tabula rasa* as campaign parties (United We Stand, Forza Italia, and the Dutch LPF). Leaders in the regime of mass-membership parties were organization men, insiders, trustees of the people, and paternalists with an interest in, and talent for pragmatism. Leaders in the regime of campaign parties (Manin's model of audience democracy) are entrepreneurs, outsiders, delegates of the people, and marketing experts, willing and able to win by means of populism. Finally, the new public sphere with capital intensive modes of collective action, competing media outlets and the web, and the new political culture of authenticity as a clue for voters in electing politicians (rather than ideological consistency) are conducive to populist representation and participation.

Populism will undermine liberal democracy when winning populist leaders reveal themselves as demagogues and dictators who crush minority voices and concerns, and abolish the checks and balances in the system of popular sovereignty. Populism will revitalize liberal democracy when they turn out to be liberators and statesmen who lead the emancipation and inclusion of second-rate citizens. To date, populist leadership seems to display neither medium dictatorship nor postmodern statesmanship, but rather something intermediate and mediocre.

Notes

1. There are important restrictions to my concise comparative study. A local politician such as the Californian Governor Schwarzenegger is excluded. Furthermore, I set aside populist leadership during original democratic revolutions and later breakthroughs of liberal democracy (parliamentary democracy, parties' democracy). I do not consider older contemporary cases, such as Kohl in Western Germany, Gonzales in Spain, Mitterrand in France, Reagan in the United States, and Thatcher in Great Britain. I leave out pioneers in one-party systems, like the Japanese Prime Minister Koizumi and the Mexican President Fox. I do not discuss populist leadership in new democracies of the 'Third Wave' in Asia, Europe, and Latin America. Nor do I include topical cases, such as the French President Sarkozy, the American President Obama or the British shadow PM Cameron, and counter-intuitive cases, like Balkenende in the Netherlands, Brown in Great Britain, Merkel in Germany, and Prodi in Italy.
2. The third campaign in 2008 was relatively moderate, indeed somewhat pragmatic, because of the dismal record of performance of Berlusconi's second cabinet and the soft populism, conciliatory tone and basic substantive agreement of his opponent Veltroni.
3. Lafontaine started as superminister of Finance and Economic Affairs in Schröder's first administration, but retreated and was dumped soon, in the spring of 1999. He would leave the SPD and establish a new and successful left party as a response to Schröder's capture of the party and 'neo-liberal' policies.

4. In November 2006, Berlusconi orchestrated a faint during a rally in a Tuscan village, which resulted in a massive demonstration of the Italian right against Prodi's second administration a week later.
5. A private man again, Schröder immediately began to maximize the private commercial potential of his political reputation by, among other things, joining a Russian oil and gas conglomerate. The publicness of such *enrichissez-moi* may be normal in American and British politics. It is, however, new in continental European democracies.

Bibliography

Albertazzi, D. and McDonnell, D. (eds.), *Twenty-first Century Populism* (Basingstoke: Palgrave Macmillan, 2008).

Aucante, Y. and Dézé, A. (eds.), *Les Systèmes de Partis dans les Démocraties Occidentales* (Paris: SciencesPo.Les Presses, 2008).

Buchanan, J. M. and Wagner, R. E., *Democracy in Deficit* (New York: Academic Press, 1977).

Burnham, J., *The Machiavellians* (New York: John Day, 1943).

Bytzek, E., 'Flood Response and Political Survival: Gerhard Schröder and the 2002 Elbe Flood in Germany', in A. Boin, A. McConnell, and P. 't Hart (eds.), *Governing after Crisis* (Cambridge: Cambridge University Press, 2008).

Canovan, M., *Populism* (London: Junction Books, 1981).

——'Trust the People! Populism and the Two Faces of Democracy', *Political Studies*, 47 (1999), 2–16.

——*The People* (Cambridge: Polity Press, 2005).

Chambers, S., 'Behind Closed Doors', *Journal of Political Philosophy*, 12 (2004), 389–410.

——'Measuring Publicity's Effect', *Acta Politica*, 40 (2005), 255–66.

Dahrendorf, R., *Die Krisen der Demokratie: Lebenserinnerungen* (Munich: Beck, 2002).

Davies, N., *Flat Earth News* (London: Chatto and Windus, 2008).

De Bonald, L., *Théorie du pouvoir politique et religieux dans la société civile* (Brussels: Société nationale pour la propagation des bons livres, [1796] 1845).

Dieball, W., *Körpersprache und Kommunikation im Bundestagswahlkampf* (Berlin: Poli-C-Books, 2005).

Dworkin, R., *Is Democracy Possible Here?* (Princeton, New Jersey: Princeton University Press, 2006).

Egle, C. and Zohlnhöfer, R. (eds.), *Ende des Rot-Grünen Projektes? Eine Bilanz der Regierung Schröder* (Wiesbaden: VS Verlag, 2007).

——Ostheim, T., and Zohlnhöfer, R. (eds.), *Das Rot-Grüne Projekt:. Eine Bilanz der Regierung Schröder: 1998–2002* (Wiesbaden: Westdeutscher Verlag, 2003).

Elchardus, M., *De dramademocratie* (Tielt: Lannoo, 2002).

Frey, B. S., *Modern Political Economy* (Oxford: Martin Robertson, 1978).

Ginsborg, P., *Silvio Berlusconi* (London: Verso, 2004).

Goldthorpe, J. (ed.), *Order and Conflict in Contemporary Capitalism* (Oxford: Clarendon Press, 1984).

Habermas, J., *Faktizität und Geltung* (Frankfurt: Suhrkamp, 1992).

Hall Jamieson, K. and Cappella, J. N., *Spiral of Cynicism* (New York: Oxford University Press, 1997).

Hall Jamieson, K. and Cappella, J. N., *Echo Chamber* (Oxford: Oxford University Press, 2008).

Hamilton, N., *Bill Clinton: An American Journey* (New York: Random House, 2003).

——*Bill Clinton* (New York: PublicAffairs, 2007).

Hirschman, A. O., *Shifting Involvements* (Princeton, New Jersey: Princeton University Press, 1982).

Hogreve, J., *Gerhard Schröder* (Berlin: Siedler, 2004).

Jacobs, L. R. and Shapiro, R. Y., *Politicians Don't Pander* (Chicago: University Press, 2000).

Katz, R. S. and Mair, P., 'Changing Models of Party Organization and Party Democracy', *Party Politics*, 1/1 (1995), 5–28.

Kazin, M., *The Populist Persuasion* (New York: Basic Books, 1995).

Keller, M., *America's Three Regimes* (Oxford: Oxford University Press, 2007).

Lukacs, J., *Democracy and Populism* (New Haven: Yale University Press, 2005).

Mackie, G., *Democracy Defended* (Cambridge: Cambridge University Press, 2003).

McCormick, J. P., 'Machiavellian Democracy', *American Political Science Review*, 95 (2001), 297–313.

——'Contain the Wealthy and Patrol the Magistrates', *American Political Science Review*, 100 (2006), 147–63.

Manin, B., *The Principles of Representative Government* (Cambridge: Cambridge University Press, 1997).

Mansfield, E. D. and Snyder, J., *Electing to Fight* (Cambridge, Mass.: MIT Press, 2005).

Mansfield, H. C., *Machiavelli's Virtue* (Chicago: Chicago University Press, 1996).

Mazzoleni, G., Stewart, J., and Horsfield, B. (eds.), *The Media and Neo-populism: A Contemporary Comparative Analysis* (Westport: Praeger, 2003).

Meng, R., *Der Medienkanzler* (Frankfurt: Suhrkamp, 2002).

Mény, Y. and Surel, Y. (eds.), *Democracies and the Populist Challenge* (Basingstoke: Palgrave, 2002).

Mudde, C., 'The Populist Zeitgeist', *Government and Opposition*, 39 (2004), 541–63.

Mulgan, G., *Good and Bad Power* (London: Allen Lane, 2006).

Notermans, T., *Money, Market, and the State* (Cambridge: Cambridge University Press, 2000).

Panniza, F. (ed.), *Populism and the Mirror of Democracy* (London: Verso, 2005).

Pels, D., *De geest van Pim* (Amsterdam: Anthos, 2003).

Phillips, K., *Wealth and Democracy* (New York: Broadway, 2003).

Posner, G., *Citizen Perot* (New York: Random House, 1996).

Rawls, J., *Political Liberalism* (New York: Columbia University Press, 1993).

——*The Law of Peoples* (Cambridge: Harvard University Press, 1999).

Rieff, P., *Charisma* (New York: Pantheon, 2007).

Rifkin, J., *The European Dream* (New York: Penguin, 2004).

Riker, W. H., *Liberalism against Populism* (San Francisco, CA: Freeman, 1982).

Samuels, R. J., *Machiavelli's Children* (Ithaca, New York: Cornell University Press, 2003).

Seldon, A. (ed.), *The Blair Effect: The Blair Government: 1997–2001* (London: Little Brown, 2001).

——(ed.), *Blair's Britain: 1997–2007* (Cambridge: Cambridge University Press, 2007).

——and Kavanagh, D., *The Blair Effect: 2001–2005* (Cambridge: Cambridge University Press, 2005).
Skowronek, S., *The Politics Presidents Make* (Cambridge: The Belknap Press of Harvard University Press, 1997).
Snyder, J., *From Voting to Violence* (New York: Norton, 2000).
Spengler, O., *The Decline of the West,* vol. 2 (New York: Knopf, [1928] 1932).
Stephens, P., *Tony Blair* (New York: Viking, 2004).
Stille, A., *The Sack of Rome* (New York: Penguin, 2006).
Stoker, G., *Why Politics Matters* (Houndmills: Palgrave MacMillan, 2006).
Taggart, P., *Populism* (Buckingham: Open University Press, 2000).
——'Populism and the Pathology of Representative Politics', in Y. Mény and Y. Surel (eds.), *Democracies and the Populist Challenge* (Basingstoke: Palgrave, 2002), 62–75.
Unger, R. M., *False Necessity* (Cambridge: Cambridge University Press, 1987).
Wansink, H., *De erfenis van Fortuyn* (Amsterdam: Meulenhoff, 2004).
Wilentz, S., *The Age of Reagan* (New York: HarperCollins, 2008).

Chapter 6

Monarchy, Political Leadership, and Democracy: On the Importance of Neutral Institutions

Douwe Jan Elzinga

Democracy disperses and fragments leadership, making possible wide and diverse sources of political authority. This observation seems to be supported by the role of monarchies in democracy. The office of the monarch, so contrary to democratic principles, is often retained in democracies, either as purely ceremonial roles, or in other instances as offices with some residual authority. Thus the very existence of the office of the monarch supports the view that democratic dispersal of leadership is so extensive and far-reaching that it even sustains those institutions apparently inimical to democracy. In this chapter I want to explore a stronger version of this argument. I want to suggest that in some cases these apparently undemocratic institutions are in fact essential for the stability and welfare of democratic politics. More specifically, I argue that a 'neutral power' or constitutional 'neutrum' of offices, such as ceremonial presidents, constitutional monarchs, parliamentary speakers, are a source of indispensable stability in modern democracies. Drawing on the theoretical work of Benjamin Constant, who first laid the foundations for the constitutional monarch as the 'pouvoir neutre' or neutral power, and subsequent scholarship of Hanna Arendt and Claude Lefort that extended this core idea by emphasizing the significance of neutral institutions, neutral rules of the game, and a neutral ritualization of politics, I will concentrate on the Dutch monarchy as an indicative case of the way neutral power has this paradoxically powerful role in modern democracies. The core thesis of this chapter is that political leadership in democratic settings can be greatly enhanced and be more strongly legitimized to the extent that the idea of a constitutional 'neutrum' has been adequately incorporated into the fabric of the polity.

Neutrality in politics

The French theorist and administrator Benjamin Constant is the spiritual father of the concept of the 'pouvoir neutre', which played an important role in the nineteenth century when the idea of representative democracy was being developed. In subsequent periods, many thinkers have elaborated upon Constant's ideas. As a liberal – with the experiences of the French revolution and Napoleon in the back of his mind – Constant underlines the importance of separation of powers for safeguarding individual freedom. In doing so, however, he adds a fourth power to the 'checks and balances' of John Locke and the 'trias politica' of Montesquieu, namely the 'pouvoir neutre et intermediaire'. From a truly independent position, according to Constant, the 'pouvoir neutre' promotes harmony and cooperation between the other state powers, and guarantees at the same time that unity and diversity are adequately balanced.

Although the 'pouvoir neutre' is not linked with monarchy as such – non-political presidents can also perform this task – Constant argues that constitutional monarchy in the modern version is a suitable example: 'the constitutional monarchy creates such neutral power in the person of the head of state. The true interest of such head is by no means to put one power against the other, but it is that all the powers support each other, understand each other and act in concert'.[1] A special element in Constant's concept of the 'pouvoir neutre' (sometimes also designated as 'pouvoir régulateur' or 'pouvoir modérateur') is that it does not function 'above the parties', but 'next to the parties'. The neutral power is placed outside and therefore no longer plays a material role in the political process; it comes into action especially when the political process does not work properly or when it needs reviving. The concept of pouvoir neutre was given substance in many nineteenth century constitutions. See, for example, the Portuguese constitution of 1826, especially Article 71, where the politically-neutral monarchy was given shape and content.[2] There were also attempts, as in a Spanish constitutional draft of 1829, to link the function of the monarchy (as 'funcion moderadora') with other neutral organs, such as councils of state or the crown. Characteristically, nineteenth-century constitutionalism depoliticized royal power and combined it with the maintenance of many formal positions of the king, such as the appointment and discharge of ministers, the issuing and promulgation of laws, dissolution of parliament, the right to pardon. In countries where the monarchy was replaced by republican institutions, these neutral and formal positions were – especially later on – attributed to politically neutral presidents.

What is especially interesting for us is the extent to which Constant's reflections on what is necessary to establish, or to maintain a 'pouvoir neutre' in democratizing political systems have been taken up by subsequent thinkers.[3] One of the best-known examples of this is Carl Schmitt who analyzes the functioning of the Republic of Weimar from this perspective in his 'Der Hüter der Verfassung'. Schmitt, then still a relatively unknown scholar, expresses his concern about the disintegration of the Republic of Weimar and argues – indebted to Constant and in debate with Hans Kelsen, who especially regards the judge as 'Hüter der Verfassung' or custodian of the Constitution – for a revaluation of the 'pouvoir neutre'. Schmitt, and later authors, such as Hannah Arendt (1972)[4] and Claude Lefort (1992)[5], broadened the scope and meaning of this neutral power. They extended the concept to include the neutral state, the general system of constitutional independencies and rules of the game (among which are incompatibilities, immunities, and the prohibition of instruction to parliamentarians), a value-free constitution, democracy as 'empty place of power', and the safeguards to guarantee that emptiness continuously. The concept of the 'pouvoir neutre' in this sense can be helpful in analyzing the rather complicated relationship between monarchy, political leadership, and democracy. It can be useful for clarifying the actual non-political leadership functions in a constitutional monarchy. With this perspective as background, I will elaborate these functions in the next sections, with a special focus on the development of the Dutch monarchy.

Transformation of the Dutch monarchy

Immunity means inviolability. This inviolability is inextricably bound with the royal function. At the time of the absolute monarchies, the monarch was regarded as the highest authority in the state, who, because of his position and authority, could not be held accountable towards others. This inviolability had a political and legal aspect. Politically, there was no subordination of the royal power to any other power in the state, and criticism of the monarch was impossible because of this inviolability. Legally, the monarch could not be implicated or be subject to legal proceedings. Thus royal inviolability existed long before ministerial responsibility was introduced in the various constitutional monarchies. For example, the Dutch Constitution of 1813/1815 regarded this inviolability as so self-evident that a constitutional provision acknowledging it was considered unnecessary.

In the Dutch Constitution of 1848, inviolability was retained with its twofold meaning, but with an important innovation. Though the legal immunity of the King was confirmed, the monarch could now be criticized by directing such criticism against the responsible minister. Although the scope of this constitutional innovation remained unclear, it would have far-reaching consequences for the royal function. Whereas in preceding periods the inviolability of the king was pre-eminently a basis for the head of state to exercise political power – after all his position was inviolable, beyond all criticism – the royal position after 1848 received a whole new interpretation. In principle, the ministers were accountable for royal actions. The intention behind the liberal 'Wende' in 1848 was to position the King outside the political sphere. Because of the combination of royal inviolability and ministerial responsibility, a new constitutional concept emerged in which the politically neutral position of the King had to make room for the primacy of political power of ministers and parliament.

For a long time, however, this constitutional theory and political reality diverged significantly. Constant in the beginning of the nineteenth century understood the decreasing power of the king ('potestas') as being compensated by an increasing authority ('auctoritas'). Most nineteenth-century monarchs, however, had great difficulty with Constant's idea, and the principle 'le roi règne, les ministres gouvernent, les chambres jugent' formulated by Thiers in 1829. They still wanted to govern and could only distinguish between the elements of 'auctoritas' and 'potestas' with the greatest difficulty. Kings who did succeed in doing so were regarded by fellow monarchs as 'weak' and were dismissed with Napoleon's famous, but crude description of a monarch without power as a 'cochon engraissé'.

In the Netherlands after 1848 there was a struggle to find a more definitive constitutional basis for the monarchy. The innovation of an inviolable King and politically responsible ministers established by the revised constitution was strongly contested. Other European countries also struggled with the positioning of the monarchy. Whereas the English constitutional monarchy was often referred to as a model, with Bagehot writing that 'royalty is not essential', the limitations of such an example were evident in the correspondence of Queen Victoria which was published later, showing that the royal influence had been far-reaching and certainly biased.[6] A number of monarchies were certainly not yet ready for the English constitutional formulas. In Central and Eastern Europe (the Romanovs, the Habsburgers, and the Hohenzollerns) strong versions of royal absolutism still existed, which made Von Treitschke sigh that the British monarchy was 'unreal' because it reduced the King to a republican official in the service of his people (Von Treitschke 1897: 141; see also Van Osta [1980]: 63–87).[7]

It is clear that in the Netherlands and elsewhere in the nineteenth century there was a powerful tension between the monarchy and the developing liberal constitutionalism. The benefits of the parliamentary democracy had to be won over from the monarch and in that struggle, the King was not the 'impartial' monarch from a political perspective that Benjamin Constant had in mind. In Dutch society, too, people thought very differently about the monarchy. The monarchy had a clearly Protestant nature and therefore it took a long time before the Catholic community could completely identify itself with the House of Orange.[8] Moreover, the monarchy had been viewed as conservative for a long time. During his long nineteenth-century rule, the Dutch king Willem III did not leave any misunderstandings about this point, and in that conservative role, he was not exactly the only one of his nineteenth-century fellow monarchs. The fear of revolutions also played an important role in their conservatism. The entire century, the incumbent monarchs had a clear memory of how Louis XVI had been taken to the guillotine as 'citizen' Louis Capet. As Kossmann (1966: 61) indicates, in the nineteenth century the monarchy was in most cases a conservative institution, guarding the existing social and political order and allying itself emphatically with social elites.

The Dutch and other European monarchies experienced an important transformation in the twentieth century, especially after the Second World War. In Holland the monarchy was finally and deeply linked with the roots of the Dutch nation and connected with Dutch democracy. This connection with Dutch democracy became the foundation of the modern monarchy and ensured that the inviolable King does not profile himself as bound by a party or interests. This entails that a general integrating performance is required, characterized by a strictly (party) political neutrality which is aimed at the general functioning of the democratic system. Although there is room for the head of state to orient himself politically and socially – in the broadest sense of the word – that orientation cannot lead to the presentation of material political convictions, and where these convictions are brought forward (e.g. in a moral sense), such as in speeches, these are to be covered fully by the political accountability of the prime minister (and therefore to be cleared by him *ex ante*). Since 1945 the Dutch monarchy has found a more definitive form concerning the content and form of the politically-neutral monarchy. Future historical research will undoubtedly bring to light that under the rule of Juliana and Beatrix situations have arisen in which these queens have not acted completely in conformity with the idea of the politically-neutral monarchy. The crucial difference with the preceding periods is, however, that occasions such as these will have to be characterized as exceptions to the rule, while in the period before 1945, the relationship between rule and exception was in most cases the other way around, especially in the context of appointments, the army, and foreign policy.[9]

An important question is whether this transformation of the Dutch and other monarchies into its current form has brought the constitutional monarchy in all respects – both in theory and practice – in line with the foundations of representative democracy. Can the discrepancy between 'monarchy' and 'democracy' – which has existed for a long time – be removed? In order to judge, we briefly return to the ideas of Benjamin Constant and the different ways subsequent authors have developed them.

The indispensability of neutrality in a multiform democracy

Benjamin Constant once called Napoleon Bonaparte 'le Roi Rousseauiste' (cited in Hoogers [1999: 147, note 47]). The implications of an unlimited and plebiscitary-oriented popular sovereignty in the spirit of Rousseau can revive an absolute monarchy or emperorship. The dictatorship of the Constituante, the Terror and the actions of Robespierre, of the Jacobins and of Bonapartism, formed for Constant – and for kindred authors like François Guizot and Pierre-Paul Royer-Collard – the frame of reference for their theories on the separation of powers. In order not to derail the political process, a series of dependencies and independencies were incorporated in the constitutional system.[10] One of the most important features of these 'doctrinal' constitutional concepts is that they create a constitutional framework within which numerous political constellations can manifest themselves. It is especially for that reason that these constitutional concepts have kept their value until today and still form the core of numerous European representative democracies. An essential element of those concepts is the presence of a strong constitutional neuter. This point needs to be understood in the context of two related observations. The first is that in the constitutional order of representative democracy, there should be both distance and proximity. The second related point of view is formed by the assumption that the political (democratic) process is not only shaped by active citizens, people's representatives, political groups, and rulers, but that it also finds expression, and not to an insignificant extent, in the institutional environment of politics, the rules of the game, the political mores, the political and non-political referees, the advisory bodies, and so on.

Illustrative of this constitutional approach is the way in which the electoral and suffrage systems were shaped in the nineteenth century. To this very day, for example, the majority of the electoral laws abstract from the influence that political parties exert on the nomination and the election of people's representatives. This creates a watershed between, on the one hand, the neutral voter's democracy and, on the other hand, the biased process of nomination, binding of people's representatives to programmes and party organizations etc. If in the Netherlands a political group would like to contest a party agreement in court (e.g. that someone who is higher on the list of candidates has to give way to someone who has a lower position) then it soon confronts the Election Act ('Kieswet') which – neutrally – maintains a certain distance between voter, political party, and representative, to secure the balance of powers.

Numerous other constitutional provisions can be interpreted in the same way, the essence of which is the free mandate of the elected representatives that Emmanuel Joseph Sieyès, Benjamin Constant, François Guizot, and others, made the central foundation of their constitutional theories. In the organization of the representative democracies of the nineteenth and twentieth centuries, this foundation of distance and neutrality fanned out to various parts of the constitutional order. The safeguards of the financial independency of parliamentarians, judicial immunity, the positions of people's representatives towards third parties guaranteed by the election laws, the legal nullity of the majority of the practised party agreements etc, create a fundamental watershed between that which is political and that which is non-political. The political domain is shaped within the framework of the actual party democracy; the formal electoral democracy (with the constitutional prohibition of instruction [free mandate] and the Election Acts as most important anchors) forms the non-political domain of the representative democracy. Proximity – of voters, party members, interest groups, all or not expressed in factual connections – is the hallmark of the party democracy; distance and independence form the essential characteristics of the formal voter's democracy.

The constitutional and legal framework of electoral democracy forms the hard core of the constitutional neuter, without which a democracy based on political diversity cannot function very well. And therein lies the crucial value of the lesson that Benjamin Constant taught to his contemporaries and which has subsequently been elaborated on in many ways. A clear and neutral constitutional order, within which power and counter-power can be adequately balanced, is the most important condition for a political process based on freedom, development, and fundamental openness.

Important for our argument is how the neuter manifests itself. On the one hand it is a constitutional neuter evident in (constitutional) legal rules, regulations of order, advising institutes, mores and cultures; on the other hand, this neuter can also be a personalized entity. Chairmen and presidia of representative bodies, senior convents, non-political presidents, in some cases courts, and not lastly constitutional monarchs, and envoys associated with them, governors, and commissioners are employed in the more or less non-political domain of the democracy to keep the system going. The regulatory function that these 'less-political or non-political' referees exercise, forms a 'pouvoir préservateur' ('eine bewahrende Gewalt') which does not aim at conservation, but serves the political process aimed at dynamism and change of policy. The core of their task comes down to an assignment which is as important as it is simple: during the political game, the rules of the game cannot be changed.

Interest in this non-political 'other side' of the representative democracy – both in its personalized and other form – is traditionally not very high. The dynamics of the political and party political processes and the way in which society provides impulses for them, understandably usurp almost all attention. Still – mindful of Benjamin Constant – the nature and quality of the constitutional neuter in their various manifestations are of decisive significance for a properly functioning representative democracy. With the absence of a well-considered and well-functioning constitutional neuter, a democratic system will soon be in a danger zone, as the republic of Weimar has demonstrated.[11]

The monarchy as part of the constitutional neuter

In various respects, heads of state in most of the European monarchies play a role within the framework of the constitutional neuter. The least-mentioned manifestation of this is that various constitutional powers and procedures require a formal (and also partly ritual) involvement of the king, while the material involvement of the king is usually absent in many cases. Bills are proposed by, or on behalf of the king (apart from the parliamentary right of initiative) and ratified and signed by the king; by, or on behalf of the king an annual explanation is given of the policy that the government has set out; members of government take their oaths or give their pledges before the king; many appointments occur by royal decree, and so on. The political decision-making process has been royally ritualized in numerous fields. The justification for this cannot be found only in the historical value of continuity, because such an appeal will not be effective in a political system that favours dynamism.

This royal ritualism calls into being some sort of heteronomy through which politicians – who are completely autonomous by the way, and of course completely justified to revise the constitutional rules of the game through the appropriate procedures – are given a stable and fixed framework. Or, as Gerhard Leibholz described this passive role of the head of state at that time: the monarchy intends to 'make a gift to the nation more in its role in pacifying and maintaining'.[12] The royal ritualization of the political decision-making process furthermore leads to light forms of 'sacralization', which makes it easier to separate political issues from the non-political. In this respect, presidents, for example those of Italy and Germany, who must personify the constitutional neuter, usually face more difficulties. They have to throw off their earlier party cloaks and still have to prove their neutrality.[13]

Besides the royal ritualization of decision-making processes, the king is in most cases a member of the government, which links the execution of numerous government powers with the monarchy. Because of the unity of the Crown, which means unity between king and ministers, and the secret character of that relation, there can be endless speculation, of course, about the influence that the royal head of state can exert within the closed context of the government. Even here, however, we see the importance of the head of state as an anchor for continuity, strict observance of constitutional procedures, and neutrality. Although this pattern is sometimes broken, the publicity and the commotion that such an event causes proves that these are exceptions that confirm that principle of neutrality, from which follows that this principle is strongly internalized.[14] The same applies for the procedural role of the head of state during cabinet formations in some political systems. Appointment of those who investigate the possibilities of, and eventually form a new cabinet (as per Belgium and the Netherlands) imply royal preferences, making the position of the head of state very vulnerable and harming the royal 'auctoritas'. This 'auctoritas' increases as the head of state succeeds in playing this role of process regulator in changing political constellations neutrally but effectively.[15]

Practice has shown that monarchic heads of state can develop into a professional and adequate part of the constitutional neuter and that they can also transfer this professionalism to successors. Problems for the constitutional monarchy are usually caused by the less professional surroundings of the head of state that are more difficult to control. Both in and outside the Netherlands, often other members of the royal family or of the royal house are the ones who bring the monarchy under scrutiny or who are detrimental to the monarchy. In that respect, the entourage of a non-political president is easier to place at a distance.

Does the positioning of the Dutch and similar European monarchies meet the requirements of the constitutional neuter across the board? To answer this question we must first examine whether the monarchy should retain the government function of the head of state. Is it not more sensible to have the monarchy focus more on its unitary and ceremonial function at the level of society? I take the position that removing the monarchy from the government function could lead, under certain circumstances, to an undesirable 'politicizing' of the monarchy. If the unitary function of the head of state manifests itself only at the level of society and no longer in the constitutional sphere, there is a greater risk that the link between the non-political and the political is broken. Put simply, one could even argue that discarding the government function of the monarchic head of state could more easily lead to a chasm between the mostly wide social support for the monarchy on the one hand, and the natural and also desirable dissent within the political game on the other hand.

The permanent involvement of the monarchic head of state in government processes – such as the formation of cabinets – creates a higher pressure on the head of state to remain neutral, than when that involvement in politics would be ended. It will then certainly become more tempting for a head of state to make a stand against certain eruptions of politics, based on an extraordinary large social popularity. More importantly, however, is the consideration that the deletion of the involvement of the head of state in the political system entails that one cannot provide for the personalization of the constitutional neuter in a different sense. After all, maintenance of a representative monarchy makes it impossible to appoint a neutral president. This implies that in such a situation one should look for another format for the personalized constitutional neuter, which would certainly lead to a more influential judiciary. Because judges are not suited to guarding political procedures and solving conflicts with respect to those procedures, this is not a very tempting alternative. Generally we can, therefore, conclude that it is preferable to give the monarchy – as expression of a personalized constitutional neuter – a permanent involvement in the functioning of the representative democracy. The current politically-neutral position of the Dutch king provides a good example of the way the long-existing discrepancy between monarchy and democracy can be neutralized.

Monarchy and dispersed leadership in democracy

For a long time a discrepancy has existed between monarchy and democracy. In the eighteenth and nineteenth centuries, parliaments had to claim their power from the monarchies, and even when the monarchy was formally 'depoliticized' (as it was in the Netherlands by the Constitution of 1848) the discrepancy remained in some respects relevant because of the orientation of the monarchy on certain parts of politics and society. Now that the monarchy has found its politically-neutral form in the Netherlands and elsewhere in Europe in the period after 1945, the monarchy has become especially problematic for those who see the democratic system as something that is enacted within legitimate limits that are set directly or indirectly by voters. If one keeps the representative democracy within this limited range, the hereditary nature of the monarchy causes an insoluble problem that can only be eliminated by abolition of the monarchy and introduction of the republic. If, however, the presence of a constitutional neuter – in whatever form – is seen as an inseparable and crucial part of the representative democracy, and if also the non-political domain which is subservient to the political machinery is positioned within the framework of the democracy, then the discrepancy between monarchy and democracy can be eliminated.

The crucial presence of a constitutional neuter presupposes a structuring and demarcation of the political playground by rules, mores, and institutions, and presupposes functionaries or offices that keep the political system going without participating in politics as such. For a personalization of the neuter, there need not be a fundamental preference for the monarchy; there are various possibilities, including presidia, judges, and non-political presidents. Nevertheless, a constitutional monarchy can fulfil such a role in the non-political domain of the democracy. In this sense a democracy needs political as well as non-political leadership. When the need of a good and adequate balance between the political and the non-political domains, fixed by rules and political culture, is accepted, one can easily discern the importance of non-political leadership.

From a democratic point of view there ought to be first, a firm and strong dominance of political leadership, legitimized by regular elections. Secondly, it is important to keep political leaders and other politicians within a constitutional framework, constructed by neutral rules, institutions, and non-political leaders. In the discussion above, it has been argued that a constitutional monarchy provides the best safeguard for an adequate distinction between the political and non-political spheres. A merely ceremonial monarchy can lead to an undesirable politicization of the constitutional monarchy more quickly, and such a mutation also impedes a personalization of the constitutional neuter in the form of a neutral presidency. And with this, we, who are prepared to follow and accept this line of thinking, arrive at the conclusion only at first sight paradoxical: democracy, which characteristically disperses leadership, can very well utilize and should value the monarchy in its current form.

Notes

1. 'La monarchie constitutionnelle crée ce pouvoir neutre, dans la personne du chef de l'État. L'intérêt véritable de ce chef n'est aucunement que l'un des pouvoirs renverse l'autre, mais que tous s'appuient, s'entendent et agissent de concert'(Constant 1997, 324–5, my translation).
2. Article 71 reads (in the French translation): 'Le pouvoir modérateur est la clef de toute l'organisation politique...'. The moderating power is the key of the whole political organization.
3. Constant is – together with François Guizot and Emmanuel Joseph Sieyès – the founder of the nineteenth-century system of political representation, in which political decision-making is shaped within the framework of free debate between people's representatives. Constant attached so much value to the free exchange of ideas that he proposed to prohibit representatives to read out written speeches. For an overview see Hoogers (1999: especially chapters 3 and 4).
4. Hannah Arendt (1972: 64) argues that the need for stability and the desire for change would always keep each other more or less in balance.
5. On the political philosophy of Lefort see Loose (1997).
6. The English Queen wrote in her letters that she 'cannot and will not be the Queen of a democratic monarchy' (Buckle 1926–28: 516). As this letter indicates, Bagehot's understanding (2001) of the 'dignified' role of the monarchy did not appear to take into sufficient account its significant and concealed political influence. It is instructive to contrast Bagehot's understanding of the 'dignified' role of the monarch with Constant's 'neutral' power. As we note below, the greater direct political authority of the dignified role the more it undermines its neutrality and therefore makes the monarchy vulnerable in democracies.
7. On the nature of nineteenth-century Dutch monarchy see generally Van Osta (1980: 63–87).
8. See generally Bank (1980: 195–209). Bank, referring to the works of L. de Jong, notes that it was common knowledge that Queen Wilhelmina could hardly bear Catholic members of government.
9. Contrast this with the actions of the Thai King, Bhumibol Adulyadej, whose strategic interventions in Thai politics, most recently in endorsing the coup by Sonthi Boonyaratglin in September 2006 while Prime Minister Thaksin Shinawatra was out of the country, has had a decisive role in Thai politics.
10. It is interesting that an author like Hannah Arendt (1963) opposed the implications of the French revolution while showing a strong preference for the American revolution and the resulting rigidity of the American '*Constitution*'. For her the political

orientation of the American revolution prevailed over the more social character of the French revolution. In her opinion, the American constitutional setting creates neutral norms and forms that are serviceable to a free political process, while the French revolution was partly focused on equality and brotherhood and showed the inclination not to determine neutrally the contents of political debate, with the consequence that free political processes were closed off and directed. Hannah Arendt draws attention in her work (especially from 1963 and *On Revolution* [Arendt 1963] to the importance of non-political and procedural items) in terms very similar to those of Benjamin Constant.

11. There is no clear demarcation between the political and the non-political sphere. A speaker of a parliament, for example, has to be neutral in his duty as a speaker; as a member of parliament the speaker can vote and take (party) political positions. The debate about, and the enactment of constitutional rules is a pure political act; but afterwards these regulations form the neutral borders of the political domain.
12. 'Die Nation mehr in ihrem ruhenden und dauernden Zustand präsent zu machen' (Leibholz 1966: 62).
13. This may be the reason that in republics people appeal to judges more quickly to solve weighty political-procedural issues. In the contest between the presidential candidates Al Gore and George W. Bush, the Supreme Court was appealed to, to decide the elections in 2000. For the US, of course, it is impossible for the president to act as constitutional referee because of his sharply political profile during the elections. In Germany it appeared during the elections of 2005 that the recently elected German President Köhler still had too little neutral authority to get the leaving chancellor Gerhard Schröder back in his cage. The latter initially refused to accept that the CDU/CSU had become the biggest party; Schröder proposed to regard the CDU and the CSU as two parties, which would make the SPD the biggest party and should therefore also have the initiative in the formation of a government. This brutalization of the rules of the game was insufficiently warded off by the German president.
14. See, for example, the Australian constitutional crisis of 1975 where the Governor General dismissed the prime minister, Gough Whitlam (Whitlam 2005).
15. See, for example, the role of the Belgian King in the 1996 Dutroux paedophile crisis. The King held an audience with the parents of the missing children, and afterwards organized a roundtable conference on child abuse and missing children. He also criticized magistrates, ministers and government, demanding an investigation and presenting a list of questions and comments to the Minister of Justice (Van Outrive 1998: 24; Fijnaut 2001: 237).

Bibliography

Arendt, H., *On Revolution* (New York: Viking Press, 1963).

——*Crises of the Republic: Lying in Politics, Civil Disobedience, On Violence, Thoughts on Politics and Revolution* (New York/San Diego: Harcourt Brace Jovanovich, 1972).

Smith, P. (ed.), *Bagehot: The English Constitution* (Cambridge: Cambridge University Press, 2001).

Bagehot, W., *The English Constitution*, in P. Smith (ed.) (Cambridge: Cambridge University Press, 2001).

Bank, J., Katholieken en de Nederlandse monarchie, Tussen staatsraison en populariteit, in C. A. Tamse (ed.), *De monarchie in Nederland* (Amsterdam: Elsevier, 1980), 195–208.

Buckle, G. E. (ed.), *Letters of Queen Victoria*, second series (London: John Murray, 1926–8).

Constant, B. (ed.), *Écrits politiques* (Paris: Gallimard, [1818] 1997).

Fijnaut, C., Crisis and Reform in Belgium: The Dutroux Affair and the Criminal Justice System, in U. Rosenthal, A. Boin, and L. Comfort (eds.), *Managing Crises. Threats, Dilemmas, Opportunities* (Springfield: Charles C. Thomas, 2001), 235–47.

Hoogers, H. G., *De verbeelding van het souvereine, Een onderzoek naar de theoretische grondslagen van politieke representatie* (diss. Groningen: Kluwer, 1999).

Kossmann, E. H., Typologie der monarchieën van het Ancien Régime, in P. H. Winkelman, P. E. Schramm, L. J. Rogier, E. H. Kossmann, J. C. de Meyer, and W. Drees Sr. (eds.), *Zes beschouwingen over de monarchie* (Amsterdam: Polak & Van Gennep, 1966), 59–74.

Lefort, C., *Het demokratisch tekort. Over de noodzakelijke onbepaaldheid van de democratie* (Amsterdam: Boom, Meppel, 1992).

Leibholz, G., *Das Wesen der Repräsentation*, 3rd edn. (Berlin: de Gruyter, 1966).

Loose, D., *Democratie zonder blauwdruk. De politieke filosofie van Claude Lefort* (Best: Damon, 1997).

Schmitt, C., *Der Hüter der Verfassung*, (Berlin: Duncker and Humbolt, [1931] 1969).

Van Osta, A. J. P., Plaats en functie van de negentiende-eeuwse monarchie, in C. A. Tamse (eds.), *De monarchie in Nederland* (Amsterdam: Elsevier, 1980), 63–87.

Van Outrive, L., The Disastrous Justice System in Belgium: A Crisis of Democracy?, in P. Gray and P. t Hart (eds.), *Public Policy Disasters in Western Europe* (London: Routledge, 1998).

Von Treitschke, H., *Vorlesungen über Politik* (Leipzig: Hirzel, 1897).

Whitlam, G., *The Truth of the Matter*, 3rd edn. (Carlton, Vic.: Melbourne University Press, 2005).

Chapter 7

The Democratic Legitimacy of Bureaucratic Leadership

John Kane and Haig Patapan

Democracy's tendency to disperse leadership throughout society presents profound challenges for elected democratic leaders. Not the least of these is that they must appear to lead decisively even while being forced to persuade, negotiate with, bully or cajole people whose independent status and authority puts them beyond simple command. Yet the dispersal of leadership among business groups, labour organizations, social movements, intellectual institutions, opposition parties and so on, merely reflects the natural pluralism of democratic society. The opposition or non-cooperation of such leadership, though it may complicate or frustrate the elected leader's task, presents no problem of principle for democratic leadership as such. In a democracy, anyone may strenuously challenge and attempt to influence particular governmental decisions without implicitly challenging the authority of the government to make them.[1]

The case is quite different, however, for one particular set of leaders upon whom democratic leaders crucially depend, and over whom they seem to enjoy, at least in theory, an undoubted authority. We are speaking here of public sector leaders. Democratic leaders need competent people to manage an effective public service; they will be judged decisively on the way the latter fulfil public expectations in matters of 'service delivery'. To appreciate the costs of administrative failure one need only consider the major political consequences of the Federal Emergency Management Agency's mishandling of the Katrina disaster in New Orleans in 2005, responsibility for which was rapidly transmitted from senior managers to President George W. Bush himself, to his lasting damage. Public sector leaders seem to need to have the freedom to act decisively on such occasions, yet if they exercise a leadership that seems too independent of, or even contrary to, government intentions, they automatically challenge the democratic authority of the elected government.

The democratic dispersal of leadership to the public sector is a problem that may usefully be compared to that of the judiciary. The extent to which judicial authority may legitimately influence politics is a topic of perennial debate, and judicial decisions often cause controversy when they challenge or overturn the policies of elected governments – precisely because this seems a denial of democratic authority. Yet judges in such controversies can at least draw, implicitly or explicitly, on the august and independent authority of law itself. This authority derives not only from a traditional view of law as immemorial and transcendent, but also from the fact that liberal-constitutionalism asserts so adamantly the principle of democratic government *under the rule of law*. Elected executives and legislatures may control the creation of statute law, but the rule-of-law principle inevitably grants special authority to those whose solemn task it is to equitably administer, interpret, and safeguard the law no matter what its origin – in a constitution, a statute, or an accumulated body of 'common' law.

Asserting any equivalent non-democratic authority on behalf of the bureaucracy is much more problematic. Law has arrived, over the course of historical time, at an uneasy but generally stable modus vivendi with democracy, but the same cannot be said for bureaucracy. Meier and O'Toole (2006: ix) begin their book, *Bureaucracy in a Democratic State,* by asking: 'Can the imperatives of an administrative system be reconciled with the norms of democratic government? Or is bureaucracy, with its expertise, insulation, and byzantine procedures, the enemy of popular control?' Though elected leaders notionally command their ever-expanding bureaucracies, the reality has always been much more complicated. According to Meier and O'Toole ibid., the tensions have not significantly dissipated even with the introduction of more complex patterns of 'governance' that encompass multiple organizations, contracting out, networks and so on – in other words, with the advent of less hierarchically 'bureaucratic' forms of administration.

Such attempts have sought to solve the problem of the democratic legitimacy of bureaucratic leadership. Consider, for example, the recent emphasis on developing 'leadership' in the new public sector. The old bureaucracy, trained in discreet subservience and thus notionally the obedient creature of elected leaders, was nevertheless often criticized for displaying an independent will capable of opposing democratic authority. Indeed, the upper layer of the service was peopled by powerful lifetime bureaucrats with the experience, knowledge, and discretionary authority decisively to influence policy. They were awesome, relatively anonymous figures who, as Rhodes and Weller (2001: 1) put it, 'worked in the shadows, advising, managing and influencing the direction of their respective countries. They were the mandarins, recognized as the real rulers, the providers of continuity'. Such hidden rulers inevitably challenged the authority of here-today-gone-tomorrow ministers, which is why the reform movement of modern times sought, among other things, to reduce their power and disperse their functions more widely throughout the service.

Yet how much more opportunity for opposition must exist in a service that disperses discretionary authority and insists that managers show a degree of creative leadership in their professional work? The inward and outward aspects of dispersed democratic leadership, addressed generally in this volume, must seem somewhat at odds with one another in the case of the public sector. Leading one's agency or organization actively, effectively, responsively, even entrepreneurially may result in better public outcomes, yet how can one be sure that such outcomes will be safely aligned with those politically desired by elected leaders? Democratic leaders seek to harness the energies of an active public sector in order to enhance the value of services even while avoiding independent challenge from a new leadership cohort. They wish to combine, in other words, administrative freedom with political control. How successful have they been, or even can they be, in achieving this?

In this chapter, we will explore the fundamental nature of the bureaucratic leadership challenge and consider what it may imply about the specific form of leadership most appropriate to the modern civil service. Public sector reforms addressed the problem of countervailing bureaucratic leadership by diminishing the authority of the old bureaucratic chiefs. We will argue that in doing this, and by dispersing leadership functions throughout the bureaucracy, they unwittingly multiplied the problem of 'democratic versus bureaucratic' leadership.

Democratic versus bureaucratic authority

The precise boundaries of any independent authority that public sector leaders may lay claim to are far from clear, though it is generally articulated in terms of an ethos of the public good, public service or, in the United States especially, constitutionalism (Bertelli and Lynn 2006). Norma Riccucci (2000: 20–1) provides the example of Eileen Clausen who served in the US Environmental Protection Agency (EPA) under President Ronald Reagan.[2] Clausen had a central role in negotiating and renegotiating the Montreal Protocol on curbing the production of Chloro-Fluoro-Carbons (CFCs), and subsequently sought to preserve the effect of this agreement when the Reagan administration became intent on watering it down, eventually gaining Reagan's formal if reluctant backing for an official signing-off on the agreement. Though in effective political contest with an executive to which she was theoretically subservient, Clausen defended the legitimacy of her actions by leaning on the established mission of the EPA and on the fact that the United States had (along with twenty three other nations) agreed to the Protocol. This was bold indeed, and Riccucci describes it as an instance of excellence in administrative leadership. The fact that Clausen got away with it, however, may have been due to the extremely fragmented nature of the American political system, in which both Congress and Executive play a role in supervising administrative agencies (Behn 1998). Similar action in other countries may more readily be regarded as a usurpation of the democratic prerogative and an exercise in 'administrative tyranny'.

This inevitably raises the question of whether anything general can be said about the relationship between democratic and bureaucratic leadership across administrations that vary markedly with national context, culture, and history. As Meier and O'Toole (2006: 13) note, a German ministry is very different from a post-socialist Russian bureaucracy, and both from the US Department of Agriculture. Certainly, comparative studies of Britain, Europe, and the antipodes reveal a striking diversity of roles among senior officials, not just between different governmental systems but within them (Rhodes and Weller 2001). The authority and influence of senior treasury officials (often these days expert economists) are always bound to be greater than that of line agency officials, while different degrees of political independence are intentionally granted to the heads of statutory authorities and, *a fortiori*, to chairs of reserve banks with the responsibility of monitoring a country's whole financial system. Nevertheless, given the fundamental assumption of democracy that ministers of government represent the electorally expressed will of the sovereign people to whom they remain accountable, the question of the proper form of interaction between democratic leaders and their unelected administrative chieftains is one that remains salient at all times and in all places.

Peters (1987) describes a continuum of possibilities for the political–administrative relationship from, at one end, formal separation within a hierarchical system dominated by political officeholders to, at the other, the government by bureaucracy that marginalizes the influence of politicians. The former, though often venerated in theory, is never observed in reality, while the latter would clearly constitute a challenge to democracy. Some have argued that the French administration, with its elite corps of professionally-trained directors and strong statist tradition, constitutes a case of bureaucratic government, though others argue the reality is more complex (Elgie and Griggs 2000; Elgie 2001). Relationships in most democratic countries are in fact located at some intermediate position along the continuum and may be characterized by either mutual accommodation or competition between elected and administrative leaders for control over policy. Adversarial relationships are certainly always possible and are usually generated by a perception among elected officials that their 'servants' are not perfectly under their direction. The American system is certainly prone to adversarialism, but Westminster and continental systems can be equally so. Margaret Thatcher's reforms of the British civil service when she was prime minister were provoked by her previous experience as Secretary of State for Education, which had made her hostile to powerful and unresponsive mandarins with strong policy preferences of their own (Peele 2004: 178). The Netherlands – a 'consensual' democracy with a bureaucracy founded on values of loyalty, merit, and political neutrality – witnessed a series of highly public confrontations between ministers and senior civil servants in the 1990s that some thought suggested a dangerous trend toward bureaucratic autonomy or even hegemony ('t Hart and Wille 2006).

The potential for mutual suspicion and conflict between political leaders and administrators has existed ever since democratic governments first adopted bureaucratic forms of administration. Indeed democracies originally took up bureaucracy with a mixture of hope and fear – hope that 'rational', meritocratic, bureaucratic government would provide improved governmental outcomes to benefit the people, and fear that it might become a rival centre of undemocratic power. This form of administration was not, after all, a democratic invention but was developed in Prussia and France under monarchical or imperial regimes (Karl 1987: 27). The Continental model of the civil service, based originally on the example of hierarchically ordered military organization, was first adopted by absolutist Prussian monarchs and elaborated over the eighteenth and nineteenth centuries into the concept of a powerfully autonomous and highly prestigious organization serving an impersonal State (the so-called *Rechtsstaat* founded on legal norms rather than personal rule: see Kickert [2005]). The democratizing Anglo-American states of the nineteenth century could not help compare the performance of their own ramshackle, patronage-ridden, inefficient administrative organizations with the impressive results achieved by professional, impartial, public-service oriented bureaucracies on the Continent, particularly in Germany. They believed they must reform their civil services to thrive in the modern world, yet feared that bureaucratic innovations developed in illiberal regimes would prove fatal for systems of popular government.[3]

Most famously, Woodrow Wilson believed it necessary to 'Americanize' the continental system 'radically, in thought, principle and aim as well. It must learn our constitutions by heart; must get the bureaucratic fever out of its veins; must inhale much free American air' (Wilson 1887: 202).[4] Wilson wanted to encourage an ethos of unpartisan, businesslike public service by officeholders technically educated in the 'science of administration' (1887: 210, 217–19). Yet he recognized the dangers in having a 'corps of civil servants prepared by a special schooling and drilled, after appointment, into a perfected organization, with appropriate hierarchy and characteristic discipline'. Would such officials not become a 'government within government', an 'offensive class' prone to 'domineering, illiberal officialism' (1887: 216, 221)? Wilson suggested a number of ways to counter such dangers, the principal one being the separation of the political from the administrative sphere. Democratic politics would set the tasks for a non-partisan administration which would be an efficient instrument 'removed from the hurry and strife of politics'.

It is important to note that the famous 'politics–administration' distinction embraced by Wilson and other democratic leaders was not one of their own conceiving. It was an idea first articulated in the early to mid-nineteenth century by French writers whose concern was the opposite of securing democratic authority (Lynn 2006: 50). They wished rather to insulate a reforming bureaucratic state from the malign influences of 'civil society' with its conflicting interests and its attachment to backward modes of thought and existence. Napoleon Bonaparte, seeking to replace unstable politics with secure administration, reconceived the national community as one no longer dependent on the electoral principle but rather on administrative integrity, unity, and the coherence of the State (Silberman 1993: 107).[5] Prussian philosopher G. W. F. Hegel (1967) spoke of civil servants, whose first loyalty was to administrative masters rather than to their own social classes, as forming a 'universal class' – meaning a class presiding over civil society and devoted to the interests of the whole community rather than to any particular interest. Both Germanic and French models nurtured a high-minded ethos of professional 'public service' that was quite divorced from any notion of serving the popular will as it might be expressed through electoral politics (Caplan 1988: 4–5). The point of Continental bureaucracy was not to give the people what they wanted, but to provide what was good for 'the nation'.

This conception of administration has retained its influence on the Continent to the present day, especially in France and Germany. Indeed, a remarkable feature of the *Rechtsstaat* tradition of constitutionally legitimized administration has been its capacity to weather extreme political crises and vast socio-economic changes over centuries. Public bureaucracies on the Continent have often maintained the only semblance of stability in times of great upheaval (König 1997). Even the great waves of managerialist reform flowing from the United States and Great Britain in modern times have broken upon the integrated, legalistic structure of the *Rechtsstaat* with merely superficial effect (Lynn 2006: 121).[6] Although this model of governance might pay allegiance to a politics–administration distinction, administrators within continental systems never believed themselves to be uninvolved in politics; on the contrary, they were always intensely involved in setting policy directions for society, and, as they thought, rightly so. (It is no accident that *politique* in French translates as both 'policy' and 'political'). Very often they were merely concerned to pursue 'rational-scientific' policy untroubled by the fractious and disruptive politicking of civil society.

By contrast, the validation of this distinction in the Anglophone world, where civil society dominated the state rather than vice versa, reflected a determination to adopt the bureaucratic model without diluting the authority of elected governments. Nevertheless, the same desire to shield 'rational' administration from the biasing or corrupting effects of selfish politics is evident in the history of Anglo-American reform movements. In mid-nineteenth century Britain, for example, the Civil Service was still a creature of Parliament and subject to a corrupt patronage system that made it, as Sir Charles Trevelyan put it, a refuge for 'waifs and strays' of the aristocracy. His famous 1854 *Report on the Organization of the Civil Service*, written with Sir Stafford Northcote, proposed that this system be replaced with a service staffed by anyone of generalist education who passed an open competitive examination (Northcote and Trevelyan [1854] 1954).[7] Once in office, these permanent officials would be non-partisan and politically neutral, ensuring a professional administration insulated from corrupting political influences.

In the United States, the thrust of administrative reform after Andrew Jackson's presidency (1829–37) had been precisely the opposite – to make the civil service *less* insulated from political pressure.[8] Jackson introduced into the Federal Bureaucracy a system of rotation in which Civil Service personnel were replaced when a new president gained office. This was supposed to make the bureaucracy more responsive to the incoming administration and to democratize official posts by making participation in government more accessible to the common man (Wilentz 2005: 315). But under this 'spoils system', as it became known, new appointments were made on the basis of political loyalty rather than merit, with deleterious effects in the long run as partisanship generally trumped competency (Hoogenboom 1959).[9] Even the passage of the Pendleton Act of 1883, strongly influenced by Britain's Northcote-Trevelyan reforms, did not eradicate this problem but tried rather to strike a balance between the professional elitism of Northcote-Trevelyan and the democratic and inclusive spirit of Jackson's original reforms (van Riper 1997).[10] Certainly Wilson, who advocated adoption of continental rational-bureaucratic structures as the basis of American administration, believed the reforms did not go far enough.

Wilson's wish for rationalization would be more or less realized with the passage of time, however, as both the British and American civil services (and those of other Anglophone nations) became increasingly bureaucratized. The typical modern civil service came to feature the familiar hierarchy of interlocking offices governed by prescriptive rules and authoritative command, safeguarded by strict documentation, staffed by career bureaucrats possessed of technical expertise, and undergirded by an ethos of non-partisan public service. To prevent this bureaucracy from becoming a 'government within a government', the democratic version of the politics–administration distinction was emphasized. The sphere of legitimate politics, dominated by elected politicians, would be clearly distinguished from a sphere of purely instrumental administration staffed by 'neutral' bureaucrats. This seemed to solve the problem in democracy's favour while promising efficient government.

The problem with this 'neutralization' of the service, as scholars soon realized, was that the politics–administration distinction could not be realistically maintained (Waldo 1948) – at least not if 'distinction' were taken to mean 'dichotomy'. 'Dichotomy' implied a strict separation in which administrators had no voice in policy matters and politicians no hand in administration, and much of the literature of the recent past, especially the American, has referred precisely to a politics–administration *dichotomy*. James Svara (1998, 1999, 2001) argued that the dichotomy idea was a 'myth', an artefact of a 1958 article by Wallace Sayre that reinterpreted the history of the politics–administration distinction in absolutist terms, derailing discussions about the proper interaction of politics and administration that had been proceeding since the founding of the modern American service. Sayre bequeathed a model of administration as a 'self-contained world' exclusively concerned with the execution of assignments handed down from the political realm. Unfortunately for the civil service this model was 'patently untenable' (Svara 2001: 178). Patrick Overeem (2005), noting that those who abandoned the politics–administration dichotomy as false did not also abandon the related value of the political neutrality of administrators, argued that the real distinction to be made, rather than one between administration and politics *per se*, was between 'partisan politics' and 'policy politics' – or we might say between *interested* and *disinterested* politics. The essential requirement is that public administration be shielded from malign partisan, sectoral, or personal interests while being disinterestedly concerned with helping create, cooperatively with elected leaders, good policy. Neutrality, in other words, need not imply passive instrumentality as has so often been assumed.[11]

As we have already noted, Northcote and Trevelyan had attempted to insulate a professional administration from malign political influences in this way, not to exclude it altogether from policy-making. The stated intention of their report (1854: 3) was the creation of 'an efficient body of permanent officers, occupying a position duly subordinate to that of Ministers...yet possessing sufficient independence, character, ability, and experience to be able to advise, assist, and, to some extent, influence, those who are from time to time set over them'.[12] Such a reflection seems to support Svara's contention that a return to Wilson and other founders might uncover a better theoretical basis for contemporary public service. Svara in fact discerned in the founders' work an intended principle of 'complementarity' between political and administrative realms, the two being joined in the pursuit of sound governance.

> Complementarity entails separate parts, but parts that come together in a mutually supportive way...Complementarity stresses interdependence along with distinct roles; compliance along with independence; respect for political control along with a commitment to shape and implement policy in ways that promote the public interest; deference to elected incumbents along with adherence to the

law and support for fair electoral competition; and appreciation of politics along with support for professional standards (Svara 2001: 177).[13]

Many senior public servants would say, of course, that this is exactly how they have always understood their role. But this raises the question of why democratic leaders have so often suspected them of larger ambitions. The central fear of democrats is that insulating expert administrators from partisan influence, even if it ensures professionalism, also vouchsafes them an independence that enables them to flout, subtly or overtly, democratic authority. Wilson, certainly, was quite aware of this danger but noted that all sovereigns, including the people, were suspicious of their servants, a problem that could not be overcome by dividing powers: 'If it be divided, dealt out in shares to many, it is obscured; and if obscured, it is made irresponsible'. On the contrary, Wilson advocated trust, with larger powers and unhampered discretion invested in the heads of the service where it may be 'easily watched and brought to book'. Such power led to better administration, according to Wilson, because 'the greater [the administrator's] power, the less likely is he to abuse it, the more is he nerved and sobered and elevated by it' (1887: 214). The aim was to make bureaucracy a 'public spirited instrument of just government':

> The ideal for us is a civil service cultured and self sufficient enough to act with sense and vigor, and yet so intimately connected with the popular thought, by means of elections and constant public counsel, as to find arbitrariness or class spirit quite out of the question. (1887: 217)

Such views of action and discretion obviously implied, even if it was never clearly stated thus, genuine leadership in the civil service. The *type* of leadership required could also be read from the responsibilities of civil servants who were supposed to act with frankness, vigour, and impartiality while remaining sensitive to their subordination within a democratic system. As administrations everywhere steadily bureaucratized along Continental lines, installing rule-governed systems of strict command and control, such leadership naturally accumulated, as Wilson foresaw, at the top.

Public sector leadership, old and new

In Westminster-style governments, the civil service mandarins were leaders very much in this mould. They were permanent career bureaucrats strategically located at the critical boundary between political and administrative spheres, able to influence the shape and direction of almost all public policy. Below them were echelons of administrators, theoretically obedient to their will; above them were political masters who had to be discreetly instructed, advised, guided, but finally (and again theoretically) obeyed. The mandarins' strength and shield, from a democratic perspective, was that their important leadership role was conducted under a screen of public invisibility, safeguarded by the Westminster doctrine of ministerial responsibility (under which ministers accepted public praise or blame for all the actions of their departments).

In the United States, senior bureaucrats were much less shielded from democratic pressures than their British counterparts. Their leadership was perennially challenged by the continuing practice of rotation, which blatantly 'politicized' the service and created an enduring division between political appointees and members of what became known as 'the permanent government'.[14] Karl (1987: 27) notes that, 'the embedding of the conflict between mass democracy and elite professionalism in the American political structure is what...shapes the American meaning of bureaucracy and American attitudes toward it'. In a liberal political culture that already harboured deep suspicions of government as such, 'bureaucrat bashing' by politicians became a favourite means of deflecting blame for political failures, producing a characteristically American hostility toward bureaucracy and professional bureaucrats. The latter, for their part, always felt themselves unfairly maligned and derided, but nevertheless clung to a vision of public-service leadership that, when exposed, was in permanent tension with democratic values.

The structural situation can be delineated as follows. Democratically elected leaders are formally servants of the people, whose service may be terminated should they fail to please or appease. The bureaucratic instruments of the civil service are, in theory, the servants of these servants, serving the public through obedience to the elected leadership. Yet the civil service does not *belong* to democratic leaders who are merely its temporary custodians. The true principal of the civil service is the sovereign people whom it serves under a higher ethos of public service, always in principle distinguishable from service to transient politicians, whatever their electoral credentials. In other words, the bureaucratic conception of guardianship of a public interest separable from private interests could only with difficulty be harmonized with the idea of serving the public through non-partisan obedience to the will of democratic representatives. Tensions would inevitably arise whenever the bureaucracy's views of what constituted the true public interest differed or clashed with those of the elected government, even if in a democracy the representative democratic will was supposed to prevail. This was a permanent possibility given the inevitably different perspectives of professional career administrators, with their technocratic expertise and long experience, and democratic leaders with their particular ideological agendas and special sensitivities to urgent public demands arising from their need to be re-elected. In cases of conflict, it is tempting for bureaucrats to see themselves as the embodiment of Rousseau's rational 'general will', a will that must necessarily oppose, for the good of all, the merely transient and arbitrary will of the majority as embodied in the elected government (Rousseau 1978: III).

Democratic leaders, on their side, were liable to view bureaucratic obstruction as usurpation of legitimate democratic authority, a problem that became more acute as the responsibilities that governments assumed grew ever larger. Modern mass democracies inevitably generate continuously expanding public demands that governments are politically obliged to meet, even as severe fiscal pressures mount. Frustrations are bound to be felt if the administrations that elected leaders must employ to respond to such demands have become unwieldy and impenetrable, and are under imperfect political control. Elected leaders become helplessly squeezed between the unrelenting pressure of the sovereign people's demands and their own incapacity satisfactorily to meet them. As for the people themselves, their attitude is inevitably ambivalent and dependent in part on the historical circumstances of the polity to which they belong. It is of the nature of democratic people (as we have argued elsewhere – Kane and Patapan [2008]) to distrust the leaders they elect to represent them. Democratic politics may be fractious or chaotic, while bureaucracies may reliably deliver essential public services. In such circumstances, people may easily hold their bureaucracies in great respect and their representatives in utter contempt (e.g. in France on occasion, or in Japan until the bursting of the economic bubble). Yet when all is said and done democratic leaders generally hold a superior hand vis-à-vis their administrations, for they have the authority to radically reorder the shape of bureaucracy and to alter the rules and conditions under which it operates. Sooner or later, bold leaders were bound to cash in this advantage and try to assert firmer control over the bureaucracy.

Indeed, in the United States, attempts had been underway since Franklin Roosevelt argued that full democratization required tying the presidency, the unique conduit for growing public demands, to an 'enlightened administration' capable of meeting them. All his New Deal efforts aimed at establishing 'a government responsive to the needs of the majority', and a presidency 'with authority over its domain' to ensure that responsiveness (Milkis 1993: 111; Cook 1996: 103–104). Most post-Second World War studies, however, emphasized the limits of presidential influence over the bureaucracy (Cronin 1980; Hooton 1997; Cronin and Genovese 2004).[15] Career officials, it seemed, had numerous ways of resisting presidents and their appointees, and worked in environments where many competitive pressures came to bear other than those of the executive. Moreover, they often personally harboured goals that were in conflict with those of the presidency. Worse, according to Lowi (1979), policy was now effectively determined by 'iron triangles' of special-interest lobbyists, appointed bureaucratic officials, and narrowly self-interested congressional sub-committees. The bureaucracy was no longer a faithful servant of elected leaders, but exercised its own leadership as an independent player in a closeted game that essentially suborned the larger public interest.

Nor was the United States alone in its dissatisfaction. Leaders in every developed country could draw on long-standing complaints against bureaucracies (in addition to their alleged usurpation of popular sovereignty) to mount an assault on them. Bureaucracy, rather than gaining a reputation for rational efficiency, had become a byword for obstinate stupidity and incompetence. The proliferation of rules mindlessly applied, and of documented procedures blindly followed, produced the familiar bureaucratic nightmare of endless 'red tape'. The entrenchment of seniority systems (the cardinal sin for Northcote and Trevelyan, who had emphasized selection and promotion based on proven merit) ensured that bureaucracies turned into sclerotic, inefficient and process-obsessed organizations (Northcote and Trevelyan 1954: 4).[16] Whether or not such critiques of bureaucracy were wholly justified, governments around the world conceived the need to regain political control of administrations that had allegedly become laws-unto-themselves, to ensure more reliable and more efficient outcomes. All the waves of reform that began in the late 1970s had (at least) those aims in view, for they were borne on the promise of solving once and for all the democratic problem of intransigent bureaucratic leadership.

The reforms of the so-called New Public Management that became familiar in liberal democracies everywhere included: a shift from inputs and processes to outputs and outcomes; more measurement and quantification; a preference for specialized, 'flat' and autonomous organizational structures; a grant of greater discretionary authority to managers at all levels of the service; substitution of contractual for hierarchical relationships; market type mechanisms for delivery of public goods; and a consumer and individual orientation (Pollitt 2003: 27–8). The aim was to create a more flexible and efficient 'entrepreneurial' organization capable of delivering enhanced services at lower unit cost. Core government responsibilities were identified and all other activities that could arguably be better (more efficiently and economically) handled by the private sector or non-governmental organizations were hived off. The old sites of leadership (and some would say of real practical wisdom) in the higher reaches of the service were dismantled by the removal of tenure and the introduction of fixed-term, performance-based contracts for senior public servants. The independence of the latter was purposely destroyed and their policy role altered to one mostly of management, their task now being to make the bureaucracy more consistently obedient to the will of elected ministers. Policy roles, meanwhile, were increasingly passed into the hands of non-administrative advisers whose personal loyalty was to the politician who had hired them.

All these aspects of reform were important, but of most interest to us here is the attempt to alter the balance of force between democratic leadership and bureaucratic leadership in favour of the former. The depth of change produced by the reforms, many of them inspired by private sector models, varied greatly from country to country, as we have noted. But the general hope guiding all reform was that responsiveness to public demands could be improved and more effective outcomes gained for tax monies spent if a new kind of public servant could be created, someone who could demonstrate qualities of flexibility, innovation, entrepreneurialism, capacity for independent and discretionary judgement, ethical competence, policy-awareness, sensitivity to political factors, and managerial competence.

The genuine appeal of these reforms lay in the fact that they aimed at replacing a blind, blundering bureaucratic machine with an intelligent and adaptive organization more serviceable to overstretched governments. The anticipated rationality of the old bureaucracy had proved (at least to the satisfaction of the reformers) highly irrational, and a different, less mechanistic conception of reason was now advanced. The general intention was to create conditions in which individuals could think for themselves and respond intelligently to the particular situations they encountered in the course of their work. What was demanded, in effect, was the exercise throughout the entire service of the kind of political prudence formerly expected only of senior officials.[17] This implied that public servants should have the courage and confidence to judge for themselves what was best and to act accordingly, thus abandoning the familiar safety of mechanical rule-following. Public servants at lower levels were now asked to understand policy and to take some responsibility for it – analysing, costing, formulating, advising, implementing, and evaluating. They were asked to manage programmes and the budgets allocated to them, reporting explicitly on the match of expenditures to outcomes achieved – in other words, to ensure that policies or particular aspects of them were expedited efficiently and effectively. The reforms therefore stressed initiative, and initiative inevitably implied leadership. Indeed, leadership was now explicitly demanded of nearly every public servant. Leadership consultants were employed, leadership training courses ordered, leadership techniques explored, and leadership retreats undertaken. Even as leadership was intentionally weakened at the top, efforts were made to disperse it throughout the whole service. If, as this volume stresses, it is in the nature of democracy to disperse leadership throughout society, then the reform process could be seen as a major democratizing initiative, though this was not in fact its intention.

Laudable as this ambition seemed, the effect was also to disperse the dilemma of democratic versus bureaucratic leadership throughout the bureaucracy. The problem of democratic legitimacy would now arise, at least potentially, every time a relatively junior public servant exercised his or her discretion. Democratic leaders were not unaware of this. They understood that distributing discretionary freedom raised the problem of maintaining control from above, a control that could not be forfeited without grave political risk. Blame for any bureaucratic initiative that created public opposition or scandal would inevitably be sheeted back to the responsible elected representative.[18] It was hoped that marketization, or quasi-marketization, of public services would introduce the automatic discipline and allocative efficiency believed to characterize the private sphere – the market would, in other words, substitute to some extent for old-fashioned rule-ordered control. But the rationality genuine markets induce in individual entrepreneurs is narrowly calculating and instrumentally geared to the production of profit. Valuable as this may be for fostering economic growth, it does not even begin to address, let alone exhaust, many of the demands placed on the reasoning powers of public servants – demands, for example, of equity, justice, need, protection, defence of rights, and environmental preservation. Public employees are always striving to do more with scarce resources than is actually possible, and in a democratic environment they must do so while being assailed by competing and often conflicting public demands.

What was not plainly recognized or admitted was that the type of leadership demanded was no longer purely bureaucratic. Like that of the senior officials of old, it had become inherently political, and was thus exposed to all perils and uncertainties of the democratic realm. Public policy is, by its very nature, political, and therefore subject to all the vagaries, pressures, and perplexities of democratic politics. Modern bureaucratic reforms, having effectively neutered the political power of senior managers, tended to distribute their political responsibilities throughout the whole bureaucratic organization, but the management of policy demands skills of prudence that can be developed only through long experience. Some of this experience is inevitably painful, and the pain is not simply that of a penalty imposed for breach of protocol or neglect of proper procedure. It is pain of an altogether different quality, more profound because touching on political matters and having political consequences that may reverberate up through the bureaucratic apparatus into the minister's office itself. The demand that public servants be 'apolitical' in their professional lives became a nonsense under these new conditions. They could no longer ignore politics once significant policy responsibility had been devolved into their hands. To properly fulfil their new role they had to inhabit the mental universe of their political masters while remaining their subordinate servants, cultivating acute political sensitivities and calculating the political dimensions of all their plans and actions (see generally Kane and Patapan 2006).

Conclusion

The general avoidance or overlooking of the political dimension of administration defines the essence of the problem facing administrators as they attempt to graft the idea of leadership onto public governance generally. It is by no means clear that democratic leaders fully understood this when they embarked upon their season of change. Their need to control the bureaucracy rather than be controlled by it, and their desire to ensure the best possible outcomes from a re-ordered administration, were perfectly comprehensible.

But it was not perhaps foreseen that the combination of these would result in a thoroughly politicized bureaucracy that, through the grant of wide discretions, would tend to reproduce and multiply the dilemmas of democratic versus bureaucratic leadership at every level. Private sector rhetoric of enterprise, risk-taking and bold vision was undoubtedly very dangerous in this regard, for it encouraged just the sort of independent action that might at any instance threaten to usurp the popular will and arouse popular ire. Public servants are not private agents and cannot behave like them.

Yet administrations, like all organizations, need good leadership if they are to perform even adequately. To bring this about requires a persuasive model of the form of leadership appropriate in the public sector if clashes with democratic authority are to be minimized. Effective leadership in the public sector certainly requires ethical integrity and technical competency, but it also demands more; it requires a particular sensitivity to the constraints imposed by a democratic political environment and an ability to act prudently within it. It is not inherently absurd to want to create a nimble and intelligently responsive public administration that depends less on command and control and more on wisely and widely used discretion, but it is not at all certain that wise discretion in a public-service environment can be taught by training in risk analysis, budget management, cost-benefit calculation, ethics, or even leadership. What is required is more general understanding of Svara's notion of complementarity and what it might take to achieve it. It is confusing for professional civil servants to be told that they are legally required to be 'apolitical' and then to demand they perform efficiently in a role that demands the most acutely political appreciation of the democratic–bureaucratic nexus.

Yet we must stress that the problem of bureaucratic leadership versus democratic authority cannot be definitively solved; it must, by the very nature of things, be perennially managed. It can, however, be managed more or less well. It is important to note that Svara's doctrine of complementarity requires a certain mutuality of understanding between democratic and bureaucratic leaders, and failures can occur on either side. Well-meaning administrators deeply imbued with an ethos of public service will achieve little without the willing cooperation of the elected leadership. This is illustrated by the abysmal level of morale reported among federal administrators in the United States after eight years of governance by a party that believed 'government is the problem, not the solution'. Civil servants complained they had felt thwarted for months or years from doing the government jobs they were hired to do by political appointees who erected roadblocks to agency goals (Leonnig 2008).[19] Commentator Ruth Marcus (2007) denounced the disastrous failures of the Bush administration and pointed to their root causes: a contemptuous attitude toward government itself, a 'fox-guarding-the-henhouse' personnel plan, disdain by appointees for the laws they were sworn to enforce, and a spoils-of-war attitude toward the government they were entrusted with overseeing.

Prudent public managers are those who are capable of acting and leading effectively without endangering democratic legitimacy. But their elected political masters must do the same or effective governance becomes impossible. Democratic leaders who fail to appreciate the ethos of public-service risk embracing the kind of failures that may be fatal to their political fortunes. Thus bureaucratic leadership presents an opportunity and a challenge not only to democratic leaders, but to democracy itself.

Notes

1. John Uhr (2005: 78–83, 111–15) speaks of dispersed or diffused leadership – or a 'lattice of leadership' – as a positive good for a democratic system, by which he means leadership not overly concentrated in the executive branch. For the contrast with autocratic governments, where dissent is by definition weakness, see generally Kane et al. (2008).
2. This section of the chapter builds upon Kane (2007).
3. 'In order to survive in the modern world, democratic governments must find ways of adopting methods associated with despotic governments' (Karl 1987: 28; see also Heper 1985).
4. Wilson (1887: 219) added: 'We can borrow the science of administration with safety and profit if only we read all fundamental differences of conditions into its essential tenets. We have only to filter it through our constitutions, only to put it over a slow fire of criticism and distil away its foreign gases.'
5. In local government, this meant reinstating the *intendant* system via the office of Prefect, rendering local government bureaucratic, not political, and ultimately accountable to the central government (Silberman 1993: 106–7). This system, where the prefect had immense powers, was to remain a central feature of French administration, and was also useful in subsequent regimes in vetting executive-approved candidates for the National Assembly.
6. Rhodes and Weller (2001: 248) note with regard to the French administrative structure that, 'It is scarcely surprising that the nostrums of the private sector recycled by the new public management failed to strike a responsive chord. The powerful officials of a strong state were unmoved and the moving finger of the new public management writ and then moved on with nary a mark to show for its pains.'
7. This was in contrast to the Benthamite school, which wanted specialist systems of administration, staffed by experts, who would deal with the problems of an industrializing and urbanizing society (Greenaway 2004: 6). The 'generalist' education (usually in the classics) of the British was in marked contrast to the specialist education provided in the French *Grandes Ecoles*, a network of elite technical and administrative schools reformed and expanded by Napoleon (Silberman 1993: 114–16).
8. On the more aristocratic concept that preceded the Jacksonian, see Henderson (2004).
9. The name arose after William Marcy, describing the system's principle, declared in Congress: 'to the victor belong the spoils of the enemy' (Wilentz 2005: 316).

10. Although a bill passed through Congress in 1871 authorizing President Grant to make rules for admission to the Civil Service, and an advisory board was established, Congress refused to fund it and the practice of patronage continued. In 1877, President Rutherford B. Hayes commissioned a New York lawyer, Dorman B. Eaton, to make a report on the British Civil Service. He published his findings in 1879 in a highly influential book *The Civil Service in Great Britain* (van Riper 1997: 199). Eaton presented another bill to Congress for the establishment of a merit based system for the Federal Civil Service, which was adopted and introduced by Senator Pendleton in 1881 (Wheeler 1919: 488). In the same year, President Garfield was assassinated by a man who had been rejected for appointment into the service, hastening the momentum for reform and assisting the passage of Pendleton's bill.
11. Brian J. Cook (1996) argues that two conceptions of public administration have coexisted in American politics from the beginning, the 'instrumental' and the 'constitutive', though the instrumental has always dominated, unfortunately in Cook's view. In the constitutive vision, bureaucracy helps shape public policy and thus the character of the political community, a responsibility that requires classical 'practical wisdom' rather than technical expertise.
12. Interestingly, Trevelyan regarded such a civil administration as a training ground for future politicians (Greenaway 2004: 9–10).
13. The observations of a Wisconsin state senator from a participant politician's perspective lend practical support to Svara's principle; Mordecai Lee (2001) argued that, in his experience, elected officials interacted with administrators on the basis of political commonsense rather than according to any ruling norm defining their relationship (though political decision-making implicitly cast administrators in a subordinate role).
14. The perennial nature of their relationship can be judged from the very title of a recent book by Robert Maranto (2005), *Beyond a Government of Strangers: How Career Executives and Political Appointees Can Turn Conflict into Cooperation.*
15. Most such studies followed Richard Neustadt's classic report (1960) on the presidency which argued that presidents had the power to persuade more than to command.
16. Apart from organizational lethargy, some critics claimed that bureaucracy worked to preserve entrenched bureaucratic interests that had nothing to do with the public interest. William Niskanen (1973), for example, argued that bureaucrats had a rational interest in increasing the size of their budgets independently of public need or demand, contributing to the growth of wasteful bureaucracy, though Patrick Dunleavy (1991) disagreed. In his 'bureau-shaping' model, Dunleavy argued that rational bureaucrats would prefer not to maximize budgets but to shape their agencies for maximum work utility, for example by having small elite agencies close to the centre of power. Even big line agencies, he said, would have incentives to unload many of the problems of management onto external agencies or private sector bodies.
17. For the importance of the idea of prudence in public service see: Formaini (1990); Cooper (1991, 2001); Hart (1984, 1994); Cook (1996); Kane and Patapan (2006).
18. It was a telling sign of the times that, in Westminster systems, the ancient rule of ministerial responsibility was in fact relaxed or in some instances repudiated under

the new regime. Public servants were sometimes publicly 'unmasked' when it suited ministers to shift blame for some scandal away from themselves. Whatever the short-term expediency of such a course, it hardly seemed to indicate an adequate general solution to the problem of democratic accountability that the New Public Management had created.

19. Morale was hardest hit, unsurprisingly, among regulatory agencies like the Departments of Interior and Labor, the EPA, the Food and Drug Administration, and the Consumer Product Safety Commission.

Bibliography

Behn, R. D., 'What Right Do Public Managers Have To Lead?', *Public Administration Review*, 52/2 (1998), 209–24.

Behrens, C. B. A., *Society, Government, and the Enlightenment: The Experiences of Eighteenth-Century France and Prussia* (New York: Harper & Row, 1985).

Bertelli, A. M. and Lynn Jr, L., *Madison's Managers: Public Administration and the Constitution* (Baltimore, Maryland: Johns Hopkins University Press, 2006).

Caplan, J., *Government without Administration: State and Civil Society in Weimar and Nazi Germany* (Oxford: Clarendon Press, 1988).

Casper, G., 'Changing Concepts of Constitutionalism: 18th to 20th Century', in P. B. Kurland, G. Casper, and D. Hutchinson (eds.), *The Supreme Court Review*, (1989), 311–32.

Chapman, R. A. (eds.), *Ethics in Public Service* (Ottawa: Carleton University Press, 1993).

Cook, B. J., *Bureaucracy and Self-Government: Reconsidering the Role of Public Administration in American Government* (Baltimore, Maryland: Johns Hopkins University Press, 1996).

Cooper, T. L., *An Ethic of Citizenship for Public Administration* (Englewood Cliffs, New Jersey: Prentice-Hall, 1991).

——(eds.), *Handbook of Administrative Ethics*, 2nd edn. (New York: Marcel Dekker, 2001).

Cronin, T. E., *The State of the Presidency* (Boston, Mass.: Little Brown, 1980).

——and Genovese, M. A., *The Paradoxes of the American Presidency* (New York: Oxford University Press, 2004).

Dorn, W., 'The Prussian Bureaucracy in the Eighteenth Century', *Political Science Quarterly*, 46/3 (1931), 403–23.

Dunleavy, P., *Democracy, Bureaucracy and Public Choice: Economic Explanations in Political Science* (Hemel Hempstead: Harvester Wheatsheaf, 1991).

Edmondson III, H. T., 'The Hyppolytus, Public Administration, and the Need for Prudence', in J. S. Bowman and D. C. Menzel (eds.), *Teaching Ethics and Values in Public Administration Programs: Innovations, Strategies, and Issues* (New York: State University of New York Press, 1998).

Elgie, R., 'France: "Dual Structure, Shared Dilemma"', in R. A. W. Rhodes and P. Weller (eds.), *The Changing World of Top Officials: Mandarins or Valets* (Buckingham: Open University Press, 2001), 11–40.

——and Griggs, S., *French Politics: Debates and Controversies* (London: Routledge, 2000).

Formaini, R., *The Myth of Scientific Public Policy* (New Brunswick: Transaction Publishers and the Social Philosophy and Policy Center, 1990).

Gillroy, J. M. and Wade, M. (eds.), *The Moral Dimensions of Public Policy Choice: Beyond the Market Paradigm* (Pittsburgh, Penn.: University of Pittsburgh Press, 1992).

Gortner, H. F., *Ethics for Public Managers* (New York: Greenwood, 1991).

Greenaway, J., 'Celebrating Northcote Trevelyan; Dispelling the Myths', *Public Policy and Administration*, 19/1 (2004), 1–14.

Hammond, K. R., *Human Judgment and Social Policy: Irreducible Uncertainty, Inevitable Error, Unavoidable Injustice* (New York: Oxford University Press, 1996).

Hart, D. K., 'The Virtuous Citizen, the Honorable Bureaucrat, and "Public" Administration', *Public Administration Review*, 44 (1984), 111–20.

——'Administration and the Ethics of Virtue: In All things, Choose First for Good Character and Then for Technical Expertise', in T. L. Cooper (eds.), *Handbook of Administrative Ethics* (New York: Marcel Dekker, Inc., 1994).

Heclo, H., *A Government of Strangers: Executive Politics in Washington* (Washington D. C.: Brookings Institute, 1977).

——and Salamon, L. A. (eds.), *The Illusion of Presidential Government* (Boulder, Col.: Westview Press, 1981).

Hegel, G. W. F., *Philosophy of Right*, trans. T. M. Knox (New York: Oxford University Press, 1967).

Henderson, K., 'Characterizing American Public Administration: The Concept of Administrative Culture', *The International Journal of Public Sector Management*, 17/3 (2004), 234–50.

Heper, M., 'The State and Public Bureaucracies: A Comparative and Historical Perspective', *Comparative Studies in Society and History*, 27/1 (1985), 86–110.

Hoogenboom, A., 'The Pendleton Act and the Civil Service', *The American Historical Review*, 64/2 (1959), 301–18.

Hooton, C. G., *Executive Governance: Presidential Administrations and Policy Change in the Federal Bureaucracy* (Armonk, New York: M. E. Sharpe, 1997).

Kane, J., 'The Problem of Politics: Public Governance and Leadership', in R. Koch and J. Dixon (eds.), *Public Governance and Leadership* (Wiesbaden: Deutscher Universitäts-Verlag, 2007), 131–49.

——and Bishop, P., 'Consultation and Contest: the Danger of Mixing Modes', *Australian Journal of Public Administration*, 61/1 (2002), 87–94.

——and Patapan, H., 'In Search of Prudence: The Hidden Problem of Managerial Reform', *Public Administration Review*, September-October (2006), 711–24.

————'The Challenge of Dissident Democratic Leadership', in J. Kane, H. Patapan, and B. Wong (eds.), *Dissident Democrats: The Challenge of Democratic Leadership in Asia* (New York: Palgrave, 2008), 1–34.

——and Wong, B. (eds.), *Dissident Democrats: The Challenge of Democratic Leadership in Asia* (New York: Palgrave, 2008).

Karl, B., 'The American Bureaucrat: A History of Sheep in Wolves' Clothing', *Public Administration Review*, 47/1 (1987), 26–34.

Kickert, W., 'Distinctiveness in the Study of Public Management in Europe', *Public Management Review*, 7/4 (2005), 537–83.

König, K., 'Entrepreneurial Management or Executive Administration: The Perspective of Classical Public Administration', in W. J. Kickert (eds.), *Public Management and Administrative Reform in Western Europe* (Cheltenham: Edward Elgar, 1997), 213–32.

Lee, M., 'Looking at the Politics-Administration Dichotomy from the Other Direction: Participant Observation by a State Senator', *International Journal of Public Administration*, 24/4 (2001), 363–84.

Leonnig, C. D., 'Widespread Complaints about a Rudderless Government', *Washington Post*, 6 November 2008.

Lowi, T., *The End of Liberalism: The Second Republic of the United States* (New York: W. W. Norton & Company, 1979).

Lynn Jr., L., *Public Management Old and New* (New York: Routledge, 2006).

Maranto, R., *Beyond a Government of Strangers: How Career Executives and Political Appointees Can Turn Conflict into Cooperation* (Lanham, Maryland: Lexington Books, 2005).

Marcus, R., 'Fox-in-the-Henhouse Government', *Washington Post*, 4 April 2007.

Meier, K. J. and O'Toole, L. J., *Bureaucracy and the Democratic State: A Governance Perspective* (Baltimore: Johns Hopkins Press, 2006).

Milkis, S. M., *The President and the Parties: The Transformation of the American Party System Since the New Deal* (New York: Oxford University Press, 1993).

Neustadt, R., *Presidential Power: The Politics of Leadership* (New York: Wiley, 1960).

Niskanen, W. A., 'Bureaucracy: Servant or Master?' (Chicago: Aldine-Atherton, 1973).

Northcote, S. H. and Trevelyan, C. E., 'The Northcote-Trevelyan Report', republished in *Public Administration*, 32 Spring (1954 [1854]), 1–16.

Overeem, P., 'The Value of the Dichotomy: Politics, Administration, and the Political Neutrality of Administrators', *Administrative Theory & Praxis*, 27/2 (2005), 311–29.

Peele, G., *Governing the UK: British Politics in the 21st Century* (Oxford: Blackwell, 2004).

Peters, B. G., *The Politics of Bureaucracy* (New York: Longman, 1987).

Pollitt, C., *The Essential Public Manager* (London: Open University Press/McGraw-Hill, 2003).

Rhodes, R. A. W. and Weller, P. (eds.), *The Changing World of Top Officials* (Buckingham: Open University Press, 2001).

Riccucci, N. M., 'Excellence in Administrative Leadership', in K. Theakston (eds.), *Bureaucrats and Leadership* (London: Macmillan Press, 2000), 17–38.

Rosenberg, H., *Bureaucracy, Aristocracy, and Autocracy: The Prussian Experience: 1660–1815* (Cambridge, Mass.: Harvard University Press, 1958).

Rousseau, J. J., *On the Social Contract with Geneva Manuscript and Discourse on Political Economy*, R. Masters (eds.), and trans. J. Masters (New York: St Martin's Press, 1978 [1762]).

Silberman, B. S., *Cages of Reason: The Rise of the Rational State in France, Japan, the United States, and Great Britain* (Chicago: University of Chicago Press, 1993).

Svara, J. H., 'The Politics-Administration Dichotomy Model as Aberration', *Public Adminstration Review*, 58/1 (1998), 51–9.

——'Complementarity of Politics and Administration as a Legitimate Alternative to the Dichotomy Model', *Administration and Society*, 30/6 (1999), 676–705.

——'The Myth of Dichotomy: Complementarity of Politics and Administration in the Past and Future of Public Administration', *Public Adminstration Review*, 61/2 (2001), 176–83.

't Hart, P. and Wille, A., 'Ministers and Top Officials in the Dutch Core Executive: Living Together, Growing Apart?', *European Forum*, 84/1 (2006), 121–46.

Terry, L. D., *Leadership of Public Bureaucracies: The Administrator as Conservator* (Thousand Oaks, CA: Sage, 1995).

Uhr, J., *Terms of Trust: Arguments over Ethics in Australian Government* (Sydney: University of New South Wales Press, 2005).

van Riper, P., 'The Pendleton Act of 1883 and the Professionalism of the US Public Service', in A. Farazmand (eds.), *Modern Systems of Government: Exploring the Role of Bureaucrats and Politicians* (Thousand Oaks, CA: Sage, 1997), 196–211.

——'The American Administrative State: Wilson and the Founders – An Unorthodox View', *Public Administration Review*, 43/6 (1983), 477–90.

Waldo, D., *The Administrative State: A Study of the Political Theory of American Public Administration* (New York: Ronald Press, 1948).

Weber, M., *Theory of Social and Economic Organization*, trans. A. M. Henderson and T. Parsons (New York: Oxford University Press, 1947).

Wheeler, E., 'The Rise and Progress of the Merit System', *Political Science Quarterly*, 34/3 (1919), 486–92.

Wilentz, S., *The Rise of American Democracy: Jefferson to Lincoln*, (New York: W. W. Norton & Co., 2005).

Wilson, W., 'The Study of Administration', *Political Science Quarterly*, 2 June (1887), 197–222.

Chapter 8

Judicial Leadership

Mark Tushnet

The separation of the judiciary from the executive and the legislature is one of the best known examples of the dispersal of leadership in democracies. In the security and independence accorded to judges, and especially in the entrenchment of the authority of constitutional courts, we see the unique institutional measures that characterize modern liberal democracies. But what implications do such a separation and independence have for judicial leadership? This chapter examines three aspects of leadership in constitutional courts: leadership by the constitutional court with respect to the political system as a whole; leadership by the constitutional court in the formulation of national policy; and leadership within the judicial system. These three aspects of leadership are loosely connected. For the constitutional court to lead the judicial system, for example, someone must either act as a bureaucratic manager or devise appropriate legal strategies of coordination. Leadership in the political system depends in large measure on the existence of, or perhaps more precisely the weakness of, exogenous political constraints on the possibility for judicial leadership, but within the space those constraints open up, a judge who seeks to guide the political system must act strategically.

The chapter begins with an overview of the conditions under which constitutional courts have the opportunity to play a leading role in the political system as a whole, and then turns to the second and third aspects of leadership. It would be misleading, though, to take this organization to convey an implicit message that judicial leadership on constitutional courts has been tending to produce constitutional courts that are increasingly active and politically independent participants in national policy-making. There is a widespread view that there has been a 'global expansion of judicial power', to use the title of one important collection (Tate and Vallinder 1995). Perhaps there has been, and perhaps judicial leadership has played some small role in that expansion. External political conditions set the parameters within which constitutional courts and their leaders have the opportunity to play an independent role in national politics. There may be as well a modest trend worldwide in the direction of greater judicial independence, and again the judges themselves may have played a small role. Yet, it is worth noting that judges in the United States have not achieved – or sought – the kinds of independence discussed in this chapter. Most judges in the United States are elected (in the state judicial systems), and the process of appointment and promotion in the national judicial system is increasingly politicized. Judicial leadership on constitutional courts, then, appears to be a highly variegated phenomenon.

Political leadership by the judiciary

The classic examples of great judicial leaders are John Marshall and Earl Warren in the United States; a modern example may be Aharon Barak in Israel. They are celebrated because they used the opportunities made available by favourable external circumstances to advance distinctive positions, that is, positions that might not have been taken by other political leaders.

Scholars have begun to identify the conditions under which this sort of leadership is possible. To condense a complex literature (Hirschl 2004), there are several arrays of external circumstances favourable to exercises of judicial leadership: (*a*) *megapolitics*: significant and almost equal divisions among elites, such that whatever the judges do will find support from an important segment of the nation's political leadership; (*b*) *delegations*: divisions within a governing coalition (perhaps threatened by a significant opposition) over one or more constitutional questions that lead the coalition to delegate decision-making authority to the courts in the hope that the courts' decisions will resolve the questions in a way that preserves the coalition's unity (Graber 1993); and (*c*) authoritarian regimes that face external pressures, usually from international financial institutions, to guarantee investment by providing a judiciary that will resolve commercial disputes on the basis of legality rather than the regime's immediate desires (Moustafa 2007). There are in addition, (*d*) failures and limitations in leadership, where judges believed they could lead but for a range of reasons failed in their attempts.

Megapolitics

The government crisis in Pakistan arose when President Pervez Musharraf removed the Constitutional Court's chief justice because he expected the Court to rule that the Constitution prevented him from running for president while he remained head of the nation's armed forces. Ran Hirschl (2004) has shown that this is just one example of judicial intervention in what he calls 'megapolitics' – conflicts over who occupies high political positions. For a US scholar, the Supreme Court's decision determining the outcome of the presidential election of 2000 is of course the central example.

Two features of judicial interventions in megapolitics deserve mention here. First, and perhaps obvious, such interventions can succeed only when the external political circumstances are favourable, and that will be true when the judges' decisions are aligned with the political interests of a substantial segment of politically active society – perhaps not a majority, but certainly a substantial minority. Otherwise the judges' decisions will simply be ignored. Hirschl's evidence is consistent with this observation.

Second, and perhaps more important, judicial intervention in megapolitics ordinarily must take the form of a *legal* ruling. The interventions must rely on accepted modes of legal analysis. This allows the judges to gain support from whatever 'middle' there is in the political dispute, that is, from people who are willing to allow a legal determination to override their political predisposition. Yet, working out an appropriate legal theory may prove difficult. As I discuss below, a court's task leader might do so, but not all courts have such a leader when the megapolitics issue arises, and the conditions for successful task leadership may not exist.

The US Supreme Court's decision in *Bush v. Gore* provides a helpful example (Toobin 2007). As the case developed there were two legal theories available to a majority that wanted to rule in favour of candidate George W. Bush. One relied on an obscure constitutional provision allocating authority to determine the rules for selecting presidential electors to state 'legislatures', which might have been interpreted to place special limits on the judiciary's otherwise available power to interpret statutes to fill gaps. This theory was at least plausible although clearly innovative. The second legal theory relied on the Equal Protection Clause to argue that equality required a higher degree of consistency in counting votes than the system used in Florida provided. This theory was a real innovation and, as the Court itself acknowledged when it adopted the theory, its implications were so unclear that the Court suggested that the decision would have no precedential effect – as indeed it has not. In the end, then, the Court relied on the less persuasive legal theory. The justices felt themselves under quite severe time pressures, which made it difficult for a task leader to develop consensus on a stronger theory. Further, the late Rehnquist Court probably had no task leader on the conservative side. And, finally, the case was so important that it was almost a necessity that leadership in writing an opinion be taken by the chief justice, but Chief Justice Rehnquist was far more interested in processing cases and getting decisions out the door, that is, in being a good administrator of the Court's business, than he was in achieving consensus on the best legal theory. He did draft and issue an opinion working out the stronger legal theory, but he lacked the time and interest in bringing along the two additional justices who would be needed to make the opinion a majority opinion. Instead, he and his colleagues joined an opinion adopting the weaker theory.

It bears noting that judges intervening in megapolitics necessarily find support from a substantial part of the nation's political forces. Their interventions might annoy other political forces, but the existence of political support for the courts' decisions inevitably reduces concerns about the legitimacy of their actions, at least to the extent that the decisions have some plausible support in extant legal materials – a condition that might not have been satisfied in the US presidential election dispute.

Delegations

Politicians cannot always resolve issues important to their constituents. There are two reasons: (*a*) Whatever the politicians do risks electoral damage: choosing one solution may satisfy one set of constituents but drive another away from the politicians' side. Yet, sometimes doing nothing is also damaging. Delegating the issue to someone visibly independent of the politicians may solve their problem. (*b*) Alternatively, politicians may delegate decisions to another institution because they do not have time to resolve the matters themselves: they know what they want, and they expect that the recipient of the delegation will provide it. Candidates for receiving these delegations may vary: specialized commissions, existing administrative agencies, and courts are among the possibilities. When delegations occur, leadership by the recipient institution is almost certain, leadership by individuals within the institution less so.

Much of the work of the US Supreme Court under Earl Warren illustrates the second type of delegation. The Warren Court worked hand-in-glove with the dominant Democratic coalition in Congress and the presidency, wiping off the statute books laws, both national and more important state, that were inconsistent with that coalition's ideology (Powe 2000).

The first type of delegation occurs because the politicians need some decisions but basically do not care what that decision is. Sometimes the delegations are intentional, as politicians self-consciously seek to avoid responsibility for difficult decisions. More often, though, delegations result from what might be called the structural logic of the politicians' problems: given the existence of an array of institutions, politicians end up making some decisions and delegating others.

How can a politician respond to a decision that outrages some constituents but satisfies others? He or she can attack the court, not so much on the merits of its decision but for taking the decision away from the political process. Mark Graber (1993) argues that this describes the response of US politicians to the Supreme Court's abortion decisions. Republicans and some Democrats could 'run against the Court' without taking responsibility for the policy outcome, while leaving that outcome in place to satisfy constituents who agreed with it.

Here too additional research is needed to determine the extent to which politicians in other constitutional systems delegate authority to the courts to ease their own political difficulties. The Canadian system of seeking advisory opinions from the Supreme Court seems well-adapted to serve the delegation function, and certainly the reference on the constitutionality of a unilateral declaration of independence fits the model. I suspect as well that similar references occasionally occur in constitutional systems that give access to the constitutional court to some specified number of members of parliament, although ordinarily that access is sought by members of an opposition party that simply lost out in the legislative vote. Perhaps one could use cases – few, I am sure – in which members of a parliamentary majority invoked the constitutional court's jurisdiction to see how prevalent the delegation phenomenon is.

Authoritarian Regimes

Perhaps surprisingly, authoritarian regimes sometimes establish constitutional courts with some degree of independence. The typical scenario involves international lenders, intergovernmental or private, who are reluctant to invest in the nation without assurances that their investments will be secure against the whims of the nation's authoritarian rulers. An independent constitutional court can provide that assurance.

Strikingly, an independent constitutional court can result in judicial leadership at odds with both the external sources of pressure and the authoritarian regime itself. International lenders may insist on a court that will follow the rule of law, and then may discover that the constitutional court invokes legality against the programmes the lenders foist on the regime (Scheppele 2004). The constitutional court's judges can use their independence to rule against the regime on matters other than finances. In Egypt, for example, a constitutional court whose primary reason for existence was to ensure against expropriations of foreign investment managed to loosen up the electoral system a bit (Moustafa 2007). Of course, exercising this sort of leadership has inherent limits: do too much, and you will find the regime restricting the court's jurisdiction to financial matters only.

Failures and limitations

Not surprisingly the literature focuses on successful exercises of judicial leadership although without distinguishing between the leadership exercised by the constitutional court as an institution and leadership by individual members of constitutional courts. Yet, that focus leaves open the possibility that the outcomes are only seemingly the result of judicial leadership and actually result from some deeper constraints, as yet not fully analysed, on national policy. For that reason it may be worthwhile to pay attention not only to successful leadership but also to failures of leadership. Failures may of course be foreordained. But they do illustrate situations in which at least one important political figure – the judge seeking to lead – believed that there was space open for leadership.

Perhaps the most interesting failure occurred in post-Soviet Russia. After the collapse of the Soviet Union the nation faced serious political questions, including questions about dealing with the Soviet legacy, the territorial integrity of the Russian Federation, and integrating former Communists into the system of governing. The political situation was quite fluid, and neither the national legislature nor the national executive clearly had either the capacity for answering these questions or the legitimacy to ensure that their answers would be accepted. There was, in short, an apparent vacuum of governing authority. Into this seeming vacuum stepped Valery Zorkin, chief justice of the Constitutional Court. Zorkin led his court in several controversial cases, all involving the management of the transition from Soviet to post-Soviet rule. The court invalidated President Boris Yeltsin's decree creating a single ministry out of the prior police and security ministries. It ordered the secessionist area Tatarstan to refrain from holding an independence referendum, which was ignored. It tried to intervene in the dissolution of the former Communist party by ordering Mikhail Gorbachev to testify about the party's affairs, but Gorbachev refused. A year later the court issued a complex ruling in a case arising out of the conflict between Yeltsin and the parliament, allowing a referendum to go forward on terms that might have resolved the conflict. The court's decisions did not, however, answer the question posed by Robert Sharlet among others, 'Who shall govern Russia?' (Sharlet 1993). Then, in 1993 the court issued an opinion after a Yeltsin speech that Zorkin considered 'an attempted coup d'ètat' (Hausmaninger 1995). It found Yeltsin's actions unconstitutional.

Zorkin also acted as a 'judicial politician' (Sharlet 1993) extrajudicially. He negotiated with Yelstin and his principal adversaries in parliament, seeking to work out a solution to the crisis. He made public speeches criticizing Gorbachev, attempting to rally public support for the court and for the new Russian legality, and in general offering the court – and perhaps himself – as the best hope for Russia to manage its way out of its crisis of governing (Hausmaninger 1995). In the 1993 crisis Zorkin, perhaps with legality on his side, opposed Yeltsin and thereby became in effect an ally of the even more authoritarian leaders of parliament.

In the end Zorkin failed, spectacularly. After Yeltsin triumphed over parliament and overcame a real attempted coup d'ètat, Yeltsin simply shut the Constitutional Court down for several years. When it reopened in a new form – with Zorkin still a member – the Court had learned its lesson. It regularly took the central government's side in disputes over the increasing centralization during the 1990s (Epstein, Knight, and Shvetsova 2002).

In retrospect it might seem that Zorkin was doomed to fail. The Russian governing crisis was so severe that, one might think, it could not be managed through the forms of legality. No court, and no judge, one might think, could supply the necessary leadership to get out of the crisis – as might be suggested by the fact that the crisis was resolved by the imposition of an increasingly authoritarian system. Arguably, some degree of authoritarianism was needed to get control over the increasingly out-of-control Russian political and economic system, but authoritarianism sits uneasily with legality and constitutionalism. Yet, this gloomy assessment may be overly deterministic. The Russian political system in the early 1990s was fluid. A talented leader might have been able to push the system's development into more democratic rather than more authoritarian channels, and the experience of democracy achieved incrementally might have led to rather different conditions later in the 1990s. But neither Yeltsin nor – my focus here – Zorkin had the requisite leadership abilities.

Perhaps Zorkin was no more than an inept politician who failed to take advantage of the opportunities made available in a relatively fluid post-Soviet regime. Yet, external conditions not only enable but also constrain judicial leadership. Those conditions sometimes allow a constitutional court to act against the enacted wishes of a current majority. Despite the image associated with the US tradition of judicial review – of a constitutional court regularly standing against contemporary majorities in the service of enduring constitutional values – constitutional courts almost inevitably operate within relatively narrow limits: they cannot go too far outside the bounds of the power delegated them, for example, and they can survive as 'independent' only if their decisions are supported by a substantial segment of the nation – perhaps not a current majority, but almost certainly a substantial minority. Both the fears sometimes expressed about aggressive constitutional courts in nations with long-standing parliamentary traditions and the hopes sometimes lodged in such courts in other nations are typically exaggerated. Constitutional courts can sometimes become leaders in the national political system, but only within limits and only when external political conditions are favourable.

Judicial leadership in developing national policy

Leadership by constitutional courts is of most interest, probably, because it can implicate the development of national policy. Constitutional courts can be participants – sometimes equal participants – in the national governing process. So, for example, US Chief Justices John Marshall and Earl Warren are widely admired because of their contributions to governing. In this aspect, leadership by constitutional courts depends on at least two components on which I focus here: the establishment of a sufficient degree of judicial independence for the constitutional court to be able to make a distinctive contribution to governing, and exercising discretion – within the domain made available by the contours of politics elsewhere in the system – successfully, that is, in a way that makes a distinctive contribution.

Securing judicial independence

The concept of judicial independence is notoriously complex (Burbank and Friedman 2002). It encompasses notions of individual and institutional independence, for example. And it implicates questions about the manner in which judges are appointed and promoted and dismissed and about how their salaries are set, as well as questions about the financing of the judicial system as a whole. An opinion by Canadian Supreme Court Chief Justice Antonio Lamer identifies 'three core characteristics of judicial independence – security of tenure, financial security, and administrative independence' and 'two dimensions of judicial independence... the individual independence of a judge and the institutional or collective independence of the court or tribunal of which that judge is a member' (Reference Regarding the Remuneration of Judges). Many questions about all these aspects of judicial independence are answered with reference to the external political environment. So, for example, recent events in Pakistan appear to have made incursions on judicial independence – the dismissal of the Supreme Court's chief justice by President Pervez Musharraf in anticipation of an unfavourable ruling from the court – key to the crisis there and the electoral success of anti-Musharraf parties. Yet, it seems to me, it would grossly exaggerate the importance of the independent courts to say that the crisis occurred because of incursions on judicial independence. The Musharraf regime was in trouble for reasons other than its actions with respect to the courts, which were probably no more than the catalyst for the crisis.

The Pakistani case, and more generally the matters discussed in the preceding section of this chapter, are ones in which judicial independence is largely exogenous to the courts. In contrast, we can examine cases where judges themselves secure their independence, given external political conditions that provide some space for doing so. I deal with appointment and promotion, salaries, and removal of judges.

Appointment and promotion

Systems of appointment to constitutional courts vary widely. Some, such as the United States, place appointment entirely in the hands of the political branches. Others give politicians some role, but include experts and judges themselves in the appointment process. The Italian Constitution, for example, gives the senior judiciary the power to select one third of the judges on that nation's Constitutional Court. The latter systems open up the possibility that judges will strongly constrain the selection process, thereby increasing their independence.

In Israel the nation's president – a largely ceremonial figure – appoints judges to the high court after receiving a recommendation from the Judges' Nominating Committee. The committee includes the Supreme Court President and two other justices, two cabinet ministers and two additional members of parliament, and two representatives of the national bar association. Neither the politicians nor the judges have a majority position. Traditionally, though, the judges voted en bloc, relying on a prior vote by all the Supreme Court's justices, which required that a president who hoped to dominate the selection process had to persuade his (or her) colleagues, an enterprise that did not always succeed. A recent amendment purports to require that each member of the committee vote independently, though it is hard to see how this requirement can be enforced against at least informal consultations and coordination. In addition, the committee's composition has been changed so that lawyers – judges and bar association appointees – are one vote short of a majority rather than one vote more than a majority.

Even with a majority, the judges' expertise and intensity of interest in who receives an appointment and the fact that the politicians are likely to have more complex agendas than the judges combine to give the judges a great deal of influence. And individual judges can take advantage of the structure to exercise even more direct leadership. According to one report, a tradition has developed 'of making no appointments against the will of [the Committee's] three judicial members' (Levy 2007: 613). Sitting on the Committee because he was president of the Supreme Court, Aharon Barak reportedly exercised a practical veto over nominations, opposing and thereby killing the chances for appointment of candidates who were insufficiently enthusiastic about his programme of judicial activism.

The Supreme Court of India seemingly has achieved even greater independence with respect to appointments. The nation's constitution gives the president the power to appoint the chief justice and the power to appoint associate justices in consultation with the chief justice. The president is, again, largely a figurehead, and effective appointment power rests in the prime minister – or so the constitutional arrangements make it seem. In fact, the justices themselves control the appointment of their successors.

The relationship between the executive and the judiciary in India has regularly been a tense one, with the courts sometimes obstructing executive initiatives and meeting resistance from the executive, and with the courts sometimes capitulating to executive demands that many observers thought inconsistent with the nation's constitution (Austin 1999). The Emergency between 1975 and 1977 was particularly damaging to the judiciary, which gave Indira Gandhi's emergency rule its approval when Gandhi seemed politically strong and then gradually withdrew approval as Gandhi's political strength waned. The result was that the courts seem to become indistinguishable from ordinary political actors. In response, the courts developed a doctrine giving them the power to set aside even constitutional amendments that in their view were inconsistent with the 'basic structure' established by the constitution. Notably, the Indian Supreme Court exercised that power in connection with restrictions on the courts' own jurisdiction.

India is of course a large country, and the central government has often experienced difficulty in ensuring regularity in the administration of the law. Local officials, including judges, are sometimes corrupt, sometimes excessively sympathetic to local concerns. The nation's chief justice serves as the highest bureaucrat in administering the court system. During the 1980s concern about corruption and excessive localism led the executive government to propose that large numbers of judges be transferred from their original homes to other states, to disrupt patterns of corruption and localism. Yet transfers can also be used as a tool of political discipline. The requirement that the executive 'consult' with the judiciary regarding judicial administration served to place some constraints on arbitrariness. But not enough – or at least so thought some judges. They challenged their transfers. At the end of 1981 the Supreme Court 'in the main upheld the government's position' (Austin 1999: 527). For present purposes the most important holding was that the chief justice had to be consulted but that his advice was not binding.

A decade later the result changed. The chief justice, the court held, had 'primacy' in both transfers and appointments. The chief justice could, in effect, veto an appointment or transfer of which he disapproved. For the court system to function, though, it had to have sufficient political support. So, consultation continued, but now on terrain favourable to the judges. Because transfers were indeed sometimes a good idea, some procedure had to be established to regularize them. The procedures were developed by a committee of judges: two from the nation's Supreme Court, two from high courts in the states, and the chief justice of the state involved in the transfer. With respect to appointments, the chief justice is supposed to meet with four senior associate justices and 'recommend' new judges for appointment. The president must accept those recommendations.

The law-in-action differs. In 2008 a scandal broke out when it was discovered that several chief justices had acted on their own, without consulting their colleagues, in appointing a total of more than 300 trial-level judges. And concerns have been expressed that judges appoint their protégés over more qualified candidates. Having created out of judicial doctrine a self-contained judiciary limited only by informal political constraints, the Indian courts may have overplayed their hand. The story of judicial leadership in achieving independence – and then, perhaps, in losing it – is a complex one, of course. What is notable, though, is that the judges have been successful for more than a decade in insulating the judiciary from political interventions.

Salaries

Governments facing difficult fiscal conditions sometimes respond by imposing across-the-board budget cuts. In the United States the salaries of judges on the national courts are protected against reductions by a specific constitutional provision, which has been interpreted to allow prospective salary freezes but not the application of a freeze retroactive to the beginning of a fiscal year (*United States v. Will*).

The Canadian Supreme Court dealt with the question in 1997 (Reference Regarding the Remuneration of Judges). Four provincial governments imposed general salary reductions for all public employees, including judges. Drawing on an 'unwritten norm' of judicial independence, the Court developed an institutional response to the issue of salary reductions. Governments could reduce judicial salaries as part of a general economic programme. Specifically observing that judges were not 'civil servants', the Court required that governments create an independent judicial salary commission 'to depoliticize the process' of reducing judicial salaries, to guarantee that the programme did not constitute an indirect assault on judicial independence. Otherwise the public might get the impression that judges were indeed merely civil servants, especially were all public employees to be subject to identical salary reductions. The commission would make non-binding recommendations to the legislature, which could not 'lightly' ignore them. Judges should not negotiate over their salaries, but they could 'make representations' to governments about their salaries. Further, to ensure that judicial salaries would keep up with inflation, the commission would have to meet and make recommendations if too much time passed without an adjustment in judicial salaries.

In the name of depoliticizing the 'relationship between the judiciary and the other branches of government', this highly prescriptive decision requires the creation of a new institution to insulate the courts from the rest of the government. That insulation enhances the ability of courts to play a leadership role in politics. I should note, too, that although the Canadian Charter seems to anticipate such a role for the courts by establishing what Canadian constitutional scholars call a system of dialogic judicial review (Hogg and Bushell 1997), the extent to which dialogue actually occurs is strongly contested (Osgoode Hall Law Journal 2007). An insulated judiciary in a monologic system, one with what I call 'strong judicial review', is well-positioned to become a politically significant actor, at least if the judges are good politicians.

Several years later the same court dealt with a problem at the border between salary reduction and removal from office (*Mackin v. New Brunswick*). The province of New Brunswick allowed judges to retire and receive a full pension, to continue to sit as full-time judges, or to serve as 'supernumerary' judges, receiving full salaries and benefits but reducing their caseloads to about 40 per cent of the standard caseload. (The United States has a similar system for what are called 'senior judges' on the national courts.) After operating this system for just short of a decade, the province changed course. It abolished the position of supernumerary judge and replaced it with a system in which a panel of retired judges could be convened, paid on a *per diem* basis, to handle cases that the full-time judges were unable to deal with. The province's reason was fiscal: it would be cheaper to operate the new system than the old one.

The Canadian Supreme Court again used the concept of 'judicial independence' to invalidate the abolition of the position of supernumerary judge, with respect to judges who had chosen to become such judges rather than retire or remain as full-time judges. (Formally, the decision simply appears to 'grandparent' sitting supernumerary judges while allowing the new panel system to operate. It is unclear to me whether this is sustainable as a practical matter, or whether, once the supernumerary judges return, the panel system will wither away.) The ability to serve as a supernumerary judge provided an economic benefit in the form of a reduced workload to judges who would otherwise either continue to serve full-time or retire. Eliminating that benefit amounted to an effective reduction in salary, which triggered the requirement of some objective assessment by an independent commission.

Removal

Political officials sometimes try to remove judges from their offices. As mentioned earlier, they sometimes fail because of politics. (In addition to the Pakistani example, one might also cite the failure of Jeffersonians to remove Justice Samuel Chase from his position because they disagreed with some of his actions as a judge; the Senate acquitted Chase of the charges when a Jeffersonian refused to vote with his party on the question.)

Of interest here, sometimes these removal attempts fail because of actions by the judges themselves to defend their independence. Recent examples come from the Czech Republic, although parallel issues have arisen elsewhere. The problem is created by giving sitting judges administrative as well as judicial responsibilities. As administrators, judges deal with budgets, court personnel, salaries, and the like. The judges who administer the courts are typically given honorific titles (in the Czech Republic, president and vice-president of the court), and can be appointed as administrators separately from their appointment as judges. In some constitutional systems, judicial administration is in the hands of the judges themselves, but in systems following older models administration is controlled by an executive ministry such as, in the Czech Republic, the Department of Justice.

Suppose the ministry wants to remove a judge from an administrative position. Formally, in the Czech Republic the ministry has that power (Bobek 2008). The Czech courts have considered several cases involving what they concluded were arbitrary removals. In one they invoked ordinary principles of administrative law to hold that the minister cannot remove a judge from his or her administrative position without providing an adequate statement of reasons (and that the mere assertion that the judge had failed 'to prevent delays' in a single pending case was inadequate).

Then, in 2006 the Czech Republic's president sent a letter to the chief justice of the Supreme Court purporting to remove her from that position. She filed a constitutional complaint with the Constitutional Court challenging her removal. The Court relied on principles of judicial independence in holding that the president could not remove her as chief justice. Michel Bobek, who discusses these cases, notes that legislative efforts to regularize judicial administration had failed, but that statutes 'to strengthen the supervision and the responsibility of the judges and judicial officials... [were] swiftly approved' (Bobek 2008). He describes the courts' decisions as going 'in the very opposite direction', limiting executive and legislative discretion: 'The political power... refuses to share its entrenched competences with respect to the vital areas of judicial administration. The (uncoordinated) reaction from part of the judiciary is to make this unfettered discretion... itself subject to judicial review'. He suggests that the desirable solution would be for the legislature to allow 'some sort of judicial self-administration'.

Conclusion: implications for judicial independence

These examples illustrate some of the ways in which judges can use their positions to secure the conditions under which they can become independent actors in the nation's political system. Additional research, and many more examples, would be needed to begin to sketch the external political conditions that enable this sort of judicial self-promotion or self-defence. The examples suggest a few considerations: some degree of prior legitimacy in the courts, perhaps resulting from the accretion of prior uncontroversial decisions that came to seem correct, and the absence of some dominating political force or party in the political branches. But more research is needed to flesh out these suggestions and to generate more substantial hypotheses.

Leadership within the judicial system

Leadership within a multimember court

A small literature in US political science distinguishes between the 'task' and 'social' leadership functions in a multimember court (Danelski 1961).[1] The task leader is the intellectual leader on the court, the judge who articulates the principles with which most of his or her colleagues can agree, across a reasonably large number of cases. The social leader is the judge who smoothes over personal conflicts within the court, who provides the explanations – more emotional than intellectual – to keep those who dissent (perhaps passionately) in one or many cases committed to the court's overall good functioning.

These two forms of leadership need not be found in the same judge. The classic example in the US literature is the Warren Court. There Earl Warren was the social leader, William J. Brennan the task leader. Nor need there be either a social or a task leader. Warren Burger, for example, was a notably ineffective social leader on the US Supreme Court, and it seems that, in part because of reasonably strong ideological differences among the justices, which intensified over time, no other judge sought to act as a social leader. His successor William Rehnquist was not the intellectual leader of the conservatives on the Supreme Court, but he was the Court's social leader. Notably, he managed to keep the Court working harmoniously even in the face of the acerbic written opinions of Justice Antonin Scalia, which might under other leaders have fractured personal relations on the Court.

Nor, finally, need task leadership flow from formal rules. The US Supreme Court's internal norms are that the chief justice has the power to 'assign' opinions when he is in the majority; that is, the chief justice can ask an associate justice to write an opinion, and the associate justice will agree unless the justice can offer extremely strong reasons why he or she should not get the assignment. (When the chief justice is in the minority, the senior associate justice in the majority has the same assignment power.) Similar, though weaker, norms apply to assignments of the principal dissent when there is one. For the central decisions on the Warren Court, Chief Justice Warren was in the majority. He regularly exercised his assignment power to delegate the writing of difficult opinions for Justice Brennan. That is probably best understood as exercising social leadership in the service of task leadership.

We know less about the division of task and social leadership on other constitutional courts, largely because distinguishing between the two forms of leadership requires access to information that has been hard to come by. Only recently for example has a biography of a Canadian Supreme Court justice appeared that relied on material from inside the court (Sharpe and Roach 2003), and even there the authors felt obliged to provide a rather apologetic explanation for their 'breach' of court confidentiality. Similarly, a study of the Australian High Court in the 1990s asserts that the perhaps ephemeral transformation of constitutional law by that court resulted from the 'sheer force of Chief Justice [Anthony] Mason's intellect and leadership' (Pierce 2006: 208), but provides no details on how Mason actually led the court.

A recent brief study by Peter Quint of the German Constitutional Court is suggestive about task and social leadership there (Quint 2006). Quint emphasizes several structural features of that Court: until 1970 separate dissenting opinions were prohibited, and opinions are assigned bureaucratically to a specific judge who specializes in dealing with cases raising specific constitutional issues. Quint notes that close observers of the Court have identified individual judges who acted as mediators, encouraging colleagues to suppress dissents or to write opinions accommodating the concerns of those who would otherwise dissent. According to Donald Kommers, for example, the Constitutional Court's first president, Hermann Höpker-Aschoff, had a 'genius' for mediation of this sort (Kommers 1976: 189, as quoted in Quint 2006: 1861).

Task leadership can of course be consequential, at least when the constitutional court has a significant role in the nation's overall political system. Task leadership may be conditioned by such things as the court's voting rules. For example, it might be more difficult in a court with a tradition of so-called seriatim opinions, in which each judge delivers his or her own opinion before or after consulting colleagues, and easier in a court with a tradition against expressing dissenting votes. It might be easier as well when the court has some significant ability to control its own docket by deciding which cases to hear (Pierce 2006).

Whether social leadership matters is, I think, an open question. Perhaps a constitutional court's smooth operation internally can sometimes have some effects on its external influence. It is sometimes asserted, though I think without much supporting evidence, that decisions by a highly fractured Court in the United States – decisions with numerous separate concurring and dissenting opinions – are more likely to provoke critical comment and less likely to have enduring effects than decisions by a more unified Court. That is one reason Chief Justice John Roberts asserted early in his tenure that he would work at getting the Court to be more unified (Rosen 2007). A judge – the Court's task leader – might of course overcome objections by sheer force of intellect and reason. More likely, though, achieving unanimity or something close to it is a job for a court's social leader.

It is worth noting the possibility that leadership within the constitutional court might lead to other political roles. In Israel and the United States, for example, judges have been chosen to lead important commissions of inquiry, because politicians hope that the commissions' reports will gain special force from the judges' prestige. Less common, but historically important in the United States at least, constitutional court judges sometimes aspire to other elective office, including the presidency (in nations where the position is not merely honorific).

Leadership of the judicial system

Constitutional courts and their leaders sometimes sit at the top of a nation's judicial hierarchy, as in Japan and, with respect to the national courts but not the state courts, in the United States. Constitutional courts on the Kelsenian model typically do not. They sit apart from the ordinary judicial hierarchy of what I will here call the 'ordinary' courts, because they are thought to engage in a kind of reasoning that mixes legal and political analysis in a way different from the way the ordinary courts reason. Such constitutional courts nonetheless must also solve coordination problems, but without the resources a bureaucratically superior court has.

Consider first an integrated judicial hierarchy headed by a constitutional court. Typically the constitutional court's official head – chief justice or president – will be the official head of the national judicial bureaucracy. I doubt that there is anything particularly special about the way in which such an official exercises leadership. The courts here are an ordinary bureaucracy, and their head has most of a manager's usual tools to keep the bureaucracy functioning well and in accordance with the directives of the highest court. The head of the judiciary must respect ordinary judges' independence, of course, but that seems to me no different from the constraints modern civil service systems place on high bureaucrats. Notably, in Japan there seems to be strong evidence that the highest court uses such tools as denials of salary increases and, more important, assignment to desirable or undesirable posts as techniques of bureaucratic discipline within a system that nominally respects judicial independence (Ramseyer 1994).

One aspect of bureaucratic leadership by a constitutional court judge is worth noting. Promotion to the leadership position is unlikely to depend on a candidate's exhibition of the bureaucrat's managerial skills. A judge selected because of his or her ideology, for example, will only by chance be a good manager, as the example in the United States of Warren Burger again demonstrates. Perhaps those who aspire to the constitutional court will train themselves in management skills. But the more rationalized the promotion process, the less sensible that investment of time will be. Specifically, if promotion to the constitutional court depends largely on seniority, as it does in many systems in which the constitutional court is hierarchically superior to the ordinary courts, a large number of judges may be eligible for each vacancy, and each is likely to be relatively senior, with a relatively short time to serve on the constitutional court before mandatory retirement rules terminate the judge's tenure. Under these circumstances few judges would rationally spend much time developing administrative skills.

Bureaucracy is one method of coordinating the courts. That method is unavailable when the constitutional court is conceptualized as separate from the ordinary courts, administering a constitution that is supreme over all the courts. The problem for the constitutional court then is to ensure that *its* interpretations of the constitution prevail over contrary interpretations generated in the ordinary courts. Dealing with this problem has caused 'battles of the courts' in numerous constitutional systems (Burnham and Trochev 2007; Tushnet 2008). The battles take several forms, the details of which are often quite technical. The general solution is clear, though. The constitutional court must assert its *authority* to supervise every decision by an ordinary court, but it must refrain from actually doing so as a routine matter. The solution, then, places significant limits on the constitutional court's power to lead the judicial system as a whole.

This solution requires the constitutional court to yield in practice some authority that it asserts in theory it has. Not every constitutional court judge will see this as consistent with the judge's understanding of his or her position in the nation's government. And we can expect the battles of the courts to be more intense and longer lasting when a constitutional court lacks a leader who can convince his or her colleagues that the solutions are best for the constitutional system as a whole. Or, put another way, it is an interesting topic for future research to determine how long the battles of the courts lasted in different constitutional systems, how they were resolved, and – importantly for the present topic – who came up with the solution and got both the constitutional court and the ordinary courts to accept it.

Judicial leadership: conclusions

As noted at the outset, it is common today to speak of a global expansion of judicial power. And, relative to judicial power as of the end of the Second World War, such an expansion clearly has occurred. Constitutional courts have proliferated because in general they are useful elements of modern constitutional design. They can do things that other organs of government might find it difficult to do. They can help consolidate democracy, for example, by articulating the importance of *limiting* as well as empowering government. Politicians might find it difficult to explain to their constituents why they refuse to do what the voters want, but judges can point to the constitution.

Yet, the significance of constitutional courts can be exaggerated. Successful constitutional courts are independent of the nation's other political leaders, but not too independent. Some degree of independence is sustained by the judges' own efforts, with respect to salaries and removal, for example. But the more important contributions to judicial independence, and therefore to judicial leadership, come from the external political circumstances in which the courts find themselves.

Notes

1. Steamer (1986: 18–28), distinguishes similarly but less helpfully between the intellectual and personal leadership roles, focusing exclusively on the office of chief justice, and so is inattentive to the possibility that other justices might perform one or both of those roles.

Bibliography

Austin, G., *Working a Democratic Constitution: The Indian Experience* (New Delhi: Oxford University Press, 1999).

Bobek, M., 'The Administration of Courts in the Czech Republic: In Search of the Constitutional Balance', (2008), unpublished manuscript.

Burbank, S. and Friedman, B., *Judicial Independence at the Crossroads: An Interdisciplinary Approach* (Thousand Oaks, CA: Sage Publications, 2002).

Burnham, W. and Trochev, A., 'Russia's War between the Courts: The Struggle over the Jurisdictional Boundary between the Constitutional Court and Regular Courts', *American Journal of Comparative Law*, 55/3 (2007), 381–452.

Danelski, D., 'The Influence of the Chief Justice in the Decisional Process', in W. F. Murphy and C. H. Pritchett (eds.), *Courts, Judges, and Politics: An Introduction to the Judicial Process* (New York: Random House, 1961), 497–508.

Epstein, L., Knight, J., and Shvetsova, O., 'The Role of Constitutional Courts in the Establishment and Maintenance of Democratic Systems of Government', *Law and Society Review*, 35/1 (2002), 117–64.

Graber, M., 'The Nonmajoritarian Difficulty: Legislative Deference to the Judiciary', *Studies in American Political Development*, 7/1 (1993), 35–73.

Hausmaninger, H., 'Towards a "New" Russian Constitutional Court', *Cornell International Law Journal*, 28/2 (1995), 349–86.

Hirschl, R., *Towards Juristocracy: The Origins and Consequences of the New Constitutionalism* (Cambridge: Harvard University Press, 2004).

Hogg, P. and Bushell, A., 'The *Charter* Dialogue Between Courts and Legislatures (Or Perhaps The *Charter of Rights* Isn't Such a Bad Thing After All)', *Osgoode Hall Law Journal*, 35/1 (1997), 75–124.

Kommers, D., *Judicial Politics in West Germany: A Study of the Federal Constitutional Court* (Beverly Hills, CA: Sage Publications, 1976).

Levy, R., 'Judicial Selection Reform in Comparative Context', *University of British Columbia Law Review*, 40/2 (2007), 591–628.

Moustafa, T., *The Struggle for Constitutional Power: Law, Politics, and Economic Development in Egypt* (New York: Cambridge University Press, 2007).

Pierce, J. L., *Inside the Mason Court Revolution: The High Court of Australia Transformed* (Durham, North Carolina: Carolina Academic Press, 2006).

Powe, L. A., *The Warren Court and American Politics* (Cambridge: Harvard University Press, 2000).

Osgoode Hall Law Journal, Symposium: 'Charter Dialogue: Ten Years Later', *Osgoode Hall Law Journal*, 45/1 (2007), 1–202.

Quint, P. E., 'Leading a Constitutional Court: Perspectives from the Federal Republic of Germany', *University of Pennsylvania Law Review*, 154/6 (2006), 1853–78.

Ramseyer, J. M., 'The Puzzling (In)Dependence of Courts: A Comparative Approach', *Journal of Legal Studies*, 23/2 (1994), 721–47.

Rosen, J., *The Supreme Court: The Personalities and Rivalries that Defined America* (New York: Times Books, 2007).

Scheppele, K. L., 'A Realpolitik Defense of Social Rights', *University of Texas Law Review*, 82/7 (2004), 1921–61.

Sharlet, R., 'Chief Justice as Judicial Politician', *East European Constitutional Review*, 2/2 Spring (1993), 32–7.
Sharpe, R. E. and Roach K., *Brian Dickson: A Judge's Journey* (Toronto: University of Toronto Press, 2003).
Steamer, R. J., *Chief Justice: Leadership and the Supreme Court* (Columbia: University of South Carolina Press, 1986).
Tate, C. N. and Vallinder, T., *The Global Expansion of Judicial Power* (New York: New York University Press, 1995).
Toobin, J., *The Nine: Inside the Secret World of the Supreme Court* (New York: Doubleday, 2007).
Tushnet, M., *Weak Courts, Strong Rights: Judicial Review and Social Welfare Rights in Comparative Constitutional Law* (Princeton: Princeton University Press, 2008).

Cases

Mackin v. New Brunswick, [2002] 1 S. C. R. 405 (Supreme Court of Canada).
Reference Regarding the Remuneration of Judges, [1997] S. C. R. 3 (Supreme Court of Canada).
United States v. Will, 449 US 200 (1980).

Chapter 9

Leadership in News Institutions

Michael Schudson

Introduction

Journalism, at its democratic best, serves to hold government accountable by making its actions (or inactions) visible to a broad public. When it is not an agency of the government or largely controlled by the government – when, that is, it operates in a liberal democracy – it is an agent in the dispersal of democratic power. Democratic news media claim to hold government accountable to the public and to the laws and other established norms of the society. Sometimes they do exactly that, often enough to make plausible their boast of being democracy's guardian. At least occasionally they offer criticism of government and revelations of where government actions fall short of accepted legal, constitutional, and moral norms. They provide the central platform of the 'public sphere', a realm in which people come together to speak freely about public issues, without fear of reprisal.

The democratic function of the news media is too complex a question to discuss in detail here (and I have discussed it elsewhere; Schudson 2008). But, in a (long) sentence, the news media in a democracy play multiple civic roles: providing the public information relevant to their decisions as voters and their participation as citizens; keeping watch on political power by investing in pertinent investigations; analysing and interpreting complex phenomena for both the lay and professional public; providing a public forum for political discussion; mobilizing viewers and readers for civic participation; and offering citizens a portrait of their neighbours at home and around the world so that they can better understand people different from themselves.

When media take on these tasks and perform them well, they provide a locus of authority outside formal governmental structures and sometimes critical of government. This makes them necessarily agents of the dispersal of power. Privately owned media, unlike public broadcasting systems, have little or no formal responsibility, neither to a voting public nor to governing boards responsible to a legislature. Their organizational form is corporate, not democratic, and generally they are hierarchical rather than collegial in operation, even if most newsrooms offer a shirtsleeve informality that is unusual among large corporations. But private as these organizations usually are, their role in democracy is indispensable and leadership of them also deserves attention. In this chapter I examine a celebrated crisis of leadership at the most important newspaper in the United States, the *New York Times*. I do not presume that the *Times* is typical, but it is a paper that takes its democratic responsibility with the utmost seriousness, and is important enough in its own right to merit close scrutiny. It therefore serves as an instructive example of how the internal leadership of a major news organization connects with its external leadership function.

The neglected topic of leadership in news organizations

Adequate performance of the democratic watchdog role – through bold public reminders that even highly placed office-holders should not and cannot act without reference to public opinion, well recognized social norms and the legitimate jurisdiction of other agencies of government – is not invariably the outcome of media attention to government. In fact, most media scholars who write about news organizations in the United States – and the literature on other liberal democracies is similar – think that when journalists cover government they do much more following than leading, reinforcing rather than dispersing the authority of government officials. In the United States, no one has greater access to the media than the president, no one receives more deference, and no one has so many tools for procuring space in newspapers and time on television and radio. Although popular wisdom attributes great independent power to the news media, journalists typically give greatest play to the views of top government officials. Study after study validates the proposition that news organizations are deeply dependent on currying favour with top government officials and that their dependence on these sources means they will mimic or 'index' the range of opinion already present in elite circles.[1]

But neither reinforcement of the authority of concentrated pockets of power nor the periodic challenges to such power happen automatically in the media. Choices of what to cover in the news and decisions about how to present or 'frame' what is covered are contested inside news organizations, and the outcomes of these internal conflicts are variable. Among the factors that make a difference in these decisions is the character of leadership in the news organizations. As in other realms of life, leadership matters. Some editors and publishers lead well and others not so well, some do better and some do worse, some protect the integrity of the journalism process well and others poorly from the influence of political and economic elites. Powerful media czars are widely recognized – the press lords, the Rupert Murdochs who seem to sit astride the globe. Obsessive megalomaniacs of the Charles Foster Kane/ William Randolph Hearst sort are legendary.

Still, academic literature on journalism essentially ignores leadership. The central questions in research on journalism concern how effective or ineffective the news product is in promoting democratic self-government – by informing citizens or failing to do so, mobilizing citizens for participation or demobilizing them through cynicism about politics or through distracting them with celebrity news and sensationalism, and offering an aggressive, fearsome presence that keeps politicians anxious not to misbehave or a timid presence that lets politicians know they will not be held to account. Studies that seek to directly gauge how publishers manage resources to keep their news organizations doing good work or how editors and producers manage people to maintain morale, focus, and professional quality are rare. There is very little work on the quality of the organizational environment in newsrooms and almost none on how editors and publishers effect change or stimulate improved output from their employees.

Mainstream academic literature focuses either on large structural conditions for the production and distribution of news – public versus private ownership, for instance, or the degree of concentration of ownership in news industries; or it focuses on the relations between reporters and the officials who are their primary sources, the conventions of the newsroom, the competition and cooperation within a newsroom and across news organizations for news gathering. There is little to suggest that editors, publishers, or others who exercise authority in news organizations make a long-term difference in news judgements, although there are occasional stories of editorial heroism that suggest that, when the chips are down, a publisher may make all the difference in the world. Thus *New York Times* publisher Arthur Sulzberger, Sr wins praise for backing his Vietnam reporters when President John F. Kennedy pointedly suggested to him that they were getting the story wrong, and Katherine Graham, publisher of the *Washington Post* from 1963 to 1979, gets credit for backing her editor in the paper's aggressive pursuit of the Watergate story when few other news organizations showed much interest in Watergate. But overall the academic literature has produced no systematic work on how owners direct or guide their editorial staff or their businesses. Much that one might investigate has never been taken up. What, for instance, is the importance of the relationship between a newspaper publisher and the executive editor he or she appoints? No one will 'be a good editor if he doesn't have a good owner', former *Washington Post* Executive Editor Ben Bradlee has said (Coffey 2007: 11). But is there a single academic article that examines this relationship? There is none that I am aware of.

And yet, everyone assumes that leadership makes a difference. Even people inside an organization are inconsistent on this, sometimes judging good leadership to be essential and sometimes finding it of only incidental significance. This is illustrated in the comic finding of a classic article by James Bettman and Barton Weitz who examined causal reasoning in the annual reports of business corporations. They found that reports issued after a profitable year frequently attributed economic success to the wise decisions of executives at the company – in other words, leadership; reports at the end of a year of decline regularly attributed losses or failures to unavoidable external conditions (Bettman and Weitz 1983).

Some literature assumes leadership in news organizations to be important and therefore finds it interesting. This is the historical and biographical literature on the great publishers of the past – the Benjamin Franklins, Horace Greeleys, Joseph Pulitzers, and William Randolph Hearsts. The less popularly celebrated Adolph Ochs at the *New York Times* (Ochs was not very colourful, just very, very good at what he did) or Eugene Meyer at the *Washington Post* (about whom there is only a tiny historical literature because the *Post* was a paper of modest influence until the late 1960s) or William Paley at CBS are also important. But just what did they do? What was the strength or weakness, efficacy or inefficacy of their labours and their styles of leadership? Scholars have not attended to the quality of these people as leaders in their organizations or leaders of journalism beyond their organizations.

News organizations face unusual leadership problems. They are often run by publishers with little or no management experience and often no journalism experience. They govern organizations that are sharply divided between the 'news' side and the 'business' side and, very often, only the publisher has an organization-wide perspective on the operation as a whole. The two sides of the house have different cultures: people on the business side like PowerPoint, while people on the editorial side roll their eyes and are immediately turned off by PowerPoint presentations, not to mention any talk of 'metrics'.[2] The executive editor and the senior business manager head different sub-organizations that may share general goals but, on a daily basis, the two subunits distrust each other. News organizations have typically had few incentives for innovation, few internal structures to foster innovation, and, through fear of making mistakes, little support for the risk-taking that some other organizations seek to foster. Journalists – according to journalists – are typically cautious and conservative when it comes to understandings of their own work lives. There is little sense of intentional organizational change built into news operations. One editor I spoke to said that news organizations as organizations are 'pathetic – every newspaper has a different system for printing your mother's obituary'. In other words, there is rarely a self-conscious culture of growth and change in news organizations, little in the way of formal reviews and institutional arrangements for taking stock, setting goals, or developing knowledge of 'best practices' elsewhere in the business.

At present, however, when everyone in the news business recognizes that the digital era places new pressures on conventional news-gathering, there is a desire for visionary leadership and new likelihood that such leadership will come from the parts of the firm most closely connected to new technology or even, more likely, from entrepreneurs who have left journalism for new opportunities or were never a part of the news establishment to begin with. Ted Turner had no news experience when he launched CNN. Michael Bloomberg had no news experience when he began Bloomberg News. Many of the pioneers in blogging had never been journalists. This is the context in which news organizations are reconsidering their obligations and capacities to contribute to democracy as they reinvent their business organizations. This is true of non-profit news organizations as well as for-profit companies as all of them compete to reach the public.

Today, with the pressures of technological change, media executives are 'forced to be visionary', as one news executive put it, they are obliged to 'retrofit the newspaper for the future'. But it is very hard to drag people out of their comfort zones. Visionary leadership is required but there will necessarily be collateral damage, particularly to people who cannot seem to adapt to the new ways. Such leadership must nevertheless rise to the challenge of achieving multiple and often conflicting goals, in particular, both improving democracy and maintaining a level of profitability to guarantee the resources that make 'improving democracy' possible.

This is the problem of news leadership that I want to ponder here, though it is in fact one that relatively few major news organizations around the world face. Quite simply, most news organizations, online, radio, television, and print, do not invest heavily in news gathering. They especially do not do much to assign reporters to topics that are not already on the agenda of leading local or national politicians. It is in this sense that the academy's disdain for the work of journalism can be justified – most journalism most of the time is responsive to cues from politicians. It takes resources, expertise, and imagination to be ahead of the game, and those few news organizations that have a vision of what matters in the world that is not slavishly tied to what is already on the agenda of the nation's president or prime minister are an inestimable resource for democracy. Some organizations have the resources but not the vision – think of the large and until very recently astonishingly profitable regional newspapers and local television stations in the United States; others have a vision focused on democratic self-government but very limited resources – think of some of the more enterprising blogs or the stalwart political weekly magazines. The analysis of leadership at the *New York Times* that follows is relevant because the *Times* is one of the most distinguished newspapers in the world and one of the few news organisations with both resources and vision, commitment both to profits and to the public trust.

Leadership crisis at the New York Times

In 2001, when Howell Raines was named executive editor of the *New York Times*, he had thought about leadership a good deal. So had Arthur Sulzberger Jr, the publisher of the *Times* and the person responsible for appointing Raines to his post. Raines saw leadership as a matter of control, energy, and focus towards a determinate goal. It was no accident that he looked to a football coach as his role model for leadership in a newsroom and quoted University of Alabama coach 'Bear Bryant' all the time. But the football coach, of course, operates with a marvellously simplified leadership task: there is essentially perfect consensus on what the goal is – to win the game. Of course, there are trade-offs between winning *this* game and winning the season championship; there are trade-offs between winning the season championship and building a team that will be a strong contender for the championship over a period of years. Still, it is much easier to know what the football coach's mission is than to identify the goal of a newspaper or television news operation. A minimal goal is to stay in business. For profit-making organizations, pleasing shareholders is another goal. But in newspapers like the *New York Times*, it is equally a goal, taken very seriously from the publisher down to the newly hired reporter, to serve the public and to uphold the cause of freedom of information in a democracy. However, there is no blueprint on how to balance these sometimes conflicting goals nor, on the 'serving the public' side, any metric by which to measure effectiveness.

Raines became executive editor of the *New York Times* on 5 September 2001 after having worked for the paper since 1978. Born in Birmingham Alabama in 1943, he grew up in the South, attended Birmingham-Southern College and after, while trying to launch a career writing fiction, he earned his living in journalism, working at a number of different papers, including the highly regarded *Atlanta Constitution* and *St Petersburg Times*. At the *New York Times*, he was the Atlanta-based national correspondent and then bureau chief, national political correspondent and White House correspondent, London bureau chief, Washington bureau chief, and from 1993 until he became executive editor, editorial page editor. He thus was very experienced and knew the *Times* well. Even so, he had never worked in the New York newsroom, the heart of the paper.

But he certainly had ideas about it – and they were critical. The *Times*, he wrote in his 2006 memoir, 'liked to wear its dullness like a merit badge'. According to Raines, 'The prevailing creed in the newsroom was that any effort to improve the paper in any way other than cosmetically was "un-*Times*ian".' The paper practised 'the journalism of tireless repetition' (Raines 2006: 31).

Elsewhere in his reflections, Raines is more positive in assessing the *Times*. He wrote about his 'almost religious sense of mission about the *Times* as an institution' (Raines 2006: 36). In his view, 'Whatever its flaws, the *Times* best embodied the kind of journalism that is essential to the future of the American nation' (Raines 2006: 36). What he fervently admired were the paper's 'ideals and superior resources', but it lacked 'energy and creativity' and in 2001 he decided to see what he could do to inject these values into the newsroom (Raines 2006: 187). The *Times* at that point, in his judgement, had 'hit a ceiling in quality, variety and vivacity'. It simply was no longer possible to prosper 'by providing a stenographic record of government-certified news events' (Raines 2006: 187). In a metaphor he made familiar, he wanted to quicken the paper's metabolism.

But how? By identifying with the football coach, Raines made a fundamental error. He assumed that competitive excellence according to the existing rules of the game was all that anybody needed. For him, people who disagreed with him were just not working hard enough, they were just not committed enough to excellence in journalism. To Raines, leadership meant motivating his staff to greater enterprise and energy; he did not see that there might be legitimate disagreements about how energy and enterprise should be deployed.

The football coach metaphor assumes total clarity and consensus on organizational goals that is not possible in news organizations. The football coach model tripped up Raines in another way, too: a college football coach or even a professional football coach is likely to be far more experienced at the game and likely also to be 20 or 30 years older than any player on the team. Coaching is invariably paternalistic – and in an arena where paternalism is accepted as legitimate. Players may disagree with the coach's style or strategy but they are not in any position to say so. In contrast, a newspaper's executive editor can be paternalistic only at considerable peril. Some of the people executive editors supervise may be older than they are or more experienced in one or another part of journalism. Veteran employees expect a degree of deference and they anticipate some serious consultation and listening. It is not simply that it is good policy for leaders to listen; it is that not-listening in an organizational unit where employees may outrank the boss in maturity and experience will cause resentment, and a lot of not-listening over time will weaken morale and even lead to rebellion, as was the case at the *New York Times*.

'Coach Bryant', Raines told reporter Ken Auletta, 'was a very influential figure for any student of leadership... When Coach Bryant walked onto a football field, everybody in that stadium knew that football would be played here today' (Auletta 2003: 5). For Raines, nothing was more important than single-mindedness – one goal, one focus, one clearly identified objective. Raines cited Bear Bryant often enough to have made his football references a part of his own self-caricature. When he gave a speech to the staff after the *Times* won an unprecedented number of Pulitzer prizes for coverage of 9/11, he acknowledged that one colleague had urged him to ban all sports metaphors from his remarks. Raines went on, 'Whenever anyone congratulated

Coach Bryant', – and the anticipated laughter followed – 'on winning a game, he always said the same thing: "I didn't play a single down. The team won the game"'. Raines lifted a glass to the newsroom in an uncharacteristic moment of humility and of recognition of a team effort.

But there is a false note in this apparently gracious remark. Remember that when Osama bin Laden's zealots hijacked the planes and flew them into the World Trade Centers and the Pentagon, Raines had been executive editor for less than a week. Surely he showed leadership and raw energy in pressing his staff to put everything into their coverage, but what had he taught them? What guidance had he provided? What had he done to mould his team into a crack outfit? Nothing. He had inherited a superb group of journalists who would have won a bundle of prizes for their coverage if the attack had come the week before Raines became editor rather than the week after.

Raines became editor 5 September 2001, and he was forced to resign 3 June 2003. What went wrong?

Raines' aim to wed energy and creativity to the newspaper's impressive resources and admirable ideals seems a fair enough objective for a new editor – except that Raines seemed to communicate (and his memoir still expresses this some years later) that he was the only one at the paper who understood energy and creativity and that little of it was to be found in the newsroom as it existed. His message was that Howell knew best and that everybody else, apart from a few favourites, was too dull, too drab, too conventional, and too bound to the past. He believed that the *Times* was culturally allergic to creativity and judged leadership to mean posing a direct threat to 'the journalism of tireless repetition' he deplored.

Raines might have learned something from his own boss, publisher Arthur Sulzberger Jr. On 11 September 2001, less than a week after becoming executive editor, Raines decided to eliminate all advertising from the 'A' section of the paper to give coverage of the terrorist attack undivided attention. That was certainly an act of leadership on Raines' part, in fact his moment of truth, and Sulzberger acknowledged it by doing nothing. Raines recalled that he had not felt a need to consult with Sulzberger or the president of the company, Janet Robinson, because he was absolutely sure that 'the publisher would throw out a half million dollars in ads to bring our kind of journalism to this massive and traumatic story'.

He was correct. But how did he know? How could he be so sure that his publisher would back him up? How had Sulzberger and his predecessors communicated to the editorial staff that, serious as they were at the *New York Times* about making profits, this was only in the context of commitment to a news organization dedicated to journalism of the highest order? The 'core purpose of The *New York Times* Company', Arthur Sulzberger has said, is to 'enhance society by creating, collecting and distributing high-quality news, information and entertainment' (Coffey 2007: 18).

On 11 September, Raines was in his element, the newspaper on a game day, on a wartime footing, throwing everything into an assault on what was obviously the world's top story of the year, the decade, perhaps the generation. The war was not against bin Laden. The war was against any news organization that dared to compete with the *Times* in covering the story. This was a 'journalistic contest', Raines said. He wanted to put everything into it. 'If I'm in a gunfight, I don't want to die with any bullets in my pistol. I want to shoot every one.' Shoot whom? Rivals on the field – the *Wall Street Journal* or the *Washington Post* or CNN or CBS, anyone else seeking to get the story.

Surely there was much to admire in Howell Raines. He had 'an ability to see around corners, an instinct for the real story', writes Ken Auletta (Auletta 2003: 29). He had energy, focus, decisiveness. Sulzberger said, 'There's a relentlessness about Howell that I admire' (Auletta 2003: 23). But his weaknesses came from that same self-assurance and doggedness. It came from favouring an inside group of buddies and favourites. It came from insisting on his own position, failing to listen well, and pushing other editors to grow fearful of confronting him. Raines was powerful enough to succeed in 'imposing his will on a great institution', as Auletta wrote (Auletta 2003: 60). But if this was success, it was also failure, because the institution was made up of human beings of character, quality, experience, and competence who resented a leader who did not take them seriously.

Perhaps Sulzberger should have known better. His father had also appointed a very strong-willed editor sure of his own instincts, Abe Rosenthal. Rosenthal, according to his successor Max Frankel, left his job after seventeen eventful years 'with a reputation for brilliant, instinctive news judgment coupled with an intimidating, self-centred management style'. He was widely acknowledged to be a brilliant journalist, someone who nonetheless 'displayed his angers and affections in ways that often terrorized subordinates and left him constantly wondering why he was not better loved'. He was criticized for judging people according to how high their regard was 'for him and his ideas'. Frankel observes, 'He boasted of keeping the paper "straight," but his measuring rod was not' (Frankel 1999: 429).

Frankel, coming into the top job as Abe Rosenthal's successor, could not help but understand himself as the 'not-Abe'. He acknowledges in his memoir that while he wanted to distinguish his style from that of Rosenthal's, 'I had the luxury of his achievements'. And so he could take a more democratic approach to managing the newsroom. 'I made myself widely accessible and gathered my own intelligence.'

> Eyes popped when I dropped into the Sports Department, which had not seen an executive editor in many moons. Tongues wagged for weeks after I appeared at a Metro reporter's rooftop beer party to get better acquainted and pick up revealing gossip. I moved out of the cavernous conference room that executive editors had always made their office, keeping a smaller space for myself and creating a

> place for others to meet without me. In free moments, I strolled the aisles of the newsroom, hoping to overcome reporters' obvious reluctance to just chat with power (Frankel 1999: 430).

Despite these efforts, Frankel complained of precisely what Raines would complain of some years later: that subordinates routinely misread his slightest suggestion or reflection as a command. 'No matter how tender my tone, my question marks were often misheard as exclamation points.' Raines said, 'One of the things I've learned in this job is if I utter the word "shorter", it comes back to me as, "All he wants is shorter!" That's not true. One of the other things I've learned about my language is when I talk about breaking stories, people say, "He's only interested in spot news!"' (Auletta 2003: 51).

These plaintive recollections, from both Frankel and Raines, suggest that hierarchy engenders its own social psychology. The chief of an organization is a person of unending fascination – and mystery – for his or her subordinates. He or she is a walking, talking machinery of meaning – and if the meanings are not clear, the subordinates will interpret them anyway, over-read them, over-interpret them. Journalists at the *Times* anxiously read Rosenthal or Frankel or Raines with all the intensity that Kremlinologists employed to decipher the significance of mute gestures in still photographs of the Kremlin leadership.

But should Sulzberger Jr have known to avoid the dangers of a driven, arrogant leader like Raines because his father's appointment of Rosenthal had so terrorized the newsroom? The younger Sulzberger, after all, believed that Rosenthal 'had become too authoritarian' at the end of his time as editor (Auletta 2003: 38). There is no task for the publisher more vital than choosing the executive editor. Still, no one can ever be sure how the person at the top of the editorial hierarchy will fare. Any subordinate position the candidate may have held, no matter how responsible, is never sufficient evidence of how a person will do as boss. Retrospectively, one can see in Raines' fascination with the leadership of a college football coach a dangerous instinct. But at the time? At the time, Sulzberger's judgement was a contextual judgement, as decisions invariably are. The question was not, what is the ideal leader? The real question was, of the likeliest well qualified candidates – Bill Keller and Howell Raines – who is the better person for the position? And Keller simply did not impress the way Raines did. 'Bill was fine,' said assistant managing editor Soma Golden Behr, 'but he seemed kind of quiet and subdued. Howell seemed exciting and daring. He took risks. I thought we could use a little of that.' Where Raines was always at the centre of a social gathering, Keller was more of a loner. He was famous for 'cracking jokes that made people feel awkward'. He himself acknowledged his lack of social graces: 'My wife sometimes refers to me as socially autistic' (Mnookin 2005: 41).

Raines finally lost his job because he was executive editor when it came out that Jayson Blair, a young black reporter, had plagiarized or invented out of whole cloth story after story in the course of his brief career at the *Times*. He began – pre-Raines – in 1999 and was promoted to full-time in early 2001, still pre-Raines. When his faked news stories were exposed, it was a profound embarrassment for the 'newspaper of record'. The *Times*' own report on the episode was damning. Although Raines had relatively little to do with Blair directly, the trauma of the Blair episode led to a great deal of soul-searching at the newspaper, and this caused much of the staff resentment of Raines to surface. Raines did not respond in a way that curbed the growing rebellion in the ranks and, in the end, Sulzberger had little choice but to hasten his exit.

No doubt, some good came from Raines' efforts to energize the *New York Times* newsroom. There may have been truth to Raines' view that the paper was desperately in need of 'energy and creativity' and that it had 'hit a ceiling in quality, variety and vivacity'. It is possible that Raines' fierce energy made a real difference even after his departure. The columnist William Safire said to Raines after he left the paper, 'There are still advocates of Howellism in the paper but they have to keep a very low profile. Whenever anybody talks about the paper's metabolism, everyone knows what it means, that's your word' (Raines 2006: 298). But by 2001 when Raines became editor, it was simply not true that the *Times* was just 'providing a stenographic record of government-certified news events' (Raines 2006: 187). If that is what he thought the *Times* was all about, no wonder the denizens of the newsroom felt misunderstood. But in the end, Raines listened too much to his own words and not enough to those of people around him. People learned that if they spoke up, they would be shot down.

Other forms of news leadership

Executive leadership in newspapers is not the only kind of media leadership. Various people can exercise leadership in news, not just the person who leads by virtue of position in a hierarchy but the person who innovates in any number of positions, setting an example or pioneering outside normal routines. Leadership at the top can help create a culture that makes this more or less possible. Often there are barriers to innovation lower down in an occupational hierarchy. ('How many middle managers does it take to change a light bulb? Uh, let me get back to you on that.') Even a freelance writer can influence the way news is written.

Theodore White did just that, though not necessarily to the good – at least, not according to White. White covered the 1960 presidential campaign, working on a book that was published quickly after the campaign as *The Making of the President 1960*. He did follow-ups on the next four campaigns, too. But what he also did was to show reporters by his examples what reporting campaign life behind the scenes looked like. And, according to White, this was not in the long run of benefit to American journalism. He wrote about covering George McGovern's campaign in 1972:

> We're all sitting there watching him work on his acceptance speech, poor bastard. He tries to go into the bedroom with Fred Dutton to go over the list of Vice Presidents... and all of us are observing him, taking notes like mad, getting all the little details. Which I think I invented as a method of reporting and which I now sincerely regret. If you write about this, say that I sincerely regret it. Who gives a fuck if the guy had milk and Total for breakfast? (Crouse 1973: 37).

Regret it or not, White's example became a model. He had an influence. He changed the way the public, at any rate the attentive public, came to know its presidential candidates.

Wall Street Journal reporter Farnaz Fassihi even more inadvertently influenced the views, values, and probably the literary forms of other reporters. Baghdad correspondent for the *Wall Street Journal*, she sent an email to friends and family in 2004 in which she described the confinement of her own life in Baghdad after the insurgency began in Iraq and the difficulties she had in breaking out of a narrower and narrower circle of (relative) security and personal safety. The email, through forwarding that Fassihi had not anticipated, became public. There was enormous response to it and typically the response was, 'We had no idea how bad things are!' Fassihi was shocked. Other reporters were shocked. Isn't this exactly what we have been reporting all along in our published news stories? Yes and no. Yes, the same assessment of the declining security of everyday life in Baghdad can be found in those dispatches. But, no, it was not personal and personalized in the way the email was. Even when it was personalized through an account of this or that Iraqi person-on-the-street, the narrative voice was disembodied and it was not clear that the reporter was in her own way deeply insecure and frequently threatened. That communicated something else entirely, something that even in an era of blogging, newspapers have been reluctant to adopt.

We must note, further, that news organizations are not alone in bearing responsibility in a democracy for informing the public and investigating the government (to centre for now on just those two democratic functions). With the growth of executive power in the twentieth century, as Walter Lippmann observed in 1920, news organizations by themselves are simply not capable of keeping tabs on government. They do not have the resources. They do not have the motivation. They do not have the accountability. They share responsibility in these functions with a variety of other agencies. Lippmann dubbed these other agencies 'political observatories' (Lippmann [1920] 2008: 56). He included in this term independent research organizations or what would later be called 'think tanks', universities, and government agencies dedicated to gathering intelligence or data about society. The civic information function in democracy is dispersed across these institutions, and more. In the United

States, the flowering of commercial (as well as non-profit) polling operations from Gallup on, the formation of public interest advocacy organizations on the left (in the 1960s and 1970s) and on the right (1970s and 1980s) and the substantial reporting, auditing, and investigative functions inside government itself that expanded significantly after 1970, all share responsibility with journalism and capacity for keeping watch on government and informing citizens about their world.

The leadership in today's news organizations, professional journalism associations, foundations, and schools of journalism might begin by acknowledging and improving the trust and coordination across these various agencies. The press shares responsibility for informing the public about the government with government itself. Yet it often fails to explain (or buries deep in a story) the fact that information was provided by watchdog agencies within the government, or by mechanisms (like the Freedom of Information Act) made possible by legislation (in 1966 and 1974) that established the mechanism and the platoons of bureaucrats who make it work. Legislatures keep a close watch (or at any rate are empowered to) on the executive branch of government. In recent decades, the executive keeps watch on itself (or has the apparatus for doing so). In the United States, since the 1970s, there has been a sharp growth of internal auditing functions in the executive that have helped make information available to the public in ways that sometimes are discrediting to the government. Today, thanks to legislation passed in 1978, there are 'inspectors general' in about sixty executive agencies and departments with a total of about 12,000 staff members whose job is to investigate the agencies to which they are assigned and report to both the President and the Congress on their findings with recommendations for change or, more rarely, recommendations for prosecution. Usually the inspectors are looking for waste and fraud and other financial mismanagement, but sometimes their efforts are far more extensive.

Consider revelations about the use of 'national security letters'. The FBI was authorized by various statutes that date to the 1970s to issue a 'national security letter' to obtain private records without a court order or court review – records like telephone records, Internet communication records, bank records, consumer credit records, but only if the FBI had specific reason to think that the entity whose records were being sought was a foreign power or agent of a foreign power. Only a very few senior FBI officials could issue national security letters. The USA PATRIOT Act in 2001 broadened this greatly – many more FBI officials could issue the letters, the information sought no longer needed to relate to a foreign power, and the threshold for seeking the information was only that it be relevant to an investigation of international terrorism or espionage.

So, what happened thereafter? We know quite a lot about what happened thereafter: the FBI abused this power many times. We know this because the

Department of Justice Inspector General, Glenn Fine, supported by a staff of 400 criminal investigators, auditors, and lawyers, issued a report documenting these abuses, submitting his report as he is obliged to by statute to the Congress as well as to the FBI and the Justice Department. And, of course, the press then reported it. That was in March 2007. At that point, the Electronic Freedom Foundation filed a Freedom of Information Act lawsuit seeking further information on the FBI abuse of its authority to issue national security letters. A federal judge ordered the FBI to release information responsive to that request. Several months later, the FBI disclosed a first batch of 1,100 pages to the Electronic Freedom Foundation, all of which one can examine on the organization's website. These disclosures show, among other things, that several cases of abuse of the national security letters that the FBI itself documented were forwarded to then Attorney General Alberto Gonzales although Mr Gonzales had denied knowledge of any civil liberties violations arising from the PATRIOT Act.

The PATRIOT Act expanded the power of government to invade the privacy of American citizens and to do so without judicial review. That this became a public embarrassment and a matter of front-page controversy owes less to the news media as we normally think of them than it does to a largely unheralded office in the federal executive branch of government that has been a contributor to public knowledge about government for only thirty years. In this case, and it is by no means unique, knowledge of government wrongdoing came to light not through the efforts of the news media but primarily through initiatives of investigative agencies internal to the government.

That this is so is, in part, a question of resources. The *New York Times* has an editorial staff of 1,200 journalists, several hundred more than the next largest American news organization, excepting the Associated Press that boasts 3,000 journalists around the globe. Compare those numbers to the staff of 12,000 people working for the inspectors general or the 5,000 Freedom of Information Act officers in the federal government or the 3,500 people who work for the General Accounting Office, 200 for the Congressional Budget Office, 700 at the Congressional Research Service. The great majority of these people are fact-finders, researchers, investigators, and analysts. One might also add, moving to government employees of a more partisan bent, 2,500 people who work for congressional committees, and 12,000 more who serve individual representatives and senators (C-SPAN.org 2000).

And these are just the in-house personnel in the federal government. I have not begun to count state or municipal employees. Nor have I included the many information gatherers and analysts who work for both partisan and nonprofit private organizations. My brief mention earlier of the Electronic Frontier Foundation will have to stand in for hundreds of other non-profits that take as part of their job or even as their primary job the monitoring of government. The dispersal of democratic authority that arises because the press keeps watch on government is today a function by no means confined to the press but spread across multiple 'political observatories', commercial and non-profit, partisan, and independent, governmental and extra-governmental.

Conclusion

All that said, the work of the political observatories invariably reaches the wider public and often reaches even insiders in government through the 'mainstream' news media, and especially, on a national level, through prestige national press like the *New York Times*, *Washington Post*, and *Wall Street Journal* – including, of course, their online as well as their print editions. This means that such traditional organs retain their central importance, and thus their crucial leadership role, in fulfilling essential functions of democratic supervision and accountability. The quality of the internal leadership of these media stalwarts is therefore of major consequence to citizens and should command more serious scholarly attention than it has till now. It has been my aim in this chapter to draw attention to this field and perhaps open it up for more extensive investigation.

We may conclude from our survey of the *Times*, however, that leadership in these organizations is as tricky as leadership in any other large organization that is hierarchical but professional (with recognition and renown possible even for individuals new to the organization and lower down in the hierarchy) and that is committed to a set of deeply held goals that conflict with one another. News organizations must, on the one hand, make money to stay in business and stay profitable and, on the other, produce news that serious journalists are proud of and that is relevant to citizens seeking to stay engaged with public affairs. As Arthur Sulzberger Jr put it, the *New York Times* Company is at once dedicated to 'contents of the highest quality and integrity' and 'creating long-term shareholder value through investment and constancy of purpose' (Coffey 2007: 34–5). The leadership task is to meet the demands of commercial necessity while fulfilling the responsibilities required by democracy. This is, like all tasks of leadership, easier said than done.

Notes

1. Among many works that provide empirical support for this view, see Gans (1979); Gitlin (1980); Hallin (1984); Bennett (1990); Zaller (1994); Schudson (2000, 2003); and Schudson and Waisbord (2005) offer a broad bibliography, citing non-US as well as US studies.
2. Observations in the next paragraphs derive especially from a discussion I held with news executives participating in a leadership training institute at the Graduate School of Journalism, Columbia University, 23 October 2007.

Bibliography

Auletta, K., *Backstory* (New York: Penguin, 2003).

Bennett, W. L., 'Toward a Theory of Press-State Relations in the United States', *Journal of Communication,* 40 (1990), 103–25.

——and Paletz, D., (eds.), *Taken by Storm: The Media, Public Opinion and U.S. Foreign Policy in the Gulf War* (Chicago: University of Chicago Press, 1994).

Bettman, J. and Weitz, B., 'Attributions in the Board Room: Causal Reasoning in Corporate Annual Reports', *Administrative Science Quarterly,* 28 (1983), 165–83.

Coffey III, S. (ed.), *Best Practices: The Art of Leadership in News Organizations* (Arlington, Va.: Freedom Forum, 2007).

Crouse, T., *The Boys on the Bus* (New York: Ballantine, 1973).

Frankel, M., *The Times of My Life* (New York: Random House, 1999).

Gans, H. J., *Deciding What's News* (New York: Pantheon Books, 1979).

Gitlin, T., *The Whole World is Watching* (Berkeley: University of California Press, 1980).

Hallin, D. C., *'The Uncensored War': The Media and Vietnam* (New York: Oxford University Press, 1984).

Lippmann, W., *Liberty and the News* (Princeton, New Jersey: Princeton University Press, [1920] 2008).

Mnookin, S., *Hard News* (New York: Random House, 2005).

Raines, H., *The One That Got Away* (New York: Scribner, 2006).

Schudson, M., 'The Sociology of News Production Revisited (Again)', in J. Curran and M. Gurevitch (eds.), *Mass Media and Society,* 3rd edn. (London: Arnold, 2000), 175–200.

——*The Sociology of News* (New York: W. W. Norton, 2003).

——*Why Democracies Need an Unlovable Press* (Cambridge, UK: Polity, 2008).

——and Waisbord, S., 'Toward a Political Sociology of the News Media', in T. Janoski, R. Alford, A. Hicks, and M. A. Schwartz (eds.), *The Handbook of Political Sociology* (Cambridge: Cambridge University Press, 2005), 350–66.

Zaller, J., 'Elite Leadership of Mass Opinion: New Evidence from the Gulf War', in W. L. Bennett and D. Paletz (eds.), *Taken by Storm: The Media, Public Opinion and U.S. Foreign Policy in the Gulf War* (Chicago: University of Chicago Press, 1994), 186–209.

Chapter 10

The Challenges of Business Leadership: CEOs and the Case of the Business Council of Australia

Stephen Bell

Business leaders are often assumed to play a major role in the national leadership of liberal democracies. In fact major political theories largely agree with such a view. Liberal pluralists, for example, would simply add the caveat that business interests, whilst highly influential as lobbyists and as policy advocates within an open democratic setting, do not dominate politics, as their more radical critics generally argue. Pluralists highlight the often-fragmented nature of business interests, and point to the welter of competing interest group pressures across a range of issues. They also highlight the challenges of collective action that business leaders confront in politics. More radical critics partly sidestep such issues, arguing that business interests have special powers, or as Charles Lindblom (1977) famously argued, a 'privileged position' in politics. This form of 'structural' power is said to stem from the fact that in a capitalist system, business owns and controls most of the economy. This is said to place business interests in a structurally powerful position because governments and society more broadly are dependent on business investment as the basis for a vibrant economy. Governments, employees, and the wider society depend heavily on successful business performance, and hence government policy must always be attentive to aggregate levels of 'business confidence' and business's willingness to grow the economy.

The other side of the coin of course is that business also relies heavily on government to provide essential market infrastructure and a supportive operating environment. Indeed, in extremis, governments will even bail out key sectors, particularly in the financial sector (witness the raft of bank rescues in

This chapter relies on material published in Bell (2006, 2007, 2008).

the current sub-prime credit crisis) in order to boost 'business confidence' and secure ongoing lending and investment. Hence, even in liberal systems that feature dispersed leadership characteristics, there is a high degree of mutual dependence between business and government. In many ways the successful operation of market systems should be thought of in these terms as a public–private partnership. In the final analysis, as Lindblom (1977: 175) argues: 'public affairs in market-oriented systems are in the hands of two groups of leaders, government and business'. To 'make the system work', Lindblom continued, these two groups of leaders must 'collaborate' and 'government leadership must often defer to business leadership'.

Whilst useful in many respects, these macro accounts of business power explain too much – business dominates or business does not dominate. Reality is more complicated and nuanced, and such approaches do not tell us enough about how business leaders actually operate in the interstices of politics. The focus in this chapter is on the question of how business leaders, especially big business leaders, operate within national politics, especially in the overt political arena of public advocacy and lobbying. The chapter uses an Australian case, that of the corporate CEOs who drive the peak business organization, the Business Council of Australia (BCA), to explore the issue. The BCA, compared to peak business associations in other liberal democracies, is somewhat specialized to the extent that it relies on direct CEO engagement in associational affairs. It nevertheless provides a very good example of how business leaders operate in a lobbying and associational environment, and sheds a broad light on the challenges and opportunities confronting business leaders in the overt political arena. The associational focus taken here does not, however, explore how firms wield structural power through their investment decision-making and the impact this potentially has on government policy-making. As argued below, large umbrella organizations, such as the BCA, cannot easily wield structural power, a form of power exercised mainly at the firm, not at the associational, level.

With this focus, the chapter asks what capacities and power resources business leaders bring to the task of exerting national influence or leadership. What impediments or constraints do such leaders confront in politics? How do they engage with governments? And how should we view the exertion of such business influence from a democratic perspective? The answers to these questions reveal how various institutional and ideological factors condition and constrain the operation of business influence and leadership in Australia, and provide a case study that invites future explorations of comparable cases internationally.

Institutional capacities?

The BCA was formed in 1983 after dissatisfaction emerged within big business over the question of effective political leadership and policy advocacy. Big business, in particular, was aware of its lack of presence in national affairs and in the national capital (McLaughlin 1991; Parbo 1993). The BCA's first chief executive, Geoff Allen, recalls that in confronting a range of new challenges, the business community in the 1970s was 'frustrated, nervous and leaderless' (author's interview, Melbourne, 23 April 2004). The formation of the BCA represents a concerted effort by big business leaders to overcome such problems of political representation and leadership. Unlike other business associations, the BCA's members are corporate CEOs, much the same as the Business Roundtable in the United States. At the time of its formation, the BCA had a membership of around eighty CEOs. The shift towards overt political engagement by CEOs under the banner of the BCA was a very significant departure in Australian business politics. Never before had such leaders played such an active role in the political arena. Established industry association leaders had argued at the time of the BCA's formation that an organization based on CEOs would not work, 'because you can't corral those stallions' (G. Polities, as quoted in BCA 1985: 1085). But the BCA did appear to corral the stallions. As an internal review of the BCA's functioning and performance in 1985 argued: 'It is a constant source of amazement to observers that bi-monthly Council meetings are normally attended by between 45 and 60 Council members, and that it is possible for a group that size to meaningfully determine or confirm policy. Despite the expectations of sceptics, after two years it is true to say that this is genuinely an organisation of Chief Executives' (BCA 1985: 6).

At present the BCA's member CEOs are drawn from about one hundred of the largest corporations operating in Australia. The full Council comprised of all CEO members, meets several times each year, and is the main deliberative and decision-making body of the BCA. The BCA is led by a president, and its research and advocacy work is supported by a secretariat. Since its inception the BCA has carved out a distinctive modus operandi in politics. The BCA is distinctive because it is not a direct service to member organizations. It does not directly lobby governments on discrete firm level or sectoral issues. Nor has the BCA attempted to enter partisan politics and pressure governments through the electoral process. Instead, as outlined more fully below, the BCA's agenda has been to engage in research-based policy advocacy aimed at a selected number of medium-term, economy-wide issues of 'national significance'.

Yet the BCA also suffers from various institutional weaknesses. Neil Mitchell (1997: 101) has argued that, 'the strength of national business associations is not the same as the political strength of business'. This is because national business associations (like the BCA) cannot exert perhaps the most significant form of business power – structural power – a form of power wielded not through business associations but through the investment decisions of companies (Block 1977; Lindblom 1977; Offe and Wiesenthal 1980; Bell 1992; Swank 1992). As Hacker and Pierson (2002: 281) point out, this form of power is exercised 'automatically and apolitically...It results from private, individual investment decisions taken in thousands of enterprises, rather than from any organised effort to influence policy makers'.

When the resources giant, BHP, threatened to disinvest in the steel industry in the early 1980s, its impact on government policy was decisive. Similarly, financial markets and the potential threat of disinvestment or capital flight also constrain national macroeconomic policy. But there is no such comparison regarding the impact of the BCA, largely because it has no direct control over the investment process and cannot directly threaten governments with economic damage. In other words, the BCA is not an institutional vehicle or portal through which the putative structural power of large corporations is exerted.

Is it correct to assume such a limited articulation between structural forms of business power and the operation of business associations? Perhaps not. For example, as Offe and Wiesenthal (1980: 86) have argued, the structural power of business might be, 'exploited and fine-tuned by the operation of business associations'. Somewhat similarly, Hacker and Pierson (2002: 282) argue: 'structural power is a signalling device; by itself it does not dictate policy choices...this signal cannot tell governments what to do' (see also Bernhagen and Brauninger [2005]). This suggests that the exact policy parameters and requirements needed to promote business confidence and investment are never clear-cut. Hence, business research, lobbying and advocacy might play a useful 'educative' role in clarifying and fine-tuning the business policy agenda and communicating this to governments; backed up of course by the structural power weapon. This is a plausible argument. Nevertheless, the capacity to make credible investment threats to government is more easily achieved by tightly focused industry or sectoral business associations, especially those with a small number of large similarly positioned firms. In such a context the relationship between a potentially negative reaction to public policy, on the one hand, and investment decision-making, on the other, is likely to be more closely aligned. However, it is hard to see how this articulation could operate effectively or credibly in a large, cross-sectoral, national association such as the BCA. The diversity of the BCA's membership, ranging across all sectors of the economy, makes it an unwieldy vehicle through which to articulate firm-level investment concerns. Moreover, the BCA is an organization that has traditionally explicitly eschewed the articulation of specific firm-centric concerns of corporate members.

Accordingly, the BCA has had to rely mainly on forms of business influence generated through activism and lobbying in the overt political arena. However, this confronts business leaders with substantial collective action problems. And the BCA's particular approach to corporate political activism confronts it with an even more substantial collective action problem than would typically confront most business associations. This is because the modus operandi of the BCA requires direct CEO involvement. Business leaders tend to operate in a world of individualism and competition. This is not usually a context that encourages collective action. CEOs also potentially face shareholder displeasure if they stray too far from the bottom line, become embroiled in partisan politics and expose the firm to political risks. Also, unless the fortunes of the company are directly threatened, business leaders typically have few incentives to join with others to engage in political mobilization.

For these reasons, business leaders typically find active engagement in such forms of politics difficult. This is so in relation to industry-wide but particularly cross-sectoral and especially class-wide forms of political activism. As Mancur Olson (1965) originally argued, business leaders confront collective action problems because the public goods or public policy benefits obtainable by any one firm are often small relative to the costs and uncertainties associated with collective political mobilization. Thus, the temptation to free ride is strong. Only when the potential benefits of collective mobilization are concentrated, Olson argues – as in the case of several large firms mobilizing in a particular industry (Olson's privileged group case) – are firms likely to engage collectively in politics.

Nevertheless, we know that under certain conditions collective organization on the part of business leaders and even instances of class-wide business political mobilization can be achieved. As Olson originally argued, solutions to collective action problems might be found if the number of actors is relatively small and if certain selective benefits to aid group activity can be arranged. In a recent paper I have extended Olson's explanatory analysis and also build on more recent work by Andrew Polsky (2000) to explain the bases of the BCA's capacities for collective action (Bell 2008). Theorists of business collective action are correct to emphasize the 'daunting conditions' required to facilitate business collective action (Polsky 2000: 460). In the case at hand, collective action was supported by the relatively small numbers of players involved and by the fact that the CEOs in question were able to muster substantial corporate resources to aid political engagement, not least their status as leaders of the nation's largest companies. Scholars have also identified other factors critical in explaining business collective action. Polsky (2000) argues that three conditions are central. First, business leaders must experience a shift in economic conditions, a perceived crisis or threat or a major opportunity born of such conditions that offers the prospect of substantial policy gains. Second, following the work of David Plotke (1992) and Cathy Jo Martin (1995, 2000), Polsky argues there must be a 'discursive process' to help business leaders arrive at a common, consensual interpretation of their situation and a shared vision and set of preferences of what might be achieved in policy terms to advance their interests. Third, Polsky (2000: 460) argues there must be political actors or entrepreneurs who are able and 'prepared to absorb the costs of mobilizing business for collective action'.

There have only been a few instances when all these ingredients have come together for the BCA since its formation in 1983. Two instances stand out: the successful collective mobilization around industrial relations reform in the late 1980s and early 1990s, and the push for taxation reform in the mid- to late 1990s (Sheldon and Thornthwaite 1993; Eccleston 2004). In both instances, business elites within the BCA reacted to a major perceived opportunity for change. In the case of taxation reform, business leaders believed they were confronting a major policy opportunity occasioned by the arrival of a conservative government in 1996, one potentially amenable to a new campaign on taxation reform. On both occasions the BCA's Secretariat and other groups were able to effectively frame the issues at hand and offer compelling policy narratives which further helped mobilize business leaders. In the case of industrial relations reform, the policy discourse was successfully shifted from discussions about Australia's traditional centralized IR system towards a new decentralized firm-centric, 'enterprise bargaining' framework. These mobilizations were led by business entrepreneurs from the BCA who encouraged an initially reluctant federal government to move on a reform agenda.

This evidence suggests Polsky's account is somewhat incomplete. His account, indeed most accounts of business collective action, emphasize the role of the state as coalition partners in helping to mobilize business. But in the case of the BCA it is clear that *business* political entrepreneurs were central in propelling surges of mobilization. Only after initial mobilization by business did reluctant governments finally come on board to forge a reformist coalition.

Indeed, the extant literature on business collective action pays too little attention to two further factors which shape the nature of business collective action. First, as outlined more fully below, in the case at hand it is clear that business leaders were strongly influenced by a decidedly liberal political ideology that warned against forging relations of dependency with governments. This wariness and arm's length posture underpinned a business-centric as opposed to a statist basis for overcoming collective action problems. Second, extant accounts say too little about the institutional basis of business collective action. The formation and subsequent organizational development of the BCA added considerable new collective institutional capacity to big business in Australia. It provided an important forum for face-to-face CEO interaction and deliberation, which was decisive in moving big business political activity beyond its former relatively disorganized, atomistic state. Through corporate contributions and the role of the Secretariat, a very substantial research capacity was also achieved; one, for the first time, that was strategically targeted at matching if not bettering the capacity of the federal bureaucracy. In some respects, then, the BCA achieved a degree of 'institutional strength'. Indeed, the BCA as an organization was able to offer business leaders certain selective incentives which aided political engagement. It offered members a ready-made

CEO networking forum as well as the chance to come in from a world of political atomization and begin to play a key organized role in national affairs, thus conferring on them a new-found status. Other scholars emphasize the selective benefit of 'institutionalized access to policy deliberations in the government' (Doner and Schneider 2000: 263). This was also significant in the Australian case. True, the CEOs of the largest companies already had access to government leaders, but the BCA provided CEOs, especially the BCA's key leaders, with alternative or additional access routes. What is also significant is that the BCA – as an organization and meeting place – helped foster collective commitments within big business, helped build trust and social capital amongst CEOs, and helped reduce the transaction costs and uncertainties regarding shared commitments that otherwise plague collectivism. As Cathy Jo Martin (2000: 30) puts it, 'Groups channel information, broaden political identities, and increase trust that others will join in politically risky action'. The BCA's organizational capacity was also instrumental in forging new networking relationships between formally disparate business associations by encouraging them to cooperate in ad hoc coalitions focused on particular policy issues, including enterprise bargaining (Bell 1995). Hence, the formation and development of the BCA provided an important organizational basis from which to launch concerted forms of business collective action.

Relations with government

During its first few years of operation the BCA worked to define a distinctive strategy of political engagement. First, a strategy of 'research-based advocacy' was formulated. This involves actively cultivating the intellectual soil, especially on a medium-term basis, with the intent to persuade elites and policy-makers to alter mind sets and even prevailing policy paradigms. Unlike much of the previous history of business advocacy and lobbying in Australia, the new approach was designed to lift the intellectual level of the business case and to match if not better the intellectual capacity of the public service. A former BCA insider sums up the strengths of the BCA's approach to political advocacy in the following way.

> I think the great strength of the Business Council was that it was 'research based'...and it positioned almost all that it did in terms of some notion of the 'national interest'. I think a second strength...was the Business Council was always best listened to when it spoke through its CEOs, through its President, and through the heads of the various policy committees. The arrival of CEOs on the political stage was a very significant shift. A third strength was that the Business Council had a good model of public policy advocacy...it never set out to influence public opinion, it set out to influence leader opinion. The other strength was...the quality of the Secretariat and its high level of intellectual capability.

> The Business Council's strength was that it could over time mostly achieve consensus on tough issues. The other thing was that the Council was patient. It was prepared to work through issues over time. In the area in which I worked, labour market reform, the Council's position was that it would take 10 years (author's interview, Melbourne, 24 April 2004).

Second, the BCA sought to play a broad leadership role on key 'national issues' rather than engage in a more reactive style of business lobbying in pursuit of particular short-term interests. This medium-term strategic approach was essentially a 'blue sky' policy approach involving an attempt to pursue a select number of issues that were forward-looking and encompassing enough to unite the membership in common cause. As the BCA has argued, 'from the start we declared our intention to get ahead of the game and to create the political agenda, not simply react to it' (BCA 1985: 8). In a definitive article outlining the BCA's approach in these terms, Peter McLaughlin (1991: 147, 157), the BCA's second Executive Director, wrote:

> While recognising the importance of working constructively with the elected government of the day, the Council has consciously eschewed opportunities to negotiate for short term advantage...We would not enter into deal-making negotiations...Rather, the Council would seek to simply offer first best practical advice and urge good policy on governments whose job it was alone to reconcile competing views...It was a principled, purist view that has never been regretted by the Council.

A major test of this approach came in the 1980s under the Hawke Labor government. Hawke was an instinctive corporatist and had joined with the unions in a corporatist pact to control wage inflation. Hawke had also made overtures to the BCA to join such an arrangement. But the BCA rejected pointed overtures from the Hawke Labor government during its first years in office to engage in collaborative corporatist deal-making (McLaughlin 1991: 153–7). As a former member of the BCA Secretariat, argues, 'Hawke thought the creation of the Business Council was a marvellous opportunity to shore up corporatism, but he was sadly disappointed because the Council position was, "this is our policy and we are not going to negotiate with you on policy. We'll advocate our position. You'll have to take a decision in government"'. This stance created tensions with the government: Hawke wanted the BCA to deliver a key constituency to the bargaining table. But the BCA would not become a corporatist interlocutor with the government, with Hawke at times publicly lamenting this outcome. Arvi Parbo (1993: 5), the BCA's first president, sums up Hawke's mood on this issue in the following way: 'Despite many attempts to explain our pluralist philosophy, there is no question that both the government and the unions – probably with the mindset of their centralized industrial relations background – came to see our refusal to deliver deals on behalf of some monolithic business entity as a sign of inadequacy, poor organization and weakness.' Arguably, however, the BCA's strategy reflected realistic judgement. The corporate sector was, on the whole, ideologically opposed to 'corporatist' collaboration and deal-making with government. Moreover, even if that path had been pursued, business associations (including the BCA), in institutional terms, are typically not centralized, disciplined or encompassing enough to be able to centrally bargain with or collaborate on such terms with government (Bell 1995; see also Gordon [1998]).

It is also the case that the BCA's activism has only ever *influenced* governments. The relationship has primarily been about cooperation, not conflict. As Geoff Allen commented, 'basically we looked to find things where there was good alignment between what we needed and what government needed'. As a former senior Labor minister, John Dawkins (1994: 4) noted in a speech in 1994, the BCA's policy advocacy work, 'would have meant nothing if government had not been receptive'. He argued the government's clear preference was for consensus building strategies. Hence, as Dawkins pointed out, 'it was important to have the BCA as part of the cheer squad' (1994: 4). Clearly, the volitions of government have been central to the dynamics of the BCA's influence.

This became very apparent under the Keating Labor government (1991–6) that quickly became hostile towards the BCA, (erroneously) seeing it as 'partisan' during the 1993 federal election. The impact on the BCA's influence was devastating. Keating publicly attacked CEOs, and ministers and senior bureaucrats were discouraged from active engagement with the BCA. Keating also engaged in divide and rule strategies amongst BCA member firms by siding with some and alienating others. Significantly, during 1993–4, after all its initial heavy lifting, the BCA was frozen out during deliberations concerning the drafting of legislation dealing with enterprise bargaining. As a former BCA Executive Director, comments: 'the philosophy that informed government's attitude was if business put its head above the parapet then it'd be kicked in. And that had the effect of causing many in the business leadership to actually retreat. They ultimately had an obligation to their own shareholders not to expose the company to retaliation at the political level... And they backed off' (author's interview, Melbourne, 25 April 2004). Similarly, the Allen Review of the BCA in 1996 stated: 'The style and agenda of the government under Keating, and the then Prime Minister's strategy to undermine the BCA as a source of national influence, contributed to a relative decline of the effectiveness of the Council in this period... CEOs retreated from public advocacy to protect shareholder interest' (BCA 1996: 1). This is clear testimony to the fact that the leaders of large firms do not like to be in the political spotlight if this involves direct confrontation with government. The fact that a federal government thinks it can afford to ignore or be overtly hostile to a peak big business organization like the BCA, speaks volumes about the power dynamics at work.

The ultimate dependence of business associations on government support, combined with the challenges outlined earlier in relation to collective action, underlines the overall difficulties that business associations and business leaders confront in politics.

CEO problems

These problems of collective commitment and political influence also partly stem from deeper institutional problems. In particular, the BCA's capacity to run on 'CEO power' is confronting institutional problems rooted in the changing nature of the corporate sector. To a point this strategy appeared to work somewhat better in the 1980s, especially when the BCA was driven by a number of pioneering corporate executives, in many cases from the increasingly ascendant resources sector. These leaders were highly committed to public life, to the opening up of the Australian economy, and they appeared as a generation of corporate leaders ideally suited to BCA's requirements for large amounts of CEO time and energy. The problem now is that since the early to mid-1990s, the corporate sector has confronted increasing bottom line pressures and shareholder demands. Consequently, resources devoted to collective action within the corporate sector, especially CEO time, have been increasingly limited. As a former Executive Director argues: 'it is a constant issue, how to get CEOs to put in the time, to get across the detail, and to perform credibly in the public domain... It is a real problem. By the time I left the BCA in 2001 the input from most of the major companies, who in the interim had radically curtailed their own public policy analytical capacity, was dramatically less than it had been even five or six years earlier' (author's interview, Melbourne, 25 November 2003). Another respondent, who has worked with the BCA and has long experience in government relations in the resources sector, said that:

> if I had to put a time on it, I would say it was a gradual process that evolved from the early 1990s... and by the late 1990s and certainly now I'd say most of the CEOs don't have the time to properly engage... there is no question at all that the larger engagement in public policy, or even arguing the role of the corporation in society, is on the backburner... And it's all very well saying why isn't the Secretariat out there forcing up the issues... only to find when they stick their head up like a parrot that there's no CEO heads sticking up with them (author's interview, Melbourne, 25 April 2004).

Compounding these difficulties, CEOs are increasingly confronting very short tenures; now down to just over four years on average, according to the BCA's own research (BCA 2003–4). As Geoff Allen comments: 'Given these pressures the capacity to think reflectively on big issues beyond their immediate situation is very, very hard... It's a hard model to sustain in the current climate.' As another former BCA Chief Executive commented:

> Some would argue that this problem is a product of the branch office economy where in fact the Australian companies increasingly are subsidiaries of global players, taking their cue from global leadership. Others would argue that it's the short-term pressure for performance reflected through institutional shareholder interests. Some would argue it's a by product of the way remuneration packages are now structured, with an emphasis on short-term share prices...Whatever it is, the reality is that today you have very few full time CEOs actively prepared to run with a public agenda...I think that you're struggling now to identify business leadership figures that have the authority, credibility and muscle...(author's interview, Melbourne, 24 April 2004).

The dynamics of structural change in the economy as well as globalization are also impacting on the performance of the BCA. The BCA was heavily influenced by the agenda of large export-oriented but relatively immobile resource companies in the 1980s. The policy focus was decidedly 'national' in orientation, with issues such as industrial relations and border protectionism high on the agenda. However, globalization, increased offshoring in the large corporate sector, the increasing multinational membership of the BCA, the fact that CEOs increasingly spend large amounts of their time overseas, as well as the growing numbers of foreign CEOs in Australia, have weakened this earlier national focus. As a former General Manager of the BCA Secretariat puts it: 'the move from a domestic membership to one which is not predominantly but certainly moving towards a large multinational membership, where CEOs come into Australia on short term circuits with varying degrees of interest in Australia...That does place a strain on how the BCA functions'.

Another issue related to structural change is that service firms in areas such as finance, banking, insurance, and law now make up a larger proportion of BCA membership. Initially, CEOs from service sector firms made up around 20 per cent of BCA membership. By 2005 this proportion had grown to 50 per cent. Some respondents commented that this was a negative for the BCA, largely because such firms do not have a substantial stake in the 'real economy'. As one respondent put it, 'it comes back to the concept of what is the legitimate voice of business or industry'. Several respondents thought that the BCA was increasingly becoming a forum for the purposes of corporate networking. A current senior officer in the Secretariat agreed that one of the rationales for joining the BCA was networking: 'When companies join the Council they often join for networking opportunities, particularly new CEOs and young CEOs.' One respondent, formerly of the Secretariat, commented that he thought some service firms simply saw the BCA as a good place 'for laying the base for attracting clientele'.

The BCA's CEOs thus find themselves in an awkward situation, pressed by onerous short-term corporate demands but expected in their role as BCA members to play a broader leadership role in business political collectivism and national affairs. This tension has become more pronounced as a result of the shifting pressures on CEOs just outlined. The pressure to pull down the tent somewhat and more directly represent short-term member interests is also growing. As a former General Manager in the BCA argued:

> I think there is now a greater short term focus because of CEO turnover and bottom line pressures, there's greater questioning of, 'what can the association do for me?' I don't think that was the case in 1983, in 1983 business was truly working in the broader national interest. If you look at the CEO turnover data, the change in the structure of the economy... the number of multinationals we now have... It stands to reason that you now have less of the top 200 corporates actually interested in national interest issues and national public policy. And therefore, ultimately, they do ask the question: 'what does the BCA do for me?' And that by its very nature must change the nature of the operating parameters of the BCA... I think this is where the difference comes through between now and in 1983. The Council was principally interested in research into major public policy issues in 1983. There is now recognition that more advocacy is required, more direct lobbying if you like. And now we have to strike a balance now between the actual research on blue sky issues, and actually advocating something on behalf of members, which is quite different (author's interview, Melbourne 25 April 2004).

Conclusion

Charles Lindblom is probably right to argue that business interests have a privileged position in politics, but this stems more from the structural capacities of business interests in a capitalist democracy and their capacity to influence government policy through what Fred Block (1977) refers to as the 'investment veto weapon'. Even here, however, there are factors which can constrain the influence of such structural power, including the priority that governments place on particular types of business investment (Bell 1992). Business interests also confront a range of problems when operating in the overt political arena. It is true that business leaders, especially leaders of big business, often have resources and influence. Yet as this chapter has argued, there are various institutional factors that constrain their opportunities to engage in politics and that provide challenging conditions for collective action. These problems are symptomatic of the particular institutional configuration of the BCA but can be extended to more basic collective action problems in corporate sectors the world over.

This chapter has argued that the BCA operates mainly as a lobbying organization, wielding evidence and argument to try and persuade governments on selected policy issues. This strategy places the BCA firmly within the pluralist, lobbying domain. The BCA's relations with government are at arm's length, reflecting liberal pluralist values. In pluralist environments, the leaders of big business form just one of a number of leadership groups in national politics, a pattern that partly accords with the themes of dispersed leadership explored in this volume. Reflecting its liberal stance, the BCA rejected overtures by the federal government during the 1980s to forge a closed corporatist alliance with the government and the unions, a strategy that would have effectively *concentrated* national leadership in an attempt to impose greater coherence and coordination on economic policy. Despite its resources and capacities, however, the BCA faces a number of institutional challenges which reflect the difficulties that all business leaders face in the world of overt political activism.

As to the future of the BCA, the BCA's first Executive Director, Geoff Allen, said in interview that, 'I just hope that it can keep going, but I think it might just need to reinvent itself in some sort of way'. Similarly, a former member of the BCA Secretariat argues, 'the BCA can perhaps recover by doing a couple of obvious things, of which the most obvious is a return to a more active research agenda...and that requires a more rounded Secretariat with genuine intellectual strengths'. However, it will be difficult to regain the kind of CEO drive and commitment that was apparent in the 1980s. If this is so, then perhaps the BCA might choose to rely more heavily for direction and advocacy from a revamped Secretariat. This approach – essentially the model adopted by the New Zealand Business roundtable – would still need to be backed by BCA member firms, especially financially, though expectations of CEO activism would be reduced. If this approach were pursued, a good deal of the earlier distinctiveness of the BCA would be lost, and the organization would look more like one of a number of corporate funded think tanks. Alternatively, if the BCA focuses more on direct lobbying in relation to firm or sectoral issues, the question arises of why firms would opt to work through a large cross-sectoral association such as the BCA rather than pursue their own more narrowly focused agendas.

Bibliography

Bell, S., 'The Political Power of Business', in S. Bell and J. Wanna (eds.), *Business-Government Relations in Australia* (Sydney: Harcourt Brace Jovanovich, 1992).

——'Australian Business Associations: New Opportunities and Challenges', *Australian Journal of Management,* 19/2 December (1994), 137–58.

——'Between the Market and the State: The Role of Business Associations in Public Policy: Evidence from Australia', *Comparative Politics*, 28 (1995), 25–53.

——'Institutional Influences on the Power of Business: How "Privilidged" is the Business Council of Australia?', *Journal of Public Affairs*, 6 (2006), 156–67.

——'A Victim of its Own Success: Internationalisation, Neoliberalism and Organisational Involution at the Businesses Council of Australia', *Politics and Society*, 34 (2007), 543–70.

Bell, S., 'Rethinking the Role of the State: Explaining Business Collective Action at the Business Council of Australia', *Polity*, 40 (2008), 464–87.

Bernhagen, P. and Brauninger, T., 'Structural Power and Public Policy: A Signaling Model of Business Lobbying in Democratic Capitalism', *Political Studies*, 53 (2005), 43–64.

Block, F., 'The Ruling Class Does Not Rule', *Socialist Revolution*, 7 (1977), 6–28.

Business Council of Australia, *Business Council: Performance and Challenges*, Background Paper for a Review of the Council's Activities and Processes (Melbourne: Business Council of Australia, 1985).

——*Review of the Business Council of Australia* (Melbourne: Business Council of Australia, 1996).

——'CEO Tenure and Turnover in Australia', *BCA Quarterly*, 2nd edn. (Melbourne: Business Council of Australia, 2003–4).

Dabscheck, B., 'The BCA's Plan to Americanise Australian Industrial Relations', *Journal of Australian Political Economy*, 27 (1990), 1–14.

Davis, M., 'BCA Gets Back on its Lobby Horse', *Australian Financial Review*, 17 February 1997.

Dawkins, J., 'Business-Government Relations: A Decade of Economic Reform and the Role of Business', Corporate Public Affairs Oration, Centre for Corporate Public Affairs, Melbourne, 14 July 1994.

Doner, R. and Schneider, B. R., 'Business Associations and Economic Development: Why Some Associations Contribute More than Others', *Business and Politics*, 2/3 (2000), 261–88.

Durie, J., 'At 20, It's Time BCA Came of Age', *Australian Financial Review*, 27 September 2003.

Eccleston, R., *The Thirty Year Problem: The Politics of Australian Tax Reform* (Sydney: Australian Tax Research Foundation, 2004).

Forman, D., 'Industry Bodies Change Gear', *Business Review Weekly*, 25 November 1996.

Frieden, J., 'Sectoral Conflict in US Foreign Economic Policy', *International Organisation*, 42 (1988), 59–90.

Galligan, B. and Singleton, G., *Business and Government under Labour* (Melbourne: Longman, 1991).

Gluyas, R., Bachelard, M., and Marris, S., 'BCA Goes into Battle', *The Australian*, 9 December 2003.

Gordon, C., 'Why No Corporatism in the United States: Business Disorganisation and its Consequences', *Business and Economic History*, 27 (1998), 29–46.

Gourevitch, P., *Politics in Hard Times* (Ithaca: Cornell University Press, 1986).

Hacker, J. S. and Pierson, P., 'Business Power and Social Policy: Employers and the Formation of the American Welfare State', *Politics and Society*, 30 (2002), 277–325.

Hooper, N., 'A BCA Milestone, But Where to Now?', *Business Review Weekly*, 15 October 1993.

Lindblom, C. E., *Politics and Markets* (New York: Basic Books, 1977).

McEachern, D., Business Mates: *The Power and Politics of the Hawke Era* (Sydney: Prentice Hall, Australia, 1991).

McLachlan, M., 'Big Business Splits Over Greenhouse', *Australian Financial Review*, 22 November 2002.

McLaughlin, P. A., 'How Business Relates to the Hawke Government: The Captains of Industry', in B. Galligan and G. Singleton (eds.) *Business and Government under Labor* (Melbourne: Longman, 1991).

Martin, C, J., 'Business and the New Economic Activism: The Growth of Corporate Lobbies in the Sixties', *Polity*, 27 (1994), 49–76.
——'Nature or Nurture: Sources of Firm Preference for National Health Reform', *American Political Science Review*, 89 (1995), 898–913.
——*Stuck in Neutral: Business and the Politics of Human Capital Investment Policy* (Princeton: Princeton University Press, 2000).
Mitchell, N., *The Conspicuous Corporation: Business, Public Policy, and Representative Democracy* (Ann Arbor: University of Michigan, 1997).
Offe, C. and Wiesenthal, H., 'Two Logics of Collective Action: Theoretical Notes on Social Class and Organisational Form', *Political Power and Social Theory*, 1 (1980), 76–115.
Olson, M., *The Logic of Collective Action* (Cambridge, Mass.: Harvard University Press, 1965).
Parbo, A., Address to the 10th Anniversary Dinner, Business Council of Australia, Melbourne, 14 October 1993.
Perkin, I., 'Business Lobbying Turns into Capital Intensive Industry', *The Australian*, 3 June 1983.
Plotke, D., 'The Political Mobilization of Business', in M. Petracca (eds.), *The Politics of Interests: Interest Groups Transformed* (Boulder: Westview Press, 1992).
Polities, G., quoted in Business Council of Australia, *Business Council: Performance and Challenges,* Background Paper for a Review of the Council's Activities and Processes, (Melbourne: BCA, 1985).
Polsky, A., 'When Business Speaks: Political Entrepreneurship, Discourse and Mobilisation in American Partisan Regimes', *Journal of Theoretical Politics*, 12 (2000), 455–76.
Sheldon, P. and Thornthwaite, L., 'Ex Parte Accord: The Business Council of Australia and Industrial Relations Change', *International Journal of Business Studies*, October (1993), 37–55.
Swank, D., 'Politics and the Structural Dependence of the State in Democratic Capitalist Nations', *American Political Science Review*, 86 (1992), 38–54.
Vogel, D., 'Political Science and the Study of Corporate Power: A Dissent from the New Conventional Wisdom', *British Journal of Political Science*, 17 (1987), 385–408.
——*Fluctuating Fortunes: The Political Power of Business in America* (New York: Basic Books, 1989).
——'The Study of Business and Politics', *California Management Review*, 38 (1996), 146–65.

Chapter 11

The Contingencies of Non-Profit Leadership

Hillel Schmid

Introduction

Non-profit organizations (NPOs) play a major role as providers of social, cultural, religious, and many other services. Some NPOs are also significant loci of social mobilization and political advocacy. To do both at the same time requires careful management of relations to political, in particular government, actors who value and often pay for NPO service delivery, but who are not necessarily enamoured of NPO activism that is critical of existing social policies and service-delivery philosophies. At the level of the political system as a whole, the public leadership exercised by the NPO sector is therefore fundamentally ambivalent: in part derived from formal, delegated or contracted roles in policy implementation through public-service delivery; and in part informal, partisan and potentially oppositional, rooted in social or professional ideologies as well as claims to representation of client and stakeholder groups.

The NPO literature discusses in great detail the mission, core activities, problems, and dilemmas faced by NPOs, as well as their developing relationships with governmental agencies and for-profit organizations. It suggests that NPOs cannot be lumped together into one category; rather, they belong to different groups and sectors, including welfare, charity, health, social services, and sports, as well as recreational, religious, and other types of organizations. They have little in common. This is particularly true of the distinction between organizations whose core activity is service provision and civil society organizations which promote social involvement and citizen participation in setting public policies and determining the public agenda.

In this chapter, I argue that the leadership challenges faced by the senior strata of various types of NPOs that can be distinguished differ greatly, and conduce to different philosophies and styles of leadership. To clarify the significance of the relationship between leadership patterns and the characteristics of NPOs, I describe the changing context in which they operate. Next I highlight the distinctive features of NPOs that set them apart from governmental agencies and for-profit organizations. Drawing upon a review of relevant parts of the leadership literature, I will propose a model linking a typology of NPOs to different types of leadership that might fit their unique attributes. The upshot of this chapter is to highlight the differentiated nature of leadership dispersal in relation to NPOs.

The changing context of non-profit organizations

As of the 1980s, there have been far-reaching changes in the policies and mechanisms for provision of social and other civil services. These changes relate mainly to the gradual transfer of traditional government powers and roles to NGOs in the for-profit and non-profit sectors (Austin 2003; Bode 2006). The changes are part of broader, more comprehensive 'hollowing out' processes of the state sector that have taken place mainly in the United States, England, Western European countries, Australia, Japan, and Israel. In those processes, the government has been diminishing its role in direct provision of services, and has encouraged and supported NGOs to enter those domains (Ascoli and Ranci 2002). These changes can be attributed to ideological considerations as well as to utilitarian and economic motives. The ideology guiding the changes is based mainly on the concept of self-reliance, which has redefined the rights and obligations of citizens vis-à-vis the state (Schmid 1988; Netting et al.1990), but also on ideas about 'reinventing government' in which the state should 'steer' (make policy) but not 'row' (deliver public services itself), as the latter can be done more efficiently by non-state actors (for-profit and NPO) competing for public contracts (e.g. Osborne and Gaebler 1992).

Even though the state is committed to citizens in various domains, liberal ideologies emphasize that citizens also have obligations to the state. From an economic point of view, the state has found that the responsibility of providing services is a budgetary burden that generates deficits as well as high unemployment rates. These problems can be avoided when resources are allocated properly, and when a new division of labour is established vis-à-vis other agencies that provide services to citizens. It has also been argued that delegating some of the traditional roles of the government to NGOs is an efficient way of reducing bureaucracy, increasing the responsiveness of the state to the needs of clients, and encouraging innovation.

Transferring the role of service provision to NGOs also serves other interests of the government. It creates a political climate that justifies cuts in government programs. It lays the groundwork for charging fees for services that were provided free of charge in the past. And it protects the government from public resistance to the policy of budget cuts, and increases the potential for

NGOs to serve as institutional intermediaries between the state and the citizens to whom they are accountable.

Changes in government ideologies and espoused policies have thus led to the rapid growth and development of the non-profit sector, as well as to the entry of private for-profit organizations into the arena of service provision, which was controlled in the past almost solely by governmental agencies and NPOs. Those changes have also led to devolution and decentralization of services, as well as to the introduction of a 'new public management' (Esping-Andersen 1999, 2000; Ascoli and Ranci 2002; Gronbjerg and Salamon 2002). Privatization of social services and contracting out of service provision to non-governmental organizations have created a new situation for the state as well as for the NPOs (Smith and Lipsky 1993). As a result of privatization, competition between non-profit and for-profit providers has gained momentum. In that situation, NPOs have been forced to restructure themselves and to reevaluate their organizational and management strategies, in order to enhance their distinctive competence and competitiveness. Competition has caused NPOs to significantly modify their strategies, pricing, and marketing policies. They have also invested more efforts in careful analysis of the cost of their services, as well as in enhancing their public relations mechanisms, in improving the quality of their services, and in responding more rapidly to the needs of clients. In those processes, they have adopted new patterns of organizational behaviour, structures, and strategies (Alexander 1999, 2003).

Privatization has been accompanied by processes of devolution, where more powers and responsibilities have been delegated to NGOs. In that way, non-governmental organizations can define the type and scope of services they provide, criteria for eligibility, and procedures for provision of services. This trend has been accompanied by processes that reinforce the need to introduce advanced systems of management in governmental and non-governmental organizations. This philosophy of management highlights the need to set measurable goals that can be evaluated within specific time periods, as well as to manage public systems more efficiently and economically, to considerably reduce costs, and to increase the transparency of the organization's activities. Consistent with this approach, emphasis is placed on performance (outcomes) rather than on administrative processes (throughputs). Moreover, efforts focus on making service units into profitable centres, whose existence is contingent on the ability to cope independently and effectively with relevant market niches, and to eliminate or cut services that are not economically feasible or profitable. All of this reflects the momentum of commercialization in the markets where NPOs operate (Weisbrod 1977, 1988; Alexander 1999; Frumkin 2002; Eikenberry and Kluver 2004).

Consequently, the ideology of non-profit social and human service organizations has changed from one that focuses on treatment and concern for others to one that focuses on efficiency and economic feasibility. The situation created by these processes was described well by Lipsky and Smith (1989–90), who argued that in comparison with governmental agencies, non-profit agencies are less concerned with serving all clients in a specific target group. Rather, non-profit and for-profit providers focus on serving clients who fall within the definition of the agency's service mission. In the same vein, Knapp et al.(1990) contended that purchase of service contracting has potential for 'fragmentation, discontinuity, complexity, low-quality outputs, poorly targeted services, productive inefficiencies, horizontal and vertical inequalities, wasteful duplication and inappropriate replication, sectoralism, and paternalism' (1990: 213–14).

As a result of these processes, NPOs, which constituted the ideological and instrumental mainstay of the classic welfare state, have become the forces to hasten its transformation or indeed as some would argue its end. They have reinforced the transition from principles of universality that guided the ideologists of the welfare state, to principles of sectoralism and individualism, which are the basis of the free market.

From autonomy to ambiguity: NPOs and the politics of care and advocacy

NPOs include 'thousands of private community groups, health clinics, schools, day care centres, environmental organizations, social clubs, development organizations, cultural institutions, professional associations, consumer groups, and similar entities that comprise what is increasingly coming to be known as the private or civil society sector' (Salamon 1999: xvii).

They are formal and institutionalized to some extent, do not distribute profits generated to their owners, are self-governing, and involve some meaningful degree of voluntary participation (Salamon and Anheier 1992). Those organizations, particularly social service organizations, are ideological in nature. They aim to realize social, humanistic, and altruistic ideologies, with emphasis on attaining social justice and closing social gaps. As such, they serve as a safety net for weak and helpless populations whose special needs are not addressed.

In the domain of human and social services, NPOs include organizations that provide individual and family services (social counselling, welfare, or referral), job training (training, work experience, vocational or rehabilitative courses for unemployed, underemployed, and physically challenged), day care (children and infants), and residential care (children, elderly, etc.). There are also many faith-based organizations that deal with low-income communities, and that provide a variety of human services from housing to drug counselling, emergency food distribution, and employment assistance (Cnaan 2002).

NPOs operate mainly in contexts characterized by social ambiguity, where they have a relative advantage over public, governmental, and for-profit organizations (Billis 1993). In theory, the distinctive and ambiguous structures of those organizations enable them to overcome problems of principal–agent gap, median voter reluctance, ambiguous messages from politicians to staff, and lack of market interest. NPOs have traditionally acted as pioneers that stake out the land and enter uncultivated, unknown domains and territories. At the same time, they try to find innovative solutions for populations whose needs have not been met by government agencies or by the organizations in the private, for-profit sector.

NPOs perform numerous functions in modern societies, and their contribution is particularly important in heterogeneous, multicultural societies with populations from diverse ethnic or religious backgrounds. In homogeneous societies where the dominant majority is one ethnic group, their contribution is less significant (Salamon and Anheier 1998). In addition to their role as service providers, they fulfil other functions such as buffering, representation, mediation, lobbying, and political advocacy vis-à-vis the state and governmental agencies. As buffer organizations, they mediate between the government and citizens, so that citizens have less direct contact with government authorities. For example, citizens can turn directly to the providers of home care services for the elderly, whereas governmental agencies are distant and unknown to the clients (Schmid 2004). As representatives of the citizens, NPOs mediate on behalf of disadvantaged and excluded populations in society, who do not have access to the political arena. Thus, for example, community service organizations not only encourage civic engagement in decisions that affect the lives of local residents, but they also represent their clients vis-à-vis formal agencies that set the public and civil agenda. In that capacity, they engage in mediation and conflict resolution, and they deal with the problems and the needs of various populations that lack know-how, expertise, and effective tools to resolve conflicts. They also engage in advocacy activities, which aim at advancing deprived populations, and promoting new legislation that establishes the rights of persecuted minorities. Those organizations are the ones that exert pressure on policy-makers to change priorities for allocation of resources available to the state, and channel resources to needy populations. As such, they are the ones that seek to ensure the principles of democracy and equal opportunity (Eisenberg 2000).

However, for example in Israel – reflecting a similar trend seen in many other Western nations – today most of the third sector NPOs are service providers (about 83% on the average), and only a few are considered civil service organizations, for example, advocacy, lobby, and social change organizations (Schmid et al.2008). Their environments are complex, political, and uncertain. Because they rely heavily on resources from the relevant institutional environments and are highly dependent on government funding, they need to attain legal legitimacy. In many Western countries, the average share of government funding is as high as 50 per cent to 55 per cent of the organization's income (Gronbjerg and Salamon 2002; Boris and Steurle 2006).

Dependence on government resources imposes constraints on the organizations, and leaves them in an iron cage where they have to conform to standards, policies, and regulations (DiMaggio and Powell 1983). Thus, the institutional environment imposes bureaucratic norms of behaviour and restrains change, creativity, and innovation in organizations (Meyer et al.1988; Davis-Smith and Hedley 1993; Deakin 1996; Edelman and Suchman 1997; Schmid 2003). In addition, NPOs have encountered competition with the for-profit organizations, and have had to adapt themselves to a new, commercialized environment. This has resulted in a tendency to imitate the technologies used by for-profits, which they not been familiar with in the past.

The conflicting pressures from governmental entities and market forces have the potential to blur the organizational identity of NPOs and turn them into a kind of hybrid organization, which combines diverse, contradictory organizational properties. In that process, NPOs also confront critical dilemmas that derive from the structural tension between their espoused ideology and social mission on the one hand, and the need to cope with the challenges of the free market by making profits and competing with commercial organizations on the other (Young 2005).

The present chapter will examine what patterns of leadership are needed in NPOs, in light of changes in their unique characteristics generated by the conflicting pressures they face. In the following section, I will present the conceptual model that provides the basis for an analysis of the types of leadership that are most appropriate for NPOs in different situations and in different types of NPOs.

Varieties of non-profit leadership

Leadership is a dynamic concept, which involves processes of constant change in the leaders themselves, their peers, and their followers, as well as in the situations and contingencies they encounter (House and Aditya 1997). Current theoretical approaches emphasize the transition from the classic traits approach (Hersey and Blanchard 1982; Bargal 2000) to new theoretical models, which emphasize the impact of changing organizational situations on patterns of leadership. According to the new models, leaders need to adapt their leadership to the unique situation of the organization (Fiedler 1967, 1977; House 1971, 1977; House and Mitchell 1974; Fiedler and Garcia 1987). Special attention has been given to the theory of charismatic leadership (House 1977; Conger and Kanungo 1987), as well as to the theories of transformational and transactional leadership (Burns 1978; Bass 1985), and to visionary theories (Bennis and Nanus 1985; Nanus 1992).

Especially in NPOs, where human resources – often including unpaid volunteers – play a critical role in ensuring the organization's success, leaders need to take various steps to articulate and transmit a vision to their followers and mobilize resources to implement their vision. NPO leaders need not only to articulate goals, but also exhibit empathy and consideration, and actively stimulate their followers.

The contingency model of NPO leadership to be presented is based on the underlying assumption that NPOs vary in their ideologies, goals and objectives, organizational cultures, and core activities as well as in the characteristics of their human resources, in the levels of their professional expertise, and in the levels of their psychological and professional maturity. Hence, different types of leadership are needed in different types of organizations. It is also assumed that across the organizational life cycle, there is a need for leaders with different qualities and different leadership styles, depending on the organization's situation at a given point in time. The presentation of the different types of leadership in this section is based on a conceptual model that provides a framework for systematic analysis of the patterns which, I surmise, are most appropriate for different types of NPOs (see Table 11.1).

The convergence of the two axes in the model depicts the unique characteristics of NPOs and their task environments. The vertical axis represents a continuum between *service provider and civil society organizations*. Most of the non-profit third sector organizations provide a wide range of services to diverse populations, either at the initiative of the government or at the initiative of their founders and board members. Through the process of contracting out, the government delegates power and responsibility for service provision to those organizations, and constitutes their main source of funding. At the other end of the continuum, we find civil society organizations, which serve as a counterweight to the state and its formal institutions. They represent disadvantaged populations and those who do not have access to government funding, in addition to struggling for civil rights and freedom of organization, and protesting against social injustice, inequality, and social gaps. They protect the rights of workers who are defined as 'transparent', blow the whistle against governmental tyranny and bureaucracy, and seek to influence and change the existing social order.

The horizontal axis represents the dimension of *formal versus informal organizations*. Formal behaviour refers to patterns of organization, management, and work in a mechanistic structure that is based on legitimation of activity by the government. The structure of those organizations is hierarchical, with a clear division of tasks as well as mechanisms of coordination, communication, and decision-making based on established principles. By contrast, informal organizations adopt an organistic structure, which is flat, non-hierarchical,

Table 11.1 Four types of NPOs: provision of services vs. civil society orientation, and formal vs. informal structure

Orientation towards service provision

Informal structure			Formal structure
	The organization is at the formative stage of the life cycle. The organization's structure is entrepreneurial, informal, not established, and organistic. The entrepreneur is the owner and director. Lack of established management processes; lack of mechanisms for decision-making, communication, coordination, and evaluation. The main function is provision of services and responses to the needs of special populations, at the initiative of the founder. The organization struggles for legal legitimation of its existence. There is a public board whose work procedures and relations with the director have not yet been established. The organization's budget is limited. I	The organization's structure is formal, bureaucratic, and hierarchical. The organization operates according to formal standards, criteria, and work procedures. A legal public board oversees the organization's management. The main function is provision of services. The organization clearly defines its target population. The organization adopts and introduces service technologies based on a broad range of areas in its work routine. Low level of political advocacy activity. III	
	II Organizations with an orientation towards strengthening the foundations of civil society. The organization's activity focuses on a charismatic leader with an informal leadership style, and is based on ideological values of involvement. The organization's structure is informal, flat, participatory, empowering, and cooperative. Emphasis is on team work, without a formal division of labour and role definitions. Ad hoc, short-term, and focused activities. An esprit de corps generates cohesion among the members and groups in the organization in the process of realizing their social and civic ideology. Democratic processes and open communication characterize the dialogue among members and groups in the organization.	IV A formal organization with a hierarchical structure and division of labour among staff members. Formal decision-making patterns (besides informal patterns). The organization's main function is political activity and advocacy. It engages in constant attempts to change the civil agenda, and exerts political pressure, and lobbying. Clients are involved in policy-making, and a constant attempt is made to increase civic engagement. Clear, organized, and systematic activities in diverse areas which relate to rights of minorities, disadvantaged, and excluded populations. Resources are channelled for promotion of public relations in order to change attitudes towards bureaucratic governments and enhance awareness of minority rights.	

Orientation towards civil society

not authoritative, and lacks formal, rigid processes. In those organizations, communication is mainly oral and verbal, as are the patterns of coordination and cooperation. Communication is multi-directional and bidirectional, and is not based only on channels that represent a hierarchical perspective of communication, flowing from the 'top down'. The work of staff members is largely based on mutual trust, while the division of labour is based on relative advantages and professional specialization. Problem-solving and decision-making processes are based on teamwork and involve all staff members. There is no official management, and in many cases, teamwork is a substitute for the existence of one director at the apex of the pyramid.

The two axes converge to form four quadrants. The *first quadrant* represents the combination of service provision and an informal organizational structure. Service providers with an informal structure are usually at the initial stages of their life cycle. They can be organizations initiated by private entrepreneurs who identify unfulfilled needs of certain populations when the services provided by the government and the market are insufficient. These organizations are usually organistic, primitive, and informal. They do not have a clear, hierarchical structure or rigid division of labour. Their professional staff is small, and workers perform various tasks without specific specializations. Decision-making and policy-making procedures are informal, and are usually concentrated in the hands of the leader, as there tends not to be a fully developed management or public board structure to share the leadership role. The leader negotiates with agencies in the task environment in an attempt to attain formal, legal legitimation and ensure a steady flow of resources to the organization.

This first type of NPO lends itself to *entrepreneurial leadership*. The leader has deeply rooted beliefs, and a vision that he/she seeks to implement by initiating new and innovative service programmes. In that situation, the leader has to have the charisma and power needed to position the organization and mobilize the human and material resources it needs to fill the vacuum when the government and markets fail to provide services. Moreover, the leader needs to have competencies that will enable him or her to maintain relationships with various constituencies and interest groups as well as with staff members in the organization. At this stage of the organization's life cycle, the leader should concentrate efforts on the institutional environment in order to attain a consensus regarding the organization's domain and the programmes it offers. Moreover, the leader has to mobilize the resources for implementation of the activities and processes, while persuading the governmental agencies of the organization's relative advantage. In fact, at this stage, an external orientation and recognition by outside entities is even more important than management of the organization's internal affairs.

The *second quadrant* represents the combination of a civil society orientation and an informal organizational structure. The activity of the organizations represented in that quadrant aims to enhance public awareness and consciousness of human rights, to protect and promote the rights and privileges of disadvantaged populations, and to represent those populations vis-à-vis governmental authorities, as well as to give those populations access to arenas where decisions are made and resources are allocated. The organizations represented in this quadrant are social and human service organizations, whose structure and administrative processes have not yet been established. They can be grass-roots advocates of social change or advocacy organizations, which are organistic in nature and democratic in their patterns. They tend to have a flat, participatory organizational structure, where members are highly involved in processes of formulating policies and making decisions. Although they are often limited in size as well as in their achievements, they play an important role in undermining the confidence of the bureaucratic government administration, which believes in maintaining the status quo. Their staff consists primarily of volunteers and activists, who view their activity as part of an ideological mission, which reflects their perception of the democratic state and their belief in the humanistic and social values that they represent. In organizations with a flat structure, there is no clear hierarchy or formal division of tasks, and communication is usually direct and unmediated. The second quadrant includes organizations that focus on social change, civic engagement, and protest activities as well as peace organizations, interest groups for social action, and organized grass-roots groups of neighbourhood residents.

This type of NPO lends itself to *democratic and participative leadership*. The leader emerges from the group, and is recognized as such by the other group members in light of his or her vision, skills, and competencies (House and Baetz 1979). Those leaders do not exert formal powers and authority; rather, they engage staff in decision-making and delegate responsibilities. Their leadership style lacks formality and ceremonial expression, and resembles a type of leadership common in social movements. Because they know the members of their team, they tend to give them powers and responsibilities with the understanding that they are followers rather than subordinates. As such, they are expected to be partners in managing the organization and influencing its environment. Evidently, the followers at this stage of the organization's life cycle are not in pursuit of a professional career, but believe in their values and in their contribution to building a society characterized by justice and equal opportunity.

Leaders are attentive to members of the group and share with them, while gathering information and ideas through brainstorming. They also provide the group members with information, which enhances their sense of involvement and participation in the decision-making process. The leaders delegate authority and responsibility, particularly in administrative and technical affairs that might prevent them from realizing their vision and goals, and from fulfilling the mission of the organization. In that way, they create an organizational culture that is based on open horizontal and vertical communication among people at different levels of the organization in order to attain support, understanding, and commitment that generates social cohesion.

As for the leaders' orientation to the external environment and governmental institutions, they tend to voice complaints, warnings, and opposition against official policies. In so doing, these leaders jeopardize their status, as the governmental institutions do all they can to minimize their influence in the best case and remove them from their positions in the worst case.

The *third quadrant* represents the combination of service provision and formal structure. Organizations in this quadrant include non-profit associations whose main function is service provision, and which have an established structure with a public board, a director, professional workers, and volunteer staff. These associations are the main providers of services contracted by the government and local authorities, and their relations with the government are largely characterized by mutual dependence. On the one hand, the government and local authorities depend on the organizations to provide services. Rather than establish new mechanisms for service provision, the government and local authorities maintain their role in setting policies and establishing the basket of services to be provided, in setting standards for the quality and quantity of services provided, and in establishing criteria for eligibility, as well as in supervision and control of the process of service provision. On the other hand, the organizations depend on government funding, which is the main source of their revenue. To ensure a steady, certain flow of resources, the organizations tend to adopt behaviour that conforms to government policy, and avoid excessive innovation in their programmes. Only a few engage in advocacy, because they prefer 'not to bite the hand that feeds them' (Mosley 2006; Schmid et al., 2008). The types of organizations in this quadrant include, among others: organizations that provide home care services to the elderly, organizations for children and adolescents at risk, and organizations that provide services to people with physical and mental disabilities, battered women, people with mental retardation, and young children, as well as vocational centres and organizations for unemployed people.

The most appropriate pattern of leadership in this type of organization is *transactional leadership* – a more administrative, technical, and bureaucratic kind of leadership, in which the leader centralizes power, and focuses on maintaining routine procedures. Thus, the leader aims to achieve economies of scale and efficiency in an attempt to ensure a steady flow of resources without undermining the agency's legitimation. This pattern of leadership is not charismatic or ideological, but is instrumental and goal-oriented with respect to external relations as well as with respect to relations within the organization. Towards that end, the leader aims to attain a high level of performance in terms of the quantity and quality of services provided, and seeks to expand the agency's domain. The leaders represented in this quadrant are not considered ground-breakers or innovators; rather, their business-like and 'managerial' behaviour reflects the attempts of the institutional environment to co-opt them and suppress attempts to promote political advocacy activities.

The *fourth quadrant* represents the combination of a civil society orientation and formal structure, and includes political-advocacy organizations, whose main function is to influence and even change the public agenda. Those organizations seek to change policies and influence the decisions of the institutional elite and government agencies through enhancement of civic participation in efforts to promote a collective goal or interest (Boris and Mosher-Williams 1998). They aim to effect changes in existing or future practices for a specific client or group of clients with a common interest (Ezell 2001), as well as to protect basic civil rights (Schoff and Stevenson 1998; Boris and Krehely 2003). In the effort to influence social, political, and civic agendas, these organizations seek to gain access to the arena where decisions that affect the lives of citizens are made. In addition, they lobby for favourable policies, and promote citizen participation in influencing decisions and changing priorities for allocation of resources (Andrews and Edwards 2004).

In contrast to Quadrant II, the organizations in Quadrant IV are highly formalized, with a hierarchical division of labour, and established processes of formulating policies and making decisions, as well as coordination mechanisms. The activities are no longer sporadic, ad hoc, spontaneous, and short-term; rather, their strategies aim at achieving long-range goals such as changing power relations, promoting legislation to ensure the rights of minorities and deprived populations, for example, organizations that deal with environmental protection, social justice, citizen participation, and community advocacy.

This last type of NPOs calls for *activist–diplomatic leadership*. It recognizes the importance of a formal organizational structure as part of the process in which the NPO matures and establishes its relations vis-à-vis the government and competitive business sectors. These leaders, in contrast to leaders of organizations in the second quadrant, have a deep understanding of the importance of the organization's formal status, because they are aware that the institutional environment prefers to grant legitimation to organizations with formal structures (Dacin et al.2002). However, the leaders in those organizations focus primarily on influencing and even changing the public agenda, and raising consciousness of social issues. As part of the effort to change power relations in the political, social, and economic arenas, they can be considered political leaders in the sense that they persist in their struggle against the governmental agencies. They don't accept official policies, decisions, and statements without question. Rather, they attempt to shift public discourse in the direction of the citizens as a means of empowering the entities that challenge bureaucratic mechanisms and force them to change their behaviour and decisions about allocation of resources. Political struggles and political advocacy are part of the leaders' espoused ideology, and their efforts focus on identifying weaknesses in the behaviour of the government and strengthening their constituencies by gaining access to the political arena, where decisions are made.

This kind of leadership is oriented towards second-order social change through radical changes in the political arena. The leaders are militant, ethical, and ideological people who faithfully represent their clients, and oppose the official, bureaucratic mechanisms. This pattern of leadership is different than the pattern that prevails among organizations in the second quadrant. Activist–diplomatic leaders understand that in order to strengthen civil society, amateur activity that relies solely on the leader's charisma and sense of mission is not enough. In those organizations, the leaders recognize the importance of establishing formal structures that are strong enough to sustain their struggles, as well as the need to form coalitions and coordinate activities with other organizations.

The power of these leaders derives from the legitimation of their struggle, as well as from the target population that they represent. In that context, they raise their clients' consciousness of civil issues, and involve them in formulating policies, making decisions, and struggling for social causes. Yet they know they head formal organizations rather than grass-roots interest groups, social movements, or protest movements, and that they also bear responsibility for a professional apparatus that needs to operate smoothly and efficiently.

However, unlike the directors of organizations in Quadrant III, they do not conform with government policy. The espoused ideology of most organizations represented in Quadrant IV discourages dependence on government funding, because reliance on the government forces them to abandon their mission, silences their protests, and prevents them from challenging official decisions. However, this ideology limits possibilities for raising funds, because not every funding source is a potential source of support for the organization's activities. Nonetheless, the emphasis on independence and autonomous operation enables the leaders of those organizations to act independently without having to follow orders from external funding sources. These leaders often pay high personal and organizational prices for adhering to their ideology and goals, but they are prepared to sacrifice their personal interests for that purpose.

Coping with environmental complexities: NPO leadership dilemmas

NPOs are becoming increasingly complex. They are no longer voluntary organizations per se, whose informal characteristics have been discussed and analyzed extensively in the theoretical and empirical literature. Nor do they comprise a group of individuals who share a common social ideology and common values. In recent decades, NPOs have become more institutionalized and formal, although most of them are still mission-oriented and espouse an ideology of enhancing the well-being of their clients.

In most developed Western countries, NPOs provide a wide range of services which governments provided directly in the past. Because most of them rely on government funding, there is also a risk that they will become not only a shadow of the state, but that they will mainly act on behalf of the government and constitute a 'Government B'. At the same time, processes of privatization, decentralization, and devolution have gained momentum. In those processes, advanced patterns of management have been adopted, in accordance with the philosophy of new public management. Additionally, the strategy of contracting out has intensified processes of commercialization and privatization in the traditional social service market, which was dominated years ago by voluntary NPOs. As a result, NPOs have been forced to compete with private, for-profit organizations for government funding as well as for funding from private foundations. They have also been forced to engage in an ideological struggle against those who advocate privatization, and who attribute operational and utilitarian advantages to private, for-profit organizations. Thus, NPOs face complex, competitive, and rapidly changing political environments.

Leaders in those organizations face a dilemma: they have to adapt their patterns of behaviour to at least two types of environments with contradictory characteristics. In institutional environments, leaders tend to adopt conformist behaviour, which ensures that the organization will gain legitimacy and resources controlled by the environment. By contrast, in competitive business environments, they need to adopt alternative leadership patterns that are more commercial, aggressive, goal-oriented, programmed, and complex, 'for by wise stratagems you shall wage war' (Proverbs 24:6). Even though it has been argued that leaders need to adapt themselves to changing situations (Schmid 2006), and to the different stages of development in the organization's life cycle, the proposed model does not necessarily support that contention.

For example, the type of leadership appropriate for the organizations in Quadrant II is not necessarily appropriate for the organizations in Quadrant IV, even if the organizations in both quadrants focus on civil society activities. The leadership pattern portrayed in Quadrant II is appropriate for informal interest groups, social movements, and grass-roots organizations at the initial stages of their life cycle. However, those informal qualities are not appropriate for organizations in Quadrant IV, where the leaders need to understand that in order to promote the organization's agenda and its civil goals, it is essential to adopt a more formal and established structure with organized, systematic, and rational work procedures. Similarly, the patterns appropriate for leaders of organizations in Quadrant II, which have a civic orientation and informal structure, are not appropriate for organizations in Quadrant III, which focus on service provision and have a formal structure. Leaders of organizations in Quadrant III need to have different skills and competencies than those in informal civil society organizations. In that connection, studies have shown that the organizations represented in Quadrant III do not engage in political or advocacy activities, because they lack the appropriate skills and abilities for that field, and their relative advantage is in the area of service provision (Schmid et al. 2008).

In conclusion, the many faces of the dispersed leadership that NPO leaders may exercise requires a high degree of contextual sensitivity and adaptability on the part of the people who occupy these roles. Also, the great variability of contexts and organizational types of NPOs raises issues of leader selection and succession. Individuals with specific characteristics and skills can be suitable for one type of NPO whereas those same sources of leadership style may be inappropriate in other types. If a leader is unable to adapt his or her behaviour patterns to the situation at hand, it is best to choose a new leader with appropriate skills and qualities. Therefore, the proposed model can be useful for boards of directors in the process of selecting and hiring leaders for their organization. This is also true of leader succession. In the process of choosing new leaders, it is necessary to consider whether their skills are appropriate for the current situation of the organization, in light of the characteristics presented in each of the quadrants of the model, and in light of the unique characteristics of the organization's external environment.

Bibliography

Alexander, J., 'The Impact of Devolution on Nonprofits: A Multiphase Study of Social Service Organizations', *Nonprofit Management and Leadership*, 10 (1999), 57–70.

——'Adaptive Strategies of Nonprofit Human Service Organizations in an Era of Devolution and New Public Management', *Nonprofit Management and Leadership*, 20 (2003), 287–303.

Andrews, K. T., and Edwards, B., 'Advocacy Organizations in the US Political Process', *Annual Review of Sociology*, 30 (2004), 479–506.

Ascoli, U. and Ranci, C., *Dilemmas of the Welfare Mix: The New Structure of Welfare in an Era of Privatization* (New York: Kluwer/Plenum, 2002).

Austin, M., 'The Changing Relationship between Nonprofit Organizations and Public Social Service Agencies in the Era of Welfare Reform', *Nonprofit and Voluntary Sector Quarterly*, 32 (2003), 97–114.

Bargal, D., 'The Manager as Leader', in R. Patti (ed.), *The Handbook of Social Welfare Management* (Thousand Oaks, CA: Sage, 2000), 303–19.

Bass, B. M., *Leadership and Performance Beyond Expectations* (New York: The Free Press, 1985).

Bennis, W. and Nanus, B., *Leaders: The Strategies for Taking Charge* (New York: Harper and Row, 1985).

Billis, D., 'Sector Blurring and Non-profit Centers: The Case of the United Kingdom', *Non-Profit and Voluntary Sector Quarterly*, 22 (1993), 241–57.

Bode, I., 'Disorganized Welfare Mixes: Voluntary Agencies and New Governance Regimes in Western Europe', *Journal of European Social Policy*, 16 (2006), 346–59.

Boris, E. and Krehely, J., 'Civic Participation and Advocacy', in L. M. Salamon (ed.), *The State of Nonprofit America* (Washington, D.C.: Brookings Institution Press, 2003), 299–330.

——and Mosher-Williams, R., 'Nonprofit Advocacy Organizations: Assessing the Definitions, Classifications and Data', *Nonprofit and Voluntary Sector Quarterly*, 27 (1998), 488–506.

——and Steurle, E., 'Scope and Dimensions of the Nonprofit Sector', in W. W. Powell and R. Steinberg (eds.), *The Nonprofit Sector: A Research Handbook* (New Haven, Conn.: Yale University Press, 2006), 66–88.

Burns, J. M., *Leadership* (New York: Harper and Row, 1978).

Cnaan, R. A., *The Invisible Caring Hand: American Congregations and the Provision of Welfare* (New York: New York University Press, 2002).

Conger, J. A. and Kanungo, R. A., 'Toward a Behavioral Theory of Charismatic Leadership in Organizational Settings', *Academy of Management Review*, 12 (1987), 637–47.

Dacin, M. T., Goodstein, J., and Scott, W. R., 'Institutional Theory and Institutional Change: Introduction to the Special Research Forum', *Academy of Management Journal*, 45 (2002), 45–57.

Davis-Smith, J. and Hedley, R., *Volunteering and the Contract Culture* (Berkhamsted, UK: Volunteer Centre, 1993).

Deakin, N., 'What Does Contracting Do to Users?', in D. Billis and M. Harris (eds.), *Voluntary Agencies: Challenges of Organization and Management* (Basingstoke, UK: Macmillan, 1996), 113–29.

DiMaggio, P. J. and Powell, W., 'The Iron Cage Revisited: Institutional Isomorphism and Collective Rationality in Organizational Fields', *American Sociological Review*, 48 (1983), 147–60.

Edelman, L., and Suchman, M. C., 'The Legal Environments of Organizations', *Annual Review of Sociology*, 23 (1997), 479–515.

Eikenberry, A. M. and Kluver, J. D., 'The Marketization of the Nonprofit Sector: Civil Society at Risk?', *Public Administration Review*, 66 (2004), 132–40.

Eisenberg, P., 'The Nonprofit Sector in a Changing World', *Nonprofit and Voluntary Sector Quarterly*, 27 (2000), 325–30.

Esping-Andersen, G., *Social Foundations of Postindustrial Economies* (New York: Oxford University Press, 1999).

——'The Sustainability of Welfare States into the Twenty-first Century', *International Journal of Health Services*, 30 (2000), 1–12.

Ezell, M., *Advocacy in the Human Services* (Belmont, CA: Thomson, 2001).

Fiedler, F. E., *A Theory of Leadership Effectiveness* (New York: McGraw-Hill, 1967).

——'A Rejoinder to Schriesheim and Kerr's Premature Obituary of the Contingency model', in J. G. Hunt and L. L. Larson (eds.), *Leadership: The Cutting Edge* (Carbondale, Ill.: Southern Illinois University Press, 1977), 45–50.

——and Garcia, J. E., *New Approaches to Effective Leadership: Cognitive Resources and Organizational Performance* (New York: Wiley, 1987).

Frumkin, P., 'Service Contracting with Nonprofit and For-Profit Providers', in J. D. Donahue and J. S. Nye (eds.), *Market-based Governance: Supply Side, Demand Side, Upside, and Downside* (Washington, D.C.: Brookings Institute Press, 2002), 66–87.

Gronbjerg, K. A. and Salamon, L. M., 'Devolution, Marketization, and the Changing Shape of Government-Nonprofit Relations', in L. M. Salamon (ed.), *The State of Nonprofit in America* (Washington, D.C.: Brookings Institution Press, 2002), 447–70.

Hersey, P. and Blanchard, K., *Management of Organizational Behavior: Utilizing Human Resources* (Englewood Cliffs, New Jersey: Prentice-Hall, 1982).

House, R. J., 'A Path Goal Theory of Leader Effectiveness', *Administrative Science Quarterly*, 16 (1971), 321–38.

——'A 1976 Theory of Charismatic Leadership', in J. G. Hunt and L. L. Larson (eds.), *Leadership: The Cutting Edge* (Carbondale, Ill.: Southern Illinois University Press, 1977), 189–207.

——and Aditya, R. N., 'The Social Scientific Study of Leader: Qua Vadis?', *Journal of Management*, 23 (1997), 409–73.

——and Baetz, M., 'Leadership: Some Empirical Generalizations and New Research Directions', in B. Staw (ed.), *Research in Organizational Behavior*, 1 (Greenwood, Conn.: JAI Press, 1979), 341–424.

——and Mitchell, T. R., 'Path-Goal Theory of Leadership', *Journal of Contemporary Business*, 3 (1974), 81–97.

Knapp, H., Robertson, E., and Thomason, C., 'Public Money, Voluntary Action: Whose Welfare?', in H. Anheier and W. Seibel (eds.), *The Third Sector* (Berlin: DeGruyter, 1990), 183–218.

Lipsky, M., and Smith, S. R., 'Nonprofit Organizations, Government, and the Welfare State', *Political Science Quarterly*, 104/4 (1989–90), 625–48.

Meyer, J. W., Scott, W. R., Strang, D., and Creighton, A., 'Bureaucratization without Centralization: Changes in the Organizational System of U.S. Public Education', 1940–1980', in L. Zucker (ed.), *Institutional Patterns and Organizations* (Cambridge, Mass.: Ballinger, 1988), 139–68.

Mosley, J. E., 'The Policy Advocacy of Human Service Nonprofits: How Institutional Processes and Environmental Conditions Shape Advocacy Involvement'. Unpublished Doctoral Dissertation', University of California, Los Angeles, 2006.

Nanus, B., *Visionary Leadership: Creating a Compelling Sense of Direction for Your Organization* (San Francisco, CA: Jossey-Bass, 1992).

Netting, F. E., McMurtry, S. L., Kettner, P. M., and McClintic, S. J., 'Privatization and Its Impact on Nonprofit Service Providers', *Nonprofit and Voluntary Sector Quarterly*, 19 (1990), 33–46.

Osborne, D. and Gaebler, T., *Reinventing Government* (New York: Penguin Press, 1992).

Salamon, L. M., *America's Nonprofit Sector: A Primer,* 2nd edn. (New York: Foundation Center, 1999).

——and Anheier, H. K. (eds.), 'In Search of the Nonprofit Sector I: The Question of Definitions', *Voluntas*, 3/2 (1992), 125–51.

————'Social Origins of Civil Society: Explaining the Nonprofit Sector Cross-nationally', *Voluntas,* 9 (1998), 213–48.

Schmid, H., *The Changing Context of Social Services and the Role of Nonprofits in the Delivery of Services* (Jerusalem: The Hebrew University of Jerusalem, The Graduate Program in Management of Nonprofit and Community Organizations, 1988).

Schmid, H., 'Rethinking the Policy of Contracting Out Social Services to Nongovernmental Organizations', *Public Management Review*, 5 (2003), 167–89.

——'The Israeli Long-Term Care Insurance Law: Selected Issues in Providing Home Care Services to the Frail Elderly', *Health and Social Care in the Community*, 13 (2004), 191–200.

——'Leadership Styles and Leadership Change in Human and Community Service Organizations', *Nonprofit Management and Leadership*, 17 (2006), 179–94.

——Bar, M., and Nirel, R., 'Advocacy Activities in Nonprofit Human Service Organizations: Implications for Policy', *Nonprofit and Voluntary Sector Quarterly*, 4 (2008), 581–602.

Schoff, R., and Stevenson, D. R., *The National Taxonomy of Exempt Entities Manual* (Washington, D. C.: Urban Institute, 1998).

Smith, S. R., and Lipsky, M., *Nonprofits for Hire: The Welfare State in the Age of Contracting* (Cambridge, Mass.: Harvard University Press, 1993).

Weisbrod, B., 'The Future of the Nonprofit Sector: Its Entwining with Private Enterprise and Government', *Journal of Policy Analysis and Management*, 4 (1977), 541–55.

——*To Profit Or Not to Profit: The Commercial Transformation of the Nonprofit Sector* (New York: Cambridge University Press, 1988).

Young, D. R., 'Mission-Market Tension in Managing Nonprofit Organizations', *Social Security*, 70 (2005), 32–55.

Chapter 12

Leadership of the Modern University

Glyn Davis and Geoff Sharrock

Democratic states distribute authority among public institutions chartered to balance the interests of citizens and protect them against the excesses of more powerful social actors, including the state itself. Democracies assume an active civil sphere where public organizations can emerge to represent sectoral interests by advocating policy that may differ from that administered by state authorities. This wide dispersal of administrative and representative authority across public institutions and community, professional, industry, media, and other non-government organizations is a feature of democracies. Collectively they inform, enable, and constrain the operation of executive government, and support a wide range of voices in pursuit of the self-guiding society.

Some non-government organizations are membership based. They use democratic methods to settle aims and choose leaders. Most public institutions are not 'democratic' in this sense, with their aims and senior offices set by legislation, and their leaders selected by a governing body. This chapter considers leadership in a university setting, with a particular emphasis on large, public sector universities[1]. Such institutions draw on a long tradition in which, since the early nineteenth century at least, intellectual freedom and considerable institutional autonomy are recognized as preconditions for the advance of knowledge and the benefits higher learning can bring to society. They claim a measure of autonomy from the state, particularly on the issue of intellectual freedom, but often depend on government funding, a favourable regulatory environment, and widespread acceptance of their value and relevance. To sustain the scholarly enterprise university leadership must explain the institution's work to the world, and speak to the university about societal demands. Endless judgements are required to balance these internal and external worlds, yet authority to make substantive decisions is widely dispersed, and often contested.

In this chapter we argue that university leadership is best understood as a *portfolio of tasks* performed on behalf of an institutional community devoted to an evolving set of public purposes, framed by a long tradition, and required to respond to competing demands from within and without. All this creates strategic ambiguity; and even where direction seems clear, leadership tasks are typically constrained by limited resources, government regulation, institutional governance processes, collegial norms of decision-making, and legacy systems and cultures. Indeed, a subtext of any discussion of leadership and the self-governing university is whether much unitary leadership is possible at all in this context. To speak of 'executive' leadership in a public university may be to presume too much.

Leadership of public institutions

Leadership is a fluid social construct. Conceptions of leadership and its acceptable forms turn in part on the nature and purpose of the organization. Much of the recent literature on leadership has focused on private enterprise rather than on public institutions. Here the leadership task is often framed around centralized authority and executive decision-making rather than the task of mediating the demands and constraints of different constituencies. The archetypes of leadership, often featuring heroic levels of wisdom, skill, and virtue on the part of exceptional individuals, are drawn from a limited number of spheres – typically political, military, and business leadership roles. Yet even this narrow set of studies generates a long and incoherent list of possible ways to understand leadership. These include:

- *trait theories* (leaders are people with *innate qualities* such as intelligence or resilience that equip them for the role);
- *behavioural theories* (leadership is a *set of stances and practices* that leaders adopt to balance the accomplishment of group tasks with the psychic needs of followers);
- *power-influence theories* (leadership is a social *influence* process, affected by the way power and authority are acquired and used);
- *situational theories* (leaders require a repertoire of *different styles* that allow them to take account of the type of problem being tackled, the abilities of follower groups, the organizational culture, and the risk environment);
- *transformational theories* (leaders are people who *articulate and exemplify* a set of compelling aspirations and attributes that mobilize follower groups to achieve great things); and
- *functional theories* (leaders are those people who play a focal role in meeting the needs of an organization, its purposes, and its people at any given moment).

Some leaders can be described using all these frames, while others appear *sui generis*. Many scholars in the field (e.g. Craig and Yetton [1995]; Yukl [1998]) see little prospect of reaching a grand unifying theory of leadership. Recognizing that ideas of leadership are likely to remain ambiguous and contested, our pragmatic view sees a leader as anyone with a constituency willing to trust the leader to make wise choices on their behalf, in ways that support their aims, hopes, and interests.

The idea that leaders exist primarily to serve the aims of those led rather than be supported in pursuit of an executive vision is of course a very democratic notion but, again, for public institutions the relationship is not so simple. When democratically structured organizations – clubs, societies, nations – elect leaders, there remains a clear relationship between leaders and led. Most public institutions, though, do not elect their leader, instead relying on the governance structure to select a leader. It is in the nature of public institutions that the leader must attend to several constituencies, at a minimum the governing board, those who appointed them and the colleagues they work with, as well as staff groups, clients, partners, and other interested parties outside the institution. Leaders thus face several sets of claims, all potentially in conflict, wherever thorny issues are delegated upwards for resolution.

This situation creates a paradox for leadership in public but internally non-democratic institutions. To perform the role effectively, leaders require authority. Along with formal power to make decisions, authority derives from wide acceptance of their legitimacy as credible occupants of the office, with the confidence of most constituencies. But on complex social issues, the problems presented to leaders for resolution may not be soluble. The centrifugal forces brought to bear on the issue by different constituencies will drag leaders in more than one direction, so that any solution will represent some form of compromise. To impose any solution at all is to undermine confidence among any constituency which feels its interests have been compromised. Yet failure to act on a social problem that lies within the institution's ambit and make at least some visible progress with it, may signify a complete lack of leadership rather than merely inadequate leadership. To decide or not to decide therefore brings the risk of diminishing credibility, and therefore legitimacy and requisite authority to act responsibly on other matters.

Hence whatever the formal powers of office and the process that appoints a person to the role, leadership legitimacy (as distinct from legal authority) must rely to some degree on personal credibility. Clearly, the charter and character of the organization defines credible images of its leadership. Credibility turns in part on the *moral* and *ethical* character of the leader's actions (the perceived integrity of her or his conduct), judged against the values and purposes that the institution and office are supposed to uphold. It also turns on perceptions of *effectiveness*, namely the leader's ability to fulfil the tasks and rituals of office capably and respond to the challenges that confront the institution. In this sense leadership in a public institution shades simultaneously towards both the representative and the instrumental – 'a person we are glad to recognize as one of us, who shares our aims and hopes, and who can somehow deal with all of that, and all of them'.

In sum, constituents want leaders they regard as good, who will also produce good results. The risk with this definition of leadership legitimacy is that in practice it may cast the leader in too passive a role. During moments of change or crisis, active leadership is both sought and feared by constituents, since the impetus to alter the settings, however unworkable they have become, means reaching decisions with larger than usual consequences, often not fully predictable. Endless conformity with accumulated protocols, and energetic pursuit of approval by every constituent, may leave a representative leader too little scope to stand apart at the boundary of the institution, look beyond its familiar routines and parochial interests, and minimize long-term risks, respond to emerging opportunities, or devise strategies so the institution can fulfil an evolving mission in a sustainable way.

This more instrumental mode of leadership exists in tension with the representative mode. In periods of crisis or reform, leaders in public institutions often find themselves trying to modify the status or practice of collegial constituents who, in more stable settings, normally expect to identify them as 'one of us', more readily attuned to their own concerns than to those of other constituencies. Institutional change is usually painful and often unpopular, even when the circumstances require it. Indeed, since public institutions by definition serve interests beyond the private interests of their inhabitants, failure to prevent a looming crisis or initiate a necessary reform is a failure to meet public purpose, and has consequences beyond the institution and its internal constituencies.

By challenging what they judge to be a damaging or ineffectual or unsustainable status quo, leaders risk violating the norms and expectations of the institutional community itself, on which much of their 'representative' legitimacy otherwise depends. Authority therefore is always tenuous, since it rests on an unstable accommodation across contending interests.

Powerful constituents or factions may simply not recognize the urgency or import of the problem the leader is seeking to solve; or they may define and diagnose it differently, conveniently shifting the burdens of adjustment elsewhere. When leadership requires unwelcome change, the leader must balance authority against legitimacy and long-term interests.

The university tradition and leadership legitimacy

Universities illustrate, and often accentuate, the dilemmas of leading a public institution. In an ideal world, universities might have developed a different approach to leadership. It would be refreshing to discover that, given the value such institutions place on the dispassionate sifting of logic and evidence, scholarly communities had found ways to govern their affairs in more enlightened and exemplary ways than (say) business or government enterprises. Such an ideal approach, of course, would leave universities immune to office politics, palace intrigue, or factional antagonism.

Yet, by most insider accounts, university leadership remains a risky business, as fraught in every way as leadership in institutions not so obviously committed to evidence and dispassionate debate. Examples abound of university leaders caught in the cross-fire between the demands of student activists, the grievances of faculty members, the sensitivities of government authorities and corporate sponsors, and public displays of wrangling among colleagues in the media. In this sense it is never lonely at the top in a university, and Machiavelli's advice remains ever relevant.

What are the tasks of university leadership, in what context are they performed, and what skills and qualities and strategies do leaders require to succeed in the role? Leadership practitioners in such settings have found these questions hard to answer:

> There's no easy way to describe a college president's job.... It involves so many often conflicting roles, played in relation to so many different constituencies, frequently constituencies with directly opposed points of view, that the result is an often laughably complex set of responsibilities... in any one day (one) must be teacher, manager, financial and investment expert, entrepreneur of knowledge, strategist, magistrate, and builder of warm and collaborative relationships with faculty, students, alumnae, trustees, media and government regulators... (Jill Ker Conway 2003: 59–61).

Clark Kerr, architect of the University of California system, summed up his leadership experience in similar terms:

> The university president... is expected to be a friend of the students, a colleague of the faculty, a good fellow with the alumni, a sound administrator with the trustees, a good speaker with the public, an astute bargainer with the foundations and the federal agencies, a politician with the state legislature, a friend of industry, labour and agriculture, a persuasive diplomat with donors, a champion of education generally, a supporter of the professions... a spokesman to the press, a scholar in his own right, a public servant at the state and national levels, a devotee of opera and football equally.... No one can be all of these things. Some succeed at being none (Clark Kerr 2001: 22).

This practitioner view emphasizes that the university leadership role has no obvious practical boundaries, mainly because the institution has so many constituencies. As Kerr stresses, the university leader must look out as well as in – building and holding external coalitions of supporters, particularly within government, is imperative. At the same time, a host of internal issues demand attention. University leaders typically attest to the centrifugal pressures which work against central authority. Like Hamlet, they seem destined forever to uncertainty about what is required if they are finally to set things right.

Yet once accepted, the very ambiguity surrounding the ambit of leadership allows university leaders scope to select and attend to a particular dimension of the work of the institution, hopefully one that matches their style and skills with the hopes and challenges of their university. No two university leaders are alike because each must make a personal choice about which parts of an impossibly wide role to pursue, and which issues can be safely parked, deferred, or delegated. If all political careers end in failure, as Enoch Powell claimed, then all university administrative careers must conclude with a sense of issues not addressed, constituencies not worked with effectively, opportunities let slip because time and energy proved elusive.

Of course, there are some elements of the role difficult to ignore. These expectations, which look continuously outwards and within, can be understood in functional terms:

- As *political leaders*, university leaders must reflect, respond to and shape community expectations, and therefore must take care to justify their institution's policy stance on matters of higher learning and its social and economic consequences. Here, the relations with government and other institutions are usually *diplomatic*. The leadership stance is to represent institutional values and purposes in an open way, while remaining attentive to social and official attitudes: being willing to listen, open to dialogue, able to debate, and reserving all judgement except at the point of decision.
- As *bureaucratic officials*, university leaders authorize administrative decisions that affect many individuals, most visibly by determining who may enrol, what they may study and how they may qualify for certain kinds of work. Here, relations with government and other institutions may be *symbiotic* and heavily negotiated and formalized. The leadership stance is to create strong alignment between the institution's profile of programmes and the various needs of employers, professional bodies, and schools.
- As *advocates*, university leaders represent the interests of their institutional constituencies, make cases for causes, form alliances, stir up debates, and pressure authorities in policy domains beyond their own administrative reach. Here, the relationship with government and other institutions may be *catalytic*. The leadership stance is activist, intervening in wider social and economic contexts, promoting an institutional agenda, and provoking realignments among other institutions. This involves making judgements with social policy implications beyond the institution's internal domain of decision-making.

None of these modes necessarily implies a single-minded or autocratic approach on the part of a leader (let alone a coherent set of actions). By long tradition and by virtue of the nature of their work, university communities resist unitary leadership. Beyond those governance structures which limit central authority and distribute decision-making, there are cultural reasons to resist 'executive' styles of leadership. Bensimon, Neumann, and Birnbaum (1989: 19–20), for example, suggest that in a university context, both task-oriented and relationship-oriented authority figures:

> ...will find it difficult to exert influence when organisational participants need independence, have a professional orientation, or are indifferent to organisational rewards; when the task is intrinsically satisfying; when the organisation includes closely knit and cohesive work groups; when rewards are outside the leader's control...

There have been notable exceptions to this view in the university tradition. President Abbott Lawrence Lowell described Harvard administration as 'tyranny tempered by assassination' (Keller and Keller 2001: 17), while Clark Kerr (2001: 24) characterized management in nineteenth century Oxford as follows:

> Benjamin Jowett as Master of Balliol could set as his rule: Never retract, never explain. Get it done and let them howl.

Leadership is most visible during crisis or reform, when the difficulty of balancing divergent expectations becomes extreme, 'crucifying' the leadership figure on impossible dilemmas of policy or strategy. After protracted student protests on campus, Clark Kerr was dismissed in 1967 by the Board of Regents as the first Chancellor of the University of California Berkeley. Kerr had found himself under attack from students and Regents alike, from opposite ends of the argument. He could satisfy neither, but announced he would leave Berkeley as he arrived, 'fired with enthusiasm'.

In less dramatic circumstances a president may survive a clash, but the Kerr example highlights the constant risk of differing constituencies – in this case students and their supporters within, and politically appointed Regents in governance roles representing the external world.

In such circumstances, university leaders often move carefully, building consensus. Even so, the leader may struggle to convey any sense of urgency to match the circumstances. Practitioners intent on institutional reform remark on the glacial pace of consultative and consensus-oriented processes as the accepted mode of decision-making in a large complex institution. Former University of Michigan President J. J. Duderstadt (2007: 127), observes, for example:

> Not surprisingly, I had my share of critics. Many believed I pushed too hard, not respecting or using the traditional university process of consultation and collegiality – or, perhaps more appropriately, delay and procrastination.

Some practitioners experience a sharp disparity between the breadth of responsibilities expected of the office, and the ambit of the office-holder's authority to act. Paradoxically, this situation may be accompanied by an inflated view of a leader's authority among certain constituents, who imagine the quickest path to a policy change is direct persuasion of the person ostensibly in charge.

Many presidents describe an amusing disjuncture as those outside expect instant responses to requests, while those within know even simple tasks can become points of contention and non-cooperation. A famous debate at Cambridge in 1902 over introducing the study of Economics saw one bemused observer list thirty opposition arguments advanced, beginning with the propositions:

- That the proposal is a new one.
- That it is therefore a bad one.
- That it is asked for by people outside.
- That it is not asked by people outside.
- That if it were, that would be all the more reason why they should not have it.

And so on, until the final but familiar argument that while scholars welcome the proposal, the process by which it has been introduced requires people of principle to vote it down. As Gordon Johnson notes (1994: 74–5), 'Such a litany of impossible, though perversely plausible, arguments blights the hopes of any would-be reformer; it seems so unfair that while there is only one reason for doing something (namely that it is right to do it), there should be so many reasons for not doing it.'

The reply to this, of course, is 'Right, in whose judgement?' Judgements must be made since every worthwhile reform is actually a replacement of an unfair or unsustainable set of compromises with a better (but less familiar and comfortable) set of compromises. Meanwhile, implicit in the expectation of problem-solving and institutional progress – by internal or external constituencies – is the idea that effective leadership in a university requires centralized authority to make final judgements and decisions. There is something in this, but it is primarily a power-oriented perspective of leadership. Such a view departs from, or at least tests, the underpinnings of legitimacy in a university setting, where dispersed authority and shared decision-making are central to institutional self-image.

Such images are shaped by a long accumulation of ideas about the work of the institution, the kind of people it attracts, and the norms which constitute academic culture. The most enduring notion of the university is a self-governing community of scholars, committed to the pursuit of knowledge. By convention university leaders, whether elected or appointed, are drawn from the scholarly community rather than from other spheres. While a leader's style and range of activities may vary widely, this requirement of scholarly expertise reflects an important source of leadership legitimacy, beyond the formal power and status of the office. Hence the widespread suspicion that putting administrators in charge rather than academics will soon derail the mission. As Selznick (1957: 27) argued half a century ago:

> A university led by administrators without a clear sense of values to be achieved may fail dismally while steadily growing larger and more secure...

The pattern of leadership appointments has changed little since Selznick's comment. Scholarly credentials signify prior membership of the scholarly community, and imply that a leader's decisions and conduct will be informed by a strong and nuanced sense of the scholarly mission and associated norms. Even leadership practitioners critical of the potentially dysfunctional aspects of collegial norms and democratic processes – such as interminable delay and indecision – confirm the importance of this. Duderstadt (2007: 119), for example, suggests that a key leadership attribute must be 'a deep understanding of the fundamental values and nature of an academic community'.

On closer examination, however, even such a self-evident principle may falter in practice. While scholars often invoke a common understanding of the nature of an academic community, in reality universities contain a spectrum of such understandings among scholars themselves, with unresolved differences about the relative priority of several distinct sets of aims and practices. The common threads are that, in every field of scholarship, intellectual freedom and intellectual honesty are accepted as essential prerequisites for contributing to the discipline, and thus the work of the institution. As two sides of the coin of academic responsibility, these guiding values inform certain institutional codes of behaviour for members of scholarly communities. In turn they have implications for the way authority relations are construed, goals defined, decisions made and tasks performed, so setting limits and shaping expectations of leadership conduct. An act of scholarly plagiarism, for example, may be more damaging to a leader's authority than an act of marital infidelity, while in a different sort of institution the converse might apply.

As in many professions, for many scholarly communities, being guided and represented by 'one of us' is a minimum condition for leadership legitimacy. Whether elected by peers or selected by an external governing body, a suitable candidate for university president, rector or vice-chancellor is typically a professor who is respected as a scholar, has enough administrative experience and political skill to meet the demands of role, and whose views and character align with prevailing rules and norms. This 'archetypal' source of legitimacy may go beyond the institution's governance structure, the powers conferred by the office, the process of office-holder selection, or even the diplomatic and organizational skills of the individual who assumes the role. All these factors may contribute to a leader's legitimacy, yet they vary widely between institutions. Rectors, university presidents, and vice-chancellors are employed in different ways and perform a different mix of functions, choosing among the menu of chief custodian, administrator, and executive responsibilities.

The nexus between institutional identity and the leader's own identity accords with Selznick's view that *institutions* form when commitments are made to a particular set of values, purposes, and practices. This helps define expectations about the proper tasks of leadership, and the criteria for leadership success:

> The formation of an institution is marked by the making of value-commitments, that is, choices which fix the assumptions of policy makers as to the nature of the enterprise, its distinctive aims, methods, and roles... The institutional leader is primarily an expert in the promotion and protection of values... Leadership fails when it concentrates on sheer survival. Institutional survival, properly understood, is a matter of maintaining values and distinctive identity (Selznick 1957: 28).

The university leader archetype, usually unstated but widely shared, takes its logic from the image of a university as a self-governing community of scholars. Though the leader must represent the institution to the external world, the emphasis remains on selecting someone acceptable within the university. This reveals something interesting about the perceived constituency of a university leader, and the propensity of scholarly communities to construct expectations of leadership in their own image. University leadership in this sense is co-constitutive, reflecting a largely self-referential social contract that implies mutual obligations and common frames of reference within the scholarly community. It looks inwards, even though the role must engage with numerous constituencies beyond the campus.

These tacit understandings are reinforced in longstanding structures and practices. They include, for example, the scholarly norms of wide consultation, collegial consent, and limited central authority in decision-making. As former York University (in Canada) President Murray Ross (1976: 160–1) notes:

> The importance of consultation, on both large and minor matters, with all colleagues, both old and young, became standard practice in the monastery during the Middle Ages. It was from this period that there emerged the belief that 'all legitimate authority is derived from the consent of the governed'. The university adopted this idea and practice. But consultation, with the exception of the Italian universities, meant consultation with the masters, and 'consultation' came to mean formal councils in which binding votes were taken to limit the freedom and the authority of the rector or chancellor... Thus the idea of self-government by the masters... emerged as the proper form of university organization.

These legacy practices of self-government by a scholarly community, derived from a tradition where scholars lived and worked in residence, are often invoked today as a value-commitment to 'democratic' principles. But this view underplays the pre-democratic origins of the modern university and its contemporary status as a public rather than democratic institution, supported by society in exchange for the many services it can provide. Like universities themselves, university leadership only looks generic from a distance, and leadership stances are shaped as much by particular relationships to funding bodies and other institutions, as by the internal normative order. Publicly funded universities especially, which assert relative autonomy by drawing their rhetoric from a long 'community of scholars' tradition, often appear to belong to a membership based, 'democratic' category of community organizations. In reality they are more usually in a distinct category of their own, set up under legislation and funded to serve a government-prescribed mission, which their governing councils are bound to observe when making decisions. This reality becomes most apparent whenever governments shift funding levels or policy setting, or when institutions respond to new conditions with painful decisions to cut valued programmes, or remove individual scholars from the institutional payroll. Neither move sits well with the idea of a fully autonomous community of scholars.

University autonomy and democratic projects

As public institutions, universities are expected to play a number of social and economic roles, and their leaders to embody values beyond the local and the scholarly. These roles are not integrated into a cogent and logical framework; on the contrary, there are overlapping differences in expectation, which play out in the public domain and internal management controversies.

The familiar touchstones of academic communities are independent inquiry and free speech, intellectual honesty, respect for logic and evidence, tolerance for diverse points of view, and formal open-mindedness on questions apparently settled. To the extent that a university community can live up to these values and standards and promote them as wider social norms, its work aligns well with democratic projects and processes. Universities train future political leaders in democratic disciplines by helping ensure that free speech in the form of public dissent remains an accepted social norm.

But universities perform these important tasks for the democratic project using an institutional form that arises from a pre-democratic tradition, organized around a hierarchy of knowledge reflected in academic rank. Indeed, former Harvard Dean Henry Rosovksy (1990: 262) lists as his first principle of effective governance in a university 'Not everything is improved by making it more democratic'. The hierarchy built into university organization sets expectations of leadership by academic seniors. It values some voices, and some advice, over others. It expects the elders of the institution to preserve the values and character of the university – even if this means resisting claims by students and others for change. Neither truth nor knowledge is ever settled by a vote.

Since medieval times, universities have built their niche as self-governing communities, supported by grants and earnings in return for the kinds of service that learning can offer a society. Self-governing, though, meant neither democratic nor independent. Universities have never been entirely autonomous, relying instead on a negotiated compact with the relevant authorities who fund them or at least, allow them to operate. Reflecting on Humboldt's reforms in early nineteenth century Germany and the Dawkins reforms in Australia in the 1980s, Huppauf (1988: 150–1) remarks that:

> The *autonomy* of the modern university was never an absolute one, but determined by a delicate ambivalence based on a careful balancing of dependence on, and a simultaneous critical distance from, society. From the early phase onwards the modern university was granted the liberty to perform this tight-rope act with the understanding that this fragile construction would eventually be much more to the benefit of the whole of society than a more clearly and narrowly defined area of performance.

Such patterns of negotiation and compromise with governments and other authorities have a long history. When in dispute with local authorities, the early scholarly communities might go on strike, or depart for another town that offered a better deal. The medieval universities engaged in active diplomacy and forum-shopping to gain privileges such as tax exemption, facilities, and funding. They appealed variously to 'king or council against pope, to pope against king or bishop, and to kings and popes alike against truculent town governments' (Ross 1976; see also Grendler [2002], Clark [2006]).

As Western universities have evolved, their ambitions and capacities have expanded, along with their resource requirements and a widening array of obligations under their compact with government. Despite periods of benign neglect by authorities, universities have always been seen by governments as instruments of public policy. This sits uncomfortably with those university presidents inclined to invoke Cardinal Newman about purity of purpose, and Einstein about the overriding value of intellectual freedom, when they address scholarly communities, but compelled to rely on other arguments when pleading to governments, legislatures, and corporations for funding and support.

The central task of the medieval university was to rediscover classical knowledge and produce trained professionals (doctors, lawyers, and clergy) to meet emerging social needs within a framework of doctrine determined by church and state. The modern nineteenth-century university took up liberal learning and fundamental inquiry as defining features, to reproduce culture and progress through scientific endeavour. Institutional processes such as Kant's 'conflict of the faculties' were supposed to allow philosophers the freedom to challenge official doctrine, as taught to and administered by doctors, lawyers, and clergy, in the name of progress.

In the twentieth century, governments (not least Australian governments) harnessed higher learning directly to national economic and industrial development. University systems expanded to deliver mass higher education and technical skills, while their research programmes were directed towards advances in techno-science, industry development, and policy innovation. With the emergence of 'big science', universities have become more dependent than ever on public investment, even if delivered through quasi-independent research funding bodies. In return, governments expect universities to be reliable sources of industrial innovation, producing inventions, graduates, and start-up companies that will yield economic growth.

Given this long evolutionary history, it is not surprising that contemporary universities often seem unfocused – a loose bundle of activities overlaid one on the other, rather than an enterprise with a coherent set of purposes. What we call tradition is a long accumulation of ideas, structures, and practices, as institutions reinvent and reorient themselves. Clark Kerr famously observed that several ideas of the university now coexisted in uneasy tension as:

> ideal types which still constitute the illusions of some of its inhabitants.... Newman's 'Idea of a University' still has its devotees – chiefly the humanists and the generalists and the undergraduates. Flexner's 'Idea of a Modern University' still has its supporters – chiefly the scientists and the specialists and the graduate students. The 'Idea of a Multiversity' has its practitioners – chiefly the administrators...These several competing visions of true purpose...cause much of the malaise in the university communities today. The university is so many things to so many different people that it must of necessity be partially at war with itself (Kerr 2001: 1–6).

As knowledge proliferates, and the social demands on the institution multiply, the task of reconciling several streams of demand becomes ever more complex. Scholarly communities pursue and promote knowledge as a good in itself. Students might want short and clear pathways to valued qualifications, businesses expect graduates ready to start work, and government demands a steady stream of practical inventions from campus. One institution, itself divided over purpose and priorities, must somehow mediate all these expectations, and perhaps disappoint all.

Nearly half a century after Clark Kerr's insightful account, none of the institutional tensions he described has been resolved. In times of stability, competing visions of the university are merely contained within a loosely coupled system that glosses over deep unresolved differences. In periods of crisis, a university community that aspires to be a model of a 'rational and just' community may suffer occasional bouts of multipolar disorder, and indulge in what Selznick (1957: 147) described as 'avoiding hard choices by a flight to abstractions'.

This more ambiguous view of the university as both a collection of communities staking claims for support, and a public institution with external obligations, raises difficult questions about the leadership task. Whose interests should a self-governing community serve to remain a credible public institution? When universities aspire, as some do, to a more democratic form, they must decide which of the university's many constituencies should prevail. Should students have a veto on curriculum, or should the hierarchy of knowledge and authority based on scholarly excellence, so deeply encoded in academic values, trump the egalitarian impulses of a democratic structure? And even with internal consensus, how does a purportedly autonomous community in a public institution deal with the expectations of external supporters, including government, whose funding makes the enterprise possible?

Continuing tensions about legitimacy and authority, about the need for patronage amid the claim to autonomy, confront every university. The scholarly vocation provides one path to integrity – the 'Polonius principle' of being true 'to thine own self'. For those drawn into internal governance, as a head of school or dean, the challenge of managing others who are committed to their own independence adds a layer of complexity. They must balance respect for personal judgement with the collective choices required in an institution which speaks to, and is supported by, numerous constituencies; someone outside the university, after all, is paying the bills. For the institutional leader, this burden of balance becomes even more acute. The leader must translate traditional ideas of how academia works into new forms to meet new external conditions (not least the digitization, commodification, and democratization of knowledge itself). The university leader must seek support externally in a world often sceptical about the value of scholarly work, while holding together the multiple and sometimes feuding groups that collectively live under the shared rubric of a university. All this must be accomplished through an office which commands respect but not necessarily obedience. Little wonder the memoirs of former presidents hint at surprise and relief in surviving for their term in such challenging circumstances.

Confronting global challenges

The constraints on university leadership described so far – external expectations, internal contests – still allow some scope for strategic choice. Between state and institution, there is room for agreements about how public money will be applied to the work of the university, and how much practical autonomy will reside within the institution. For public universities, as for their private counterparts, though, a further dimension looms – the influence of external markets.

Public universities have always *managed* – found ways to marshal resources towards agreed goals. At least in the Australian setting, this has occurred within a public sector context where close regulation of institutions has been accompanied by guaranteed minimum income. As this familiar world fades, universities find themselves operating in a mixed economy setting, more alone and more dependent on their own judgement than ever before. For publicly funded institutions, a fall in government funding relative to growth now places a sharper institutional focus on raising revenue, resource management, quality assurance, innovation, and market responsiveness.

The new emphasis in universities on *managing* is often decried as a displacement of collegial-democratic values by business ideology. It is better understood as perhaps the only rational response available to new challenges facing institutions in an era of mass higher learning, growth in enterprise scale and complexity, and the need for multiple income streams from public and private sources. Nonetheless, the risks of relying on commercial income evoke worry at even the most wealthy institutions. As former Harvard President Derek Bok (2003: x) observed, 'if more and more "products" of the university were sold at a profit, might the lure of the marketplace alter the behaviour of professors and university officials in subtle ways that would change the character of Harvard for the worse?'

Yet facing the markets for higher learning proves just the first challenge. As markets develop they create space for other types of institutions to emerge, grow, and challenge the pre-eminent position of universities as credentialing agencies and knowledge gatekeepers. In an era of global online providers, open source knowledge production and research consultancies, universities cannot assume their traditional public standing will endure (see Waks [2007]).

No wonder the times seem out of joint. Such shifts threaten a major break with the tradition in which the archetypal community of scholars acts as society's keeper of knowledge, enabler of learning, certifier of competence, and source of expert advice. For much of its history, the university's compact with government was shaped by the relative scarcity of texts and expertise, its capacity to regulate access to higher learning, and the leverage this gave scholarly communities to set terms and conditions conducive to their aims and interests. Governments accepted claims of university autonomy, at least in part, because they had few alternative sources of training and expertise. The producer was able to define the terms on which knowledge would be made available.

In a global knowledge economy, universities no longer exercise this degree of leverage. With so many enterprises now in the knowledge business, the archetype is being reconfigured. Once an island of knowledge in a sea of ignorance, the university now competes with an archipelago of choice. Knowledge is instantly available and skilfully packaged by suppliers not burdened by the formidable overheads of libraries, lecture rooms, gargoyles, and tenured staff (Davis 2006). As universities learn to manage in a new market context by adapting the disciplines of business enterprises to their own operations, they face the kinds of dilemmas familiar to smaller nation states. The rising tide of globalism may leave universities culturally swamped or economically stranded.

Scholarly authority, identity, and practice also come under threat. While time-poor students Google first and ask later, librarians worry about how quickly to digitize their physical collections, and professors debate what policy to adopt on the uses of Wikipedia. Meanwhile unions contend that while universities are central to the nation's capacity to innovate, as older academics retire they will take their institution's knowledge and 'intellectual infrastructure' with them (National Tertiary Education Union 2008). Once grounded in tradition and localism, scholarly communities now meet new knowledge players from other spheres, alien invaders of the territory they once called their own. Marginson (2007: xii) remarks that:

> Global convergence means that processes conducted in isolation in localities and nations no longer absorb us as they once did... Direct cross-border relations subvert the old distinctions between national and international, and remake the relations between government and higher education institutions.... Amid the first open information environment in history, national policy and local culture can no longer be isolated.

For public universities, the most pressing contemporary strategic dilemma is whether to seek exemption from market conditions by constructing and defending a separate sphere (much as they had done in the past, to gain relative independence from church and state), or to opt for greater interdependence as other kinds of knowledge enterprises emerge across society.

To some this may seem a choice between learning how to surf and holding back the tide. To the extent that higher learning and knowledge production are subject to global flows of information, expertise, students, and knowledge projects, attempts to reclaim the institution as an island of expertise, supported by governments while standing apart from the social and economic mainstream, seem risky indeed. The pattern of interdependence is likely to continue, with universities mediating their position through constant negotiation with government, private supporters, students, and staff. Projects such as the recently launched 'iTunes U' 'transforming learning on campus, off campus and where there's no campus at all' illustrate the new consumer power – and with it, the threat to traditional forms of provision – of the digitization of scholarly knowledge, where texts can be browsed and expert lectures watched or heard from leading universities 'in session 24/7'.

Such developments harness technology to extend the university mission of pursuing and promoting knowledge as a public good to be shared as widely and freely as possible. The irony of course is the 'boomerang effect' (Sharrock

2007), whereby traditional universities democratize knowledge and in doing so, diminish the competitive advantage that scholarly communities historically relied on in their dealings with other social actors. Strategic dilemmas, and the need to make difficult institutional choices, present new challenges for university leadership. In a context of flux and uncertainty leadership may be understood as an essentially *supplementary* and *makeshift* activity, one that improvises when a social system encounters novel, urgent, or intractable problems for which no ready solution is apparent. Considine (2006: 265) suggests that university leadership is needed to help guide the social system through transitions, finding ways to translate potentially dysfunctional relations into productive ones:

> Surely, the diversity of actor positions inside the university makes any individual or group claim unstable. Paradoxically, it is precisely because actors will disagree and will promote different projects that translation must occur and, once in motion, can produce new actions. Occasional failures to agree, conflicts over projects, and the expression of different values are part of this process of diplomacy. When systems engage in such interaction but fail to reach new positions, they find themselves in a state of emergency... Leaders... cannot shift this burden onto the process of legislation or rule making because the whole point of emergencies is that they are exceptional.

This contemporary dilemma for university leaders, accentuated by markets and global competition, only underlines an old and unavoidable challenge. The 'community of scholars' tradition – the cultural DNA of most Western universities – is at odds with the emerging strategic context for universities. The central institutional leadership task described by Selznick – protecting a set of values, assumptions, methods, and identities from forces that threaten to subvert them – may need to be recast as a process for supporting considered adaptation in response to new conditions, required to sustain an evolving mission. This task cannot be delegated to the decision-making routines of the institution. A central task of leadership is to enable successful transitions from older forms of organization and identity into new ones.

Exceptional circumstances bring leaders into the spotlight. At points of institutional transition, staff communities turn to authority figures to contain uncertainty, ambiguity, and anxiety, until adaptation to a new situation can occur. Finding a way to handle the novel within inherited patterns of decision-making becomes the challenge. New kinds of problems usually fall outside the routines and repertoires of institutional governance, management, and administration structures. Somehow they must be accommodated by the leadership, and communicated back to the organization in language which connects them to tradition cogently enough to resonate within a community of scholars. Walking forward while looking backwards is a difficult skill to acquire.

Tasks and styles of university leadership: what is to be done, and how?

The task of leading a university has always been complicated by the institution's sheer range of public purposes – teacher, trainer, library, laboratory, economic catalyst, social critic, site of innovation – and the different relationships each creates with other social institutions.

Internally matters are no less complex. A defining feature of the university has always been the diversity of viewpoints its communities express, since much fundamental inquiry proceeds by constructive dissensus, largely unconstrained by administrative authority. Developing an expert opinion, distinct from the opinions of others, is a powerful source of scholarly identity. This aspect of academic culture, combined with the institution's protean external relations, creates a multiplying series of strategic and policy dilemmas for institutional leadership.

A university leader can offer only provisional and contestable answers to these challenges. Leaders of earlier generations lamented an already impossible array of tasks. Contemporary circumstances add still more: to the familiar tasks of sustaining the enterprise, developing its mission, dealing with its beneficiaries, engaging with staff communities, representing the institution to external constituencies, various forms of cross-border partnering and entrepreneurship now require leadership attention. 'Global knowledge economy strategist' has now been added to the list.

Distributing institutional authority widely in the hope that all parties and projects will somehow muddle through may help sift some of the issues. But as practitioners have experienced it, this may also amplify the prospect of distress, paralysis, and stalemate. The distinct repertoire of tasks and styles and strategies required can never fully be defined. Leadership in a public university will always be makeshift, responding to events and creating agendas that require endless adjustment.

Perhaps the most useful task any leader can perform in a context of change is educative, naming the issues and extending the vocabulary of the institution to deal with them. Preparing for change means making it clear to people there are risks and costs associated with deflecting hard realities, delegating problems, or vetoing every solution. To procrastinate is to surrender to fate; in the memorable phrase attributed to British Prime Minister Harold Wilson, 'a decision deferred is a decision made'.

Leaders presiding over disruptive change who run ahead of expectations, or step too quickly into the unknown, soon find themselves at odds with their constituents. Universities are full of clever people, and argument is prized, sometimes above logic or evidence. Persuading people in a successful institution that change is required is difficult, particularly when the change proposed responds to external change. A critical task for university leaders is to find ways to encourage like-minded allies into the debate, and engage directly with the views of dissidents and critics, not to quell but to clarify. On new policy or strategy proposals, dissidents and critics help 'ripen the issue' (Heifetz 1994) and reality-test solutions that have been too narrowly conceived.

Hence university leadership groups spend considerable time framing institutional problems and designing engagement processes to work through the issues. Once defined as projects, the work of engagement can be distributed, by selecting what to do directly, what to delegate, what to refer to working parties and committees, and what to outsource entirely. Such sharing of responsibility helps prepare the ground for decisions. An engagement process on seemingly intractable issues can be educative for all concerned. While such a process typically aims to consult with people and hear their views, making people conversant with the details of a problem is one way to develop leadership capability close to the constituencies affected, and build adaptive capacity across an institution.

This dispersed and decidedly unheroic view of leadership in a public university conceives of it as a *portfolio* of roles and tasks performed by a group of people in key institutional positions. The leadership task is not a personal solitary matter but a shared responsibility. The leadership team needs to include active membership of key constituencies, an extensive repertoire of skills and resources, a common vocabulary for the leadership agenda, and a wide informal network. This group in turn may be supported by informal coalitions of contributors, inside and outside the institution.

The weakness of such an approach is the need for greater central effort to keep every group member well-informed and able to respond in a consistent way to the various constituencies as issues develop, an emerging strategy is refined, and engagement processes are conducted on several fronts at once. Leaders who stand at the centre have far greater information and advice at their fingertips, but also far less time to process it. Email helps, but also swamps. Traffic control via Blackberry becomes a vital skill but invites endless distraction from the more reflective tasks of thinking and planning ahead.

Despite its manifest advantages, a common problem for a widely dispersed leadership group with an agenda for change is that engagement processes designed to glean what afflicts each constituency soon take the agents of leadership into unscripted and unrehearsed territory. An otherwise well-planned consultation process on a sensitive matter can easily spread confusion and distress, due to unscripted answers to thorny questions in public discussions. An incoherent message or undiplomatic response to questioning may soon be relayed beyond the forum, or amplified by the media. At best, constituents receive mixed signals about the intentions of the leadership group. At worst, it appears to an increasingly suspicious audience that the leadership group is merely pretending to have answers when it has none, or has solutions in mind so unthinkable they cannot be declared openly.

This may be why university leaders are sometimes cast as overly powerful but tragically misguided figures, fixed on strategies that reflect either flawed ideology or a failure to grasp the essential nature of their institution. The reality may be more prosaic – leaders who see the complexity of the choices required, but struggle to create recognition of problems and consent around solutions.

Conclusion: the subjectivity of university leadership

Leadership of a public university, we have suggested, places an individual at the uncomfortable point where external pressures for change meet familiar internal stances and unresolved debates. It requires a leader to explain the institution's mission and methods to the world, and the world's expectations to the university. This cannot be done alone. Leadership in a public university requires a collective effort, and so subverts the usual notions of a single person making brave calls about institutional direction. Inherited traditions about the role of a university, the dignified arrangements of autonomy, the contrasting demands of governance, students, and scholars – all constrain choice, while demanding attention. Nothing is simple, at least in the world of academe. Agreement across constituencies is negotiated constantly, and may fail – as Clark Kerr found, there may be no middle path between warring expectations.

What is it like to play a leadership role, and survive to tell the tale? Most personal accounts stress the difficulties: lack of time, lack of shared understanding, inflated expectations of what is possible, self-interested policy positions, irrational resistance to change, and occasional public abuse. Meanwhile, practical prescriptions for good leadership rarely rise above platitudes worthy of Polonius.

There is agreement that the span of a university leadership role is now very wide, and certainly beyond the capacity of any individual. This requires some humility for leaders once valued by peers primarily for their expertise. In this kind of role, leaders inevitably will lack sufficient knowledge to offer authoritative judgements on most of the complex issues confronting their institution.

There is no science of university leadership, no set of reliable, empirically tested practices. Any list of suggestions communicates an important underlying message – that an impossible role can only be handled by sharing the task, accepting fallibility, and recognizing limits to authority and control.

Neither the idea of the public university nor the idea of leadership can be readily defined, much less settled. With so many purposes and constituencies in need of attention, no single leader can deal with all successfully. The factors that keep such institutions in a state of flux demand flexible leadership. The team – and not just the individual with the formal title of leader – must draw on extensive informal networks to deal with constituents, structure problems, and get things done.

Meanwhile the leadership process involves translation of new institutional problems into the vocabularies of purpose and value at play within the institution. In Aristotelian terms, good leadership becomes a blend of *praxis* with *poiesis*, channelling culture while negotiating change, and translating old into new. As Hamlet learned, sadly too late, 'the readiness is all'.

In a sense universities have learned to accommodate intellectual pluralism, and create space for the voices of unheard minorities. But for the university and for society it is precisely their embrace of pluralism as a social virtue, as much as their acceptance of external conditions, that brings them to this pass. The attempt to contain competing value sets derived from different traditions, cultures, and belief systems creates space for endless ambiguity and anxiety as each faction pursues its projects and worries about its status and prospects. No leader can embody all the virtues and priorities required by all constituencies, let alone an identity that would somehow mirror their diversity. Since pluralism cuts both ways, the socially desirable characteristics of credible and legitimate leaders ('one of us, who can somehow deal with all of them') are all too clearly a mirage.

The portfolio of activities we label leadership can, and must, be widely distributed to have any hope of achieving connection with disparate constituencies. The ultimate task of leaders in a public institution, beyond leading adaptive change to meet new circumstances, is to make central monolithic authority increasingly redundant, a routine reassurance that wise choices are being made as close to the people and the problem as possible, and that these are visible enough to inform the choices of other groups.

We have suggested that this less visible form of distributed leadership is more prosaic than heroic, and we should add that it is not new:

> A leader is best/When people barely know that/he exists,
> Not so good when people obey and/acclaim him,
> Worst when they despise him.
> Fail to honor people/they fail to honor you;
> But of a good leader, who talks little/When his work is done,/his aim fulfilled,
> They will say/'We did this ourselves.'
> (Lao Tzu)

Perhaps it is time to call for a new academic field and training ground to emerge, focused on combining leadership with management in contemporary tertiary institutions. After all, a similar process of globalization, technological change, and new markets encouraged widespread interest in the study of leadership in business enterprises from the 1980s (Kotter 1996). Strong corporate governance and capable management of enterprise systems and routines, while still needed, were no longer deemed sufficient in the business world. Such now seem the circumstances of public universities. There are now many personal accounts and case studies to illustrate the kinds of challenges leaders face in this arena, but structured programmes of inquiry and leadership training are still rare.

Notes

1. While our principal focus in preparing this article has been publicly chartered universities, we suspect the argument offered applies more widely to modern universities. Indeed, some of the supporting material produced derives from significant private institutions in the United States. It is likely the shared characteristics among universities are more significant than differences arising from ownership.

Bibliography

Bensimon, E. M., Neumann, A., and Birnbaum, R., *Making Sense of Administrative Leadership: The 'L' Word in Higher Education,* ASHE-ERIC Higher Education Report 1 (Washington, D. C.: Association for the Study of Higher Education, 1989), 663–84.

Bok, D., *Universities in the Marketplace: The Commercialization of Higher Education* (Princeton: Princeton University Press, 2003).

Clark, W., *Academic Charisma and the Origins of the Research University* (Chicago: University of Chicago Press, 2006).

Considine, M., 'Theorizing the University as a Cultural System: Distinctions, Identities, Emergencies', *Educational Theory*, 56/3 (2006), 255–70.

Conway, J. K., *A Woman's Education* (New York: Knopf, 2003).

Craig, J. and Yetton, P., 'Leadership Theory, Trends and Training: Summary Review of Leadership Research', *Enterprising Nation: Renewing Australia's Managers to Meet the Challenges of the Asia-Pacific Century.* Report of the Industry Task Force on Leadership and Management Skills (the *Karpin Report*) (Canberra: Australian Government Printing Service, 1995), 1183–221.

Davis, G., 'The Rising Phoenix of Competition: What Future for Australia's Public Universities?', *Griffith Review*, Autumn (2006), 15–31.

Duderstadt, J. J., *The View from the Helm: Leading the American University during an Era of Change* (Ann Arbor: The University of Michigan Press, 2007).

Grendler, P. F., *The Universities of the Renaissance* (Baltimore: John Hopkins University Press, 2002).

Heifetz, R. A., *Leadership without Easy Answers* (Cambridge, Mass.: Belknap Press of Harvard University, 1994).

Huppauf, B., 'Universities and Postmodernism', *Arena,* 83 (1988), 135–58.

Johnson, G., *University Politics: F. M. Cornford's Cambridge and His Advice to the Young Academic Politician* (Cambridge: Cambridge University Press, 1994).

Keller, M. and Keller, P., *Making Harvard Modern: The Rise of America's University* (New York: Oxford University Press, 2001).
Kerr, C., *The Uses of the University*, 5th edn. (Harvard: Harvard University Press, 2001).
Kotter, J., *Leading Change* (Harvard: Harvard Business School Press, 1996).
Marginson, S. (ed.), *Prospects of Higher Educations: Globalization, Market Competition, Public Goods and the Future of the University* (Rotterdam: Sense Publishers, 2007).
National Tertiary Education Union (NTEU), *Submission to the Innovation Review* (Melbourne: National Tertiary Education Union, 2008).
Rosovksy, H., *The University: An Owner's Manual* (New York: W. W. Norton & Company, 1990).
Ross, M. G., *The University: The Anatomy of Academe* (New York: McGraw-Hill, 1976).
Selznick, P., *Leadership in Administration: A Sociological Interpretation* (New York: Harper and Rowe, 1957).
Sharrock, G., 'After Copernicus: Beyond the Crisis in Australian Universities', *Australian Universities' Review*, 49/1–2 (2007), 2–14.
Waks, L. J., 'In the Shadow of the Ruins: Globalization and the Rise of Corporate Universities', in S. Marginson (ed.), *Prospects of Higher Education* (Rotterdam: Sense Publishers, 2007), 101–19.
Yukl, G., *Leadership in Organizations,* 4th edn. (New Jersey: Prentice-Hall, 1998).

Chapter 13
Leadership of International Organizations

Bertjan Verbeek

Leadership in search of legitimacy: the rise of IGOs

Intergovernmental organizations (IGOs) have become more salient actors both in international and in national policymaking. The consequences of globalization have made national governments increasingly look upon IGOs to help them solve global, regional, and national policy problems (Scholte 2001). In addition, the end of the Cold War has reinforced the effects of globalization as IGOs are no longer paralyzed by the East–West conflict (Berridge 1991). Moreover, the 'third wave of democracy' (Huntington 1991) which started in the 1970s has increased the number of governments that are politically vulnerable to the effects of global events. In democratic societies constituents affected by such events enjoy more opportunities to pressurize their national leaders into demands to IGOs (Risse-Kappen 1991). Finally, the increased weight of international law in world politics has changed the calculus of many states at multilateral gatherings. States can be charged in front of a variety of international courts and commissions. Fear of loss of reputation makes it more difficult for states to simply ignore policies agreed upon in IGOs (Joachim et al. 2008).

The more frequent delegation of tasks to IGOs has allowed the international bureaucracy to become autonomous actors in their own right, although this autonomy varies across IGOs (Reinalda and Verbeek 1998). The increased weight of IGOs has important leadership implications, whether that leadership is exercised by Secretariats-General (like in most UN organizations), Commissioners (such as in the European Union [EU]), or (quasi-)judges (such as in the European Court of Justice [ECJ], or the World Trade Organization [WTO]).

This chapter deals with two related, fundamental IGO leadership problems that derive from the increased prominence (and controversiality) of IGOs. Both problems jeopardize the authority of IGOs in the long term. First, leaders of an IGO find it increasingly difficult to perform the balancing act between meeting the raised expectations of member states and avoiding antagonizing some of them in the process. This is related to the foundations and design of their leadership. Formally, the dispersed power that IGOs represent, rests on a logic of delegation: IGOs are founded by sovereign nation states and are subject to their control. And to mollify these principals, the most important norm guiding IGO performance is impartiality, which IGO leaders are expected to embody and enshrine within the bureaucracies they preside over. Impartiality refers to avoiding taking sides against one or more member states over substantive issues. However, the increased reliance of nation states on IGOs to help solve global (as well as domestic) problems makes it more difficult for them to meet the norm of impartiality. Tackling serious regional and global problems often requires IGOs to take a stand, and thus take sides vis-à-vis (some) nation states. It is then that the imperatives of impartiality and effectiveness may clash – a tension IGO leaders have to negotiate (cf. Barnett and Finnemore [2004: 168]).

Second, the delegation to IGOs by democracies of an increasing number of transnational leadership tasks raises the issue of democratic control. Critics complain that some international agencies control 'vital aspects of life' without a possibility for those affected to control these agencies in a democratically meaningful way (e.g. Hirst [2000: 15–16]). Indeed, the systems of accountability of IGOs and their leaders are often opaque and well beyond the reach of individual citizens. The perceived lack of democratic control may in the long run weaken the authority an IGO's leader enjoys and thus the legitimacy of the organization itself. We thus have to address the issue how an increased role for IGOs and their leaders is related to the issue of democratic control.

In sum, the increased role for IGO leaders since the end of the Cold War and the advent of globalization may actually undermine their authority and the long-term legitimacy of their organizations. In addressing this matter it is important to distinguish between IGOs which are highly intergovernmental in nature such as the UN and those that are highly legalized in nature such as (elements of) the EU (cf. Goldstein et al. [2000]). The different institutional nature of such IGOs is an important element in assessing and explaining the system of accountability under which an IGO's leader has to perform his/her balancing act. Two important examples of strong leaders of IGOs are discussed: the leadership displayed by UN Secretary-General Boutros Boutros-Ghali (1991–6) in shaping the international agenda of the 1990s and early 2000s and the role European Commissioner Peter Sutherland played in shaping EU competition policies during his term between 1985 and 1989. Both cases underline the tightrope IGO leaders have to walk in order to remain perceived as impartial and thus to preserve their authority.[1]

Several preliminary remarks are in order regarding the notion of leadership employed in this chapter and the consequences of this choice for assessing the leadership of IGOs. For one, political leadership is a specific manifestation of power. Leadership refers to the ability of individuals to mobilize followers to perform certain deeds that they otherwise would not have done. Yet, leadership goes beyond Dahl's notion of the individual who wields the 'greatest influence in the political system' (Dahl 1976: 59), because leadership operates within the boundaries set by the motives that urge his/her followers (Blondel 1987: 4–5). Indeed, it is the purpose of power that sets leadership apart from naked power wielding (Burns 1978: 19). I here follow Burns who argues that leadership is about leaders mobilizing followers in order to effectuate goals held by both of them. Burns labels such successful mobilization 'transactional leadership'. Under specific circumstances, however, leaders succeed in establishing lasting social change, while elevating followers to a higher level of motivation and morality. This phenomenon Burns calls 'transforming leadership' (Burns 1978: 18–23, 251, 455–7). In assessing transforming leadership, it is important to distinguish between degrees of change leaders seek to establish (moderate or large) as well as between scopes of the changes they aim for (wide, moderate, or narrow) (Blondel 1987: 87–96). Transforming leadership can only be said to exist if the changes brought about by leaders are of a lasting nature. Because of the close watch member states keep on the IGOs they have created and because of their diverging interests, it is generally considered unlikely that leaders of IGOs can ever be transforming leaders, particularly those operating in highly intergovernmental settings.

A second preliminary issue regards the relationship between formal position and leadership (Blondel 1987: 19–26). Some leadership scholars assume that occupying a formal top level position equals to being a leader. Others point out that leadership does not come with a position, but has to be earned, for instance when it is tested during crisis situations. Also, individuals can exercise leadership without holding formal power positions. It is true that sometimes leadership in international politics is exercised by individuals who do not occupy any formal position, including celebrities (e.g. Bono, Princess Diana, Angelina Jolie, see further 't Hart and Tindall, this volume) and former government leaders (Jimmy Carter, Tony Blair, see further Keane, this volume). However, intergovernmental organizations remain primarily forums where international civil servants have to strike a balance between various national interests. Therefore, in this chapter I focus on the leadership role played by specific key high-level office-holders within IGOs.

Securing authority: IGO leaders' resources

Intergovernmental organizations are created by sovereign states by international treaty. By definition, they consist of an assembly with decisional authority in which all member states have a seat and a secretariat to which stipulated tasks have been entrusted (cf. Archer [2001]). Assuming that the states call the shots, many theories of international relations ignore the role of leaders of an IGO. Still, it is clear that people working for an IGO are not simply their home country's tools. In fact, in the 1920s sovereign states accepted that international civil servants are supposed to be independent from their home countries and to serve the international organization they work for. In order to ensure their independence international civil servants are rewarded diplomatic status, tax exemptions, and competitive salaries. This international norm was wrung out of a fierce battle with its member states by the League of Nations' first Secretary-General Sir Eric Drummond, and has remained a key principle of international organization ever since (Barros 1979). As a matter of fact, the same principle is applicable to the employees of the institutions of the EU. Internally, therefore, IGO staff will expect leadership from their top officials. Externally, an IGO leader will be closely watched by the member states and by the global audience. Member states will be wary of leaders who ignore their preferences, while the general public will look at the IGO for leadership in helping solve pressing problems (cf. Tallberg [2006: 19–29]).

How much policy freedom does an IGO leader enjoy when faced with these mixed expectations? Principal–agent theory suggests that IGO leaders always enjoy some room for manoeuvre. Because of cost-effectiveness a principal delegates certain tasks to an agent. A principal will have to invest some resources in order to monitor the agent's performance. Knowing that a principal will be prepared to invest only a limited amount of resources into monitoring (up to the point where it could perform the task itself), an agent knows it has a certain amount of discretion in performing its task. This allows the agent to pursue part of its own policy preferences (called 'shirking') (Bendor 1990). When applied to IGOs, member states are principals delegating tasks to the international secretariat.

Member states hold three weapons when they are dissatisfied with the international civil service: they can withhold finances, they can alter or withdraw the mandate, or they can refuse to confirm candidates for international positions, such as the Secretary-General (S-G) of the UN. In the 'politicization' era (1970s and 1980s), the United States (as well as Malaysia and Great Britain) used the power of the purse to change practices at IGOs that were charged with nepotism, inefficiency, and bias, such as UNESCO and ILO. The United States even withdrew formally from the latter in the hope of altering its course. It returned a few years later, despite the fact that no policy changes had occurred. The latter example indicates that, as observed elsewhere, the power of the purse is not absolute. Principal–agent theory thus suggests that IGOs and their leaders certainly enjoy policy discretion under all circumstances, but that clear outer boundaries of such autonomy exist.

Indeed, the factors that have contributed to states turning to IGOs more frequently since the mid-1980s have enlarged the room for manoeuvre for many an IGO. IGO leaders have been able to affect the preferences and policies of states at the agenda-setting, decision-making as well as implementation stages of international policymaking.[2] Sometimes the direction of these instances of influence is rooted in the substantive policy visions IGOs may have developed regarding certain transnational problems (cf. Tallberg [2006: 37]). For instance, in the early 1990s General Secretary of the International Maritime Organization (IMO), William O'Neil, played a key role in persuading member states to adopt as an international standard IMO's policy perspective, which focused on human error rather than technical deficiencies as causes of shipping accidents (Dirks 2004). Yet, knowing that any particular international bureaucrat has room for manoeuvre is not sufficient in understanding why some IGO heads display leadership whereas others do not. So, what are the sources of IGO leadership?

Formal competencies and expertise

Formal competencies matter, because they bestow a degree of authority on senior IGO officials. IGOs differ widely in terms of the competencies conferred upon them (cf. Joachim [2008: 178, figure 13.1]). Several European institutions, most notably the EC, the ECJ, the European Central Bank and the European Veterinary Committee have been given exclusive authority in particular policy domains. The same is the case with WTO trade panels, the North American Free Trade Agreement (NAFTA) trade dispute resolution mechanism, and the International Criminal Tribunal for the Former Yugoslavia (ICTY). The UN S-G has the unique competence to call for an emergency meeting of the Security Council if s/he believes a certain situation endangers international peace and security. However, most IGOs have been given the task to monitor implementation of agreements, collect information, or to provide technical assistance. Many IGO leaders, because they often formally chair multilateral gatherings, enjoy 'asymmetrical control over negotiation procedure' (Tallberg 2006: 29), including determining the format and frequency of such negotiations as well as the allocation of speaking time. They thus have access to potentially formidable agenda-setting tools.

An IGO leader's authority may also be based on the technical expertise his/her organization represents. For instance, Director-General of the International Atomic Energy Agency (IAEA) Hans Blix played a crucial role in the international community's relations with Iraq, because member states held his expertise in high esteem. Moreover, because small member states often lack the administrative clout to obtain and process information regarding international issues, they often turn to IGOs to be briefed on the issue. By consequence, an IGO's use of its expert knowledge may help forge a specific alliance during an international conference. Similarly, IGOs often invite national civil servants or experts for training at an IGO site or on the spot. This helps them convey a certain perspective on policy issues and on the role an IGO can play to solve them. Examples include the regular visits of member state judges to the ECJ in Luxembourg and the training of civil servants of prospective EU member states (cf. Tallberg [2006: 41–3]).

Routines and reports

Once an international policy has been agreed upon (even if only as a declaration of intent), the institutionalized routines of multilateral diplomacy ensure that the issue will resurface on the agenda within foreseeable time. Most international conferences are followed by a monitoring conference in which progress is being reported upon. International civil servants thus have considerable agenda-setting powers, not only because the issue is raised again, but also because IGOs usually do the actual monitoring and reporting. Often, in their reports IGOs choose to report in a neutral way, like, for instance, in the WTO's Trade Policy Review Mechanism (Conzelmann 2008). Sometimes, however, they engage in benchmarking or shaming. The latter technique denounces noncompliant member states; the former praises well-performing member states. Shaming and benchmarking affect the domestic and international reputation of states and thus their cost-benefit calculations regarding future compliance. For instance, the Financial Stability Forum (FSF) and the Financial Action Task Force (FATF) (both created by the G7 countries) blacklisted so-called tax haven states for 'harmful tax competition' (Sharman 2006).

Personal characteristics

Undoubtedly, personal characteristics of leaders also matter, even in IGOs. Even though it is likely that such personal elements become relevant only to the extent that they may make leaders promote specific policy goals (Blondel 1987: 28), it is also the case that some officeholders prove more effective than others despite the fact that they are facing similar environmental constraints (Kille and Scully 2003: 178). In the field of IGOs, the most studied leader must be Jacques Delors who held the Presidency of the EC between 1985 and 1994, with the possible exception of UN Secretary-General Dag Hammarskjöld (1953–61). In many accounts Delors is credited for the successful 'Russian doll strategy' of deepening European integration by strategically exploiting the logical consequences of the adoption of the idea of a single European market. Delors's 'leadership by ideas' (Drake 1995) was based on a clear vision of a social Europe and an active role for the Commission, his sociability in dealing with other Commissioners and member states and his sense of timing (Cini 1996: 72–91; Endo 1999; Van Assche 2005).

As yet, however, little systematic research has been conducted on the personal qualities of IGO leaders and much less into the question of whether such qualities can be said to have made a difference for an IGO's policy. As a matter of fact, Andrew Moravcsik has argued that the lack of advanced research designs has caused us to simply assume that IGO leaders are salient actors because of their personal qualities. He even doubts the importance of Delors's leadership in European integration (Moravcsik 1999: especially 275–8). Several strands of research in political psychology and foreign policy analysis have focused on the measurement of belief systems of individual leaders in order to account for their policy preferences and decisions. A first application to the field of IGO leaders has been the description of the ethical frameworks of UN Secretaries General between 1945 and 2007 (Kille 2007). In recent years, however, most advancement has been made in studies of leadership styles of foreign policy decision makers, pioneered by Margaret Hermann (Hermann and Wilburn 1977). This line of research has established that specific individual traits of leaders relate to how they will exercise their leadership. These traits are combined into several leadership styles (Hermann and Preston 1994; Preston 2001). Kille and Scully have tested the hypothesis that IGO leaders equipped with an expansionist leadership style are likely to pursue an expansion of their organization's role. They investigated the leadership styles of six UN S-Gs and four Presidents of the EC. They found clear differences in leadership styles and observed that the most expansionist IGO leaders (Hammarskjöld, Boutros-Ghali and Delors) are mostly associated with pursuing policies that strengthened the role of their organizations (Kille and Scully 2003). Impressive though their findings may be, they fail to account for the changes in fortune Boutros-Ghali and Delors experienced during their final years in office.[3] This requires us to have a closer look at the crucial balancing act IGO leaders have to perform.

Impartiality

Many IGO leaders seem well equipped to exercise transactional leadership. They command important organizational resources and personal skills that may help them mobilize a variety of actors to help bring about specific substantive international policies. It seems much more difficult for them to exercise transforming leadership, because their influence remains embedded in their relationship with their member states, which at heart remains a principal–agent relationship. This implies that although member states delegate a certain amount of policy discretion to IGOs, they will have great difficulty accepting that their leaders overstep their boundaries. This is even the case in a highly legalized environment such as the EU. In particular since the adoption of the Single European Act in 1985, the EC, on the basis of its competency to initiate regulation in order to complete the internal market, has been accused of incrementally widening the domain of European policymaking, thus extending its own discretion (so-called 'creative legislation',

Leibfried and Pierson 1995). As a result, during the 1990s and early 2000s EU member states successfully put pressure on the EC to limit its enthusiasm and to some extent tamed the Commission by inventing new modes of more intergovernmental forms of policymaking, such as the Open Method of Coordination (Van Kersbergen and Verbeek 2004).

The tightrope IGO leaders walk resembles the balance that has to be struck between, what Selznick called, organizational autonomy and responsiveness. While autonomy is necessary to preserve an organization's integrity in terms of its mission and goals, an organization must not step out of bounds with the wider community it is serving. It is the organization's elite that has to ensure that autonomy does not lead to distancing from its direct environment (Selznick, as paraphrased by Terry [1995: 45–8]). In the world of IGOs and their member states, most of the time, this issue surfaces as a debate on an IGO leader's impartiality. Member states claiming IGOs and their leaders are stepping out of line by extending their policy discretion will question an IGO's authority by raising doubts about their impartiality. This is why senior IGO officials have to operate so carefully and why many IGOs, during implementation, prefer to not always use their strongest enforcement mechanism. Enforcement often entails the risk of being accused of taking sides, and thus of losing one's authority (Bauer 2006). Interestingly, many IGOs thus prefer to rely on more managerial implementation styles in order to cajole member states into policy implementation (Joachim et al. 2008). For example, in an attempt to curtail tax havens the Organization for Economic Cooperation and Development (OECD) and FSF switched from shaming tactics to offering technical assistance, when the former proved ineffective (Sharman 2006). Similarly, some observers fear that the WTO trade panels may lose authority, and thus endanger the legalized system as a whole, when they seem to convict systematically certain states rather than others (Alter 2003). And the legitimacy of the Yugoslavia Tribunal was only established when it indicted and prosecuted (Bosnian) Serbs, (Bosnian) Croats as well as Bosnian Muslims suspected of war crimes. Most IGOs, then, are basically subject to an odd form of democratic control by member states. In most UN organizations member states check their international bureaucracies on the principle of one vote per member state. Only a very weak, indirect accountability link exists between national citizens and IGO. One might argue that the American Congress, funding 20 per cent of the UN budget, comes closest to holding the UN democratically accountable. Within the EU member states exercise different votes on the basis of size. In some EU policy arenas the European Parliament (EP) and, indirectly, national parliaments, serve as instruments of democratic control. Nevertheless, the EC is not a government held accountable to an elected assembly. The Commission's main opponents are the member states.

The need to preserve authority through maintaining a reputation for neutrality and impartiality makes it difficult for IGO leaders to display transforming leadership, as the latter requires them to lift followers (such as member states) to higher levels of morality and motivation and to establish lasting social change. It might be a bit easier for the EC as this institution officially is the guardian of the treaty. This might give it the necessary moral authority to put forward grander schemes of change.

In the next sections, I will discuss two cases that can be seen as the attempts of IGO leaders to engage in transforming leadership. UN Secretary-General Boutros Boutros-Ghali attempted to carve out a new role for the UN in the post-Cold War era. His legacy is much debated. European Commissioner Peter Sutherland succeeded in establishing the Commission's lasting authority in competition policy. Both reached 'the boundaries' of their relationship with their member states. Both had to fight the accusations of being partial. Both cases will be discussed by first sketching the outline of the 'principal–agent' relationship they were embedded in, followed by an analysis of their attempts at transforming leadership.

Boutros Boutros-Ghali

The UN Secretary-General's balancing act

Any UN S-G has to cater to many different constituents. Countries from his/her region of origin usually look upon them as 'their representative at the UN'. Countries that were instrumental in having him elected as S-G expect special attention. Furthermore, the S-G is expected to help implement the decisions taken by the Security Council and the recommendations made by the General Assembly. In addition, he is the manager of the UN organization and as such responsible for its personnel and finances (and thus accountable to its creditors, the member states). The S-G was meant to serve, not to lead. Yet over the years the S-G has effectively become an influential political figure, because Security Council members expect the S-G to take the lead to implement its resolutions and because many new UN offices and programmes have to report to him directly (Trent 2007: 138–9). However, in a world where numerous eyes closely watch the S-G's (or any UN official's) steps it is extremely difficult to pursue substantive policies without being accused of partiality by one or the other party. This is increasingly the case since the end of the Cold War, as public opinion everywhere is looking to the S-G for moral guidance and problem solving capacity regarding pressing issues, global as well as local.[4]

This increase in the number of stakeholders complicates the accountability problem any S-G is facing. The S-G is held accountable effectively by the UN member states, not by the organizational staff and not by the general public. This implies that s/he will be closely observed by countries with clout in the UN: the five permanent members of the Security Council, regional leaders such as Brazil, South Africa, and India, as well as countries which contribute large sums to the UN and its specialized agencies, such as Canada and the Netherlands. Even though s/he may use international public opinion as a weapon against critical member states, in the end it is those same member states which decide about the future of the S-G's contract.

Boutros-Ghali's leadership moment: transforming the UN's role

The Egyptian Boutros Boutros-Ghali was appointed S-G in December 1991. He held the position until 1996, when the United States vetoed a proposed second term. His appointment underscored that it was Africa's turn to occupy this position. At the same time, Arab countries considered Boutros-Ghali a representative from their region, even though many were wary of him because of his active involvement in the 1979 Egyptian–Israeli peace settlement (Meisler 1995: 184).

When Boutros-Ghali entered the UN, the organization was facing a difficult situation. On the one hand it had gained new legitimacy because of its successful involvement in resolving various regional conflicts since the mid-1980s. Moreover, the UN's role during the Gulf War (1990–1), condemning Iraq's occupation of Kuwait, formally branding it an aggressor and allowing the use of force under Chapter VII of the UN Charter, had made the United States less weary of the organization. At the same time, however, the UN was experiencing severe internal troubles. Because many states were in arrears with paying their membership dues, its organization was crippled at the very moment when costly peacekeeping operations were being agreed upon. In addition, the UN bureaucracy was generally considered to be highly inefficient and ineffective, occasionally accused of nepotism. Taking office at this critical juncture Boutros-Ghali had a window of opportunity to carve out a new role for the UN in a new era of international politics, while at the same time he knew he would be closely watched by its main creditors and by his own traditional constituents, Arab and African states.

Boutros-Ghali was a Coptic-Christian from Egypt. Trained as an international lawyer, he took up an academic career before he became Foreign Secretary under President Anwar Al-Sadat. He was Sadat's major aide during the 1978 Camp David peace talks, and had established close links with Israelis like Shimon Peres and Ezer Weizman. Between 1979 and 1992 he was member of the UN Commission of International Law.

Because his performance as S-G infuriated the Clinton administration, eventually leading to an American campaign to prevent him from serving a second term, sources differ considerably in their judgment of Boutros-Ghali's character and leadership style. James Traub describes him as not having 'the temperament for self-effacing adjudication or for the patient searching out of common ground. He was condescending, arrogant, secretive, status-conscious.

He was prone to interrupt an ambassador in the midst of a presentation' (Traub 2007: 67). Others would praise Boutros-Ghali for his legal expertise, wit, and stamina. Boutros-Ghali himself was well aware of the risk of being considered paternalistic, a tone which he attributed to his many years as a teacher (Boutros-Ghali 1999: 156). His leadership style has been described as expansionist (Kille and Scully 2003: 185). In terms of his belief system, his religious background and early career experiences allegedly provided Boutros-Ghali with a particular perspective on international affairs, based on tolerance, reconciliation, respect for human rights and democracy and a notion of the central role that the nation state should play in bringing about such values (Lang 2007: 266–74).

Clearly, Boutros-Ghali was well aware of the 'outer boundaries' of his role. He knew that everyone would closely monitor his behaviour, in particular where the fate of Africa or Muslims would be concerned, as well as the Arab–Israeli problem. He therefore decided to base his policies upon a strict interpretation of UN resolutions. In addition, he would always form a team or task force so that the outer world would look upon his policies as taken by consensus and not by the S-G alone (Boutros-Ghali 1999: 181). He created an eight-member team of close advisors (from each continent) in order to keep an eye on the variety of interests involved (Boutros-Ghali 1999: 29). Boutros-Ghali thus knew that his authority was intimately linked with member states perceiving him as impartial.

Boutros-Ghali wanted to be more than an administrator. He intended to use the window of opportunity offered by the end of the Cold War to help reshape the international order by strengthening the role of the UN. He sought to derive authority from the UN's principles set out in its 1945 Charter. Indeed, his critics would accuse him of seeking 'independence': at best they considered his principled interpretation as 'extremely naive' (Traub 2007: 68). Boutros-Ghali wanted to make the organization more efficient; to improve the coordination of the efforts of UN workers in New York City with those in Geneva; to ensure that the funding of the UN would suffice to meet the needs of the increased number, and complexity, of its missions around the globe; and to strengthen the commitment of every member state to the UN. He also sought to widen the S-G's formal competence by asking for a mandate to seek advisory opinions from the International Court of Justice (Weiss et al. 2001: 129). His most important objective, however, was to broaden the UN's peacekeeping role.

By setting these goals Boutros-Ghali mobilized a lot of resistance. Many UN civil servants opposed the administrative reforms Boutros-Ghali proposed. His perennial 'shaming' of member states, in particular the United States, of lagging behind in their contributions, contributed to the negative attitude in the American Congress towards the UN. His proposal to activate the UN Military Staff Committee, which had been defunct since 1945, and thus ensure a ready intervention capacity for peacekeeping operations, aroused suspicion in the US, where his critics accused him of being more of a general than a secretary.

Boutros-Ghali proved more successful in agenda-setting. First, his 1992 *Agenda for Peace,* giving an analysis of the problems of international peace and security, contributed to the overall acceptance (after his term) of a new UN role in peace and security. Peacekeeping, where UN troops would separate fighting parties, had proven to be of only limited use and dependent on the permission of the sovereign states involved to welcome blue helmets. Boutros-Ghali's report helped the embracing of the concept of peace enforcement, in which the international community could intervene in conflicts at a much earlier stage, and in which it could also intervene in a state's domestic affairs. *Agenda for Peace* and its 1995 *Supplement* thus contributed to the notable alteration in the legal weight accorded to the notion of state sovereignty (Weiss et al. 2001: 111–19).

Boutros-Ghali's success was mainly based on seizing the opportunity given to him by the Security Council members. In the 1990s the Council adopted many resolutions dealing with intra-state conflicts leaving their precise implementation to the S-G. Boutros-Ghali took on that challenge and used this room of manoeuvre to widen the UN's policy domain.

Second, his decision to hold six major conferences that were supposed to set the agenda for accomplishing the other objectives of the UN Charter: the 1992 environmental conference in Rio de Janeiro, the 1993 human rights conference in Vienna, the 1994 population conference in Cairo, the 1995 social development world summit in Copenhagen, the 1995 women's rights conference in Beijing, and the 1997 cities conference in Istanbul. Boutros-Ghali wanted these summits in order to be able to set the agenda and in order to avoid the creation of yet further UN bureaucracies (Boutros-Ghali 1999: 165). Some of these conferences, in particular those in Rio and Beijing have had important lasting effects and have set in motion important international regulation (Weiss et al. 2001: 317–26).

Boutros-Ghali's activist vision had a lasting effect, and as such constituted a form of transforming leadership. At the same time, his style of 'shaming' and frankness made him powerful enemies, none more so than the Clinton administration. It is unclear whether President Clinton explicitly endorsed the removal of Boutros-Ghali proposed by his foreign policy team (including Secretary of State Warren Christopher and UN representative Madeleine Albright) or felt entrapped by Christopher's leaking to the press of American opposition to a second term for Boutros-Ghali (cf. Christopher [1998: 328–34]). Regardless, Boutros-Ghali served as the major culprit in the 1996 Presidential campaign of Republican candidate Bob Dole and Clinton could not afford to look weak on the issue of the UN. It is also clear that Boutros-Ghali had not been sufficiently aware of the effect of his behaviour on the American Congress and of the pivotal role it played in American policies towards the UN. In that sense, he overstepped his boundaries and faced the consequences. Ironically, Boutros-Ghali refused a face-saving compromise of serving for one more year until his seventy-fifth birthday and stepping down voluntarily. Instead, in a final act of 'shaming' it, he forced the United States to use its veto in the Security Council, exposing that it stood alone in its desire to block his second term.

Boutros-Ghali's leadership left changes that endured, however, as they were strengthened under his successor Kofi Annan. Indeed, the development of international law, the increased use of his policy principles by international and transnational actors, including national leaders such as British Prime Minister Tony Blair, ensured that the principle of non-interference in domestic affairs weakened and that peace enforcement became a more common practice.

Peter Sutherland

The European Commissioner's balancing act

It is commonplace to argue that the twenty-seven EU member states have delegated wide policy discretion to the EU. The EU has not yet by far evolved into the supranational state that some fear and others desire. Rather, the EU consists of various policy arenas which differ in many respects. Some policy areas, such as the EU Common Foreign and Security Policy, remain exclusively intergovernmental, meaning that European law and the European institutions are of little or no consequence. In other fields, supranational institutions have been given exclusive competencies. This hybrid character of the EU complicates the discussion of its powers and its accountability. One might argue that in intergovernmental arenas little dispersion of leadership has occurred and that member states are held accountable by their national parliaments. In supranational policy areas, such as competition policy, the European Commission(EC) and the ECJ are highly salient. Here, member states have delegated important powers to institutions that operate in a shady system of accountability (Verbeek 2006).

Regarding matters concerning the internal market, the EC enjoys the exclusive right to initiate legislation, giving it important agenda-setting powers. In addition, the Commission has important exclusive competencies in the fields of competition, and in ensuring that member states implement European legislation (Cini 1996: 13–33). Even so, the Commission will be closely watched by the EP and the member states, which hold a number of weapons to prevent the Commission from engaging in legislation that would endanger their vital interests. First, the member states appoint Commissioners. As most Commissioners are career politicians, they will have to take the view of their individual domestic constituents into account, even though the Commission has to act in the interest of the EU as a whole. Every Commission is therefore a coalition of liberals, social-democrats and Christian-democrats (Cini 1996: 106–11; Hix 2005: 41–6). Second, the member states have designed an elaborate system of some 224 advisory committees on which national government officials have a seat. This system of 'comitology' was designed to closely monitor and direct the Commission's agenda-setting and implementing activities (Hix 2005: 51–8).

Finally, member states can change the rules of the game by reducing (or widening) the formal competencies of the Commission by intergovernmental treaty. Commissioners, even in supranational policy areas like Sutherland's (see further below), thus have to proceed cautiously when they seek radically new policies or seem to enlarge the organization's policy autonomy. This holds true also for the domain of competition. The EU's competition policy is aimed at establishing a truly internal market by creating a level playing field among enterprises. It rules on mergers and state subsidies and thus may affect issues that are highly sensitive to individual member states.

The EP holds a veto over the appointment of the Commission and has the right to censure it, the latter requiring an absolute majority of EP members and a two-thirds majority of the votes cast. In the late 1990s the EP showed increased assertiveness in holding the Commission accountable, as was best demonstrated by the resignation of the Santer-Commission in 1999 when the adoption of a motion of censure was likely after the publication of a report filed by independent experts on allegations of fraud, corruption, and nepotism by Commission officials (Hix 2005: 60–1).

Lastly, individual Commissioners are closely examined by their fellow Commissioners. The President of the Commission is likely to make an attempt at directing the policies of his/her Commissioners. The Commissioners themselves differ in outlook because they most of the time come from different ideological strands, as every Commission displays a balance between social-democrats, Christian-democrats, and liberals. Commissioners also jealously guard their bureaucratic turf and raise difficulties when a colleague seems to encroach upon their domain.

Sutherland's leadership moment: institutionalizing neoliberal competition policy

Peter Sutherland was European Commissioner for Ireland between 1985 and 1989. He was appointed by the Irish government led by his party Fine Gael. Sutherland had been a member of the Strategic Committee of Fine Gael between 1978 and 1981 and had twice served as Attorney-General for Ireland (a political function) between 1981 and 1984. Irish Commissioners usually are strong national politicians who 'would have fitted badly inside the governing coalition' (Middlemas 1995: 725 note 16). Sutherland, a lawyer by training, had proven a tenacious proponent of the principles of a free market economy. Generally seen as highly ambitious, he acknowledged 'to hav[ing] wanted to run [Europe] all [his] life' (Martinson 2007). Indeed, in 1985 he became Commissioner at the European Community's Directorate-General IV (now DG Competition) at his own insistence, because DGIV held real powers (Ross 1995: 160).

When entering the Commission, Sutherland faced many opponents. Several member states were weary of his free market ideology and its implications. France, Italy, and Greece, having suffered during the economic recession of the early 1980s, considered competition policy a protective device to strengthen 'national champions' (McGowan and Cini 1999: 179). Other member states, including Germany, feared that DGIV might seek an expanded role at the expense of national cartel authorities. In addition, Sutherland faced internal rivalry from the powerful DGIII (now DG Enterprise and Industry). DGIII had long favoured a more protectionist attitude (Middlemas 1995: 232; McGowan and Cini 1999: 189). Finally, Sutherland had to deal with the attempts by the President of the EC, Jacques Delors, to micromanage the course of the various DGs. Delors, a social-democrat, who did not fully share Sutherland's outspoken free market principles, sought to lead his Commissioners by turning his own *cabinet* (advisory unit) into a power house by preventing them from strengthening their own *cabinets* (Middlemas 1995: 232; Cini 1996: 181–91).

Under Sutherland, however, DGIV succeeded in expanding the interpretation of its competencies under articles 85 and 86 of the Treaty of Rome. While until 1985 it dealt with minor issues like agreements between firms, its authority was widened to include mergers, takeovers, and state aid (McGowan 1996: 15–16). Sutherland exercised transforming leadership particularly in designing and promoting the Merger Control Regulation (MCR). When the Single European Act entered into force in 1987, the EC was committed to creating an internal market, yet this did not imply that competition policy should include preventing the development of market-dominating firms: indeed, to many actors the creating of big European champions was supposedly a major strategy to thwart American, Japanese, and South Korean competition (Wigger 2008). Indeed, this was a policy line much favoured by Delors. The MCR thus met with fierce resistance, but was eventually adopted in December 1989 after Sutherland's departure from the Commission. The MCR allotted the authority to investigate and judge large-scale mergers to the EC and took it out of the hands of national jurisdictions (Cini 2002: 240–1).

In four years' time, Sutherland had succeeded in making first DGIV, next the EC, then the member states accept a strict interpretation of EC competition policy based on the notion of creating the necessary conditions for a truly open market (McGowan and Cini 1999: 179). Furthermore, he made them accept additional competency in mergers and acquisitions. His success proved also to be lasting, partly because he was succeeded by a like minded and equally energetic Commissioner, Leon Brittan (1989–94). In the mid-1990s even the more protectionist leaning Commissioner Karel van Miert would accept Sutherland's and Brittan's competition standards, despite the fact that several member states had favoured Van Miert's appointment assuming that this social-democrat would promote a less strictly neoliberal competition policy.

Sutherland's leadership was rooted first of all in his forceful personality and firm convictions. Known for the style that he had developed as a barrister, Sutherland tended to approach opponents aggressively before locking them up in legal arguments. Delors nicknamed him 'the little sheriff' because of this style (Schwartz 1993: 639). Sutherland truly believed that Europe needed a level playing field regulated by the European institutions if it was to remain a serious player in a globalizing world economy.

Sutherland also carefully exploited the institutional weapons handed to him by the EC treaties. Basically, he chose as his strategy to seek to regulate mergers and state aid on the basis of the existing Treaty Articles in the absence of any formal competency. He reckoned that the ECJ would choose his side if he were to be taken to court.

And Sutherland displayed craftsmanship in various ways. He ensured that the civil servants working at DGIV would be dedicated to his perspective of the internal market. Indeed, in later years German DGIII Commissioner Martin Bangemann was to refer to DGIV officials as 'the Ayatollahs of competition' (Middlemas 1995: 249–50, quote from 506). In addition, he promoted the development of a common outlook by having organized staff meetings between DGIV and national agencies (Middlemas 1995: 509–10). Furthermore, he introduced a strategy of naming and shaming of state aid practices by member states (Wilks 2005: 124). Finally, he succeeded in building important coalitions, in particular with European industries and their representatives at the national and European level. European business had a keen interest in creating 'one counter' for cartel and merger matters in Europe, rather than having to deal with many different national competition authorities (Wigger 2008). In persuading his fellow Commissioners and reluctant member states Sutherland conveyed this point not by just preaching neoliberal principles, but by insisting that liberalization would be the only way of ensuring that European industries would be able to compete with American and Asian firms on the global market.

Conclusions: the tightrope of IGO leadership

This chapter offered two arguments why the increased involvement of IGOs in solving global and domestic problems may threaten their authority in the long term. First, greater involvement entails the danger that IGOs and their leaders will be perceived as partial. Second, it raises the awareness among the general public that IGOs engage in substantive policymaking, yet are hardly subjected to democratic control. The two cases presented here offer mixed results. The case of UN Secretary-General Boutros seems to underscore the argument. Boutros-Ghali faced an increase in member states' demand for UN policies, laid down in numerous Security Council resolutions. Initially, he moved carefully, by sticking to strict legal interpretations and with his strategy to engage in agenda-setting by organizing encompassing conferences. These set the stage for important treaties in the 1990s and early 2000s. Yet, his authority waned as he neglected the interests of the United States and of a majority within the American Congress, thus crossing the boundaries of the principal–agent relation. The choice for Kofi Annan in 1997 was meant to ensure that the next UN S-G would respect these boundaries.

The case of European Commissioner Peter Sutherland suggests that IGO leaders can actually change the boundaries between principal and agent. Sutherland managed to institutionalize, and give teeth to, a robust neoliberal EU competition policy. He succeeded despite the resistance of powerful member states and of competitors within the Commission. Even though his policies eventually strengthened the overall position of the Commission, EU competition policy was never subject to attempts to reduce the Commission's powers, as happened, for instance, in the fields of agriculture and the environment. The key to this lasting success was Sutherland's use of the idea of creating a level playing field. This concept suggested that impartiality could be maintained. Sutherland thus never risked being accused of partiality.

Both Boutros-Ghali and Sutherland displayed distinct qualities in terms of style, vision, and craftsmanship. Nevertheless, Boutros-Ghali, in the end, proved the least successful, because his style was instrumental in antagonizing his largest opponent in the UN, the United States, but also because a UN S-G enjoys much fewer formal competencies than the Commissioner of DG Competition. Furthermore, contrary to international law, the EU legal system is strongly entrenched, making it more difficult for member states to ignore EU policies. In addition, the EU political system allows a Commissioner to build powerful alliances, not the least with the courts. A UN S-G lacks such weighty allies. In sum, IGO leaders walk a tightrope between various constituents by maintaining an air of impartiality. In such a game a leader of the UN has to be more careful than an EU Commissioner, because s/he has been invested with little formal authority.

Notes

1. Both cases are also interesting because in 1996 Boutros-Ghali was denied a second term when the United States cast a veto in the Security Council, and Ireland did not reappoint Sutherland in 1989 as the Commissioner to the Delors Commission.

2. For example, Barnett and Finnemore [2004]; Dijkzeul and Beigbeder [2003]; Joachim et al. [2008]; Reinalda and Verbeek [1998, 2004].
3. Hammarskjöld died in a plane crash in 1961 but had become the object of severe criticism and resistance in the year preceding his death.
4. Proponents of a cosmopolitan perspective on international justice are much in favour of a widened role for the UN as part of a wider system of global civil society that is instrumental in effectuating individual rights in an interdependent global society (e.g. Dower [1998: 185–7]). For some it might even be a stepping stone to reaching cosmopolitan democracy (Colás 2002: 143–7). A weightier UN would imply a more important role for its chief executive.

Bibliography

Alter, K. J., 'Resolving or Exacerbating Disputes? The WTO's New Dispute Resolution System', *International Affairs*, 79/4 (2003), 783–800.

Archer, C., *International Organizations*, 3rd edn.(London and New York: Routledge, 2001).

Barnett, M. and Finnemore, M., *Rules for the World: International Organizations in Global Politics* (Ithaca, New York: Cornell University Press, 2004).

Barros, J., *Office Without Power: Secretary-General Sir Eric Drummond, 1919–1933* (Oxford: Clarendon, 1979).

Bauer, S., 'Does Bureaucracy Really Matter? The Authority of Intergovernmental Treaty Secretariats', *Global Environmental Politics*, 6/1 (2006), 23–49.

Bendor, J., 'Formal Models of Bureaucracy: A Review', in N. Lynn and A. Wildavsky (eds.), *Public Administration: The State of the Discipline* (Chatham: Chatham House, 1990), 873–96.

Berridge, G. R., *Return to the UN: UN Diplomacy in Regional Conflicts* (London: Macmillan, 1991).

Blondel, J., *Political Leadership* (London: Sage, 1987).

Boutros-Ghali, B., *Unvanquished: A U.S.-U.N. Saga* (New York: Random House, 1999).

Burns, J. M., *Leadership* (New York: Harper and Row, 1978).

Christopher, W., *In the Stream of History: Shaping Foreign Policy for a New Era* (Stanford: Stanford University Press, 1998).

Cini, M., *The European Commission: Leadership, Organisation, and Culture in the EU Administration* (Manchester: Manchester University Press, 1996).

——'The European Merger Regime: Accounting for the Distinctiveness of the EU Model', *Policy Studies Journal*, 30/2 (2002), 240–51.

Colás, A., *International Civil Society* (Cambridge: Blackwell, 2002).

Conzelmann, T., 'Beyond the Carrot and the Stick: State Reporting Procedures in the WTO and the OECD', in J. Joachim, B. Reinalda, and B. Verbeek (eds.), *International Organizations and Implementation: Enforcers, Managers, Authorities?* (London, New York: Routledge, 2008), 35–47.

Dahl, R. A., *Modern Political Analysis*, 3rd edn. (Englewood Cliffs, New Jersey: Prentice Hall, 1976).

Dijkzeul, D. and Beigbeder, Y. (eds.), *Rethinking International Organizations: Pathology and Promise* (Oxford and New York: Berham Books, 2003).

Dirks, J., 'Decision Making in the International Maritime Organization: The Case of the STCW 95 Convention', in B. Reinalda and B. Verbeek (eds.) Decision Making within International Organizations (London: Routledge, 2004), 201–14.

Dower, N., *World Ethics: The New Agenda* (Edinburgh: Edinburgh University Press, 1998).

Drake, H., 'Political Leadership and European Integration: The Case of Jacques Delors', *West European Politics*, 18/2 (1995), 140–60.

Endo, K., *The Presidency of the European Commission under Jacques Delors: The Politics of Shared Leadership* (Basingstoke: Macmillan, 1999).

Goldstein, J., Kahler, M., Keohane, R. O., and Slaughter, A-M. (eds.), 'Legalization and World Politics', *International Organization*, 54/3 (2000), 385–703.

Hermann, M. G. and Preston, T., 'Presidents, Advisers, and Foreign Policy: The Effect of Leadership Style on Executive Arrangements', *Political Psychology*, 15/1 (1994), 75–96.

——and Wilburn, T. W. (eds.), *A Psychological Examination of Political Leaders* (New York: The Free Press, 1977).

Hirst, P., 'Democracy and Governance', in J. Pierre (ed.), *Debating Governance: Authority, Steering, and Democracy* (Oxford: Oxford University Press, 2000), 13–35.

Hix, S., *The Political System of the European Union*, 2nd edn. (Houndmills: Palgrave Macmillan, 2005).

Huntington, S. P., *The Third Wave: Democratization in the Late Twentieth Century* (Norman and London: University of Oklahoma Press, 1991).

Joachim, J., Reinalda, B., and Verbeek B., *International Organizations and Implementation: Enforcers, Managers, Authorities?* (London and New York: Routledge, 2008).

Kille, K. J. (ed.), *The UN Secretary-General and Moral Authority: Ethics and Religion in International Leadership* (Washington, D.C.: Georgetown University Press, 2007).

——and Scully, R. M., 'Executive Heads and the Role of Intergovernmental Organizations: Expansionist Leadership in the United Nations and the European Union', *Political Psychology*, 24/1 (2003), 175–98.

Lang, Jr., A. F., 'A Realist in the Utopian City: Boutros-Ghali's Ethical Framework and its Impact', in K. J. Kille (ed.), *The UN Secretary-General and Moral Authority: Ethics and Religion in International Leadership* (Washington, D.C.: Georgetown University Press, 2007), 265–97.

Leibfried, S., and Pierson, P. (eds.), *European Social Policy* (Washington, DC: Brookings, 1995).

Martinson, J., 'OK, He Chairs BP, But Really He Wants to Run Europe', *The Guardian*, 19 January 2007, available at: <http://www.guardian.co.uk/business/2007/jan/19/oilandpetrol.news>.

McGowan, L., 'Unmasking a Federal Agency: The European Commission's Control of Competition Policy', *European Business Review*, 96/5 (1996), 13–26.

——and Michelle C., 'Discretion and Politicization in EU Competition Policy: The Case of Merger Control', *Governance*, 12/ 2 (1999), 175–200.

Meisler, S., 'Dateline U.N.: A New Hammarskjöld?', *Foreign Policy*, 98 Spring (1995), 180–97.

Middlemas, K., *Orchestrating Europe: The Informal Politics of the European Union 1973–1995* (London: Fontana, 1995).

Moravcsik, A., 'A New Statecraft? Supranational Entrepreneurs and International Cooperation', *International Organization*, 53/2 (1999), 267–306.

Preston, T., *The President and His Inner Circle* (Princeton: Princeton University Press, 2001).

Reinalda, B. and Verbeek, B. (eds.), *Autonomous Policymaking by International Organizations* (London: Routledge, 1998).

——— (eds.), *Decision Making Within International Organizations* (London and New York: Routledge, 2004).

Risse-Kappen, T., 'Public Opinion, Domestic Structure, and Foreign Policy in Liberal Democracies', *World Politics*, 43 July (1991), 479–512.

Ross, G., *Jacques Delors and European Integration* (New York: Oxford University Press, 1995).

Scholte, J. A., 'The Globalization of World Politics', in J. Baylis and S. Smith (eds.), *The Globalization of World Politics: An Introduction to International Relations*, 2nd edn. (Oxford: Oxford University Press, 2001), 13–32.

Schwartz, E., 'Politics as Usual: The History of European Community Merger Control', *Yale Journal of International Law*, 18 (1993), 607–62.

Sharman, J. C., *Havens in a Storm: The Struggle for Global Tax Regulation* (Ithaca, New York: Cornell University Press, 2006).

Tallberg, J., *Leadership and Negotiation in the European Union* (Cambridge: Cambridge University Press, 2006).

Terry, L. D., *Leadership of Public Bureaucracies: The Administrator as Conservator* (Thousand Oaks, CA: Sage, 1995).

Traub, J., *The Best Intentions: Kofi Annan and the UN in the Era of American World Power* (New York: Picador, 2007).

Trent, J. E., *Modernizing the United Nations System: Civil Society's Role in Moving from International Relations to Global Governance* (Opladen and Farmington Hills: Barbara Budrich, 2007).

Van Assche, T., 'The Impact of Entrepreneurial Leadership on EU High Politics: A Case Study of Jacques Delors and the Creation of EMU', *Leadership*, 1/3 (2005), 279–98.

Van Kersbergen, K. and Verbeek, B., 'Subsidiarity as a Principle of Governance in the European Union', *Comparative European Politics*, 2/2 (2004), 142–62.

Verbeek, B., 'Democracy and European Integration', in C. Ahn and B. Fort (eds.), *Democracy in Asia, Europe, and the World: Towards a Universal Definition?* (London/Singapore: Marshall Cavendish, 2006), 87–105.

Weiss, T. G., Forsythe, D. G., and Coate, R. A., *The United Nations and Changing World Politics* (Boulder: Westview, 2001).

Wigger, A., *Competition for Competitiveness: The Politics of the Transformation of the EU Competition Regime* (Amsterdam: Vrije Universiteit, 2008).

Wilks, S., 'Competition Policy: Challenge and Reform', in H. Wallace, W. Wallace, and M. Pollack (eds.), *Policy-Making in the European Union*, 5th edn. (Oxford: Oxford University Press, 2005).

Chapter 14

Leadership by the Famous: Celebrity as Political Capital

Paul 't Hart and Karen Tindall

'When a celebrity talks, people listen; there is no better messenger.'

(Ford and Goodale, cited in Cooper 2008: 114)

Star power

Many of us care about refugees and displaced children.[1] Tens of thousands of us spend considerable amounts of time and money improving their situation. But few of us have been as effective in drawing attention to these issues and keeping them on the agenda of political elites and institutions around the world as celebrities such as Angelina Jolie. In the last six years she has evolved into a formidable agenda-setter, a tenacious lobbyist, and a grand benefactor. A regular fixture in the last few instalments of the *Time* 100 list of the year's most influential people, Angelina Jolie is no longer just an actress and a celebrity figure. She has come to be seen as a public leader.

In fact, she is a public leader *because* she is a valuable Hollywood commodity. She deftly uses her famous name, physique, and performative qualities to gain clout in the world beyond Hollywood and to advance the causes she has come to embrace ever since shooting a movie in Cambodia. Jolie understands that a celebrity is not just someone hounded by tabloid journalists but also 'an individual whose name has attention-getting, interest-riveting and profit-generating value' (Rein, Kottler, and Stoller 1987: 15). She is by no means the first big-name humanitarian activist (cinema icon Audrey Hepburn is considered one of the pioneers of humanitarian activism in Hollywood), but Jolie has succeeded on a much larger scale than Hepburn ever contemplated. Jolie represents a paradigmatic example of 'star power' at work in the world of international politics (Cooper 2008: 32–5). She and other modern day 'celebrity diplomats' such as Bono, Bob Geldof, and George Clooney know that 'celebrity sells' (Pringle 2004), but instead of (or as well as) selling watches, jewellery, fragrances, and cars they have chosen to 'sell' humanitarian causes and other political messages.

Star power defies conventional accounts of democratic leadership. It epitomizes the notion of leadership dispersal, although not one that is the product of institutional design let alone constitutional foresight. It rests upon personal rather than institutional moral capital. That capital is derived from fame, dramaturgy, and personality marketing in the non-political sphere, rather than by democratic election, representation, and accountability. It is a form of leadership by the well-known, not necessarily leadership by the well-qualified. In an era of boundless mass communication worldwide and 'entertainment culture' merging seamlessly with 'high culture' star power feels a lot more potent, connected and 'in tune' than electoral power. Unless of course, the two are aligned, with the one reinforcing the other and vice versa.

Many on both sides of the divide have seen this potential, and many have tried to exploit it. Rock stars rub shoulders with presidents and bankers to eradicate poverty. Politicians keenly seek endorsements of talk show hosts to get (re-)elected. NGOs lobby musicians and football stars to become their public faces. A former politician teams up with film makers to produce an Oscar-winning documentary and helps stage the world's biggest rock concert to push for action on global warming. A pro wrestler and a bodybuilder-turned-actor both get themselves elected as state governors in the United States. A poet becomes prime minister of the largest democracy in the world. In Australia, a former news presenter unseats a four-term prime minister at the ballot box.

There is no dearth of opinions about celebrity leadership, perhaps because it is clearly an emergent phenomenon that straddles 'democracy's edges' (cf. Shapiro and Hacker-Cordon 1999). But among the clamour of opinions on offer, there is surprisingly little in the way of empirical analysis. Where, how, and why do the worlds of celebrity and politics merge to produce forms of celebrity political leadership? These elementary questions have been given almost no coverage in the celebrity literature, which is scattered across disciplines such as cultural studies, media and communications, sociology and social psychology, with political science contributions modest in number and scope. In the first part of this chapter we shall try to lay some much-needed groundwork for a comparative analysis of celebrity politics in established democracies. We present four different forms of celebrity politics, and then dissect them in greater detail. We look at their critical features, how they are situated within democratic institutions and practices, and identify the sources of their leadership potential. Throughout the chapter, we formulate empirical propositions purporting to identify the institutional, cultural, and situational conditions of their occurrence and impact. These propositions are strictly explorative; they intend however to stimulate and inspire the kind of systematic comparative research that is presently lacking. In the final section, we assess the rise of celebrity politics as a form of dispersed leadership.

Celebrity and politics: how the twain meet

We should not make the mistake of thinking that we are dealing with a (post) modern phenomenon here. People who have already gained fame in another sphere of life have always been looked at to play public leadership roles. Quite a few of them have actively sought public office, or have been encouraged to do so by power brokers. Every epoch and culture produces its own 'stars' or at least skews the distribution of stardom in particular ways (Braudy 1986). When, as in ancient Rome, societies depended on armies and/or conquest for their survival and prosperity, successful military leaders were likely to be key heroes and potential recruits into political leadership positions. And this has extended into modern times: the United States has repeatedly turned to generals whose credentials for political office were largely that they were famous 'warriors'. Among others, generals Harrison, Grant, Eisenhower ('I like Ike') and, for a while, MacArthur and Powell were courted by parties (often both major parties at the same time) to be their standard bearer, and in some cases ended up as president.

Yet there have long been alternative bases for celebrity. When societies value achievement in science and the arts, inventors, investigators, painters, sculptors, and composers become celebrities (although historically relatively few of them seem to have sought or achieved formal public leadership positions). When societies are oppressed, dignified dissidents become popular heroes, and, after liberation, almost irresistible candidates for executive office (Mandela and Havel). And when the culture and economy of societies are permeated by an all-encompassing and increasingly global sports and entertainment industry, high-profile people within that industry – today's sports, television, movie, rock, pop and hip-hop 'stars' – are handed a golden opportunity structure for political advocacy and/or careerism.

It is therefore important to acknowledge the contextual and contingent nature of celebrity. Firstly, whilst one may usefully analyse celebrity in terms of individual stardom and the political opportunities and choices of the people involved, it remains necessary to understand this as a broader social phenomenon embedded in and indicative of industries, cultures, and regimes (Turner 2004). Secondly, regardless of the original source of fame, celebrity involvement in politics itself can take very different forms (Monaco 1978; Rojek 2001; Mukherjee 2004; Street 2004). Therefore no grand, one-size-fits-all interpretation is sufficient. It is necessary to drill down into the specific circumstances and problems of different manifestations of celebrity politics: the celebrity activist, the celebrity endorser, the celebrity politician, and the politician-turned-celebrity. Each has its own distinctive contingencies, challenges, and implications for political

Table 14.1 Celebrity leadership: a comparative overview

	Celebrity advocate	Celebrity endorser	Celebrity politician	Politician-celebrity
Foundations	*Issue-focused*: agenda-setting and/or policy-seeking behaviour by high-visibility figures from traditionally non-political spheres (entertainment, arts, sports, civil society, journalism, and science)	*Office-focused*: high-visibility figures from traditionally non-political spheres offering financial and/or public support for a political candidate and/or party	*Office-seeking*: legislative or executive offices sought by high-visibility figures from traditionally non-political spheres	*Office-transforming*: office-holder whose public behaviour, purposeful association with celebrities, and/or private life alter his public persona beyond the traditional political sphere into the celebrity sphere *Subtypes:* P-C1: active (by intent); P-C2: passive (by accident/scandal)
Nature of leadership exercised	*Political mobilization*: Watchdog Agenda-setter Educator Energizer	Electoral momentum-building	Achieving formal legislative or executive leadership positions	Not applicable. (P-C1: power consolidation or expansion) (P-C2: political survival)
Relation to institutional politics	Informal; not embedded *System-confirming*: refocusing public and political agendas; supporting existing NGOs/IGOs *System-eroding*: vocal criticism of incumbent elites and institutions	Informal; partially embedded *System-confirming*: mobilizing support for candidates in electoral contests	Formal; embedded *System-confirming*: celebrity chooses the path of conventional, electoral politics to exercise leadership	Informal; embedded *System-expanding*: P-C1 seeks to widen his/her (and his/her policies') appeal by reaching 'beyond politics' P-C2's private life is propelled into the public limelight, and becomes a political issue
Leadership capital	'Concentrated star power' Has easy access to (free) publicity, is a known and liked public figure. Enjoys personal wealth and/or easy access to funds as well as advocacy professionals. Few constraints on ability to pursue 'unorthodox', 'direct', 'controversial' advocacy methods in the service of a cause.	'Selective star power' Has easy access to (free) publicity, is a known and liked public figure. Enjoys personal wealth and easy access to other high-profile donors and/or endorsers.	'Constrained star power' Has easy access to (free) publicity, is a known and often liked public figure, and not (yet) 'tainted' by politics as usual. Enjoys personal wealth and easy access to high-profile endorsers and donors Has 'outsider' status, and can draw on references to 'former life' to garner support and/or avoid punishment for unorthodox political behaviour.	'Borrowed star power' P-C1 uses privileged access to celebrity circles/events that comes with office-holding, and is in fact key target for celebrity activists' political lobbying activities. The smell of 'something big' in P-C2's personal life attracts entertainment, gossip, tabloid journalism that would otherwise not cover politicians.

leadership. Table 14.1 provides a thumbnail sketch of each of these types, and its political leadership potential. We tackle each in turn.

Celebrity activists and endorsers: leadership by mobilization

While most celebrities today associate themselves with one or several charities, some put in a much greater effort for their chosen cause and seek to display public leadership on selected issues and causes. Celebrity activists and endorsers possess the potential resources to have a significant impact in the political process. These resources (both intangible and material) allow them easier access to the many echelons of democratic society (the leaders, the policy makers, and the public). They have time and money that they can devote to a limited number of causes. They are not constrained, as politicians are, by the need to cater to various segments of voters and keep interest groups on side. The difference between the two types is to a large extent one of degree: the endorser offers money and moral support to causes and candidates; the activist actually organizes campaigns, lobbies power-holders and turns up in the field to publicize causes. For our purposes here, however, we can treat them as two sides of the same coin.

Celebrity endorsers and activists face the same constraints that have hindered effective action on their chosen causes in the past (bureaucracy, congress/parliament, organized interests, and geopolitics). The difference between them and professional politicians lies in the methods celebrities may employ to bypass or overcome these constraints. Celebrities do not have institutional power, but do tend to have money, or easy access to it. They can use it to make large, publicity-generating donations. It also enables them to 'buy in' issue expertise that they themselves (initially) lack (e.g. economist Jeffrey Sachs working with Jolie and Bono). More importantly they can use their fame to orchestrate intense media coverage, evoke public emotion, and thus mobilize large numbers of people. Their ability to sell products to the public, which is keenly sought by many firms, can be used to sell public ideas and political campaigns. Their own activist writings (or those they endorse) can be turned into best-seller books (Cheadle and Prendergast's *Not On Our Watch: The Mission to End Genocide in Darfur and Beyond*; Jolie's *Notes From My Travels*), and they can not only produce but also effectively market humanitarian/political documentaries (Clooney's *Darfur Now*; Jolie's *The Diary of Angelina Jolie and Dr Jeffrey Sachs in Africa*; DiCaprio's *11th Hour*) that would otherwise easily be overlooked.

Persona: the importance of seeming earnest

Celebrity endorsement and activism are exercises in leadership by mobilization. Speaking out on a cause or donating money to it are necessary but not sufficient conditions for effective leadership of this kind. Like all advocates they need to captivate and energize their target audiences (whether it is the public or a political leader and his staff). In order to do so they need to be seen to 'know their business' and 'to be in it for the right reasons' (for instance, not to polish their own image and brand or to revive flagging careers).

These claims are easier to make for some celebrities than for others. Is their persona associated with intelligence, seriousness, and social responsibility, or does it epitomize quite the opposite? It takes no Platonic elitist to argue that on the required brainpower alone celebrities such as former Spice Girl Gerri Halliwell or tabloid favourite Lady Sarah Ferguson were out of their league when taking on ill-fated UN ambassadorial roles on the world political stage (cf. Cooper 2008). And it does not take a cynic to discern the hand of spin doctors and image consultants in 'socialite' Paris Hilton's sudden (and short-lived) interest in the plight of African children following her brief prison sojourn. Clearly, there is a publicly perceived and politically consequential distinction between 'activist leadership' and 'jumping on the bandwagon' by celebrities spurred by their managers. Some are hailed as 'serious' and 'dedicated', others are dismissed as lightweights and opportunists.

Like all political actors, celebrity endorsers and activists need to negotiate the world of facts as well as that of appearances and image in their quest for the authority they need to be able to persuade and mobilize. The difference among celebrities in doing so is that some are famous because of evident merit (even in 'non-high brow' sectors such as sports) whereas others, well, only because they are well-known (cf. Boorstin 1961), in however fleeting a fashion. One would expect these different starting points to affect the political capital they enjoy when turning their attention to public causes. Some examples illustrate the point. The polished public persona of 1970s German soccer star Franz Beckenbauer required very little adjustment for him to become *Salonfähig* in German and global sports leadership roles. To elevate Mike Tyson to a similar sort of stature is surely impossible. Earnest, never too wild rock stars like Bono and Peter Gabriel who both had penned fame-generating political anthems (*Sunday Bloody Sunday* and *Biko*, respectively) early in their careers had impeccable celebrity activist credentials. For a Marilyn Manson (shock rocker), Michael Jackson ('Wacko Jacko'), or Britney Spears (compromised teen idol) to take the same route would not be impossible but would require a substantial and convincing 'image makeover'.

There is, however, an alternative interpretation. Perhaps power is simply in numbers and not so much in cultural capital. This is sometimes referred to as the difference between 'A-list' and 'minor' celebrities, depending on the pervasiveness of their fame. Brad Pitt and David Beckham are known in all corners of the world, whereas Peter Gabriel's or cyclist Lance Armstrong's fame is more limited to particular niches of fans but equally enduring among them. At the other extreme there are the 'celetoids' (Rojek 2001) whose fame is artificially created by the entertainment industry (reality TV 'stars' for example) and usually mainly local as well as short-lived. Consequently, the former should enjoy a competitive advantage over the latter in the market of celebrity activism.[2] Hence a first set of propositions can be offered:

Proposition 1: The more merit-based the source of a celebrity's initial fame, the more likely that this celebrity's charitable and political activities will be seen as significant and successful.

Proposition 2a: The higher the social prestige of the cultural sphere in which a celebrity gained fame, the more likely that this celebrity's charitable and political activities will be seen as significant and successful.

Proposition 2b: The broader (geographical, numerical) and wider (across social strata and cultural groups) a celebrity's fame, the more likely that this celebrity's charitable and political activities will be seen as significant and successful.

Proposition 2c: The more enduring a celebrity's fame, the more likely that this celebrity's charitable and political activities will be seen as significant and successful.

Tactics: Penetrating the public mind and the corridors of power.

As stated, in at least one respect, celebrity endorsers and activists come from behind when trying to lead: they cannot make a simple claim to represent 'the people', as any elected politician can. Although Street (2004) has rightly criticized the narrow notion of representation that lies behind such claims (see also Saward 2006), the argument continues to be raised. In fact, segments of the public seem to have become more critical of celebrity endorsement and activism for that reason: a September 2007 *CBS/New York Times* News Poll showed that 49 per cent of Americans think celebrities should stay out of politics (up from 38% in 2003).

Lacking formal authority, celebrities find numerous other ways to influence policy makers. Some are simply variants on traditional diplomacy. For example, politicians are willing to meet with celebrities to raise their profile (or they may genuinely want to meet them), and in turn celebrities can use this opportunity to have access to powerful policy makers. U2 front man Bono is the undisputed master at this game (Tyrangiel 2005). Celebrities play on their own popularity and target top politicians who are fans, or have family members who are fans. Celebrities can also gain access to high-level meetings, such as the World Economic Forum in Davos, as they are thought to inject colour into otherwise bland, arcane events.

Another strategy is for celebrities to formally affiliate with established organizations, such as the UN (as 'Goodwill Ambassadors' or 'Messengers of Peace'). Former UN Secretary General Kofi Annan supported this development. His successor Ban Ki-Moon continued the policy. In 2008, he named actors George Clooney and Charlize Theron 'UN Messengers of Peace'. Legitimacy is also conferred on some celebrity activists by other institutions. Bill Gates has been awarded numerous honorary doctorates. Bono, and Bill and Melinda Gates were named *Time's* 'Persons of the Year' for 2005 (billed as 'The Good Samaritans'). Furthermore, celebrities also have the resources to create their own organizations to consolidate and 'corporatize' their activism, such as Bono's (PRODUCT)^RED and DATA (Debt AIDS Trade Africa), or the Michael J. Fox Foundation for Parkinson's Research.

Some use their 'home ground' – the stage on which they perform, the television show they present, award ceremonies – as an institutionalized platform for their activism. The most conspicuous example of this is Oprah Winfrey, whose endorsement allegedly boosted Barack Obama's votes in the 2008 Democratic primaries by approximately one million (Garthwaite and Moore 2008). Not only does Oprah financially support her own causes (e.g. 'The Oprah Winfrey Leadership Academy for Girls' in South Africa) and publicly endorse those of others, she also uses her show – a global institution of sorts in its own right given its durability and audience size – to provide an effective vehicle for other celebrity activists (Clooney got precious airtime to draw attention to the crisis in Darfur; actress Lucy Liu did the same for the 2005 Kashmir earthquake) and for candidate endorsement. Some celebrities choose different tactics and deliberately eschew institutional affiliations. Actor Sean Penn, for example, pursues a more radical form of activism, spending US$56,000 to take out a full-page advertisement in the *Washington Post* that berated Bush and his Iraq policy, visiting Iraq in 2003, reporting on the Iranian elections for the *San Francisco Chronicle* in 2005, and meeting with Venezuelan President Hugo Chavez in 2007. People like Penn and Bob Geldof receive criticism for their 'antics', but this, of course, is publicity too, and may serve to keep the public engaged with the underlying issues.

Some people are not colourful personae but have enormous financial clout. Lindblom (1977) and many others may rightly lament the disproportionate power of business in many contemporary democracies, but would they also object to the influence wielded by wealthy businessmen who choose to become do-gooders? People who own billions in personal fortune can advance political causes in a dramatic fashion. Much has been made of George Soros' role in furthering democracy in former-Soviet states. Yet eyebrows were raised when Soros then used his money and his access to media to forcefully oppose – one might say negatively endorse – George W. Bush's 2004 re-election campaign.

Which of these two tactical stances work best (or under which conditions)? We simply do not know. Hence we offer two competing propositions:

Proposition 3a: The more strongly affiliated a celebrity is with well-entrenched socio-political and cultural institutions, the more likely his/her political activities will be seen as legitimate, consequential and successful.

Proposition 3b: The more explicitly a celebrity activist eschews being (portrayed as) aligned to well-entrenched socio-political and cultural institutions, the more likely his/her political activities will be seen as authentic, independent and successful.

Celebrity politicians: towards leadership through election

Some celebrities go beyond staying on the political sidelines and embark on full-time political careers. Quite a few of them succeed in getting elected to legislative or executive office. In India alone, the total number of celebrities and socialites that have become political office-holders runs into the hundreds (Mukherjee 2004: 80). In the United States, the cases of Ronald Reagan (president), Clint Eastwood (mayor), Jesse Ventura (governor), Fred Thompson (senator), and Arnold Schwarzenegger ('governator') and even astronaut John Glenn (senator) have been widely publicized, applauded, condemned, and analysed (West and Orman 2003; Indiana 2005; Drake and Higgins 2006). In the Philippines, Mexico and many other developing nations, numerous figures of the entertainment industry have likewise made it into politics.[3] Electoral success is, however, by no means guaranteed. For example, global stars such as chess champion Gary Kasparov and world renowned footballer George Weah, both failed in their high-profile bids to achieve public office in Russia and Liberia. Popularity does not necessarily translate into local electability, since 'political success requires qualities beyond a famous name and celebrity background' (West 2003).

The distinctive feature of celebrity politicians is that they go all the way: they often completely abandon the world in which they gained fame – movies, music, sports, entertainment – and enter that of politics on a full-time basis. In doing so, they subject themselves to the laws of electoral politics and public office-holding, unlike celebrity activists and endorsers who tend to combine their original careers with part-time political advocacy. Once elected, celebrity politicians gain one important advantage over their counterparts: they can shrug off many of the questions about the legitimacy of their leadership that dog celebrity activists and endorsers. They are now formally representatives of the people.

Getting there: the road to election

To get there, celebrity politicians tend to capitalize on their position as popular public figures, combining it with self-conscious posturing as 'political outsiders', not 'tainted' with the awkward compromises, linguistic obfuscation, and endemic opportunism that, they claim, professional politics imposes upon its practitioners.

They are known, they are liked, and quite often they are rich – all attributes any ordinary newcomer to political campaigning craves. They are new, they are exciting, they are unpredictable – all attributes an incumbent politician they may run against has often long since lost.

Celebrities running for office face challenges that are different from other newcomers to electoral politics. They do not have to gain a public profile by courting publicity. Instead, they need to find a way of exploiting and at the same time subtly refashioning their existing personae to suit their new professional ambitions. It is not always easy to get the balance right. Being well-known and admired by segments of the public does not make celebrities immune from attacks by opponents and criticism by observers. Implicitly or explicitly, celebrities taking the road into professional politics are open to charges of being ill-informed, political lightweights, dreamers, not serious, and so forth.

As is the case with celebrity advocates, running for political office may require quite considerable restyling of celebrities' public behaviour and public image to make them into credible candidates. The image makeover required is partly a function of the nature of a celebrity's pre-political profession and reputation. One could speculate that, *ceteris paribus*, the more meritorious the basis of a celebrity's fame, and the higher the social esteem accrued to the profession at which the celebrity excelled, the easier it is to credibly portray that celebrity as a future political leader. This proposition can predict the electoral success of high-culture celebrities such as poets (A. B. Vajpayee) and erstwhile literary 'dissidents' (Václav Havel). But it does not really account for the political ascent of 'low-culture' celebrities like Joseph Estrada (Philippine schmalz actor-turned-president), and Jesse Ventura (television pro wrestler-turned-state governor). Arnold Schwarzenegger would be a borderline case. His celebrity status is derived not from one but from two sources: his status as a Hollywood success (but in the typically lowbrow genres of action and family comedy), and a marriage to a Kennedy clan celebrity (hardly an asset in the Republican circles which he sought to penetrate).

And so we need to turn to other factors to help explain cases of success and failure of celebrity politicians, as well as the differential incidence of celebrities-turned-office-holders across countries. One set of factors is widely discussed in the literature: the public *culture* in which celebrities seek office. Clearly, media culture is a key force at work here. To what degree have politics and entertainment been merged already in the public consciousness and in the reporting practices of both political and entertainment journalists (cf. Gamson 1994; Marshall 1997: 240; Meyer 2002; Schudson 2003)? Celebrity politics presupposes an institutionalized blurring of the boundaries between politics and sports, show business and the arts, as evident from patterns of media coverage (Street 2004). West and Orman (2003) coined the term 'celebrity regime' for such a state of affairs, and argue the United States is a prime case of it. Mukharjee (2004) does the same for India. In contrast, in a media landscape where broadsheets stand firm, the state operates or controls the key television stations, and/or there is a living norm among journalists of all kinds that politicians' private lives are off limits, it is more difficult for celebrities to capitalize on their fame (Stanyer and Wring 2004: 5–7).

But there is arguably also an autonomous role for political culture. How much does the voting public respect and trust its current office-holders as compared to other famous people? Perhaps it is no coincidence that the case of the first ever porn star to be elected into parliament occurred in Italy, where trust in politics has been an issue for a long time. And perhaps it was no coincidence that erstwhile 'B-movie' actor Ronald Reagan was elected president at a time of a deep crisis in American public life. Hence proposition 4: *The more endemic public disaffection with 'politics as usual', the bigger the political space for even the most unlikely types of celebrities to run for office successfully.*

Overlooked by almost all scholars on the subject, political *structure* comes into play too. Are celebrities running for president or for parliament? Are they in a single-winner (e.g. single-member constituency) or multiple-winner (e.g. party list) system, and in a majority-voting or proportional representation environment? The rules of the electoral game affect the scope for celebrity power via the ballot box. In countries with multiple-winner constituencies and proportional representation, and a robust party system, celebrities can often only gain office through an existing political party. To be pre-selected, they must be 'team players' and abide by the requirements of party discipline imposed by its leaders. Once elected they may end up in opposition, or on the back benches along with the party's other novice parliamentarians.

In many polities therefore, celebrities cannot run their own (electoral) show. This may put off many of them who have become used to doing precisely that. So we are more likely to see celebrity politicians seeking and achieving office in countries with single-member constituencies (where the ultimate battles are between individual candidates), majority voting (where they are not so dependent upon arcane vote aggregation rules) and/or relatively weak political parties (which are more prone to co-opt political outsiders). Celebrities – with high profiles, but quite often big egos to match them – might not be prepared to submit to a political apprenticeship before they can exercise a significant leadership role. Used to the limelight, and having that limelight as their main asset in politics, they may be ill-prepared for instructions from above to shun it for the greater good of the party. Party hierarchy, party programmes, and party discipline: not a good habitat for the celebrity politician. Hence proposition 5: *The more aspirants to political office are dependent for their election on entrenched catch-all political parties, the less widespread the incidence of celebrities running for office.*

The United Kingdom provides a good example of this. Even though it is a single member, majority-voting system, its party organizations are well entrenched and for the most part deeply conservative in their recruitment practices. Other than Glenda Jackson (Labour MP since 1992) and Sebastian Coe (Conservative MP 1992–7, currently in the House of Lords) almost no celebrity from the world of entertainment, the arts, and sports has successfully attempted a VIP-entry into politics. This applies in even stronger degree to the smaller West-European countries, where multi-member constituencies and proportional representation make celebrities entirely dependent on party hierarchies for an electable spot on the party list. In the Netherlands, for example, the number of celebrity politicians in parliament has always been zero or close to it; at the same time, since members of the government can be recruited from outside politics, (minor) celebrity academics and business leaders have sometimes entered politics in this way, but they tend to disappear quickly when their terms as ministers are up. In contrast, in Finland, where there is open-list, preferential voting, the number of celebrities in representative institutions is comparatively high (Hautamäki and Kaarto 2006).

There are two ways for celebrities to overcome the barriers created by party gatekeeping practices. One is to 'take over' an existing party and enter it right at the top, as Schwarzenegger to some extent did in the Californian Republican Party. The celebrity can then sidestep the conservers in the party machine, and make the party hierarchy work for him (or reform it to consolidate his leadership). When are they most likely to be able to pull this off? Perhaps the most evident situation is when a party is suffering electorally. As a matter of survival, its power brokers will start to look around for potential saviours to pull it out of oblivion. In these circumstances, criteria such as ideological purity, appropriate gravitas and grass-roots experience quickly lose relevance. Outsiders with money or fame (but preferably both) are well placed to pose as saviours and be believed.

The other option for office-seeking celebrities is to simply bypass existing parties and form one's own. The personalist party has been around for a long time in, for example, Latin America (Vargas in Brazil, Peron in Argentina, see Lewis 1973), but it is a relatively new and rare phenomenon in many Western European countries, whose PR-systems offer potentially good prospects for it. The sagas that do exist are revealing though. Sweden had its New Democracy party founded by and built around two celebrities (an aristocrat–industrialist and a record company owner) in the early 1990s. The Netherlands saw the rise and fall of the List-Pim Fortuyn in the early 2000s. It was formed by the eponymous public intellectual cum extravagantly gay socialite Pim Fortuyn, after he repeatedly failed to gain a prominent position in virtually all of the main existing political parties. Both parties took radical right-wing positions on issues like immigration and Islam, both were highly successful at first in capitalizing upon the charisma of their celebrity founders. Both, however, proved short-lived. New Democracy's two figureheads had a very intense and very public falling out, and the party disintegrated after just one term in parliament (one of the founding duos ironically went on to develop a successful TV show called *Fame Factory*). Fortuyn was assassinated a few days before he contested his first election; the party nevertheless received almost 20 per cent of the seats in the 2002 parliament and found itself a member of the new coalition government. An intense and widely reported power struggle between Fortuyn's hitherto anonymous lieutenants helped decimate its popular support within four years. Although often meteoric in their rise, charisma-based personalist parties are latently unstable, and tend not to last, although exceptions (Peronism in Argentina and Gaullism in France; Berlusconi's Forza Italia) do exist.

In whichever form celebrities choose to make the run to office, they all face the same key dilemma: how to position their past life (the extra-political source of their celebrity) in the frame of their new, political life. Before entering politics the celebrity may have lived in ways that can be a source of political embarrassment. Shadows from their past have a way of catching up with celebrities in general, and even more so with those who now have to get elected by large numbers of ordinary, law-abiding heartland citizens. Pictures and stories of sexual exploits, drug habits, 'bad' company, personal profligacy, past partners, and neglected children may arise. Such 'revelations' (often old stories known among insiders but now dramatized through fresh evidence or ruthless journalistic framing) can turn the celebrity's past life from a great asset into a potential liability virtually overnight. Did Arnold take drugs on his road to become bodybuilding champion? And was he 'rough' in sexual encounters? What casualties did he make on his road to bodybuilding and acting glory? Were Arnie's parents Nazis? And what exactly were young Arnold's political beliefs? In fact, celebrity politicians who first were celebrity activists may be haunted by the very purity and radicalism of their early political stances. Midnight Oil singer-turned-Australian Labor MP and then Environment minister Peter Garrett is a case in point (*Daily Telegraph* 2007; *Sydney Morning Herald* 2007).

Schwarzenegger overcame all that with apparent ease. Perhaps he simply has more political savvy than Garrett. Perhaps he has better spin doctors to advise him how to cope with these shadows of the past. The challenge for celebrity politicians is to draw political capital from the idiosyncrasy credit (Hollander 1978) they enjoy because of their star status, and avoid being dragged down by it. Covering up or lying about aspects of their past that may reduce their electability, as ambitious political newcomers sometimes do, is hardly an option for celebrity-newcomers: the details of their lives are a matter of public knowledge. Their job is to frame the story of their past life, so as to make it work for, and not against their current political aspirations. Some resolve this potential tension by perfectly matching a rather outrageous pre-political life with an equally outrageous political persona, like Italian porn star-turned-parliamentarian Cicciolina, who among other things offered to have sex with Saddam Hussein in exchange for peace. This will only work in a parliamentary system where niche popularity (local or sectional) is enough to ensure election; this strategy would be near impossible for those running for executive office. Overall, proposition 6 may best capture the dynamics: *The larger the discrepancy between a celebrity politician's past and current life styles, espoused political values and policy preferences, the greater the likelihood that this celebrity will suffer credibility damage from selective media exposure of his past.*

Being there: celebrity leaders in office

To achieve high political office is one thing; to hold on to it over time and to utilize it to display effective leadership are quite different challenges. There is no systematic research available that compares the length of tenure of celebrity politicians to the average in their respective jurisdictions, but our hypothesis is that particularly in established democracies, celebrities on average do not last very long. None of the previous Dutch, Swedish, and Italian examples lasted longer than five years, although counterexamples (Glenda Jackson, Silvio Berlusconi among them) are not difficult to find either. One could argue that for the reasons set out above, celebrity politicians in parliamentary systems with strong cadre parties are likely to find their time in politics frustrating rather than uplifting. They may fare better in presidential systems, where legislators can build up much more of an individual profile; and even better when elected to executive office, where they can – within limits – actually call the shots. Hence the logic of proposition 7: *In established democracies, the average tenure of celebrity politicians is shorter than that of professional ones; and it is shorter in presidential than in parliamentary systems.*

The art of executive leadership is markedly different from that of campaigning or legislating, although perhaps in a fully developed 'celebrity regime'that distinction becomes increasingly obsolete (the 'permanent campaign' syndrome). Are celebrities good at governing? Again, systematic research is lacking and the total number of cases in the Western world is still too limited, so no empirically founded generalizations are possible. Talking about the US context, West (2003) argues that the record of celebrity leadership in government is mixed: 'To win office, celebrities often assemble unconventional coalitions that transcend normal party alignments. Unlike established politicians who most appeal to conventional political constituencies, celebrities can build coalitions that are more broad-based... [T]his same quality harms them in the governing process. The presence of broad voter support often is based on an allegiance that is not very deep'. Likewise, 'the very qualities (independence and unconventionality) that voters find appealing often alienate the media and legislators. When these individuals start complaining, voters sometimes see the celebrity as an amateur and a novice who is not up to the governing task. If that perception becomes widespread, it is hard for celebrity politicians to govern very effectively'.

Still, Ronald Reagan consistently pops up in the upper ranks of almost every 'presidential greatness' poll taken since the end of his presidency. In office, he displayed a remarkable capacity to overcome gaffes, setbacks, and outright fiascos (such as the Iran-Contra affair) and retain personal popularity (see Schwartz 1990). A celebrity war hero-turned-president, Dwight Eisenhower is up there as well, ever since historians discovered that behind the veneer of the disengaged, golf-playing president lies a man whose 'hidden-hand' leadership style was far more pervasive and effective than generally assumed during his time in office (Greenstein 1982). Both these celebrity presidents achieved relatively high popularity scores whilst in office; both had no problems getting re-elected. But their enduring esteem as effective policy-makers owed perhaps less to their celebrity status as to relevant experience of governing (Eisenhower as supreme allied commander during the Second World War and Reagan as governor of California). At the state level, Jesse Ventura's initially sky-high popularity did not last for more than a year or two, and he retired as governor of Minnesota after one term. Arnold Schwarzenegger on the other hand proved comfortable with leading America's most populous state, was re-elected in 2006, and appears well-entrenched at the helm of Californian politics. In all, although the record is mixed and broad cross-national variation is as yet lacking, we might offer a final proposition 8: *Celebrity politicians are more likely to exercise effective leadership in executive rather than legislative roles.*

Politician-celebrities: leader self-dramatization and victimization

The fourth type of celebrity politics is fundamentally different from the other three. In its case, the direction of the flow between the two spheres is reversed: now we are looking at established politicians who enter the sphere of celebrity – by their own intent and design (in Table 14.1: P-C1s) or by somehow appealing to the cohort of celebrity (rather than just political) journalists and commentators, unwittingly becoming subjected to celebrity-style media coverage, commentary and gossip, and thus acquiring a new level of public visibility and/or undergoing a significant 'reframing' of their 'images' as professional public leaders – for good or for bad (in Table 14.1: P-C2s).

The P-C1s are a manifestation of traditional institutional politics coming to terms with the media age and consumer culture. So much has been written about this already that we can be brief here (Graber, McQuail, and Norris 1998; Perloff 1998; Meyer 2002). Personalizing authority through projecting 'the person behind the leader' in every possible media outlet reflects the transformation in political communication in an age where policy struggles and electoral fates are no longer resolved in the classic corporatist and parliamentary arenas but in increasingly open, fluid, deliberative, symbolic ones. In those arenas 'politics as usual' is not necessarily the main game (and perhaps not more than a sideshow). Political actors – executives, legislators, bureaucrats, advocates, stakeholders – have had to adapt to several such transformations over time, as radio, television, and the internet came along, greatly affecting the media landscape and patterns of mass communication. All of them have worked in the same direction: towards an increasing emphasis on the personal and the dramatic, and towards an increasing convergence between the logics of political leadership and business marketing. Democratic politics, like marketing, has always been about persuasion; but these days the techniques used in persuading publics of the merits of certain ideas, parties, and people have become almost indistinguishable from those used in 'branding' firms, products, and indeed 'stars' (Needham 2005).

Of all the (sub)types of celebrity politics discerned in this chapter, the P-C2s are the only ones who have celebrity happening to them rather than either seeking and/or exploiting it. P-C2s are people whose life outside politics inadvertently triggers attention well beyond the niche market of political journalism. Normally, this would be behaviour deemed to be unsuitable, outrageous, and in short 'scandalous': hard drinking or drug use, conspicuous partying, association with dubious characters, sexual adventurism, and loss of composure in public. Although this results in them and their lives getting covered by the celebrity stratum of journalism, they are first and foremost notorieties instead of celebrities. And in politics, notoriety often comes at a high price: relentless scrutiny, decline of political capital, legal battles and retribution, and not seldom loss of office (Markovits and Silverstein 1988; Tiffen 1999; Thompson 2000). In a sense, P-C2s end up as the casualties of contemporary media democracy: prior to the widespread blurring of political and entertainment journalism, their private vices would not have turned into public issues at the same speed, scale, and intensity.

The epitome of the leader who will be remembered as much for his scandals as for his record, Bill Clinton's 'colourful' persona and private life turned him into a celebrity, a notoriety even, and ended up crippling his presidency, although his personal approval ratings remained remarkably high throughout the ordeal. Despised by many yet liked by even more, he could continue to function as a public leader in some arenas, but was forced throughout his second term to fight an energy-sapping battle for political survival.

Celebrity, leadership, and democratic politics: normative reflections

Having mapped out the various forms of celebrity politics, it is time to reflect on their relevance for democratic leadership. Two questions are in order. To what extent and how do these manifestations of celebrity politics amount to distinctive forms of *leadership*? And in as far as they do, do they amount to a form of leadership *dispersal* that strengthens or detracts from the democratic authenticity of politics?

The answer to the first question, not surprisingly, is 'it depends'. For one, we should not confuse either influence or office-holding with leadership. Influence and power imply causing specific 'targets' to think and act in certain ways; leadership is about acquiring, maintaining, and affecting followers. Arguably, celebrity activists are sometimes influential in swaying legislators' and executives' attention and opinion on certain issues, but many of them do not seek, service, respond to or direct 'followers'. Their political activism is at best an expression of their individual beliefs, values, and aspirations, at worst a form of self-promotion masterminded by others. Few of them explicitly claim to represent a broader constituency – perhaps intuitively knowing how problematic such a claim turns out to be (Saward 2006, see further below). Likewise, the mere fact that celebrities may have a comparative advantage in attaining legislative or executive office does not necessarily mean that they effectively use these offices to exercise significant leader*ship* in terms of public, policy, and political impact. Some remain back-benchers; some executive celebrities fail or refuse – Jesse Ventura is a case in point here – to sufficiently adjust to the rules of the game of institutional politics, or fail to transcend those rules once in office.

So any assessment of celebrity politics in terms of leadership has to be a cautious and contingent one. With that in mind, let us revisit the various archetypes of celebrity politics discussed here, and weigh their significance in terms of four logics of dispersed leadership (checks and balances, fragmentation, and emancipation being the most important one; delegation is not at stake here); (see further chapter 16).

Celebrity endorsement and activism revisited

Celebrity endorsement and activism can and do frequently serve to harness and even reinvigorate democratic politics. They may be actively aimed at stimulating public involvement and demanding greater transparency from policy-makers. They force politicians and bureaucrats to take into account the demands and opinions of a wider societal – indeed sometimes global – demographic. On the downside, it can exacerbate the pathology of politics as a popularity contest, which greatly disfavours social problems and groups that celebrities choose not to pay attention to or shy away from (unpopular, controversial, or unglamorous causes). In-depth analysis and careful deliberation may give way to star power, clever marketing, rock concerts, and cleverly made but ultimately shallow docu-pics and blogs.

On the front stage of democratic politics, celebrity activism does, however, offer an unorthodox but potentially effective way of breaking the hold of established elites on political agendas and public discourse about policy. Celebrities have a unique capacity to reach out to and mobilize otherwise apathetic publics. They sometimes manage to give powerful voices to the disenfranchised in society and at the world stage. Where legislatures and other institutional watchdogs may be fully co-opted by executive dominance, celebrity-led initiatives can help 'keep the bastards honest'.

Celebrity endorsement and activism has the potential to contribute to the intelligence and deliberative quality of democracy by educating segments of society about public issues they would otherwise remain ignorant about (George Soros's extensive programmes in Central and Eastern Europe come to mind). At the same time, celebrity-focused publicity tends to gloss over crucial facts and complexities. And the strong amplification that celebrity voices receive in the public discourse may crowd out the perspectives provided by other, less famous interlocutors. Top celebrity activist Bono, for example, is advised on economic policy by Jeffrey Sachs – the man whose ardent belief in 'shock therapy' has brought various 'new democracies' economic chaos and political turmoil, and who has since revised his theories (see Klein 2007). Policies on debt relief masterminded by Sachs and amplified by Bono are the ones that get beamed to the public through mega-spectacles such as the Live 8 concerts. Other theories and policy formulas hardly compete on a level-playing field.

There is also considerable scope for scepticism. As noted, the fact that celebrity activists and endorsers are essentially leaders without followers raises thorny issues of representation. Who or what can the Jolie's and Bono's of this world legitimately claim to represent? Their fame is as boundless as the scope of their political causes, but it would be a stretch to argue their leadership is embedded in some form of cosmopolitan democracy (Held 1995; Saward 2006). In contrast, celebrity politicians seek to obtain institutional (party preselection, electoral mandate) backing for their public leadership aspirations, albeit at the price of – eventually – having to become more of an 'ordinary politician' in the process.

Other critics question whether celebrities are really usefully understood as (political) actors in their own right. Perhaps they should be seen more as cultural emblems or as not more than products of an entertainment-industrial complex that creates, sustains, utilizes, and discards them when economic logic so dictates. Turner et al. (2000: 9), for example, follow Alberoni's analysis of 'stars' to argue that while they enjoy some of the privileges of an elite, celebrities are an institutionally 'powerless elite' – objects of interest over which they have no control.

Some have gone much further in their critique, not just of celebrity activists but of the entire entertainment culture and celebrity politics of which they are but one manifestation. Public intellectuals such as Daniel Boorstin and Neil Postman dismiss all of these as a despicable trend that epitomizes the banal and the mindless in public life, empowering image over substance and producing pseudo-charismatic leadership (cf. Weiskel 2005).

Celebrity politicians revisited

Whether we like it or not, there can be little doubt that celebrity entails potentially significant political capital for people seeking to exercise public leadership. This is particularly so for celebrities seeking to attain high public office. Two long-time students of celebrity politics note: 'Even though Americans tend not to trust politicians, they have great respect for and confidence in celebrities who enter the world of politics... These individuals have a fame that transcends public service and a reputation for personal integrity. This allows them to succeed politically in ways that are unavailable to more conventional kinds of politicos' (West and Orman 2003). It makes celebrities particularly well-suited to play the Weberian game of plebiscitarian politics, which many have argued has regained prominence as established patterns of electoral democracy – voter alignment, voter participation, party stability; party competition – weaken. Silvio Berlusconi is a classic case in point.

But the Berlusconi example in many ways also feeds the fire of critics who point out that celebrity politics thrives by virtue of the public behaving as admiring fans rather than discriminating citizens. The undiluted admiration that comes with fandom may in some cases develop into charismatic forms of leader–follower relations (cf. Marshall 1997: 20–6; Hughes-Freeland 2007) which, as Weber suggested, is not necessarily an authority pattern that comfortably sits within institutional democratic politics. There is even plenty of evidence to suggest that celebrity frequently gives rise to psycho-pathological phenomena among both the famous and their fans (Giles 2000; Ferris 2007). Obviously, being widely known and admired can be a great asset for a leader who wants to get elected and get things done. But: What if the causes pursued by charismatic celebrity-leaders are not so noble? Who or what checks the power of celebrity leadership?

We are not to worry, according to economist Tyler Cowen. In *What Price Fame* (2000: 170) he has argued that 'the burdens of fame provide a new means of limiting political leaders, a means overlooked by Hobbes and subsequent classical liberal commentators. The separation of fame and merit is part of the price we pay for modern democracy, which relies heavily on media to monitor our leaders'. Insofar as they seek to utilize their own 'star power' or exploit that of others, political leaders of both the conventional and celebrity kind will have to submit to relentless public scrutiny of their lives that goes far beyond the accountability regime of parliamentary scrutiny and political journalism. Far from empowering the famous to lead without restraint, celebrity instead provides a relatively fickle and fleeting form of leadership capital, Cowen argues. This is because of the media-entertainment complex's insatiable appetite for not only building up certain people as celebrities but also bringing them down and replacing them by other, fresher faces. Albeit unwittingly, it provides a strong mechanism for cutting rascals down to size and throwing them out when their 'sell-by' date has elapsed. Perhaps democrats should not condemn celebrity leadership out of hand?

Politician-celebrities revisited

Cowan's 'checks and balances' interpretation of celebrity politics is perhaps best tested by examining the fate of politician-celebrities. Are they being kept in check by the pressure of celebrityhood, or do they succeed in exploiting celebrity to maximize personal power? If the latter holds, celebrity politics takes us about as far away from leadership dispersal as one could get. The fates of politicians acquiring celebrity features are, of course, mixed. Cowan got it at least half right. Blair's mastership of 'spin' was arguably a big asset to him in his early years, but when spin itself became part of the Blair story it turned against him and constrained him. And French president Sarkozy embraced celebrity in his courtship of Carla Bruni, only to find significant backlash against him among the French public, which apparently valued the dignity of the office more than the joy of reading daily gossip about the exploits of its current holder. But after marrying Bruni and resorting to a more classic presidential style, he began to appear more Kennedy-esque again. The incidence of personal gossip and the air of scandal that are part and parcel of celebrity life can therefore be seen as a taming force on political leaders in the manner suggested by Cowan, particularly for P-C2s.

However, there are sharply contrasting views on the other side of the politician-celebrity coin, the P-C1s. An optimistic assessment of it emphasizes that it is all about 'professionalization' of the persuasive tool kit that democratic politicians need to have in the contemporary age. If this requires that they themselves become a pivotal part of the story, so be it. Hence, we acknowledge the skill of leaders such as Tony Blair, Gerhard Schröder, and Barack Obama (see De Beus, this volume). P-C1 leaders surround themselves with political marketers and communication advisers, and project non-traditional political personae, reach out to all corners of the media and Internet spectrum, and do not hesitate to highlight their personal histories, idiosyncrasies, and families. Their objective: not just to get (re-)elected but to become a 'strong brand', one that receives the benefit of the doubt when it launches a new product line (proposes a new policy) or one that endures through tough times (fiasco and scandal).

The pessimistic accounts of P-C1s come in various shapes. One stresses that this so-called professionalization of political communications and personalization of public leadership is really nothing but a desperate, and in the end ineffectual, move by political parties and public institutions to stay relevant in a society that governs itself increasingly without them. Leadership dispersal through the rise of governance and 'netizens' is the big trend; centralizing the paraphernalia of state power around executive celebrity leaders is essentially a defensive and increasingly trivial move (Frissen 1999; Bang 2003; Bevir and Rhodes 2006). Another stresses that the rise of the media-savvy politician-celebrity amounts to a 'dumbing down' of public deliberation. Politics comes to many today in the form of hollow talk about 'pseudo events', for instance the lives and antics of leaders instead of substantive discussion about issues, ideas, and policies (Boorstin 1961). A third suggests that the rise of P-C1s in fact constitutes a significant yet sinister development: in a world saturated with political 'spin' and 'soap' the active citizen is deliberately reduced to a passive consumer–spectator, prone to be efficiently manipulated by the politics of distraction and misinformation (Edelman 2001).

Concluding observations

We cannot settle these debates in this chapter. There is simply too much to be learned about the causes, incidence, forms, and effects of celebrity politics and leadership across democratic polities. The eight propositions offered here hopefully provide a viable starting point for the kind of systematic empirical analysis that the literature is so sorely lacking (Duvall 2007), which should also include the two forms of celebrity leadership not covered here (cf. Table 14.1). We need to know more about the similarities and differences between various national systems of political celebrity production, as well as the degree to which transnational celebrity power affects national political processes. Let us not forget that even in this day and age, completely and in fact deliberately 'traditional' politicians can and do remain very effective in getting elected and exercising leadership, despite the pressures of the media-cultural complex to 'personalize' their persona (Van Zoonen 2006). We need to acquire a more fine-grained picture of celebrity politics, and compare different types of celebrities, different celebrity leadership tactics, and different electoral and executive settings.

Only when we have a firmer empirical footing can we fully address the normative question raised by Cowen and others: is the emergence of a celebrity regime at the intersection of entertainment and politics a bad or a good thing for democracy? If we deplore the power of money in election campaigns and seek to curtail monetary donations to parties and candidates, how do we view the increasing number and scope of political endorsements by celebrities? Which forms and extent of celebrity activism do we regard as democratically desirable, and which not? And when do the celebrity antics of incumbent politicians (such as Bill Clinton or Nicolas Sarkozy) begin to erode the institutional legitimacy of the offices they hold?

Notes

1. We would like to thank Rod Rhodes, Harald Wydra, Bob Goodin, Michael Schudson, John Kane, the other participants at the authors' workshop in Utrecht, and partici-

pants at this paper's presentation at the Political Science Program Seminar at the Research School of Social Sciences of ANU for helpful comments and suggestions.

2. The impact of a celebrity's activism can also be dependent on what happens in their 'regular' careers and their private lives. If they are out of the spotlight professionally they may lose their power to gain interest for a cause. If they become embroiled in personal scandals or controversies this can tarnish their cause. But, paradoxically, the latter may also benefit it. Tabloid coverage of their personal travails does raise the profile of celebrities, and this in turn consolidates their main political resource – their attention-getting potential. It depends on the kind of publicity involved: the odd marital breakdown will probably not hurt a celebrity's 'market value'; personal tragedies in fact enhance it and may give celebrities personal credibility in specific areas (former US first lady Betty Ford and stricken actors Christopher Reeve and Michael J. Fox are prime examples of this). But when publicity is consistently negative, a celebrity's standing with the public suffers, and so too the potential for effective activism. The spectacular disintegration of Michael Jackson's or O. J. Simpson's public persona surrounding their alleged involvement in major crimes made them unsuitable to promote any product, let alone pursue good causes. Although under some circumstances celebrities that are mainly notorieties have the potential to be political marketing assets (the 'reformed criminal', the 'former junkie'), originally meritorious celebrities that become notorieties because of personal aberrations (or worse) are clearly non-starters in the world of celebrity activism.
3. Other countries, particularly those of Western Europe as well as Australia and New Zealand seem remarkably impervious to such celebrity inroads into electoral politics – although the Australian Labour Party successfully launched former rock star Peter Garrett (of *Midnight Oil* fame), and then high-profile television journalist Maxine McKew in the national election of 2007. The cross-national differences between high and low incidences of celebrity politicians are an interesting phenomenon worth studying in its own right, particularly since standard explanations of the phenomenon tend to emphasize universal trends in the media technology, ownership, and culture as the chief causes. Obviously, these cannot account for such differences, which suggests that elements of political structure (e.g. electoral systems and party systems) and political culture (e.g. attitudes towards 'traditional' politics and politicians) should be factored into the explanation.

Bibliography

Australian Associated Press Pty Limited, 'Garrett Denies Selling Out Beliefs', *Daily Telegraph*, 1 April 2007, available at: <http://www.news.com.au/dailytelegraph>.

——'Garrett Pathetic Over Pulp Mill: Howard', *Sydney Morning Herald*, 9 October 2007, available at: <http://www.smh.com.au/news>.

Bang, H., (ed.), *Governance as Social and Political Communication* (Manchester: Manchester University Press, 2003).

Bevir, M. and Rhodes, R. A. W., 'Prime Ministers, Presidentialization and Westminster Smokescreens', *Political Studies*, 54/4 (2006), 671–90.

Boorstin, D. J., *The Image, or, What Happened to the American Dream* (London: Weidenfeld and Nicholson, 1961).

Braudy, L., *The Frenzy of Renown: Fame and its History* (Oxford: Oxford University Press, 1986).

Cooper, A. F., *Celebrity Diplomacy* (Boulder: Paradigm Publishers, 2008).

Cowen, T., *What Price Fame* (Cambridge, Mass.: Harvard University Press, 2000).

Drake, P. and Higgins, M., '"I'm a Celebrity, Get Me into Politics": The Political Celebrity and the Celebrity Politician', in S. Holmes and S. Redmond (eds.), *Framing Celebrity* (London: Routledge, 2006), 87–100.

Duvall, S-S, 'A Star is Made: News Coverage of Celebrity Politics in the 2000 and 2004 US Presidential Elections', Paper presented at the Political Studies Association Conference, 2007.

Edelman, M., *The Politics of Misinformation* (Chicago: Chicago University Press, 2001).

Ferris, K. O., 'The Sociology of Celebrity', *Sociological Compass*, 1/1 (2007), 371–84.

Frissen, P., *Politics, Governance and Technology* (Cheltenham: Edward Elgar, 1999).

Gamson, J., *Claims to Fame: Celebrity in Contemporary America* (Berkeley: University of California Press, 1994).

Garthwaite, C., and Moore, T., 'The Role of Celebrity Endorsements in Politics: Oprah, Obama, and the 2008 Democratic Primary', September 2008, available at: http://www.econ.umd.edu/~garthwaite/celebrityendorsements_garthwaitemoore.pdf

Giles, D., *Illusions of Immortality: A Psychology of Fame and Celebrity* (New York: Macmillan, 2000).

Graber, D., McQuail, D., and Norris, P. (eds.), *The Politics of News: The News of Politics* (Washington: CQ Press, 1998)

Greenstein, F. I., *The Hidden-Hand Presidency: Eisenhower as Leader* (New York: Basic Books, 1982).

Hartley, J., *Popular Reality: Journalism, Modernity, Popular Culture* (London: Edward Arnold, 1996).

Hautamäki, J. and Kaarto, H., 'Politics Goes Entertainment,' *Helsingin Sanomat*, 3 December 2006, available at: <http://www.hs.fi/english/article/Politics + goes + entertainment/1135223472392>.

Held, D., *Democracy and the Global Order: From the Modern State to Cosmopolitan Governance* (Cambridge: Polity Press, 1995).

Hollander, E. E., *Leadership Dynamics: A Practical Guide to Effective Relationships* (New York: Free Press/Macmillan, 1978).

Hughes-Freeland, F., 'Charisma and Celebrity in Indonesian Politics', *Anthropological Theory*, 7/2 (2007), 177–200.

Indiana, G., *Schwarzenegger Syndrome: Politics and Celebrity in the Age of Contempt* (New York: New Press, 2005).

Klein, N., *The Shock Doctrine: The Rise of Disaster Capitalism* (Victoria: Allen Lane, 2007).

Lewis, P. H., 'The Durability of Personalist Followings: The Vargas and Peronist Case', *Polity*, 5/3 (1973), 401–14.

Lindblom, C. E., *Politics and Markets: The World's Political-Economic Systems* (New York: Basic Books, 1977).

Marshall, P. D., *Celebrity and Power: Fame in Contemporary Culture* (Minneapolis, Minn.: University of Minnesota Press, 1997).

Markovits, A. S. and Silverstein, M. (eds.), *The Politics of Scandal: Power and Process in Liberal Democracies* (New York: Holmes and Meier, 1988).

Meyer, T., *Media Democracy: How the Media Colonize Politics* (Cambridge: Polity Press, 2002).

Monaco, J., *Celebrity: The Media as Image Makers* (New York: Doubleday, 1978).

Mukherjee, J., 'Celebrity, Media and Politics: An Indian Perspective', *Parliamentary Affairs*, 57/1 (2004), 80–92.

Needham, C., 'Brand Leaders: Clinton, Blair and the Limitations of the Permanent Campaign', *Political Studies*, 53/2 (2005), 343–61.

Perloff, M. R., *Political Communication: Politics, Press and Public in America* (Mahwah, New Jersey: Erlbaum, 1998).

Pringle, H., *Celebrity Sells* (London: Wiley, 2004).

Rein, I., Kottler, P., and Stoller, M., *High Visibility* (New York: Dodd, Mead and Company, 1987).

Rojek, C., *Celebrity* (London: Reaktion Books, 2001).

Saward, M., 'The Representative Claim', *Contemporary Political Theory*, 5/3 (2006), 297–318.

Schudson, M., *The Sociology of News* (New York: Norton, 2003).

Schwartz, B., 'Ronald Reagan Misremembered', in D. Middleton and D. Edwards (eds.), *Collective Remembering: A Social Psychological Approach* (London: Sage, 1990), 108–19.

Shapiro, I. and Hacker-Cordon, C. (eds.), *Democracy's Edges* (Cambridge: Cambridge University Press, 1999).

Stanyer, J. and Wring, D., 'Public Images, Private Lives: An Introduction', *Parliamentary Affairs*, 57/1 (2004), 1–8.

Street, J., 'Celebrity Politicians: Popular Culture and Political Representation', *British Journal of Politics and International Relations*, 6/4 (2004), 435–52.

——'Politics Lost, Politics Transformed, Politics Colonised? Theories of the Impact of Mass Media', *Political Studies Review*, 3/1 (2005), 17–33.

Tiffen, R., *Scandals: Media, Politics and Corruption in Contemporary Australia* (Sydney: University of NSW Press, 1999).

Thompson, J. B., *Political Scandal: Power and Visibility in the Media Age* (Cambridge: Polity, 2000).

Turner, G., Bonner, F., and Marshall, P. D., *Fame Games: The Production of Celebrity in Australia* (Cambridge: Cambridge University Press, 2000).

——*Understanding Celebrity* (London: Sage, 2004).

Travers, P., 'George Clooney', *Rolling Stone*, 673 January (2008), 61–3.

Tyrangiel, J., 'The Constant Charmer', *Time*, 166/26 (2005), 46–62.

Van Zoonen, L., 'The Personal, the Political and the Popular: A Women's Guide to Celebrity Politics', *European Journal of Cultural Studies*, 9/3 (2006), 287–301.

Weiskel, T., 'From Sidekick to Sideshow: Celebrity, Entertainment, and the Politics of Distraction. Why Americans are "Sleepwalking Towards the End of the Earth"', *American Behavioral Scientists*, 49/3 (2005), 393–403.

West, D., 'Arnold Schwarzenegger and Celebrity Politics', *InsidePolitics.org*, 6 October 2003, available at: <http://insidepolitics.org/heard/westreport903.html>.

——and Orman, J., *Celebrity Politics* (Englewood Cliffs: Prentice Hall, 2003).

Chapter 15

Life after Political Death: The Fate of Leaders after Leaving High Office

John Keane

Understood as forms of government and ways of life in which no body rules because power is subject to periodic elections as well as publicly monitored and contested from a multiplicity of sites, contemporary democracies are remarkable in the way they dispense with the fetish of leaders. Democracies certainly need leaders, multiply their numbers, respect them, follow them, learn from them – but they do not worship them as leaders blessed with metaphysical powers. Democracies specialize in bringing leaders down to earth. They manage to do this – as we shall see in this chapter – by using a variety of formal methods and informal customs that require leaders to leave office peacefully, without staging ruthless comebacks, so enabling other leaders to take their place without kidnappings or gunfire, bomb blasts or street upheavals.

The principle that leaders should periodically be replaced using peaceful means has its origins in the birth of representative democracy in the Atlantic region, at the end of the eighteenth century. It is well known that this new type of polity was formed by splicing the classical spirit and language of democracy with medieval European ideals and institutions of representative government; that the new language and institutions of representative democracy fundamentally transformed the meaning and significance of political leadership; and that the resulting hybrid turned out to be one of the primary inventions of modern politics (Keane 2009). Representative democracy signified a new form of government in which people, understood as voters faced with a genuine choice between at least two alternatives, were free to elect leaders who then acted in defence of their interests. Much ink and blood was to be spilled in defining what exactly representation meant, what counted as interests, who was entitled to represent whom, and what had to be done when representatives snubbed or disappointed those they were supposed to represent. But what was common to the new age of representative democracy that matured during the early years of the twentieth century was the belief that good government was government by elected representatives of the people.

Representative democracy was not simply a functional response to territorial imperatives, a practical solution to the problem of how to exercise power responsibly over great distances, as is still commonly supposed today. The case for democratic leadership was much more interesting than this. Thomas Paine's intriguing remark 'Athens, by representation, would have outrivaled her own democracy', is a vital clue to the entirely novel case for the superiority of representative government made by eighteenth- and nineteenth-century publicists, constitution makers, and citizens; so too is Thomas Jefferson's insistence that 'there is a fullness of time when men should go, and not occupy too long the ground to which others have a right to advance' (Jefferson [1811] 1905: 204; Paine [1791] 1925: 273; Urbinati 2006). Usually in opposition to monarchy and despotism, representative democracy was praised by its supporters as a way of governing better by openly airing differences of opinion, not only among the represented themselves, but between representatives and their electors. Representative government was applauded for its emancipation of citizens from the fear of leaders to whom power is entrusted; the elected representative temporarily 'in office' was seen as a positive substitute for power personified in the body of unelected monarchs and tyrants. Representative government was hailed as an effective new method of apportioning blame for poor political performance – a new way of encouraging the rotation of leadership, guided by merit and humility. In open defiance of talk (by Thomas Carlyle and others) of hero worship as rooted in the human condition, representative democracy was thought of as a new weapon against pandering to the powerful, a new form of humble government, a way of creating space for dissenting political minorities and levelling competition for power, which in turn enabled elected representatives to test their political competence and leadership skills, in the presence of others equipped with the power to sack them.

The leap of imagination that accompanied the invention of representative democracy was astonishing. Yet it had some puzzling features, including an odd silence within theories of representative democracy about the fate of political leaders after their term had expired, or after they had been booted from office. It is true that there were some observers who warned that ex-leaders would be troublemakers. They drew the conclusion that representative government should not apply term limits to the highest offices of state.[1] This strangely anti-democratic argument was to lose the upper hand during the course of the nineteenth- and early twentieth-century struggles for the extension of the franchise; in the case of the United States, the argument was finally rejected in 1951 by the ratification of the 22nd Amendment, which limits presidents to a maximum of two terms. That innovation left untouched the whole issue of what was to become of political leaders after they had left office. The sources of this strange silence about life after leadership are unclear. Perhaps it was due to the belief that monarchy was the prime enemy of the principle of rotation of office holders at the executive level. The experience of lunatic kings like George III or Austrian Emperor Ferdinand I (who suffered up to twenty seizures a day, which made ruling difficult) convinced many of the pertinence of the great slogan of the Dutch Patriots and the French revolutionaries: 'Death to Aristocrats, Long Live Democrats!' There was also the passionate conviction, in some nineteenth-century liberal circles, that the spirit of monarchy could be replaced by the public-spirited power of educated reason that would apply to leaders and former leaders alike. James Mill (according to his son John Stuart) 'felt as if all would be gained if the whole population were taught to read, if all sorts of opinions were allowed to be addressed to them by word and in writing, and if by means of the suffrage they could nominate a legislature to give effect to the opinions they adopted. He thought that when the legislature no longer represented a class interest, it would aim at the general interest, honestly and with adequate wisdom; since the people would be sufficiently under the guidance of educated intelligence, to make in general a good choice of persons to represent them, and having done so, to leave to those whom they had chosen a liberal discretion' (Mill [1873] 1969: 64–5). The odd silence about life after high office perhaps probably rested as well on the presumption that leaders would always be getting on in years, and that given life expectancy patterns markedly different from those today the autumn of their lives after office would be short (a presumption that has been invalidated by the fact that for the past four decades in OECD countries two and a half years have been added to people's lives each decade, on average). Or perhaps the strange silence was based on the belief that the holding of office is supervised and protected by God, that (as Edmund Burke famously put it in a much-neglected passage in his 'Speech to the Electors of Bristol' [1774]) the 'unbiased opinion', 'mature judgement' and 'enlightened conscience' that ideally come with the holding of office were 'a trust from Providence', with the corollary that the abuse of these qualities by incumbent and former leaders would be punished by divine wrath.

Whatever the reasons for the silence, it is my opening conjecture that in the field of political thinking there is something like a classical Greek bias that clouds our inherited understanding of representative democracy: a mentality of ostracism, it could be called, a presumption that leaders who give up or are ousted from office are simply stripped naked and banished to the Land of Oblivion, just as happened in ancient Greek democracies. The method of ostracism (*ostrakismos*) was a distant cousin of modern efforts to apply limited terms of office to political incumbents. Ostracism represented a definite break with the old Greek custom of elites hounding their elite opponents into exile. It was a new form of democratic compromise, a clever method, under the control of citizens, of transforming the ugly blood sport of hunting down enemies into the milder practice of treating opponents as mere competitors for power. Ostracism was also seen by Greek citizens as a potent remedy for a pathology that was peculiar to democracy: that self-government of 'the people' could seduce 'the people' into choosing leaders who had no interest in 'the people', except for abusing 'the people'. Resting on the principle of one man, one vote, one victim, ostracism involved annually banishing unduly popular leaders from a city for ten years, if a minimum number of voters favoured their expulsion. Those banished in the unpopularity contest were given ten days to quit the city – leaving the *ekklēsia* to get on with the business of self-government.

It is unimportant here why the weapon of ostracism failed and was subsequently abandoned (it had the effect of stirring up political vendettas and was misused by rival political figures bent on shoving their opponents off the political stage). The crucial thing is to see that contemporary realities are quite at odds with the mentality that framed the Greek theory and practice of ostracism. Out of office, out of sight, out of mind is a rule that no longer applies in actually existing democracies. 'All political lives', Enoch Powell used to say publicly and in private conversation, 'unless they are cut off in midstream at a happy juncture, end in failure, because that is the nature of politics and of human affairs' (Powell 1977: 151). That is no longer true. Life after office is becoming commonplace, for several reasons. Under democratic conditions, former leaders are not typically forced into exile, although that practice has not entirely ceased (Roniger and Sznajder, forthcoming). With a bit of luck and regular exercise in the gym or pool, former top political leaders are living healthier and longer lives, so that when they leave office they find they still have many extra years on their hands. Democracies that impose term limits reinforce the trend towards life after high office, either because ex-leaders tend in consequence to be younger or because term limits often produce leaders who in the final period of office are turned into lame ducks (an expression invented by eighteenth-century bankers and later applied to elected representatives). For these and other reasons, former leaders do not usually go quietly. No longer are they relegated to the ranks of nobodies, or simply forgotten. They instead enjoy rising public prominence; and they are the source of a growing problem – and perhaps a resource opportunity – for actually existing democracies.

For reasons of space and clarity, I will concentrate exclusively upon political figures that once occupied the highest offices of state. I am aware there are other and probably different patterns of life after holding office at lower levels of both government and civil society, inside and beyond territorial state boundaries. The concentration on executive office holders is however not just an analytic convenience; it is justified by the very considerable powers that they usually enjoy when in office, and (so I claim) by the growing opportunities of exercising powers of leadership after they leave or are removed from office. Put differently: there are empirical, strategic, and normative reasons for thinking in fresh ways – hard and deeply – about the dialectics of life after political office holding at the highest levels. The subject of ex-office holders is under-theorized, under-researched, under-appreciated, and – in many cases – under-regulated. What follows is a rough sketch of a field of research that is new, undeveloped, and arguably of growing importance in shaping the future of contemporary democracies.

Office dependency

The starting point of this research is that the experience of political office holding at the highest levels induces habits that are difficult to kick after leaving office. The experience of being removed from office is often synonymous with the collapse of a personal world. 'You know how hard it is. I've given my whole life to politics', says the key character in Václav Havel's *Leaving* (2008), a play scattered with references both to Chekhov's *The Cherry Orchard* and to Shakespeare's *King Lear*, two plays that also deal with the theme of the painful personal costs produced by the loss of power. Office dependency, as it might be called, is particularly virulent among former presidents, prime ministers, and other top jobholders, but the malady may afflict office holding at all levels.

What triggers office dependency? It is arguably not just the perks of office – guaranteed salary and discretionary budgets, administrative back-up, the chauffeured time management, good dinners, access to women and men, potential bribes – but also the deep personal satisfaction of winning public recognition (or fond memories of 'honeymoons') that together function as a type of snuff whose consumption is not easily relinquished when one's time is up. Political leaders come to be hooked on the stuff of office; they are prey to what is usually called hubris; they hanker after honours (such as the peerages, knighthoods, the Order of the Garter and other prizes much coveted by former British prime ministers). Psychoanalytic reasons usually figure in the manic or narcissistic clinging to office (as Angus McIntyre [1988] has insightfully pointed out). It was Tito who remarked that 'political death is the most horrible death of all', a comment that clarified why he not only dyed his hair, sported gleaming white false teeth and regularly used a sunlamp to top up his tan, as if to build a grandiose self that recognized no death; Tito so equated departure from office with bodily death that he secured lifelong tenure of office and ordered a constitutional change to collective leadership, so that after he had moved on (so he thought) nobody could hijack or mothball his fame, or ruin his reputation.

My point about office dependency can be expressed differently: the capacity to concede power gracefully to others – the 'politics of retreat' is the term I invented for analysing the different cases of the post-1985 Gorbachev reforms in the Soviet Union, and Václav Havel's difficult presidencies in the former Czechoslovakia – is neither a divine nor a 'natural' gift (Keane 1990; Keane 1999). Of course, there are exceptions, in the form of political office holders who are mentally and viscerally committed to observing time limits on their power; know that the rotation of office holders is an unqualified democratic good; grasp the pitfalls within the illusion of indispensability; and who are blessed with the wisdom that political genius consists in knowing when to stop ('In der Beschränkung zeigt sich erst der Meister', was Goethe's way of saying that the master triumphs by holding back). But stepping down is a capacity learned reluctantly, and with the greatest difficulty, usually in trying circumstances; it is a talent that has few supporting role models and virtually no philosophical mentors or political guidebooks.

The perceived perils of losing power are well known. The grimness of defeat is not just linked to the enforced abandonment of policies that may have been fought for with great energy and purpose. The fear of political death has much more to do with the loss of constantly challenging work; mourning the lengthening of days where once minutes were sliced thinly; empty diaries and silent phones; the inability to make up lost time with families and loved ones; and the emotional difficulty and fears of outright depression (suffered by Lyndon Johnson, for instance) caused by exiting a macho world where thick skin is a job requirement and confessions of vulnerability are reckoned a liability. The resulting 'relevance deprivation syndrome' (a phrase coined by a former Australian foreign minister, Gareth Evans) undoubtedly fuels the unwillingness to leave office, and that is why the history of representative democracy brims with concrete attempts to force soldiers of high politics to shoulder their arms, to prevent hubris by erecting political and constitutional limits upon leaders. The mid-nineteenth-century invention (in the Canadian province of Nova Scotia) of the formal role of 'leader of the opposition' (Michaud 2000; Kaiser 2008) can be seen as an early attempt to constrain hubris by simultaneously offering an incentive to competitors for office and providing a formal role for leaders who find themselves thrown from office. More recent methods of regulating office dependency include informal restrictions, such as public exposure through investigative or muckraking journalism and the observance of rules of propriety concerning private dalliances. There are also formal rules, such as laws against the acceptance of bribes and payments, recall and initiative mechanisms, impeachment, time limits on office holding and (practices designed supposedly to ease the transition to the role of an incorruptible ex-leader) the payment of pensions, the provision of free travel and medical benefits, office accommodation, security protection and (as in Belgium and Canada) restrictions on membership of supervisory boards or management of companies in receipt of state contracts.

Self-recycling political elites

The extent to which these checks on leaders are put in place, or are practically effective, is of course highly variable and context-dependent in today's democracies. Yet there is ample evidence that the more any democratic political system gives a free hand to their top political leaders, the more that system typically turns a blind eye to the doings and misdoings of their former office holders. That in turn has the effect of minimizing, or eliminating outright, the difference between holding top elected office and life after political leadership, an elision that is not usually good for democracy.

The political art of keeping tabs on leaders and enforcing the distinction between holding and leaving office is a key indicator of whether or not a form of government can be considered democratic. The contrast with anti-democratic governments, eighteenth-century European monarchies, and twentieth-century totalitarian regimes for instance, is revealing. Think for a moment how hard-core monarchies symbolically represented the power they wielded over their subjects. The physical body of kings like Charles I and Peter the Great was conceived both in the figure of God the Father and Christ the Son. The monarch's body was divine, and therefore immortal and unbreakable. It could not be admitted that kings died; they lived on forever. Their bodies symbolized perfection. Like God and his Son, kings could do no wrong, which is why the violation of their bodies – through ungodly acts ranging from unsolicited touching by their subjects through to attempted regicide – were harshly punishable. The body of kings also symbolized the unbreakable quality of the 'body politic' over which they ruled. Like God, kings were omnipresent and their bodies coterminous with the polity itself. Monarchs were God-given givers of laws. But they also resembled God the Son. Sent by God to redeem humankind, kings had a 'body natural' – the sign of God in the world – as well as a body politic. Just like the persons of the Trinity, the two bodies plus the authority they radiated were immortal and one, inseparable and indivisible.

It is a strange historical fact that twentieth-century totalitarianism thrived on a version of the same fiction of a unified body politic, 'pure as a diamond', as the butcher Great Leader Pol Pot explained in a little-known 1949 pamphlet, *Monarchy or Democracy*. In the name of 'the people', but like the monarchies of old, totalitarianism put the body of the Great Leader on a grand pedestal for the grand purpose of establishing Him as the ultimate source of wisdom, strength, knowledge, and power. The embalming and public display of Lenin's corpse in the Soviet Union in January 1924 was a foretaste of such practices, which reached something of a climax in the huge Memorial Hall edifice in T'ienanmen Square constructed in memory of the Great Helmsman of the Chinese people, Mao Zedong. Those who have seen it will agree that it is no simple grave for a common corpse. It more than resembles the royal mausolea reserved for the Sons of Heaven who were at once elevated persons and divine persons, in whose bodies time figuratively stood still, forever. The T'ienanmen edifice preserves this custom for a revolutionary saint. It contains a marble statue and a crystal-covered sarcophagus containing Mao's embalmed remains, together with an inscription in the green marble of its southern wall:

a telling phrase dedicated to the memory of 'our great leader and teacher Chairman Mao Zedong: forever eternal without corrupting'.

This kind of worship of rulers is anathema to democracy. That is why democracies that permit their leaders to stay on indefinitely – sometimes to get away with blue murder – potentially compromise democracy itself. A positive example that springs to mind of how drawing a line between holding and not holding office is vitally important for democracy is the way the British parliamentary system has become gradually less tolerant of prime ministers hanging on to high office. Although Tony Blair, John Major, Margaret Thatcher, James Callaghan, Edward Heath, and Harold Wilson by no means disappeared from public sight after their removal from power, they did not seek to return side stage to the highest office. In the history of the office of prime minister, a history that stretches back to Robert Walpole in the eighteenth century, this is a new and significant trend. It stands in striking contrast to the eighteenth and nineteenth centuries, when nine prime ministers served at the helm of subsequent governments under other prime ministers, and (prior to the election of Harold Wilson) the twentieth century saw just five (Douglas-Home, Chamberlain, MacDonald, Baldwin, and Balfour) who managed to do the same thing. Although their moves were typically justified as giving governments under pressure greater strength based on experience – Hamilton's argument – the continuity stood at right angles to the rotation principle of representative democracy. In democratic terms, it comes as a welcome surprise that during the past half-century what might be called the Balfour syndrome has been shattered: it is now virtually unthinkable that a prime minister would be allowed to behave like Arthur James Balfour, the political chameleon who after serving as prime minister for three years (1902–5) excelled at playing the role of imperial elder statesman by serving eleven years in such high ministerial posts as Foreign Secretary (1916–19) and Lord President of the Council (1919–22; 1925–29) under both Liberal and Conservative governments.

A negative example of the political dangers posed for democracy by the fudging of the line between holding and giving up office is the case of contemporary Italy. Described by the noir author Carlo Lucarelli as a country 'where you can pull one string and it leads you to a garbled skein of interlocked groups of power', its political system is of course a 'freak' case within the world of contemporary democracy (Povoledo 2007; Rizzo and Stella 2007). But its exceptional qualities, its pathologies in matters of top office holding, should be carefully studied, if only because Italy provides some good examples of what is arguably bad practice, including an unusually high degree of recycling of top political leaders. It is perhaps not surprising that there exists no detailed study of life after political office holding in that country; it is as if the topic is taboo among political scientists. All presidents of the Italian republic become *senatore a vita* after leaving office (article 59.1 of the Constitution); presidents themselves enjoy the power to appoint *senatore a vita*; and all eleven presidents since 1948 have either been prime ministers, or presidents of the Chamber of Deputies or the Senate, or active as leaders or founders of political parties. The same pattern of recycling is evident among prime ministers; most of them leave and return quickly to top political jobs. Virtually all of the twenty-two prime ministers since 1948 have remained in politics after the end of their mandates, either as presidents, vice-prime ministers, ministers, or senators. The recycling process is anchored in the patterns of political party patronage; and it is strongly reinforced by the fact that representatives in both houses, the Chamber of Deputies and the Senate, are elected for five-year terms of office, with no limitation on the number of terms, either for deputies or ministers or prime ministers.

The upshot is that through time, past and present political leaders in Italy have formed something like a self-enclosed governing elite that easily survives changes of government, which come and go, with regular monotony. The elite is male-dominated, unusually old and wealthy. Some 60 per cent of Italy's politicians are over the age of seventy (in France, the figure is 20%; in the Scandinavian democracies about 38%); among major member states of the European Union, Italy has the lowest number of female politicians; earning more than twice as much as representatives in the US Congress, Italian politicians are driven around in chauffeured cars, enjoy free train and air travel and mobile phones, and are entitled to a handsome pension after only two terms in office, despite the fact that many hold outside jobs and often never show up in the legislature. When established Italian politicians fail to get re-elected, they are normally recycled into government or business positions, protected by top leaders through revolving-door systems of patronage. Naturally, the Italian political elite resists any effort to impose public controls on the recycling of office holders. That is why it is only in moments of profound crisis that their degree of public unaccountability is exposed. The *Tangentopoli* scandal of the early 1990s was certainly the biggest, and (so far) the most revealing. The upper layer of the political elite was either forced into retirement, committed suicide, exiled, or skulked off into the political shadows. Under pressure from the courts and investigative journalism, the two dominant political parties, the Christian Democrats and the Socialist Party, in effect collapsed. Their respective leaders were badly shaken. After four decades of leadership, Giulio Andreotti, prime minister seven times, found himself facing a ten-year trial linked to his alleged mafia involvements. His dream of becoming President of the Republic failed to come true; but he remained defiant (as Paolo Sorrentino's film *El Divo* documents). Reminded by a journalist that power has exhausting effects on people, he replied by quoting Talleyrand: power exhausts those who do not have it (*il potere logora chi non ce l'ha*). His counterpart on the Socialist Party side, Bettino Craxi, fared less well. On the day that parliament denied judges based in Milan the authority to proceed with investigations of his alleged criminal activities, a large crowd gathered outside his place of residence, the Hotel Raphael in Rome. That evening, as he left the hotel, the crowd mockingly chanted, 'Bettino, do you want these as well?', and 'Thief! Thief!' They then hurled thousands of coins and waved 1000-lire banknotes in the air. He seemed never to recover from that moment of humiliation; to save his skin he ostracized himself and remained until his death in political exile.

The contrasting cases of Britain and Italy contain many morals, but this one is of particular interest: in the absence of strong legal restrictions and informal rules governing both office holding and the departure from office, top political leaders who leave office never really do so. They in effect stay on or, like Silvio Berlusconi, expect to stay on, if need be by calling into question the results of elections, all the while complaining about the excessive controls on those who want to wield power from the top. The upshot is the formation of a self-perpetuating political class whose unelected power contradicts some basic principles of representative democracy – and through time injects a measure of sclerosis into the whole system of government. The case of Italy in particular suggests a new maxim: *the level of formal public regulation of former top political office holders, the overall degree of awareness of the need in practice to monitor and to circumscribe their duties and powers, and periodically to rein them in, serve as a vital index of the strength or weakness of democratic controls placed more generally upon representatives within any given polity*. Indirect confirmation of this political maxim – that democracies are advised to put former top office holders under a pedestal – can be found in regimes where no such controls exist. The absence of formal limits on former office holders is matched by the absence of formal controls on incumbent leaders, which is why the public demand for either typically causes a big stir in authoritarian regimes (as happened in China during the 1970s, when for the first time unofficial magazines like *Beijing Spring* took advantage of the normalization of diplomatic relations with the United States to call for American-style limited-term presidents).

Revolving doors

Even when formal and informal controls upon top political leaders are strong, ex-office holders potentially remain powerful figures. This is not just a function of good health and increasing life expectancy, though in some contexts (Japan's 'silver democracy' is an example) the declining average age of exit from office, sometimes called the 'younging' of politics, are important trends. The power thirst of former office holders is slaked above all by their battle-hardened egos, their dreams of running or governing again, their seduction by the fantasy of returning to governmental office 'through the back door', by redeploying an arsenal of skills and contacts gleaned from their time in office. Herbert Hoover's meddling in White House politics during Franklin

Roosevelt's unprecedented third term of office counts as an example; so too does Bill Clinton's fraught 2008 campaign in support of a Hillary Rodham Clinton presidency – a campaign that triggered alarm in the minds of some voters that dynasty was not good for democracy, especially when the former president tried to offer explanations of his future role. 'I wouldn't be in her cabinet – that would be unlawful', he said clumsily on one occasion. 'And I wouldn't be in a fulltime staff position – that wouldn't be wise. But if there's something specific I can do for Hillary then I would do it in a heartbeat' (Luce 2008).

There are times when this will to resume office as an *unelected* broker of governmental power potentially clogs the open pores of rotated representation that are vital for the health of representative democracy. The growing involvement of former top political leaders in government by moonlight, for instance in the flourishing multimedia lobby industries upon which all democratic governments have become invisibly dependent, is a troubling case in point. Ken Silverstein's rare study of former political leaders' involvement in the Washington lobbying scene shows just how important these ex-office holders are in providing what is sometimes called 'the secret handshake that gets you into the lodge' (Silverstein 2007). Little seems to have been written about the subject, but as the drafters of the Canadian Federal Accountability Act (2006) and those pressing for its tougher implementation have correctly spotted, legal regulation of former office holders' involvement in the shadows of governmental power – closing the revolving doors through which public officials sell their expertise and inside knowledge when they leave public office – is vital for nurturing the ethos and procedures of open government that is routinely subject to public monitoring. That is why in Canada, and in several other democracies, there are calls for the implementation of a new package of reforms, including: a public register of details of the activities of all lobbyists; stringent bans on their gifts and political donations; a several-year ban on former top political office holders taking jobs as lobbyists; and the creation of an independent agency that is responsible for monitoring the overall system, enforcing a code of conduct and imposing sanctions on those lobbyists who cover up, or fail to register, their activities.

Civil society pathways

Other former political office holders are learning to cope with life after being at the top by cultivating new leadership roles within the nooks and crannies of civil society; for a growing number of still-youthful political leaders, politics is becoming a job followed by a career. A careful examination of former US presidents, for instance, shows that right from the beginning of the republic this was an option that could earn private respect, public fame, but rarely dollars for ex-presidents (examples include Thomas Jefferson's commitments to the establishment of the University of Virginia; Theodore Roosevelt's prolific writing, including his autobiography; and Lyndon Johnson's founding of a library and museum). The full realization of the potential of civil society as a grazing ground for ex-office holders is however only being felt in our times. The media saturation of contemporary societies is among the powerful forces enabling former top leaders to enjoy life after political death by becoming celebrities. The age when former leaders lapsed into mediocrity (spent their time 'taking pills and dedicating libraries', as Herbert Hoover put it) or enjoyed untrammelled privacy, sometimes bathed in self-pity ('after the White House what is there to do but drink?', Franklin Pierce reportedly quipped), is over. Former leaders of government and heads of state find it virtually impossible to stay offstage, or to remain invisibly silent.

That is why growing numbers of top political leaders, attracted by the magnets of stardom, discover that there is much life to be lived after holding high office. They sense that the heterogeneity of their media-saturated civil societies provides them with choices, with possibilities of leading others in new ways, outside the sphere of government. They befriend fame, for instance by exploring star roles on the global lecture circuit, setting up foundations, hiring their services to businesses and signing lucrative book contracts (Margaret Thatcher's memoirs brought her £3.5 million advance royalties; Tony Blair reportedly signed for £5 million; Bill Clinton received a record $12 million royalty advance for *My Life*). There is nothing in principle objectionable about any of this (quite a few who leave high office have huge debts to pay off), and actually existing democracies ought on balance cautiously to welcome the trend. Ex-office holders' involvement in civil society leadership serves as an important reminder that during the course of the past century the word leadership was excessively politicized, to the point where we have forgotten that the words *leader* and *leaderess*, from the time of their first usage in English, were routinely applied to those who coordinated such bodies as singing choirs, bands of dancers and musicians, and religious congregations.

The opening up of pathways that lead towards civil society serves as an important corrective to the undue dominance of state-centred definitions of leadership. We should not be instantly dismissive of the involvement of former political office holders in civil society, for instance by sourly lamenting the disappearance of true charisma (as Philip Rieff [2007] has done), or by condemning the quest for fame, as if it was merely a cunning means of earning money or simulating the retention of office long after leaving behind the real thing. The evidence rather suggests that by exploring various civil society leadership roles, whose substance and style are often in tension and sometimes contradictory, former top office holders are (*a*) challenging and pluralizing prevailing definitions of (good) leadership, partly by freeing it from guilt by association with government; (*b*) stretching the boundaries and meaning of political representation, especially by putting on-message parties, parliaments, and government executives on their toes; (*c*) contributing to the contemporary growth of 'monitory' forms of democracy, for instance by drawing the attention of publics to the violation of public standards by governments, their policy failures, or their general lack of political imagination in handling so-called 'wicked' problems that have no readily agreed upon definition, let alone straightforward solutions (Keane 2009); and (*d*) generally helping both civil societies and governments to make sense of the growing complexity of democratic decision-making under conditions of dispersed power, so bringing a greater measure of nuance and coherence to policy-making and administration (Mishra 2007).

Leadership in the non-governmental domain is of course tricky business; former top office holders find this when attempting to juggle different roles, which are sometimes in tension with the egalitarian ethos and public openness of democratic ways of doing things. It is also the case that leadership of civil society organizations raises tough, but intellectually interesting and politically important questions about the legitimate scope of parliamentary prerogatives and the powers of political parties and government executives in representative democracies. One trend is however unmistakable: we live in times (as Frank Ankersmit [2009], Michael Saward [2009] and others have shown) marked by the multiplication and dispersal of different and conflicting criteria of representation that confront us with problems (such as whether unelected leaders can be held publicly accountable for their actions using means other than elections) that were unknown to the earliest champions and architects of representative democracy.

Ethical responsibility

What range of choices do ex-office holders have in the field of civil society? Some former leaders cultivate the style and message of *ethical responsibility*. Contemporary examples include Al Gore, Nelson Mandela, Adam Michnik, Mary Robinson, but the trend has been developing for some time. The case of Pierre Trudeau is instructive: shortly after his departure from office, he joined the Montréal law firm Heenan Blaikie as a counsel. Though he rarely gave public speeches or spoke to the press, Trudeau's measured interventions into public debate had a significant impact, as when he wrote and spoke out against both the Meech Lake Accord and the Charlottetown Accord proposals to amend the Canadian constitution, on the ground that their implementation would weaken both federalism and the Charter of Rights. His opposition proved to be crucial in producing the defeat of the two proposals.

Trudeau's behaviour set an example of ethically responsible leadership after holding office: those who have followed in his footsteps like to be seen as seasoned sages, as public witnesses of suffering and injustice, as endorsers of prospective new leaders, advocates of policies, and ways of thinking that do not yet command majority support. These ethical former office holders sublimate their political leadership skills into the arts of communicating with publics about the strengths and limits of government policies and structures. We can leave aside here questions about the merits of their causes, for what is striking is the way that ethical ex-leaders are not simply using the bully pulpit (a peculiarly American term coined by Theodore Roosevelt to describe the use by leaders of a 'superb' or 'wonderful' platform to advocate causes and agendas). The experiments of ex-leaders in non-governmental or civil society leadership roles have profoundly transformative effects on the meaning of leadership itself. Leadership no longer only means (as it meant ultimately in Max Weber's classic state-centred analysis) bossing and strength backed ultimately by cunning and the fist and other means of state power – a *Realpolitik* understanding of leadership that slides towards political authoritarianism (and until today has given the words *Führer* and *Führerschaft* a bad name in countries such as Germany).[2] Leadership instead comes to be understood as the capacity to mobilize 'persuasive power' (as Archbishop Desmond Tutu likes to say). It is the ability to motivate citizens to do things for themselves, the learned capacity to win public respect by cultivating 'narrative intelligence' (Denning 2007), an intelligence that includes (when leaders are at their best) a mix of formal qualities, such as level-headed focus; inner calm; courteousness; the refusal to be biddable; the ability to listen to others; poking fun at oneself; and a certain radiance of style (one of the confidants of Nelson Mandela explained to me his remarkable ability to create 'many Nelson Mandelas around him'; the same thing is still commonly said of Jawarhalal Nehru). Such qualities also include the power to combine contradictory qualities (strength and vulnerability; singularity and typicality, etc.) simultaneously, and apparently without effort, as if leadership is the embodiment of gestalt switching; and, above all, an awareness that leaders are always deeply dependent upon the people known as the led – that true leaders lead because they manage to get people to look up to them, rather than leading them by the nose.

Unelected wealth

The age when former leaders passed away in penury has come to an end. It is astonishing to think that this was the fate of James Madison, who left the presidency poorer than when he entered, due to the steady financial collapse of his plantation; or that Harry Truman was quoted in 1957 as saying to then-House Majority Leader, John McCormack: 'Had it not been for the fact that I was able to sell some property that my brother, sister and I inherited from our mother, I would practically be on relief, but with the sale of that property

I am not financially embarrassed'. Growing numbers of former top office holders now prefer to make money, usually in the guise of good causes, but sometimes in gung-ho ways that are frowned upon in the world of business itself, certainly when measured (for instance) against the much-discussed Toyota business model, whose executives, by all accounts, are encouraged to live by the values of parsimony, customer focus, and humility; or when measured against the present-day talk in the United States of CEO Version 3.0, according to which good managers are neither empire builders with boardroom-sized egos nor narrow-minded clean-up specialists, but innovative team builders equipped with a strong sense of personal responsibility.

There are moments when gold-digging former office holders are turned into scandalous parodies of the most vulgar money-grubbers. Gerald Ford was among the first former leaders of the United States to make huge sums of money (at least $1 million a year) from what he called the 'mashed potato circuit' of speaking engagements, and from corporate directorships. More recent examples include Gerhard Schröder's earning of undisclosed large sums behind the scenes after accepting Gazprom's nomination for head of the shareholders' committee of Nord Stream AG, a gas pipeline business venture that he had approved just weeks before leaving office; Tony Blair's widely reported three-hour visit to China's southern province of Guangdong, sponsored by the Guangda Group of property developers, who allegedly paid the former British prime minister a net cash payment of US$330,000 and offered him a luxury villa worth US$5.39 million (whether he accepted the latter offer is unknown, but the gist of his unusual decision to resign his parliamentary seat, in part to avoid disclosing his outside earnings, and his new role as a price-tagged travelling publicist who reportedly earns up to half a million pounds sterling per month, is profiled on the Washington Speakers Bureau web site <http://washingtonspeakers.com> ; and (to illustrate that the trend is bipartisan) Margaret Thatcher's reported consultancy fee of £1 million paid annually by the American tobacco giant, Philip Morris. Gold digging on this scale, variously dubbed 'after-dinner mints', the rubber-chicken circuit or, in Blair's case, the Blair Rich Project, arguably tends to breed discomfort and to arouse public suspicions of politicians in existing democracies. In certain contexts, it feeds political disaffection, the sense that political crooks happen, the belief that the lavish lifestyle of ex-leaders proves that all political office holders misuse office by kicking away the ladders of election, in order to climb to new heights of unelected wealth, and the power it brings.

Cross-border leadership

There is one other interesting and important development in the contemporary politics of life after office holding, a development whose effects are literally the most far-reaching: the systematic involvement of former top office holders within governmental and non-governmental structures that operate at the regional and global levels, in ways that have never happened before in the history of democracy. Elsewhere I have attempted to analyse the rapid contemporary growth of cross-border civil society networks and new tangled architectures of law and government ('cosmocracy') that defy all previous empire- and state-centred accounts of institutionalized power (Keane 2003). What is interesting is that growing numbers of ex-office holders are taking advantage of regionalizing and globalizing trends by getting involved in cross-border government, business, think tanks, charities, media, and public affairs. It is hard to interpret the long-term viability and significance of this trend, which is now a well-established feature of political life within and among the European Union and its member states. With its growing density of cross-border institutions, the European region may be thought of as a laboratory in which experiments are conducted in the arts of carving out political futures for former high office holders. The appointments of Paddy Ashdown as High Representative for Bosnia and Herzegovina and Peter Mandelson as European Trade Commissioner are exemplary of the trend; so too is the active commitment of Jacques Delors (the only politician to have served two terms as President of the European Commission) to the think tank Notre Europe, which he helped to found; Carl Bildt's role as special European Union envoy to the former Yugoslavia; and the career of Karel Van Miert, who went from holding office as president of the Flemish Socialist Party to appointments as European Commissioner responsible for transport, credit and investment, consumer and environmental policy and (from 1993 until 1999) as vice-chairman of the European Commission responsible for competition policy.

Is the trend a new form of sinecure system for former leading office holders (as might be thought of Edward Heath's propagandizing for two decades on behalf of the Chinese regime, for undisclosed sums)? Might it be a new and improved version of the old Greek method of sending dangerous or disgraced ex-leaders into exile? Is the trend perhaps a solution to the Peter Principle, that is, a way of getting rid of incompetents who have managed to rise to the top of domestic politics? Are former leaders who embed themselves in cross-border settings simply flash-in-the-pan celebrities, mere mutants who will probably not survive the entangled contradictions and hostilities of the current round of globalization? Or might their involvements be the seed of new forms of cross-border political representation and public opinion formation? The evidence is inconclusive, but think for a moment of the role played by former German Chancellor Helmut Schmidt, who helped found (in 1983) the InterAction Council, a group of over thirty former high office holders; Mikhail Gorbachev's and Nelson Mandela's running commentaries on world affairs; Al Gore's *An Inconvenient Truth* campaign; the Africa Progress Panel and peace negotiation efforts of Kofi Annan (most recently in Kenya); or of Jimmy

Carter, whose self-reinvention as an advocate of human rights makes him the first ex-president of the United States to realize that the world is shrinking, and therefore in need of new ways of doing politics in more negotiated and principled ways, nurtured by bodies like The Elders, which he helped to found in 2007. Is it just possible that by their actions these former leading political office holders are trying to show the world that it resembles a chrysalis capable of hatching the butterfly of cross-border democracy – despite the fact that we currently have no good account of what 'regional' or 'global' or 'cross-border' democratic representation might mean in practice?

Some implications

This chapter has pointed to an unexplored aspect of the question of dispersed leadership: the growing social and political importance of former political leaders engaged in a variety of activities after leaving high office. The trend is fairly ubiquitous but by no means straightforward. Public recognition is growing – this is undoubtedly something new in the history of democracy – that there is life after political death, and that former political leaders can make comebacks in ways that raise questions about their capacity for re-entering government and meddling with its structures and policies, their propensity to give politicians a bad name by engaging in dubious matters, or by foolish wrongdoing. On the more positive side, it is clear that life after political death provides opportunities for democracies. Former political leaders can do good works for democracy. They can serve as an inspiration to their colleagues and to citizens alike. Especially in times in which politicians as representatives are suffering (to put it mildly) a mounting credibility gap, ex-leaders can set new and higher standards for public office holding. Out of office, they can demonstrate to millions of people what ideally office holding is about.

There is something wholly unprecedented about this trend, for it challenges static conceptions of leadership through office holding. The notion of office and office holding was among the great inventions of medieval Europe (Keane 2009). It was within the Church in particular that a basic principle of representative democracy took root: the rule that specified that holding office implied faithful performance of a specific set of tasks. The point was that office holding carried with it certain expectations and obligations. That in turn meant that an office resembled a depersonalized or 'disembodied' role; it was not identical with its holder. Jobs and persons who did jobs were not the same. To hold an office was not to 'own' that office – not even when the office was held for life. On the contrary, office holding was a contingent matter because it implied the ongoing possibility, subject to certain procedures, of removal from office. The removal rule, let us call it, was a basic ingredient of what later came to be called bureaucracy. Yet (contrary to Max Weber and those influenced by him) the removal rule had equally strong affinities with the theory and practice of modern representative democracy. Think for a moment of elected city mayors, or members of parliament who are elected for a fixed term of office, or presidents or prime ministers who are forced to resign. Each one of these political roles rests upon the old Christian presumption that office holders are not synonymous with their office, that they do not privately 'own' their position, that every holder of political office, from the most humble to the most powerful, are in post only for a specified time – such that in a representative democracy (to paraphrase lyrics from the famous song by Bob Dylan, *It's Alright, Ma (I'm Only Bleeding)*) even presidents of the most powerful democracy on the face of the earth are periodically forced to stand naked before their citizens, and the whole world.

The real normative significance of the growing power of former political leaders is that they force existing democracies to think twice, and more deeply, about what counts as good political leadership. The old maxim, a favourite of Harry Truman when he was out of office, that money, craving for power and sex are three things that can ruin political leaders, now applies with real force as well to leaders after they have left office. If that is so, then politically alert former leaders can teach by positive example the need for renewing and crafting new standards of public integrity. The days are over when former leaders could summarize their new occupation using the same staid words as Calvin Coolidge when asked (in 1930) to fill out a membership form for the Washington Press Club: 'Retired. And glad of it'. Life after leadership has become more complicated, more challenging, and more able to set standards for others left behind in office. A sign of our times is the wise remark of a distinguished Portuguese former politician who later directed a remarkable non-governmental foundation that is by world standards a pacesetter in its active support for public accountability and pluralism in matters ranging from political power to aesthetic taste. When asked to define the ideal qualities of life after leadership in a democracy he replied that they were the same as the qualities to be expected of incumbent political leaders: 'A determination to be courageous; an ability to anticipate situations; the inclination to dramatize political effects, so as to warn citizens of actual or potential problems; above all, the willingness to admit that mistakes have been made, to urge that they must be corrected, without ever being afraid of making yet more mistakes.'[3]

Notes

1. Writing as 'Publius' ('The Same Subject Continued, and Re-Eligibility of the Executive Considered', *New York Packet*, 21 March 1788, later known as Federalist Paper 72), Alexander Hamilton defended the principle that elected heads of state should enjoy unlimited time in office, so long as 'the people' consented to their 'perpetuation in

office'. Hamilton said that 'inevitable annihilation', the strict application of term limits, would have perverse effects. Short-term stays in office would produce unwelcome changes of policy and unstable administration; and weaken the state in times of crisis, when the wisdom of experienced leaders is vital. Term limits would also stir up trouble among 'the people', who might feel deprived of their favourite leaders; and tempt incumbents 'to make the harvest as abundant as it was transitory' by engaging in 'peculation, and, in some instances, to usurpation' (an odd argument that critics of Hamilton tried to turn on its head, by pointing out that the temptations of power could only be cured by placing strict limits upon its use). Hamilton went on to warn that 'inevitable annihilation' would inevitably result in disgruntled former leaders 'wandering among the people like discontented ghosts'. The warning rested upon several questionable assumptions, but it correctly pointed to a difficulty that defenders of representative democracy were initially reluctant to address: the problem of finding meaningful public and private roles for former holders of high office.

2. Max Weber's famous account of the qualities of competent political leadership (*Führerschaft*) in parliamentary democracies is sketched in 'Politik als Beruf' (originally delivered as a speech at Munich University in the revolutionary winter of 1918/1919), in *Gesammelte Politische Schriften* (Weber 1958: 493–548). During the speech, Weber said that democracies require leaders to display at least three decisive qualities. Genuine leadership first of all necessitates a passionate devotion to a cause, the will to make history, to set new values for others, nourished from feeling. Such passion must not succumb to what he called (Weber here drew upon Georg Simmel) 'sterile excitation'. Authentic leaders – this is the second imperative – must avoid 'self-intoxication' all the while cultivating a sense of personal responsibility for their achievements, and their failures. While (finally) this implies that leaders are not merely the mandated mouthpieces of their masters, the electors, leaders' actions must embody a 'cool sense of proportion': the ability to grant due weight to realities, to take them soberly and calmly into account. Passionate, responsible, and experienced leaders, Weber urged, must be relentless in 'viewing the realities of life' and must have 'the ability to face such realities and... measure up to them inwardly'. Effective leadership is synonymous with neither demagoguery nor the worship of power for its own sake. Passionate and responsible leaders shun the blind pursuit of ultimate goals; such blindness, Weber noted sarcastically, 'does rightly and leaves the results with the Lord'. Mature leaders must be guided instead by the 'ethic of responsibility'. Recognizing the average deficiencies of people, they must continually strive, using state power, to take account of the foreseeable effects of particular actions that aim to realize particular goals through the reliance upon particular means. Responsible leaders must therefore incorporate into their actions the prickly fact, in many contexts, that the attainment of good ends is dependent upon (and therefore jeopardized by) the use of ethically doubtful or (in the case of violence) even dangerous means.
3. Interview with Emílio Rui Vilar, former senior minister of the first democratic governments after the defeat of the Salazar dictatorship, former Deputy Governor of the Bank of Portugal and former Director-General of the Commission of the European Union (Keane 2006).

Bibliography

Ankersmit, F., 'On The Future of Representative Democracy', posted at http://www.thefutureofrepresentativedemocracy.org/files/pdf/resources/Ankersmit%20comments.pdf

Burke, E., 'Speech to the Electors of Bristol (3 November 1774)', *The Works of the Right Honourable Edmund Burke* (London: Nimmo, 1899), 89–98.

Denning, S., *The Secret Language of Leadership* (San Francisco: Jossey-Bass, 2007).

Jefferson, T., 'Thomas Jefferson to Benjamin Rush (17 August 1811)', in W. B. Parker and J. Viles (eds.), *Letters and Addresses of Thomas Jefferson* (New York: Kessinger, [1905] 2008).

Kaiser, A., 'Parliamentary Opposition in Westminster Democracies', *Journal of Legislative Studies*, 14/1–2 (2008), 20–45.

Keane, J., 'The Politics of Retreat', *The Political Quarterly*, 61/3 (1990), 340–52.

—— *Václav Havel: A Political Tragedy in Six Acts* (London and New York: Bloomsbury, 1999).

——Interview with Emilio Rui Vilar (Calouste Gulbenkian Foundation, Lisbon, 27 October 2006).

——*Global Civil Society?* (Cambridge: Cambridge University Press, 2003).

——*The Life and Death of Democracy* (London, New York and Madrid: Simon and Schuster, 2009).

Luce, E., 'Bad Cop Bill Gives Hillary Deniability', *Financial Times*, 25 January 2008, 7.

McIntyre, A., *Aging and Political Leadership* (Melbourne and Oxford: Oxford University Press, 1988).

Michaud, N, 'Designating the Official Opposition in a Westminster Parliamentary System', *Journal of Legislative Studies*, 6/4 (2000), 69–90.

Mill J. S., *Autobiography*, Jack Stillinger (ed.) (London: Houghton Mifflin, [1873] 1969).

Mishra, V., 'Nuclear Nehru', *Indian Express*, 1 November 2007.

Paine, T., 'Rights of Man, Part the Second (1792)', in W. M. Van der Weyde (ed.), *The Life and Works of Thomas Paine* (New Rochelle, New York: Thomas Paine National Historical Association, 1925).

Povoledo, E., 'Unsolved Crimes a Novelist's Fodder', *International Herald Tribune*, 24 October 2007, 19.

Powell, E., *Joseph Chamberlain* (London: Thames and Hudson, 1977).

Rieff, P., *Charisma: The Gift of Grace, and How It Has Been Taken Away From Us* (New York: Pantheon, 2007).

Rizzo, S. and Stella, G. A., *La casta: così i politici italiani sono diventati intoccabili* (Milan: Rizzoli, 2007).

Roniger, L. and Sznajder, M., *The Politics of Exile in Latin America*, (Cambridge and New York: Cambridge University Press, 2009).

Saward, M., 'Representative Claims', in S. Alonso, J. Keane, and W. Merkel (eds.), *The Future of Representative Democracy*, (Cambridge and New York: Cambridge University Press, 2009).

Silverstein, K., 'Their Men in Washington: Undercover with DC's Lobbyists for Hire', *Harpers*, July 2007, 53–61.

Urbinati, N., *Representative Democracy: Principles and Genealogy* (Chicago and London: Chicago University Press, 2006).

—— Weber, M., *Gesammette politische Schriften* (Tübingen: Mohr 1958).

Chapter 16

Dispersed Democratic Leadership Revisited

John Kane, Haig Patapan, and Paul 't Hart

We began this study by observing that most democratic theorists have difficulty in articulating a proper role for leadership, largely because none among democratic equals has any *innate* or *inherent* right to rule over others. Democracy requires good leadership if it is to function effectively, yet the very idea of leadership seems to conflict with democracy's egalitarian ethos. The more democratic leaders lead from the front, the less democratic they appear; the more they act like good democrats, the less they seem like true leaders. Confronted with this dilemma, the general tendency among scholars has been to accept the need for leadership in practice while overlooking it in theory and consequently failing to offer a yardstick for assessing leadership within democracy (Ruscio 2004; Wren 2007; Kane and Patapan 2008). Meanwhile many explore paths towards wider participation and deliberation in search of a social consensus that would arguably make democracy 'more democratic' (Barber 1984; Cohen 1989; Dryzek 1990; Benhabib 1996; Lijphart 1999; Gutman and Thompson 2004). However, none of them articulate a clear role for leadership. Indeed their unexpressed aim often seems to be to eliminate the need for leadership altogether.

Leadership cannot, however, be eliminated, at least not without endangering the polity. This volume shows that in practice democracy's tendency is not to eliminate leadership but to multiply it and disperse it throughout society to a rather extraordinary degree. The volume's chapters have uncovered the unique opportunities – as well as constraints – that a variety of leaders confront in negotiating the demands of their specific offices within the larger expectations of a democratic regime. Here we reflect on these contributions and their implications. Our discussion is in four parts. First we trace the effects of the two main drivers of leadership dispersal in democracy: popular sovereignty and liberal constitutionalism. We then explore the implications of leadership dispersal, particularly the need to understand and manage the often sensitive relations between various loci (e.g. heads of government, top officials, international organizations, and non-profit leaders) and the various forms (e.g. political, administrative, judicial, and civic, as discerned in Table 1.1) of public leadership in democratic systems. We will see, for example, that some leadership offices (and their holders) have a tendency to resist the realities of distributed leadership that democratic dispersal imposes upon them by attempts to centralize power resources, demarcate and enlarge professional autonomy, and expand their authority while trying to diminish that of others. Third, we discuss various normative criteria for assessing the effects, beneficial and otherwise, of leadership dispersal, and note the importance of sustaining a subtle balance between them all. Finally, we suggest three avenues for future research on the nature of leadership in democracy that follow on from the dispersal perspective developed in this volume.

Leadership dispersal

As we noted in the introduction and have seen reinforced in many of the chapters, the dispersal of leadership in modern democracies has two seminal sources. One is the doctrine of popular sovereignty whose egalitarian premises allow potentially anyone an influential voice in public affairs. The other is the liberal constitutional division of powers designed to moderate and control authority in the modern state. Let us revisit both.

The impulse from popular sovereignty

In addressing the first of these, it is important to note that much of the dispersal that has occurred under this impulse has been in the nature of an historical achievement, usually the result of long political struggle. Most Western liberal democracies grew out of monarchical and patriarchal systems in which individuals ruled with, at most, only partial express consent of the governed. As the moral and political authority of monarchical systems declined, an increasing number of popular voices clamoured to be heard. Monarchs for their part were increasingly compelled to listen and, in listening, to cede authority, as noted long ago by Antoine de Rivarol: 'From the day when the monarch consults his subjects, sovereignty is as though suspended... When people cease to esteem, they cease to obey. A general rule: peoples whom the king consults begin with vows and end with wills of their own' (cited in Godechot 1981: 33; see also Elzinga, this volume). The democratic thrust of Western history has been, through many trials and upheavals, to release a multitude of individual wills from the thrall of traditional authority while yet contriving to assemble them into the collective will necessary for effective government. Those who have sought to exercise leadership in this new and difficult political domain have had to learn to cope with an increasing number of wills that can no longer be simply commanded or ignored, even while they fend off rivals from an ever-expanding pool of contenders for office.

That the struggle towards equality continues today for hitherto overlooked or actively discouraged social groups is shown in Sykes' chapter on women ministers, which can be read as emblematic of many other possible examples: Catholic, African American, and Latino penetration of US high public offices; Magreb, Turkish, and Moroccan immigrant representation in top public positions in France, Germany, and Holland, respectively; lower caste penetration of the Indian corridors of power; indigenous office-holding in Latin America, Canada, Australia, and New Zealand. All these could provide stories of slow numerical growth over time in the face of entrenched bias, institutional stickiness and elite attempts to marginalize, co-opt, and normalize would-be leaders from 'out-groups' (De Zwart 1994). Incidental cases of success (e.g. Thatcher, Meir, Gandhi, and Clarke among women; Obama the most recent conspicuous breakthrough in the United States' racial divide) serve to remind us how far democracy's dispersal, not just of leadership roles, but of the opportunities to fill them has yet to go.

Nevertheless, the process of dispersal continues, sometimes denoted these days as the 'displacement of politics', or the 'hollowing out' of the state, or the 'fragmentation' of governance (Bovens, Derksen, Witteveen, Becker, and Kalma 1995; Frissen 1999). The tendency throughout has been to expand the field, not only of who gets to *be* a leader but, by virtue of the very clamour of competing voices, the loci of leadership in society. Dispersion gives unprecedented and in some instances unexpected authority to a large and growing number of offices that are often contingent on, yet distinct from, conventional political offices. The chapters by Schudson, Bell, and Schmid, for example, discuss the importance of leaders in the media, business, and other non-governmental fields in influencing politics and policy. Nor is dispersal confined to the domestic arena, as demonstrated by Verbeek's chapter on the post-Second World War rise of international regimes and the international organizations dedicated to making them work. These have created a whole new set of public offices offering leadership possibilities to Inter-Governmental Organization (IGO) executives adept at operating in the multi-level governance settings thus created. This proliferation, remarkably, affects even authoritarian regimes that choose, for appearances' sake, to dress themselves up as democracies – tolerating a semi-independent judiciary as proof of the alleged adherence to the rule of law, building a façade of parliamentarism, and affording some measure of freedom of speech. In thus tolerating diluted forms of opposition and oversight, they occasionally produce genuinely competing centres of leadership (Kane and Patapan 2008).

The democratic dispersal of leadership has been hugely assisted by advances in technology, particularly technologies that radically improve ability to communicate, persuade, and monitor at ever-increasing speed. From Gutenberg to Google, each wave of communication technology has widened the public sphere and enabled more people and groups to perform public leadership roles. Perhaps the most entertaining example of this trend is the rise of celebrity leadership, as discussed here by 't Hart and Tindall. Here the public activism of 'stars' is immeasurably helped by their ability to capture huge audiences on all mediums of communication, often right across the globe. In fact, much of the high public profile and indeed public leadership of former government leaders rests on them achieving a similar kind of 'celebrity' status, and some of them have practically become one-man brands (Needham 2005). As we see in Keane's chapter, they can cleverly exploit the multitude of contemporary communication channels at their disposal to stake out new leadership roles for themselves even after leaving office. The Bonos and Mandelas of the world can thus draw on, and exploit, one another's distinct public auras to advance their own particular civic leadership ambitions.

At the same time, new technology has placed a burden of adaptation on conventional leaders in existing institutions. Erwin Hargrove's trend survey of British and US heads of government clearly suggests that over time politicians have had to command an ever-widening range of communication skills. Indeed, leaders and would-be leaders ignore the ever-transforming carriers of communication at their peril. During the 2008 presidential campaign in the United States it proved damaging, for instance, for the Republican candidate John McCain to admit he did not do emails or even know how to operate a computer, when his much younger rival was using state-of-the-art Web and mobile phone technology to engineer an upset in the presidential primaries.

Clearly, the relative importance of mass (as opposed to inter-elite) communication as a sine qua non for acquiring political authority has increased exponentially. At the same time, the diversity of communication channels has burgeoned: FDR could focus on a few key set piece speeches and casual 'fireside' radio chats; Obama (aided by a massive and highly skilled communications staff) had to cover many more bases. The latter's successful use of SMS-texting during the 2008 presidential campaign revealed the shape of things to come. Everywhere now, Web-based communication allows well-equipped political elites to 'cut out the middleman' (e.g. journalists and television stations) in communicating with mass constituencies.

Just as importantly, the very character of public communication has changed. From the age of the printing press to that of television, new channels of communication have tended to simply provide ever more powerful 'bullhorns' amplifying leader message to audiences. But this requires leaders who really understand the possibilities. Australian Prime Minister John Howard looked hopelessly out of touch when on the cusp of his bid to win a fifth consecutive election he began his inaugural YouTube message by saying 'Good Morning' to what he imagined must have been the people viewing his message 'live' (Cunningham 2008). The recent explosion in interactive forms of communication has changed the nature of the leadership game much more widely, however. It has lowered the threshold of skills and resources required from those who seek to play it. In fact, many people typically confined to audience roles in twentieth-century democracies can now realistically aspire to play leadership roles on at least some public issues some of the time – if they are Web-literate. Some even get to play the role by accident (see Schudson's story about Farnaz Fassihi's email from Baghdad). This fragmentation of the public sphere has challenged political parties, interest groups, social movements, administrative agencies, and news organizations alike.

Schudson suggests that the fast-increasing transformation of the civic information function in and indeed across contemporary democracies means that leaders of conventional news organizations like the *New York Times* or major television networks face significant challenges relating to their mission, technologies, and market share. The once unshakeable hold of 'the press' on 'the public', and thus the great dependency of political leaders on political journalists, is fading fast. Nor is it just journalists and news organizations that are thus challenged; all agents and loci of political, civic, administrative, and judicial leadership must now reinvent their modus operandi. Those that do stand to gain exposure, credibility, and clout; those that do not, risk irrelevance and indeed oblivion.

The impulse from liberal constitutionalism

Clearly some of the key manifestations of dispersed leadership covered in this volume are the product of deliberate and often long-contested efforts to build a system of checks and balances around early monocratic rulers or colonizers. Absolute monarchies were tamed by certain key fruits of liberal political thought: the rule of law; the rise of parliamentarism; and the constitutional protection of freedom of speech that permitted the press and the academy to flourish. Institutional designs founded upon liberal conceptions of individual rights and freedoms account for the familiar political offices secured by liberal constitutionalism and the separation of powers – parliament, the executive, and the judiciary. The chapters in this volume addressing the role of the executive, the opposition, and the judiciary in effect explore this liberal democratic aspect of dispersal. In each, however, we also discern the perennial tendency of each office to broaden the scope of its authority, thus creating tensions between the offices and imposing considerable 'diplomatic' demands on the respective office-holders. These are perhaps the best-known examples of dispersal of leadership and, as such, the focus of extensive scholarship and debate.

Dispersed leadership of the checks and balances variety trades off the short-term decisiveness of monocratic rule against the benefits of more time-consuming, piecemeal, and at times 'messy' processes of a system with multiple institutional veto players at its core. (Its logic also dictates a preference for federal above unitary systems, and within unitary systems for maximal autonomy for lower levels of government.) The diffusion of sites at which agenda-setting, public policy-making, and public service delivery occur (roughly the political and administrative leadership functions) we might call the 'first face' of leadership dispersal. A 'second face' comprises rapidly multiplying sites concerned with vetting and opposing political and administrative office-holders (the dispersal of 'watchdog' forms of public leadership).

Taken altogether these sites constitute what John Uhr calls a 'lattice of leadership', a set of public offices and roles that can each claim a certain amount of public legitimacy for their holders to engage in leadership activities. In effect this has created a 'mutually supportive arrangement of diversified leadership, consistent with the constitutional principles we associate with separation of powers doctrines' (Uhr 2008: 41). In every contemporary democracy this trajectory of leadership dispersal has been far advanced, although its nuances and institutional manifestations may differ and may be subject to periodic expansion or revision (e.g. New Zealand's switch to an electoral system of proportional representation, or the European Union's continuing attempts to broaden, deepen, and democratize its governance arrangements).

Both democratic thought and liberal democratic institutional design foster the idea that public power is at once a precious and a dangerous resource, best divided across different institutions and office-holders. With power dispersed and the wielders of that power forced to bargain with one another, be accountable to one another, and to deliberate together before collective action is possible, democratic societies are arguably governed in less intimidating, more predictable, and smarter ways. As noted above, this is an historically evolving process. But there is strong evidence to suggest that, slowly but surely, even the strongest bulwarks of hierarchy, patriarchy, and 'government knows best' mentality are having to come to terms with the realities of 'shared power' in contemporary, globalized 'network societies' (Crosby and Bryson 2005; Morse and Buss 2007). The world over, governments and bureaucracies are trying to reshape themselves to accommodate more participative, deliberative ways of engaging with citizens (OECD 2008). They try to seduce other public and private actors into horizontal (as opposed to top-down) forms of coordinated, collaborative, networked governance (Rhodes 1997; Goldsmith and Eggers 2004; Koppenjan and Klijn 2004; Agranoff 2007). And they attempt to absorb the large and increased demands for transparency and public accountability imposed upon them. Even within the judiciary, many a 'strategy session' is devoted to how the institution and its officers can continue to project authority in the face of less automatic deference and more intense public scrutiny (Huls, Adams, and Bomhoff 2009).

The more democratic ideas take root in constitutional and institutional practices, the greater the number and diversity of public leadership loci likely to be found within the political system. In established democracies, leadership dispersal becomes its own cause: we like the idea of it, we feel it 'works', and so we create more of it.

Responses to dispersed leadership

The democratic tendency to disperse offices explored above would appear to have no obvious limits. Yet the very strength of such a drive may conceal equally powerful countervailing influences that resist such diffusion of leadership. Some of these countervailing forces have their origin in principles that may challenge, or contend with, the notion of democracy itself. For example, the idea of the 'knower' or the 'expert' questions the very premise of popular sovereignty: authority should be vested in those who know, rather than in the many (Willard 1996). Thus the notion of the 'expert' becomes a principled basis for resisting the dispersion of leadership and authority. Similar principles include the idea of efficiency, of the rule of law, and inviolable principles, such as individual dignity or rights. In addition to these principles, however, we contend that there is a countervailing dynamic in the very notion of 'office' itself. Hence dispersion inevitably fosters attempts by the new office-holder to retain such authority, and thereby resist the movement towards greater democratic dispersion. Often such resistance will be articulated in terms of principles – for example, as we will see, bureaucracy will claim that it should retain its authority because of its superiority in knowledge and expertise. Nevertheless, the persistent evidence of the resistance to dispersal is found in struggles over control of political agendas and policies, and will generally involve leaders in some sites trying to maintain their independence against assaults upon it by leaders in another, usually those in the elected branch. The range and complexity of this dynamic of dispersal and resistance means that we can only indicate some of the important ways dispersal of office is countered in democracies. Our selection is intended to show the diversity in the nature of offices and thereby the complexity of the dynamic of dispersal and resistance.

The monarchy

There are some offices that seem, by their very nature, to resist democratic dispersal. Foremost among them is that most pre-eminently undemocratic of institutions, the monarchy, which by definition implies concentrated authority. This may seem of little consequence given that constitutionalized monarchs have purely ceremonial duties and a merely 'dignified' role (Bagehot 1873). Yet as Elzinga argues the matter is not so simple, and that the monarchy continues to play an important 'neutral' role essential for the smooth functioning of modern democracies.

Elzinga shows that contemporary kings and queens must be exceptionally circumspect in navigating their particular political leadership dilemma. Their formal powers – including the power to speak out – are usually extremely limited, so they have to rely on tradition-based, symbol-driven public affection as their only fount of authority, a shaky resource in rapidly modernizing and postmodernizing societies. Nevertheless, as 'managers of last resort' during acute crises of the democratic polity – for example, during periods of sustained political paralysis, unrest, or coup attempts – monarchs like Juan Carlos of Spain, Albert of Belgium, Bhumbol of Thailand and Gyanendra of Nepal have had to make tough judgement calls. The choices of these monarchs did not just affect the immediate course and outcomes of the crises at hand, they also proved fateful in either solidifying (Juan Carlos) or fatally undermining (Gyanendra) their own leadership and indeed the future of their monarchies. Not touched upon by Elzinga, but equally significant from a dispersed leadership perspective, is the reverse situation, when crises of the monarchy compromise its moral authority or constitutional integrity. In those circumstances – the Lockheed bribery scandal involving Dutch Queen Juliana's husband Prince Bernhard, the Charles and Diana scandal in the United Kingdom, and the crisis over Diana's death – political and sometimes judicial leaders are faced with fateful judgement calls on whether and how to help the monarch, and thereby the monarchy, save face. If Elzinga is right, then the constitutionalized monarchy should be seen as a prime example of the democratic dispersal dynamic – an office that serves and respects the democracy precisely when it resists through 'neutral' adjudication. Democracies have paradoxically created a new, predominantly symbolic and moral leadership niche for the very monarchs they first helped strip of their active powers of authoritarian rule.

The executive

Much more seriously resistant to leadership dispersal is the democratic office which inherits most of the prerogatives and functions formerly reserved for monarchs, the political executive. Indeed the executive arm of government seems to harbour an enduring impulse to amass institutional power unto itself. There has been much critical discussion, for example, of the increasing 'presidentialization' of the prime ministership in parliamentary systems. The accuracy of this label has been questioned, as has the geographical extent of the phenomenon (see chapters by Hargrove and Sykes; Rhodes 2007), but certain features have been observed in many Westminster systems: the steady growth of prime ministerial staff to form a 'shadow bureaucracy'; the personalization of the government by prime ministerial dominance of public communication; and the increasing prevalence of prime minister-dominated 'short cuts' to full cabinet deliberation and collective responsibility (Foley 1993, 2000; Poguntke and Webb 2005; Walter and Strangio 2007).

In the United States, meanwhile, there has been fierce debate about the tendency towards the formation of an 'administrative' or even 'imperial' presidency (Nathan 1983; Schlesinger 2004). The George W. Bush administration's rather blunt attempts to endow a 'unitary executive' with quasi-monarchical prerogatives by putting it beyond ordinary legal controls has deepened the bitterness of this debate. Hargrove argues that attempts at presidential rule by executive order rather than legislative negotiation with Congress are predominantly a Republican phenomenon – and indeed the early period of the Obama presidency has seen fewer examples of outright presidential imposition and a return to persuasion and bargaining.

Nevertheless, such attempts to (re)assert executive dominance should not be written off as mere renegade, ultimately futile efforts to turn back the clock. They are rather a symptom of, and response to, the inherent difficulties of democratic leadership. The tendency to dispersal grows out of a permanent licence of members of the sovereign body, the people, to dissent. The consequence of this is the multiplication of loci where dissent can be made effective in questioning, obstructing, or countermanding the actions of a government that will, nonetheless, be held strictly responsible for its failures to act. The desire of executives with a heavy burden of responsibilities would seem quite naturally to lean towards gathering more securely into their own hands the reins of effectual power. Such attempts will, just as naturally in democracies, sooner or later be effectively resisted. There is no a priori reason, moreover, why continued dispersal in some domains – judicial or civic, say – may not coexist with robust trends towards centralization in another – for instance, the political executive. The tug of war between dispersing and centralizing tendencies should therefore be regarded as a permanent feature of liberal democratic government. It is a manifestation of the always inconclusive trade-off between principles of efficiency and democratic inclusion, and between principles of efficiency and liberty.

The bureaucracy

Modern bureaucracies provide unique insights into the dynamic of democratic leadership dispersal and resistance. Bureaucratic leaders (administrators at the highest echelons of the civil service) necessarily perform a delicate balancing act between the twin imperatives of maximizing their organizations' responsiveness (to political masters, clients, and partners) and safeguarding their own professional autonomy and integrity. But if the balance appears to slide too far towards autonomy, their organization risks appearing as an independent centre of power challenging the authority of the elected government. In recent years, this drama played out in a series of administrative reforms with interesting consequences for our story of dispersal versus concentration of leadership.

Wise administrators will not, of course, bite the hand that supplies their organization with its lifeblood – mandate, money, tasks, and legislative support. But professionalism and expertise nevertheless always allow a measure of independence and some capacity for resistance. With distinctive missions, sophisticated professional technologies and tight-knit stakeholder coalitions, established bureaucratic institutions can wield a licence for recalcitrance vis-à-vis governments, central agencies, and watchdogs of various kinds. They may feel secure enough to voice concerns to political principals and to appear front-of-stage in democratic deliberations – to act, in other words, as 'public entrepreneurs' (Lewis 1980; Boin and Goodin 2007). Nevertheless, as Kane and Patapan argue, the risk that democratically elected leaders would come to resent and wish to tame the power of a professional bureaucracy capable of opposing their will is always a real prospect. Throughout the late twentieth century, governments around the world conceived the need to regain political control of administrations that had allegedly become laws-unto-themselves. This was done, importantly, by dismantling the main locus of the old bureaucratic leadership at the most senior levels of the service. Lifetime career bureaucrats, who had always performed a crucial gatekeeping and thus leadership role in policy processes, were replaced by executives on time-fixed performance contracts that made them theoretically more amenable to political direction.

This greater responsiveness was argued to be necessary to achieve greater efficiency and effectiveness in public service than the old bureaucracy, for all its declared professionalism, seemed capable of delivering. Certainly it was undeniable that administrators faced a daunting task in trying to induce the massive machinery of government successfully to implement political choices and deliver services. Zealous reformers argued that the task required, in today's complex and fast-moving environment, much more than the technically competent 'administration' envisaged by Woodrow Wilson. It presupposed both transactional and at times transformational leadership aimed at institution-building, stewardship, reform, networking, and alliance-formation (Selznick 1957; Lewis 1980; Terry 1995; Moore 1995; Boin 2001). Ironically, then, the emasculation of the old bureaucratic leadership was accompanied by a much more pronounced emphasis on leadership throughout the entire service, so that centralization at the top was balanced by general dispersal of discretionary authority below. This dispersal of the leadership function throughout the whole service, however, created multiple sites (rather than the few that has previously existed) that might potentially evade the effective control of elected governments. After several decades of reform, and with an undoubted decline in professional expertise in many administrative spheres, it is not clear whether what we might term the de facto 'democratization' of the service has gone too far or not far enough (Kane and Patapan 2006).

The judiciary

Judicial leaders sit on top of micro-political systems full of potentially recalcitrant professionals. Judges enjoy strong positional protection, and are traditionally inclined to jealously guard their professional autonomy against 'managerial' attempts by their institution's executives to tell them what to do or change the way they do things. But as Tushnet indicates, the real litmus test for judicial leadership is in managing its relations to the political system at large, particularly the executive and legislative branches of government.

The judiciary, like the bureaucracy, forms a site of authority which is partly complementary to and partly independent of elected authorities. Judicial leaders are more securely situated than bureaucratic ones because they can draw on the ancient authority of the law itself, and especially because liberal constitutionalism insists so strongly on the separation and independence of the judicial power. (The notable exception, as Tushnet points out, are those State judges in the United States who must be elected to office, and who thus have no real autonomy from the democratic political system.) Judicial power is considerable because liberal democracies exist under the rule of law, and judges get to determine authoritatively what laws mean. Though held to be strictly 'legal', their interpretations nevertheless implicate the judiciary in every area of policy – tax, business, regulation, land tenure, and so on. Of most political consequence, however, are the judges who sit atop a federal system with powers of constitutional interpretation. These can act as genuinely political leaders because they may make authoritative findings on matters of great social consequence that are very difficult or even impossible for elected governments to overrule or alter. This is inevitably a cause of considerable tension, controversy, and even anger. Judges will generally be very circumspect about how and when they exercise such power in a democratic system. Tushnet in his chapter identifies the external conditions that make such occasional forays into judicial political leadership possible.

Because of the separation of powers, the real struggle over control versus autonomy in the judicial realm occurs in the process of appointments. Elected leaders who get to appoint judges to fill vacancies on important courts can have a political influence that long outlasts their tenure. Of course, control is hardly perfect here, for securely independent judges may judge in unanticipated ways, but a series of either 'conservative', 'liberal', or 'activist' appointments can certainly alter the tenor of the judiciary for many years to come.

Civic leadership

The civil society leaders who run community organizations are actively engaged in delivering services to those who need them, either in conjunction with – as contractor or partner – or as an alternative to government service provision. They would seem to represent, therefore, a paradigm case of democratic dispersal. But Schmid's chapter teaches us that the reality is more complicated. The drama of dispersal versus autonomy occurs in the sector because Non-profit Organization (NPO) leaders experience tension between engaging with their constituents as political activists and serving them as clients. Indeed, this dual function produces a certain strategic dilemma. The more passionately leaders perform advocacy and watchdog roles, the more likely they are to collide with government elites. As service providers, however, their dependency on government resources may incline them towards pragmatic cooperation. Yet to appear effectively co-opted erodes the aura of independent partisanship that forms the moral capital they need to be credible to followers. Large service-oriented NPOs tend to be strongly reliant on 'soft money'. They are more likely to be docile creatures of government than a locus of alternative leadership contributing to the public scrutiny of governments, certainly when compared to their more advocacy-oriented or philanthropy-funded counterparts.

In many ways, the same dilemma affects the university leaders described by Davis and Sharrock. Not only is their office not a product of democratic dispersal – universities antedate the spread of democracy by centuries – the very office itself entails a complex blend of executive power within their own micro-political systems and civic duty in their roles as defenders of academic freedom and 'voice' in the larger democratic polity. Many university administrators within and beyond the United States wrestled with this tension during the political escalation of the Vietnam War: would they defend the students' rights to hold (large-scale, repeated) protest rallies against the US government's war policy, or would they use or invoke executive power to maintain order and minimize disruption on campus?

NPO and university leaders both wrestle with the civic leadership dilemma of purity versus pragmatism. Civic leaders may choose to 'deal with the devil' in order to do some tangible good', but at the risk of being seen to have 'sold out', losing their credibility as a result (Baraket 2008; Shergold 2008). As Davis and Sharrock argue, civic leaders need courage, one way or the other: the courage to assert academic autonomy when governments of the day seek to curtail it, but also the courage to 'do deals' with government and/or business in the face of purist opposition within their own ranks.

Assessing leadership dispersal

Granted that dispersed leadership is an inevitable consequence of liberal democratic development, we might nevertheless inquire what its value is for democratic government. Is dispersed leadership, in short, actually good for democracy, and does it make governance 'more democratic'? The answer we give to such questions will depend on the normative yardstick we use to judge, and it should be evident from all that has been said above that no single agreed yardstick is possible. We have argued that dispersal occurs both under the force of the principle of popular sovereignty and under that of liberal constitutionalism; the quality of a government will be differently judged depending on which of these is used as the relevant yardstick. Moreover, we have seen that dispersal, however motivated, causes recurrent tensions and contests over ultimate control of political agendas. These are all, in the end, struggles to achieve coherent government by resisting the natural fragmentation of democracy, thus providing a third yardstick, effectiveness. We thus arrive at three normative bases for assessing the effects of dispersal, as identified by Bovens, 't Hart, and Schillemans (2008): popular control; checks and balances; and effective governance. Leadership is important in all three, but each has different concerns about leadership in democracy: accountability, harm minimization, and effectiveness, respectively (see Table 16.1).

First, the idea of *popular control* has been theoretically defined, in contemporary terminology, on the principal–agent model. According to this, a modern representative democracy can be described as a concatenation of principal–agent relationships (Strom 2000, 2003; Lupia 2003). The people (the primary principals in a democracy) have delegated their authority to popular representatives, who, in turn, have delegated the drafting and enforcement of laws and policy to the government. Ministers subsequently entrust policy implementation to their ministries, who proceed to delegate parts of these

Table 16.1 Evaluating democratic leadership: three perspectives

	Democratic responsiveness	Democratic constitutionalism	Democratic resilience
Key criterion	Leaders to be recruited and sensitized to serving citizens	Leaders' power to be checked by watchdogs	Leaders to be induced to communicate, reflect, and collaborate
Favours	Representation as key design principle for all public offices (leader recruitment as well as office-holding practices) Representative democracy	Independent, strong civic 'voice', and judicial 'accountability' forums and leaders Monitory democracy	Variety and overlap in public leadership offices, and strong inducements to leader reflexivity and dialogue Deliberative democracy
Fears	Preponderance of 'technocratic' (e.g. administrative and judicial) over 'democratic' (e.g. political and civic) leadership forms Technocracy	Executive (political and administrative) capacity to escape independent scrutiny and/or avoid sanction of past performance Oligarchic authoritarianism	Weak civil societies; homogeneous elite recruitment and socialization practices; charismatic and other forms of strong and 'greedy' leadership Plebiscitary, charismatic rule

tasks to more or less independent bodies and institutions. Public servants at the end of this chain of delegation end up spending billions in taxpayers' money and using their discretionary powers to furnish licences and subsidies, distribute benefits, impose fines, prosecute people, and a host of other tasks. Each set of leaders–principals in the chain of delegation seeks to monitor the execution of the delegated public tasks by calling the agent–leaders to account. At the end of the chain are the citizens, who pass judgement on the conduct of leaders and who indicate their pleasure or displeasure at election times.

Of prime importance to effective accountability are all the organs of the modern media, one of whose tasks is to investigate, expose, and judge all the acts of government. The aim of this whole system of accountability is to ensure that the leadership is kept as closely as possible in touch with the sovereign people's expressed wishes. In other words, this criterion for judging the value of democratic dispersal is primarily concerned with the democratic responsiveness of leaders (Przeworski, Stokes, and Manin 1999). Leadership dispersal that improves responsiveness is, by definition, good. Dispersal that does not may or may not be good for other purposes but that is irrelevant to this perspective.

The second set of criteria derives from the liberal idea of *checks and balances*. As we have seen, liberal constitutionalism is concerned with preventing tyrannous behaviour by leaders that would inevitably infringe individual rights. The main remedy against dangerously overbearing or improper government is the institutionalization of countervailing powers. Other public institutions, such as an independent judicial power, special tribunals, legislative committees, and so on act as complementary political watchdogs. There are, indeed, a whole host of such monitory institutions and forms not covered in this volume – Freedom of Information provisions; audit offices; Ombudsmen; an entire wave (some call it an 'explosion') of 'horizontal' accountability mechanisms (Power 1994) – that give citizens opportunities to hold to account actors and networks exercising discretionary administrative power (Bovens 2007; Bovens et al. 2008).

Under this liberal model, power is granted to leaders but the prime concern is to constitutionalize power, which means to keep it securely in check. This criterion of judgement therefore earns the label democratic constitutionalism. Dispersal that improves checking ability is good, by definition. As in the previous case, other forms of dispersed leadership may be good after their fashion but of no moment under this perspective.

The third perspective is that of *effective governance*. It is concerned with actually getting useful or necessary things done. Though leaders may often feel this requires rising above or even silencing the democratic cacophony, taking effective power into a single set of hands, democracies inevitably resist such attempts sooner or later. Leadership dispersal might be seen as beneficial from an effectiveness perspective, however, if it contributes to what Lindblom

(1965) called 'the intelligence of democracy': that is, the capacity to arrive at appropriate solutions to complex predicaments and to adapt to changing circumstances. Defenders of this view argue that leadership structures and processes should facilitate this key aim, an achievement that depends on maintaining and strengthening leadership learning capacity (van der Berg 1999: 40; Aucoin and Heintzman 2000: 52–4). Leaders' awareness that they inhabit a world in which many others play crucial public leadership roles serves, it is argued, to focus their minds and stop them becoming inward looking ('t Veld, Schaap, Termeer, and van Twist 1991). They are forced to consider feedback about their own performance (Behn 2001) and to genuinely communicate with 'outside actors' (O'Loughlin 1990). The public nature of the dialogue between overlapping and competing leaders teaches all what is expected, what works and what does not.

There is a public accountability aspect to this criterion of judging dispersal that emphasizes responsiveness, but the mechanisms involved are less adversarial than 'exhortative'. The prime concern is with democratic resilience. It is not, in other words, about 'keeping them honest' but about keeping them smart and sharp.

Thus weighing the pros and cons of dispersal from each different perspective, we may arrive at quite different judgements as to value, as noted in Table 16.1. These criteria, though distinct, are not mutually exclusive, in the sense that it is quite possible for citizens to want responsiveness *and* checking *and* effectiveness. Yet having more of one may easily mean having less of another, forcing people to prioritize. For example, the proliferation of public accountability arrangements in many democracies may be warmly embraced by proponents of democratic constitutionalism who welcome the trend towards 'monitory democracy' (Keane 2009). Defenders of a democratic responsiveness perspective would be concerned to maintain a balance between democratic and liberal constitutional forms of accountability arrangements; many of the new checking mechanisms are of a purely technocratic kind and do not necessarily keep public leaders attuned to the needs of clients and stakeholders in society at large. Proponents of the democratic resilience perspective, however, may argue that more accountability is 'too much of a good thing', pointing to the risk of accountability overload and overzealous behaviour by public watchdogs. Indeed, critical accounts of the growing size, prominence and complexity of the transparency and accountability 'industry' (overview in Bovens et al. 2008) argue that too many watchdogs render the system M.A.D. (suffering from 'Multiple Accountabilities Disorder', see Koppell 2005).

As another example, consider the trend towards 'presidentialization' discussed above. From a democratic responsiveness perspective, this may be judged the self-assertion of a democratically elected leader embodying the popular will who is concerned to counter the creeping technocratic rule of shadowy administrators. Democratic constitutionalists may take a bleaker view, seeing presidentialization as a new manifestation of oligarchic tendencies that threaten to shred the carefully woven web of accountabilities (Körösényi 2005, 2007; Higley and Pakulski 2008). Finally, those judging from a democratic resilience perspective might note that cosy cliques built around dominant leaders have a tendency to develop a distorted picture of reality, indulging in Groupthink and leaving prudence and responsibility by the wayside. Recent examples in the United Kingdom and the United States have reconfirmed what we have known for a long time: that when crucial decisions about complex and controversial matters are made by narrowly composed 'inner circles' to the exclusion of relevant stakeholders, expert analysis, and public accountability, policy fiascos result ('t Hart 1994).

We may conclude, therefore, that the question of whether greater dispersal is a good or a bad thing for a democracy is too simplistic. It all depends. Obviously the question of balance is critical here. Concentrating power may seem superficially more efficient and effective, but the dangers of concentration are not figments of liberal democratic imagination. Successful liberal democracies attempt to occupy a difficult middle ground between excessive concentration and excessive fragmentation of authority, with sufficient channels that connect leaders meaningfully to citizens, sufficient mechanisms for checking and balancing, and sufficient flexibility and intelligence to provide genuinely good governance. Of course, this moderate position is easier to state than to achieve, especially in a system as dynamic as a democratic one. It is often difficult to judge new developments when one is in the midst of them, yet it is wise to keep the ideal of balance always before one's mind.

Implications for the study of democratic leadership

Contemporary studies of leadership in democracy tend to be dominated by political psychologists on the one hand, and students of executive government on the other. Looking at leadership in democracy through the lens of dispersal offers several key advantages over these. First, it helps us move away from a narrow preoccupation with leadership in the executive branch, and in particular with heads of government. Many public leaders help shape debate and policy in a democracy, and it is helpful to balance a person-centred approach with more contextual, institutional, and relational approaches to leadership analysis. We are rewarded with a surer grasp of the manifold ways in which leaders and leadership operate in democratic societies.

Second, our examination of dispersed democratic leadership brings to light important and contending notions regarding the merits of such dispersion and its implications for democratic governance. In allowing us to see more clearly the different expectations at stake, we are better placed to understand

and appraise the extraordinary opportunities as well as onerous demands placed on leaders in democracies.

Third, the focus on dispersal allows us to explore the extraordinary range of offices made possible in democracies. In addition to the variety of office, this research reveals the extent to which each office is itself subject to the demands of democratic leadership – to ensure accountability, inclusion, indeed dispersal of authority, while attempting to retain important features of coherent, efficient and technically sound and professional leadership.

Fourth, dispersal reveals that public office-holding is neither a necessary nor a sufficient condition for exercising public leadership. The Hargrove, Uhr, Sykes, Verbeek, and Tushnet chapters all provide ample illustrations of this proposition. Only a subset of the presidents, prime ministers, opposition leaders, women ministers, IGO leaders, and court presidents covered in their accounts has been widely understood to have managed to utilize their offices to exercise effective leader*ship*, that is, to perform one or several of the key leadership roles distinguished in Table 1.1 in non-trivial and widely supported ways. Some office-holders simply lack the appropriate skills (Greenstein 2000; Lord 2003; Keohane 2005) or luck (Dowding 2008). Others end up being short of political momentum (Skowronek 2008), time in office (Bynander and 't Hart 2007), or situational opportunities (Boin, 't Hart, Stern, and Sundelius 2005; Boin, 't Hart, and McConnell 2009) to actively lead and bring their followers and non-followers along. In contrast, consider Pim Fortuyn's brief but paradigm-shattering political ascendancy, the post-presidency peacemaking of Jimmy Carter, or Oprah Winfrey's political kingmaking. These and the many other examples discussed in this volume by de Beus, Keane, and 't Hart and Tindall illustrate the leadership potential of individuals who do not hold public office but nevertheless possess many or all of the above leadership resources.

Vibrant civil societies provide democracies with a rich mosaic of non-office-based public leadership: watchdogs, moralists, dissidents, clergy, revolutionaries, and social entrepreneurs. Some rely on personal charisma to build momentous social movements, others effectively exploit the moral capital of already established non-government institutions to perform civic leadership work. Some work alongside existing office-holders and regimes, others in stark opposition to them. Some self-consciously craft a public persona in the limelight of democratic deliberation and political controversy; others self-effacingly accomplish significant feats of public service unseen by the larger public but keenly welcomed by beneficiaries and followers (Barker, Johnson, and Lavalette 2001; Kane 2001; Elkington and Hartigan 2008; Kane, Patapan, and Wong 2008).

Future research

Future studies of leadership dispersal need to deepen our understanding of how democracies reconcile the challenge of dispersal of office and authority with the demands of stability, efficiency, and accountability; how such accommodation evolves under different systemic and situational conditions; and how different office-holders perceive and tackle it. In particular, we suggest three avenues for further research. First, we need studies examining the way democracies appear to manage the formidable centrifugal and centripetal leadership forces that shape contemporary politics (Wren 2007; Gerring and Thacker 2008). Given the powerful tendency to dispersal, the sheer number of leadership loci and the potentially deeply conflictual relationships between them, how do democracies manage to combine and safeguard responsiveness, resilience, and constitutionalism? When and why do they fail to do so? We need to infuse the comparative analysis of democratic transition, consolidation, and possible breakdown (as pursued by scholars like Linz and Stepan 1978, 1996), as well as the normative study of democratic design – even its leadership-eschewing strand of deliberative democracy – with a more explicit and certainly more sophisticated leadership perspective that takes into account the importance of democratic dispersal of office. Such an approach has the potential to contribute new insights into the study of democratic theory, democratization, and constitutionalism.

Second, we need to re-balance the study of leadership in political science, which is currently dominated by a preoccupation with executive government leaders (presidents, prime ministers, and senior bureaucrats). Whilst not abandoning this endeavour, a supplementary research programme should focus on the nature, forms, and implications of leadership that goes beyond these forms to include an ever-expanding range of non-executive- and non-office-based leadership. Democratic polities around the world have been experimenting with institutional innovation (decentralization, delegation, democratization, and internationalization). In the process, many new structures and opportunities for public leadership have been created: new venues for agenda-setting, policy design, authoritative choice, service delivery, and conflict management. From a democratic leadership perspective, future research needs to track these developments and map these changes. What are these venues? How if at all are leadership roles institutionalized within them? Which informal leadership practices develop in and around them, and how can these be assessed from the perspective of democratic responsiveness, constitutionalism, and resilience?

Finally, the dispersal perspective affects our notions of good and bad leadership. Existing research tends to evaluate leadership in terms of the performance of individual office-holders, exemplified by the apparent irresistibility of efforts to assess presidential or prime-ministerial 'success' or even 'greatness' (Simonton 1987; Greenstein 2000; Landy and Milkis 2000; Theakston and Gill 2006; Theakston 2007; Cozma 2008). Quite aside from the immanent critique such efforts may elicit, we suggest that at the very least they need to be supplemented by studies looking at leadership success as a feature of institutional design at the level of the polity. The nature and scope of the office inevitably empowers and constrains leaders. As such it defines the moral potential of leadership. A focus on dispersal of democratic office corrects the tendency to impose strict moral codes and templates on leaders, providing an important contextual flexibility in judgement that takes into account the ethical potential of office and institutions and therefore a more nuanced appreciation of the moral dimension of political leadership. It makes possible a new approach to the understanding of moral leadership.

These three new avenues of research are intended to be no more than an indication of the range of possibilities opened up by the notion of dispersed leadership – the list can easily be expanded. Yet all such approaches will inevitably confront and address a core democratic challenge. Democracies give voice and power to a wide range of people and offices. How they manage to reconcile this dispersal with high expectations of accountability, efficiency, and transparency remains the continuing challenge of dispersed democratic leadership.

Bibliography

Agranoff, R., *Managing Within Networks: Adding Value to Public Organizations* (Washington: Georgetown University Press, 2007).

Argyris, C. and Schon, D., *Organisational Learning: A Theory of Action Perspective* (Reading, Mass.: Addison Wesley, 1978).

Aucoin, P. and Heintzman, R., 'The Dialectics of Accountability for Performance in Public Management Reform', *International Review of Administrative Sciences*, 66 (2000), 45–55.

Bagehot, W., *The English Constitution,* 2nd edn., (1873), available at: <http://socserv.mcmaster.ca/econ/ugcm/3ll3/bagehot/constitution.pdf>.

Baraket, J. (ed.), *Strategic Issues in the Non-Profit Sector* (Sydney: University of New South Wales Press, 2008).

Barber, B., *Strong Democracy* (Berkeley, CA: University of California Press, 1984).

Barker, C., Johnson, A., and Lavalette, M. (eds.), *Leadership and Social Movements* (Manchester: Manchester University Press, 2001).

Bauman, Z., *Liquid Modernity* (Cambridge: Polity Press, 2000).

Behn, R., *Rethinking Democratic Accountability* (Washington, DC: Brookings Institution Press, 2001).

Bendor, J., *Parallel Systems: Redundancy in Government* (Berkeley, CA: University of California Press, 1985).

Benhabib, S. (ed.), *Democracy and Difference: Contesting the Boundaries of the Political* (Princeton, New Jersey: Princeton University Press, 1996).

Berg, J. van der, *Verantwoorden of Vertrekken: Een Essay over Politieke Verantwoordelijkheid* (The Hague: VNG uitgeverij, 1999).

Boin, A., *Crafting Public Institutions: Leadership in Two Prison Systems* (Boulder, Col.: Lynne Rienner Publishers, 2001).

——and Goodin, R. E., 'Institutionalizing Upstarts: The Demons of Domestication and the Benefits of Recalcitrance', *Acta Politica,* 42/1 (2007), 40–57.

Boin, A., 't Hart, P., and McConnell, A., 'Crisis Exploitation: Political and Policy Impacts of Framing Contests', *Journal of European Public Policy*, 16/1 (2009), 81–106.

———Stern, E., and Sundelius, B., *The Politics Of Crisis Management: Public Leadership Under Pressure* (Cambridge: Cambridge University Press, 2005).

Bovens, M., 'New Forms of Accountability and EU Governance', *Comparative European Politics*, 5/1 (2007), 104–20.

——'t Hart, P., and Schillemans, T., 'Does Accountability Work? An Assessment Tool', *Public Administration*, 86/1 (2008), 225–42.

——Derksen, W., Witteveen, W., Becker, F., and Kalma, P., *De verplaatsing van de politiek; een agenda voor democratische vernieuwing* (Amsterdam: Wiarda Beckmanstichting, 1995).

Braithwaite, J., 'On Speaking Softly and Carrying Big Sticks: Neglected Dimensions of a Republican Separation of Powers', *University of Toronto Law Journal*, 47/3 (1997), 305–61.

Bynander, F. and 't Hart, P., 'The Politics of Party Leader Survival and Succession: Australia in Comparative Perspective', *Australian Journal of Political Science*, 42/1 (2007), 47–72.

Cohen, J., 'The Economic Basis of Deliberative Democracy', *Social Philosophy and Policy*, 6/2 Spring (1989), 25–50.

Cozma, R., 'Presidential Greatness Reconsidered: How Modern Great Presidents Differ From The Old Ones In Terms Of Leadership Style', Paper presented at the annual meeting of The ISA's 49th Annual Convention, Bridging Multiple Divides, San Francisco, San Francisco, California, 26 March 2008, available at: <http://www.allacademic.com/meta/p252080_index.html>.

Crosby, B. and Bryson, J. D., *Leadership for the Common Good: Tackling Public Problems in a Shared Power World*, 2nd edn. (San Francisco, CA: Jossey Bass, 2005).

Cunningham, S., 'Political and Media Leadership in the Age of YouTube', in P. 't Hart and J. Uhr (eds.), *Public Leadership: Perspectives and Practices* (Canberra: ANU E Press, 2008), 177–88.

Curtin, D. and Wille, A. (eds.), 'Meanings and Practice of Accountability in the EU Multi-Level Context', Connex Report Series Vol. 7, Mannheim, 2008.

De Zwart, F., *The Bureaucratic Merry-go-round: Manipulating the Transfer of Indian Civil Servants* (Amsterdam: Amsterdam University Press, 1994).

Deutsch, K. W., *The Nerves of Government* (New York: The Free Press, 1963).

Dowding, K., 'Perceptions of Leadership', in P. 't Hart and J. Uhr (eds.), *Public Leadership: Perspectives and Practices* (Canberra: ANU E Press, 2008), 93–102.

Draper, T., *A Very Thin Line: The Iran-Contra Affairs* (New York: Simon and Schuster, 1991).

Dror, Y., *Policymaking under Adversity* (New Brunswick: Transaction, 1986).

——*The Capacity to Govern: A Report to the Club of Rome 2002* (London and Portland, Oregon: Frank Cass, 2001).

Dryzek, J. S., *Discursive Democracy: Politics, Policy and Political Science* (New York: Cambridge University Press, 1990).

Elkington, J. and Hartington, P., *Power of Unreasonable People: How Social Entrepreneurs Create Markets that Change the World* (Cambridge, Mass.: Harvard Business School Press, 2008).

Fisher, E., 'The European Union in the Age of Accountability', *Oxford Journal of Legal Studies*, 24/1 (2004), 495–515.

Foley, M., *The Rise of the British Presidency* (Manchester: Manchester University Press, 1993).

——*The British Presidency* (Manchester: Manchester University Press, 2000).

Frissen, P., *Politics, Governance, and Technology* (Cheltenham: Elgar, 1999).

Gerring, J. and Thacker, S. C., *A Centripetal Theory of Democratic Governance* (Cambridge: Cambridge University Press, 2008).

Godechot, J., *The Counter-Revolution: Doctrine and Action* (Princeton, New Jersey: Princeton University Press, 1981).

Goldsmith, S. and Eggers, W. D., *Governing by Network: The New Shape of the Public Sector* (Washington, DC: Brookings Institute, 2004).

Goodin, R. E., 'Democratic Accountability: The Distinctiveness of the Third Sector', *European Journal of Sociology*, 44/3 (2003), 359–96.

Greenstein, F., *The Presidential Difference: Leadership Style from FDR to Clinton* (New York: Free Press, 2000).

Gutmann, F. and Thompson, D., *Why Deliberative Democracy?* (Princeton, New Jersey: Princeton University Press, 2004).

Higley, J. and Kapulski, J., 'Toward Leader Democracy', in P. 't Hart and J. Uha (eds.), *Public Leadership Perspectives and Practices* (Canberra, ANUE Press, 2008), 45–55.

Huls, N., Adams, M., and Bomhoff, J. (eds.), *The Legitimacy of Highest Courts' Rulings: Judicial Deliberations and Beyond* (Cambridge: Cambridge University Press, 2009).

In't Veld, R., Schaap, E., Termeer, C., and van Twist, M. (eds.), *Autopoiesis and Configuration Theory: New Approaches to Societal Steering* (Dordrecht: Kluwer, 1991).

Kane, J., *The Politics of Moral Capital* (Cambridge: Cambridge University Press, 2001).

——and Patapan, H., 'In Search of Prudence: The Hidden Problem of Managerial Reform', *Public Administration Review*, 66/5 (2006), 711–24.

————'The Neglected Problem of Democratic Leadership', in P. 't Hart and J. Uhr, *Public Leadership: Perspectives and Practices* (Canberra: ANU E Press, 2008), 25–36.

————and Wong, B., *Dissident Democrats: The Challenge of Democratic Leadership in Asia* (New York: Palgrave Macmillan, 2008).

Keane, J., *The Life and Death of Democracy* (London, New York and Madrid: Simon and Schuster, 2009).

Keohane, N., 'On Leadership', *Perspectives on Politics*, 3/4 (2005), 705–22.

Koppell, J., 'Pathologies of Accountability: ICANN and the Challenge of "Multiple Accountabilities Disorder"', *Public Administration Review*, 65/1 (2005), 94–108.

Koppenjan, J. and Klijn, E.-H., *Managing Uncertainties in Networks* (London: Routledge, 2004).

Körösényi, A., 'Political Representation in Leader Democracy', *Government and Opposition*, 40/3 (2005), 358–78.

——'Political Leadership: Between Guardianship and Classical Democracy', Paper presented at ECPR Workshop on 'Political Leadership: A Missing Element in Democratic Theory', Helsinki, Finland, 7–12 May 2007.

Landau, M., 'Redundancy, Rationality, and the Problem of Duplication and Overlap', *Public Administration Review*, 29 (1969), 346–58.

Landy, M. and Milkis, S. M., *Presidential Greatness* (Kansas: Kansas University Press, 2000).

Lewis, E., *Public Entrepreneurship: Toward a Theory of Bureaucratic Power* (Bloomington, Indiana: Indiana University Press, 1980).

Lijphart, A., *Patterns of Democracy* (New Haven, Conn.: Yale University Press, 1999).

Lindblom, C. E., *The Intelligence of Democracy: Decision Making Through Mutual Adjustment* (New York: Free Press, 1965).

Linz, J. J. and Stepan, A. K. (eds.), *The Breakdown of Democratic Regimes* (Baltimore, Maryland: Johns Hopkins University Press, 1978).

——*Problems of Democratic Transition and Consolidation: Southern Europe, South America, and Post-Communist Europe* (Baltimore, Maryland: Johns Hopkins University Press, 1996).

Lord, C., *The Modern Prince: What Leaders Need to Know Now* (New Haven, Conn.: Yale University Press, 2003).

Luhmann, N., *Theorie der Verwaltungswissenschaft: Bestandsaufnahme und Entwurf* (Köln-Berlin: Grote, 1966).

Lupia, A., 'Delegation and its Perils', in K. Strom, W. C. Müller, and T. Bergman (eds.), *Delegation and Accountability in Parliamentary Democracies* (Oxford: Oxford University Press, 2003), 33–54.

March, J. G. and Olsen, J. P., *Democratic Governance* (New York: Free Press, 1995).

Moore, M., *Creating Public Value* (Cambridge: Harvard University Press, 1995).

Morse, R. S. and Buss, T. F., 'The Transformation of Public Leadership', in R. S. Morse, T. F. Buss, C. M. Kinghorn (eds.), *Transforming Public Leadership for the 21st Century* (Armonk: M. E. Sharpe, 2007), 3–19.

Nathan, R. P., *The Administrative Presidency* (New York: John Wiley and Sons, 1983).

Needham, C., 'Brand Leaders: Clinton, Blair and the Limitations of the Permanent Campaign', *Political Studies*, 53/2 (2005), 343–61.

O'Donnell, G., 'Horizontal Accountability in New Democracies', in A. Schedler, L. Diamond, and M. Plattner (eds.), *The Self-Restraining State: Power and Accountability in New Democracies* (London: Lynne Rienner, 1999), 29–51.

O'Loughlin, M., 'What is Bureaucratic Accountability and How Can We Measure It?', *Administration and Society*, 22/3 (1990), 275–302.

OECD, *Focus on Citizens: Public Engagement for Better Policy and Services* (Paris: Organization for Economic Cooperation and Development, 2008).

Pakulski, J. and Higley, J., 'Towards Leader Democracy', in P. 't Hart and J. Uhr, *Public Leadership: Perspectives and Practices* (Canberra: ANU E Press, 2008), 45–56.

Poguntke, T. and Webb, P. (eds.), *The Presidentialization of Politics: A Comparative Study of Modern Democracies* (Oxford: Oxford University Press, 2005).

Power, M., *The Audit Explosion* (London: Demos, 1994).

Przeworski, A., Stokes, S., and Manin, B. (eds.), *Democracy, Accountability, and Representation* (Cambridge: Cambridge University Press, 1999).

Rhodes, R. A. W., *Understanding Governance: Policy Networks, Governance, Reflexivity and Accountability* (Buckingham: Open University Press, 1997).

——'Blair and Governance', in R. Koch and J. Dixon (eds.), *Public Governance and Leadership* (Wiesbaden: Deutscher Universitäts-Verlag, 2007), 95–116.

Rosenthal, U., 'Politics and Administration: Max Weber and the Quest for Democratic Order', in A. Kouzmin and N. Scott (eds.), *Dynamics in Australian Public Management: Selected Essays* (Melbourne: Macmillan, 1990), 392–408.

Ruscio, K. P., *The Leadership Dilemma in Modern Democracy* (Cheltenham: Edward Elgar, 2004).

Schlesinger, A. M., *The Imperial Presidency* (Boston: Mariner Books, [1973] 2004).

Selznick, P., *Leadership in Administration* (New York: Harper and Row, 1957).

Shergold, P., *Dealing with Governments: The View from the Not-for-Profit Sector* (Sydney: Australian and New Zealand School of Government, 2008), unpublished speech.

Simonton, D. K., *Why Presidents Succeed: A Political Psychology of Leadership* (New Haven, Conn.: Yale University Press, 1987).

Skowronek, S., *Presidential Leadership in Political Time: Reprise and Reappraisal* (Lawrence, Kansas: University Press of Kansas, 2008).

Strom, K., 'Delegation and Accountability in Parliamentary Democracies', *European Journal of Political Research*, 37/3 (2000), 261–89.

——'Parliamentary Democracy and Delegation', in K. Strom, W. Müller, and T. Bergman (eds.), *Delegation and Accountability in Parliamentary Democracies* (Oxford: Oxford University Press, 2003), 55–106.

Terry, L. D., *Leadership of Public Bureaucracies: The Administrator as Conservator* (Thousand Oaks, CA: Sage, 1995).

't Hart, P., *Groupthink in Government: A Study of Small Groups and Policy Failure* (Baltimore, Maryland: Johns Hopkins University Press, 1994).

Theakston, K., 'What Makes for an Effective British Prime Minister?', *Quaderni di scienza politica*, 14 (2007), 39–61.

——and Gill, M., 'Rating 20th-Century British Prime Ministers', *The British Journal of Politics and International Relations*, 8/2 (2006), 193–213.

Thompson, M., Ellis, R., and Wildavsky, A., *Cultural Theory* (Boulder, Col.: Westview, 1990).

Uhr, J., 'Distributed Authority in a Democracy: The Lattice of Leadership Revisited', in P. 't Hart and J. Uhr, *Public Leadership: Perspectives and Practices* (Canberra: ANU E Press, 2008), 37–44.

Walter, J. and Strangio, P., *No, Prime Minister: Reclaiming Politics from Leaders* (Sydney: University of New South Wales Press, 2007).

Willard, C. A., *Liberalism and the Problem of Knowledge: A New Rhetoric for Modern Democracy* (Chicago, Illinois: Chicago University Press, 1996).

Witteveen, W., *Evenwicht van machten* (Zwolle: Tjeenk Willink, 1991).

Wren, J. T., *Inventing Leadership: The Challenge of Democracy* (Cheltenham: Elgar, 2007).

Index

The letter t indicates a table

Index

Index